THE WORLD'S CLASSICS

276

COMEDIES BY

WILLIAM CONGREVE

Oxford University Press, Amen House, London E.C.4

GLASGOW NEW YORK TORONTO MELBOURNE WELLINGTON
BOMBAY CALCUTTA MADRAS KARACHI KUALA LUMPUR
CAPE TOWN IBADAN NAIROBI ACCRA

COMEDIES BY
WILLIAM CONGREVE

EDITED

WITH INTRODUCTION AND NOTES

BY

BONAMY DOBRÉE

LONDON
OXFORD UNIVERSITY PRESS

William Congreve

Born, Bardsey, near Leeds (baptized 10 Feb.) 1670
Died, Surrey Street, Strand, London 19 Jan. 1729

Congreve's Comedies *were first published between the years* 1693 *and* 1700. *In* The World's Classics *they were first published in* 1925, *from the text of the edition of* 1710, *and reprinted in* 1929, 1934, 1939, 1944, 1949, 1951, 1957 *and* 1959.

PRINTED IN GREAT BRITAIN

WILLIAM CONGREVE

1670. Born at Bardsey, near Leeds.
1685. Goes to Trinity College, Dublin.
1692. Publishes *Incognita*, under the name of *Cleophil.*
Translates the 11th satire of Juvenal for Dryden's translation.
Writes complimentary verses for Dryden's *Persius. On Mrs. Arabella Hunt Singing.*
1693. *The Old Bachelor.*
1694. *The Double Dealer.*
Obtains a post in the Pipe Office (*circa*).
1695. *The Mourning Muse of Alexis.*
Love for Love.
Ode to the King.
Letter to Dennis *Concerning Humour in Comedy.*
Becomes commissioner for licensing Hackney Coaches.
1697. *The Mourning Bride.*
The Birth of the Muse.
1698. *Amendments of Mr. Collier's False and Imperfect Citations.*
1700. *The Way of the World.*
1701. *The Judgment of Paris.*
Ode for St. Cecilia's Day.
1704. *Squire Trelooby*, an adaptation from *Monsieur de Pourceaugnac*, in collaboration with Vanbrugh and Walsh.

1705. *The Tears of Amaryllis.*
Is given a place in the Customs.

1706. *A Pindaric Ode to the Queen*, with *A Discourse on the Pindaric Ode.*

1710. Publication of his Works, with *Semele.*

1714. Place in the Customs bettered.
Receives in addition the Secretaryship of the Island of Jamaica.

1720. Pope dedicates his *Iliad* to him.

1722. Steele dedicates to him his edition of Addison's *The Drummer.*

1726. Is visited by Voltaire.

1729. Dies.
Epistle to Lord Cobham posthumously published. Written 1728.

INTRODUCTION

I

RESTORATION COMEDY

SINCE the year 1698, when Jeremy Collier flung his fulminations into the strongholds of the English drama, it has been the habit to tag Restoration comedy with the epithet 'licentious'. Macaulay scrawled the word in flaming characters throughout a full-length essay; and Lamb, in elaborating his nimble excuse, admitted the black indictment. What has happened that to-day we can face without flinching the prospect of seeing a comedy by Wycherley, and that Congreve touches our emotions instead of seeming a monster of callousness?

The first thing to recognize is that Restoration comedy was not merely licentious, even if the adjective is useful in revealing that its chief subject is the intimate relations between men and women. It is a mistake to confuse subject with treatment; one might as well say that *Vanity Fair*, *Madame Bovary*, and *Crime and Punishment* are licentious, because the characters in those books do not behave with the perfect propriety of the ladies in *Cranford*. The truth is—perhaps it was this that really shocked the moralists—that the comedy written from 1660 to 1700 dealt somewhat coldly with human love and lust, something cavalierly with the marriage tie. For there are, in the main, two attitudes one can take up in face of man's inability to live up to his ideals: one that of amusement in the comic spirit, which implies that man's ideals need modification, or at least that his attitude towards them does; the other that of horror, which implies that man himself needs modification—a task in which the risks of failure are discouraging.

The comic writers of that time took for subject the relations between the sexes not only because it lends itself so easily to jest (the earliest recorded laughter is on this subject) but because at that time it was one of crying importance. This was due to the fact not so much that society was lax, as that it was experimental. And this is perhaps why so much of this work seems to speak very directly to us, for it is the expression of people endeavouring to readjust their values after a great upheaval, trying to see themselves clearly, not as they might wish to be, or as a previous generation had said they ought to be, but as they really were. There is an extraordinary ring of intellectual honesty about the comedy of this period, an attempt to get down to bed-rock in these matters, which we find in the previous age only, perhaps, in Chapman fully, though we see it partially in Marston. It is the prominence of this subject, and the manner in which it is treated, that makes Restoration comedy different from any other.

But if the social assumptions of the previous

age were broken down, Charles II's courtiers made others of their own, because without assumptions of some kind on every point society cannot exist at all. Being leisured, they were much preoccupied with love : being sceptical, their emotions were of the first importance to them, for when man's communings with God cease to matter intensely to him, his personal relations are bound to gain significance. They took as established that passion and affection were separate things, and that it was foolish to confuse them ; they looked upon love as a purely personal reaction, marriage as a social performance—and the writers of comedy dissected the resulting complications. Under the surface, of course, the normal life of social acceptance went on ; but what flared before the public eye was the behaviour of the Rochesters, Buckinghams, Killigrews, and, chiefest of all, that of 'the best good man that ever ruled a throne'. Licentiousness of course there was ; but it was rationalized, argued, made subject to scientific tests. And if the most brilliant and amusing statement of the experiment is given in Dryden's *Marriage à la Mode* ; the most profound and biting, and still more laughter-provoking in Wycherley's *Country Wife* ; the most graceful in Etherege's *She Would if She Could*, in none of these cases is the result aphrodisiac. As regards licentiousness there is nothing in the whole dramatic literature of this period, not in Sedley, Otway, or Aphra Behn, that goes farther in this direction than certain scenes in *Pericles* or *Romeo and Juliet*.

It is often said that Restoration comedy was an offshoot from France, but no one who has seriously studied either French comedy or the later Elizabethan in relation to that of Charles II's time can agree that this is more than a very partial statement. French plots, it is true, were taken in abundance, but they were always transformed, doubled, reworked, so as to become, as works of art, or parts of works of art, something totally distinct. *The Plain Dealer* is as far from *Le Misanthrope* as *All 's Well that Ends Well* is from Boccaccio's tale. A general influence there was, but it was linguistic rather than anything else, for the English stage has always been impatient of classical construction and economy, even when handled by such a master as Jonson. Congreve also is a classic in this respect, and he comes not from Molière but from Terence.

The chief source of Restoration comedy is the late Elizabethan—Massinger, Shirley, Brome, D'Avenant being an easy link with Cokain, Wilson, and Shadwell. Much also came from earlier sources, such as Marston; and if something in the working of intrigue came from Spain, in structure, in treatment, in the types chosen, in general movement and moral, this comedy everywhere betrays its national ancestry. Indeed it is not altogether foolish to say that the Restoration writers completed what the Elizabethans began: that Dryden is the fitting successor of Jonson; and Rymer, with his dramatic criticism of Shakespeare, the proper descendant of Webbe with his

Arte of Poesie. It is to be noted that in this period the centre of literary interest, the object of criticism, was not poetry, as it had been for the last hundred years, but the drama, which up to this time had undergone hardly any criticism at all. It was in many ways a timely change.

There is, of course, a difference in kind between the work of the two periods ; the names Comedy of Humours and Comedy of Manners themselves indicate this ; but there is no rigid dividing line, and the difference is only very obvious at the extremes. The Comedy of Manners also took types, human qualities, and worried them into all sorts of distortions, as the names Sir Fopling Flutter, Sir Positive At-All, Horner, Lady Fancyful, Mrs. Marwood are enough to show ; indeed, Congreve was the one writer of his period to subtilize the ' humour ' into a person. But the names, it will be noticed, are slightly different ; the qualities taken are more superficial, less separated, than those of Volpone or Sir Giles Overreach. For the Restoration writers were far more realistic ; they drew their characters, copied their situations, from the life they saw around them ; they were much less abstract. They were concerned to bring things to earth, to test them by immediate actuality ; they had none of the metaphysical background of the Elizabethans. Their comedy, therefore, is lighter, racier, more spinning ; the action is brisker, the wording sharper and more epigrammatic. Their wit sometimes became wearisome, but it had its point, which was the 'acquired follies' of man, not his deep characteristics ; their criticism was from a social angle, not from a humanitarian one

For Restoration comedy was, with the exception of Etherege's work, what is known as critical comedy ; it tried to 'cure excess', to find the happy mean by laughing exaggeration out of court and vice out of countenance. This is in itself a limitation, for the greatest minds do not want to change anything ; Shakespeare wanted to alter Falstaff about as much as Bardolph did ; and if Molière held Arnolphe up to scorn, one feels he understood Tartufe to be a necessary ingredient in the general make-up of the world. It is true that Wycherley in one play, and Congreve in another, achieved this more divine comedy, and we need not blame the rest for not succeeding in something they were not trying to do. Rather we have every reason to be grateful for the restraint which kept them making something they could make supremely well and amusingly, for the result is a gallery of entertaining, and partly immortal types, involved in situations which never cease to divert mankind. The Restoration comedy writers, with their keen observation, their quick, even too facile, deductions from externals, their capacity for seizing character from a gesture, keep us dancing along to a gay tune that is often irresistible. The fop, the idler, the preposterous man of importance ; the philanderer, his feminine counterpart, the sham scientist, the astrologer; the town elegant, the country clod-pole, the seaman and the professional man; the Spanish knot, the Chedreux wig, the fruz-toure, and the 'fanatic's' robe—all conspire to leave the busy world and appear before us on the stage in a lively medley of action, with robust outpouring of words.

Congreve is not wholly of the type of Restoration dramatist; he is in some sort the descendant of Etherege and Wycherley; he is more mature. But the material he used for his comedies hardly differs from that of his companions. Like theirs, his people are the men and women who talked in the boudoirs and coffee-houses of King William's reign, and took their exercise in the Park, the Piazza, or the Mall. They may be met in the comedies of Crowne, Shadwell, and Dryden, in the diaries of Evelyn and Pepys, even in the letters of Dorothy Osborne. They were not very different from ourselves. Superficially their conversation seems different because the idiom has changed; we no longer rail, or hunt elusive simile to the death: but were the Petulants, the Carelesses, the Belindas, and the Brisks to appear at our own dinner-tables, we should find them natural enough. They would, with just the same zest as ourselves, use the discoveries of Dr. Freud pleasurably to widen the limits of gossip, and charitably to interpret the failings of our friends.

But part of the material an artist has at his disposal is his philosophic make-up, and here Congreve differs from his contemporaries. Not much, for his was not a profoundly original mind ; he had no new orientation to declare, no revelation to make, wherewith to stir the people of his day to revision, as Signor Pirandello drives us now. But he differed in two points. His intellectual fastidiousness made him loath to portray ' fools so gross, that they should rather disturb than divert the well-natured and reflecting part of an audience ' ; and secondly, his passionate sense rebelled against the rationalization of love. The attempt had proved a failure, and Congreve, born somewhat late in the day, could only feel the disillusion of peace, while missing the joy of battle.

But more important than the material of an artist is the use he makes of it ; how else could we distinguish between Jonson and Brome, between Etherege's lace-work, and the turgid periods of Crowne ? By this is shown a writer's sensibility, his affective wealth ; in this alone artistic creation makes so close the fusion of mind with sensibility, that thought merges into feeling, and we enter that realm where it really is true to say *Le style, c'est l'homme même.*

To achieve a style argues a passionate nature ; it cannot be coldly constructed or artificially put together ; for passion means not the noisy tearing of the heart to tatters, but the deep-rooted impulse which drives a man to labour continually in the same road. And here we hit the amazing paradox about Congreve—that not even in spite of, but actually because of his style, which almost without a gap gives evidence of exquisite feeling, he is accused of being cold, heartless, wicked. Some have seen in him nothing but a social snob, and have entered his works in the stud-book as being by Pride out of Urbanity. The reason may be that, endowed with a passionate and selective nature—in this, but for fear of exaggeration, one would like to compare him with Racine—an element of physical weakness prevented its full realization either in life or in literature. Under such conditions the mind turns ever inward upon itself, continually discerning and refining, dwelling upon possibilities of relationship, making ramifications of increasing subtlety. We see this carried to its farthest point in Proust. This would account for the strong element of wistfulness in Congreve's work, that constant fear of disillusion, that 'against fruition' note, we find so often on the lips of his women, of Cynthia, Angelica, and Millamant. Yet because Congreve was not a sentimentalist, he applied his clear, strong mind, his discerning, if not very wide or deep imagination, to his emotions; he never deluded himself. Thus he made every effort to be dry, and his last comedy, though based on sentiment rather than on the 'humours', is far from sentimental. This is not by any means to say that it is heartless.

In discussing Congreve, then, it must be insisted that he belongs to the type of 'pure' creator, who is to be judged solely on aesthetic grounds, that is, by the quality of delight which he imparts. He and Dickens are not to be measured by the same instrument, any more than Dostoievsky and

Miss Austen, in spite of the elements they may possess in common. It is, when all is said, the province of art to delight the spirit, and it is, finally, the aesthetic pleasure we get from Congreve that earns him his high place. It is on that plane, and not on the moral or philosophic, that he has something to give.

II

THE STYLE OF CONGREVE

The most evident pleasure we obtain from the drama is in the interplay of character, by the colours woven together to make up an objective view of humanity ; but though in this, too, Congreve must be ranked with the masters, he does not take a very high place among them. His first piece, *The Old Bachelor*, has all the obviousness of Jonson without the especial creative purpose that made it necessary ; Bluffe is a version of Bobadill, Fondlewife is modelled on Kitely ; we detect patches of Brome, we scent the influence of Marston. Congreve had learned much from the old masters, but he had not yet made them his own, nor entered into the Restoration inheritance. As characterization the play adds nothing to our riches ; we are still in a late Elizabethan world. In *The Double-Dealer* there is a new set of contrasts that are almost too striking, of the harsh unredeemed villains with the rightly-named Froths, and with the candid Cynthia. *Love for Love* again is a return, not to

Jonson, but to the purest Wycherley. *The Way of the World,* however, soars above all, and the characterization becomes subtle and individual; too subtle almost, since even Pope was constrained to ask 'Tell me if Congreve's fools are fools indeed'. For here Congreve broke through the rules he had laid down in that happy piece of constructive criticism, the *Letter Concerning Humour in Comedy,* and made his people three-dimensional. The greatest triumph, of course, is Millamant, many-faceted, spontaneous, who hides her feeling beneath her gaiety, and is so well set off against Lady Wishfort, Mrs. Marwood, and Mrs. Fainall, not containing within herself the springs that move those others, but alive with the possibility of containing them.

Characterization, however, is not a solely dramatic element: as an ingredient it is equally important in the novel; but what we may hazard as being specifically dramatic is the changes of speed, of movement, which constitute the rhythm of a piece. You can have 'great still novels' like those of Richardson, you cannot have a play that those adjectives will suit. It may even be said that a dramatic moment is definitely that where the rhythm changes, of which the knocking at the gate in *Macbeth* may be taken as one *locus classicus,* and Cleopatra's 'Peace! Peace! Dost thou not see my baby at my breast That sucks the nurse asleep?' as another, in the reverse direction. For, as in physical life, it is not motion that we feel, but change of motion. In the drama this varying of speed may be achieved by the introduction of new persons, by changes of tempo, or by the quality of the phrasing, this last consciously and most superbly done by Jonson in *Catiline*. Of all these methods Congreve was a master, producing results of delicious beauty. When his works were reprinted, he made the addition or loss of a person upon the stage constitute a new scene, not to borrow a French habit, but to emphasize the change of tempo, and to allow each scene to be itself a separate jewel. To give only one example of how, by phrasing alone, he could alter the speed, it will be enough to point out the staggering finale of *The Double-Dealer*. The play has been proceeding at a glorious and ever-increasing pace ; until the last moment we are borne along in a tremendous rush ; it seems incredible that the curtain should not come down upon a tumult : but then :

Brisk. This is all very surprising, let me perish !
Lady Froth. You know I told you Saturn looked a little more angry than usual.

This shows his strength : we are suddenly pulled up sharp. A technically similar, but in tone vastly different, ending to *The Way of the World* illustrates his grace, like that of a pigeon, which hurtling through the air with closed wings, opens them to alight on the selected branch. It is all done by phrasing ; for it is in prose that Congreve most surely excels.

Dryden's panegyric, contained in the lines that preface *The Double-Dealer*, was no affected piece of homage such as grey hairs sometimes pay to gold. For the hoary monarch of Will's had, in a famous phrase, found the language brick and left it marble, and he saw in Congreve a young man working unerringly in the new medium. Here, at last, was a poet 'lineal to the throne', an artist who realized that his material was words, who loved words, glorying in their proper and beautiful use. He could not but admire a boy who began a first comedy with:

> Vainlove, and abroad so early! good morrow; I thought a contemplative lover could no more have parted with his bed in a morning, than he could have slept in't.

He immediately rejoiced in the amazing skill, so surely shown, in the difficult matter of spacing stresses.

To any one who has not thought about stage dialogue the speech may not seem very striking; yet it is a sound piece of craftsmanship. For stage prose, like pulpit, or even law-court prose, is not to be judged in the same way as chamber prose, or that written for the inward ear. Browne so enthralling to murmur to oneself; Swift so delightful to read to one's friend; Gibbon so effective and amusing to quote, would empty box and gallery alike; while the grandiose periods of Burke sent the Mother of Parliaments to dinner. For stage prose must be easy to say at once rapidly and loud; it must suit the human lungs working under specialized conditions. The weight must always be brought naturally, and rather obviously, onto the important word. That is why, if we compare a passage from *The Silent Woman* with one of Jonson's dedications, or a description of a masque, we find the prose so markedly different ; and why, if we put a speech from *Marriage à la Mode* against an extract from the *Essay of Dramatick Poesy* we get the same variance. That Congreve understood how the rhythm of stage writing had to differ from the balance of other forms can be proved in a moment by any one who cares, however cursorily, to turn over the pages of this book.

But in his first play, for prose as well as for persons, Congreve chose Jonson for his master. If we take a typical piece of the latter's work, we can see that the same kind of beat runs through *The Old Bachelor* :

> Yes, faith. The fellow trims him silently, and has not the knack with his sheers or his fingers : and that continency in a barber he thinks so eminent a virtue, as it has made him chief of his counsel. (*The Silent Woman*, I. 2.)

For Congreve's lighter touch, however, Jonson was too fond of accented syllables ; and his prose, though rarely blank verse, in beat-structure resembles his own to an extraordinary degree. Moreover, he was inclined to come down too heavily on the last syllable :

> If she be short, let her sit much, lest when she stands, she be thought to sit, &c. (*The Silent Woman*, IV. 1.)

and this sometimes gives his work a kind of gaunt,

hammered stiffness, admirable for what he was trying to do, but lacking in the lilt Congreve required for his differently felt persons. He wanted something more fluid, and perhaps he applied to Dryden :

> You speak more truly than you think : I have shown it. For, since I must confess the truth to you, I am no fortune : my father, tho' he bears it high, to put me off, has mortgaged his estate. We keep servants for show, and when we should pay their wages, pick a quarrel with their service, and turn 'em off penniless (*Love Triumphant*, IV).

That is a fair average sample of Dryden's stage prose ; it is charming enough to the inward ear, but is not of quite the first class for stage enunciation. In his prose plays Dryden never seemed quite sure of his rhythm, and, perhaps through fear of slipping into the ' other harmony ' of verse, often ran too many unstressed syllables together. He here lacked the splendid assurance of his critical and controversial essays, as much as he did the irresistible march of his verse. But Congreve learned something of flexibility from him, and how to deal with runs ; as he learned, it may be, a certain swing from Etherege, and how to introduce the note of lyrical sadness into comedy :

> Did you not tell me there was no credit to be given to faces ? That women nowadays have their passions as much at will as they have their complexions, and put on joy and sadness, scorn and kindness, with the same ease as they do their paint and patches.—Are they the only counterfeits ? (*The Man of Mode*, v. 2.)

Etherege more nearly approaches Congreve for a sensitive ear than any other dramatist of the period, but he had not the rich polyphonic mastery of vowels; while Wycherley, giant as he was, something neglected his surface in the bigger scale of his conceptions.[1]

But to have done with Congreve's predecessors, and to come to his own progress. The attentive reader will, I think, see that in *The Old Bachelor* he definitely tried to soften the angles of his model:

> Lard I have seen an ass look so chagrin, ha! ha! ha! (you must pardon me I can't help laughing) that an absolute lover would have concluded the poor creature to have had darts, and flames, and altars, and all that in his breast (II. 3),

a passage in which he veered away from Jonson to write nearly pure Dryden. Again, he did not always avoid the pitfall gaping for those who wish to write swift, rhetorical prose, and occasionally fell into blank verse:

> Methinks I feel the woman strong within me,
> And vengeance kindles in the room of love (III. 1).

His measure, too, sometimes missed the right balance of prose to hit upon that of poetry:

> and called him aloud in your sleep (II. 3)

reminding one over-forcibly of such metres as:

> And left him alone in his glory.

[1] The curious may like to trace Congreve's descent from Cowley. It is an opinion I would maintain after dinner, supported by *Cutter of Coleman Street*, IV. 5, 6, but for which I would not go to the stake.

But his next play shows an enormous advance :

> My mind gives me it won't—because we are both willing ; we each of us strive to reach the goal, and hinder one another in the race ; I swear it never does well when the parties are so agreed.—For when people walk hand in hand, there 's neither overtaking nor meeting. We hunt in couples where we both pursue the same game, but forget one another ; and 'tis because we are so near that we don't think of coming together. *The Double-Dealer* (IV. 1).

Here he achieved a larger rhythmical unit than was common with Jonson, but yet preserved an admirable stress spacing ; and in the second part of the paragraph varied the phrase endings to contrast beautifully with those in the first. He was more aware, too, of the value of vowel changes. *Goal* with *race* is effective ; and if *agreed* and *meeting* constitute an experiment that does not quite come off, we shall see later what he could do, in the plenitude of his power, by playing on the same sound.

Love for Love was an attempt to re-create *The Plain Dealer's* scenes of Manly rage ; but who would lash the follies of the time is compelled to use a certain medium, and some of the earlier passages of this play are pure Wycherley. Congreve's rhythm, however, was vastly superior once he plunged into his own atmosphere :

> What a bustle did you keep against the last invisible eclipse, laying in provision as 'twere for a siege ? What a world of fire and candle, matches and tinderboxes did you purchase ! One would

> have thought we were ever after to live under ground, or at least making a voyage to Greenland, to inhabit there all the dark season (II. 3).

In this play, too, the listening reader will find a blank verse couplet (IV. 19) as he may have noticed some in *The Double-Dealer* (e.g. V. 13), but it is in *Love for Love* that we really begin to hear the melody that pervades *The Way of the World*—that melody which was most readily Congreve's in the tenderer passages, for instance in the one which begins 'You're a woman—one to whom Heaven gave beauty, when it grafted roses on a briar' (IV. 16), or that wonderful paragraph 'Would any thing but a madman complain of uncertainty' (IV. 20), much of which *could* be twisted into blank verse, and which perhaps gains its effect because it does all the time seem to skim perilously along the brink.

The Way of the World is throughout authentic Congreve, and is of incomparable beauty in its kind. Here, whatever he may have learned from his predecessors, he made something peculiarly his own, impossible to imitate. For sinewy flexibility and point, combined with seductive gentleness; for the full gamut of vowel sounds and the varied spacing of stresses, English literature had to wait for Landor until it once more heard a voice that had something of the especial quality of Congreve. Addison, for instance, made far too flat a country out of Congreve's beautifully accidented landscape, and one has only to read *The Drummer* to see how short he fell.

For his satiric passages Congreve could still use the Jonsonian regular ring, coming down thump on the last syllable with a spondee; or 'keen iambics, i'Gad', like locking the door upon a prisoner:

> For a fool's visit is always a disguise; and never admitted by a woman of wit, but to blind her affair with a lover of sense (III. 10).

But when he came to the more delicate passages, especially when he wished to move to sympathy, he nearly always closed upon a trochee, with that plaintive, almost melancholy effect Landor used so well, and that Fletcher tried to get with the feminine double-ending in blank verse. In the same way he transformed down the rather too marked contrasts in the vowel sounds in the antithetical parts of the sentence, the broad distinction having become too common a trick, and wearisome in the writings of such as the Marquis of Halifax. Take even that torrential passage at the beginning of the last act, wherein Lady Wishfort is not only 'at once concise and voluble', but a poetess:

> Out of my house, out of my house, thou viper, thou serpent, that I have fostered; thou bosom traitress, that I have raised from nothing—begone, begone, begone, go, go—that I took from washing of old gauze and weaving of dead hair, with a bleak blue nose, over a chafing-dish of starved embers, and dining behind a traverse-rag, in a shop no bigger than a bird-cage,—go, go, starve again, do, do.

Facit indignatio versum! and it was certainly no

ordinary inspiration that imagined that splendidly incisive 'bleak blue nose', with its deepening sound to clinch the delicious modelling of 'from washing of old gauze and weaving of dead hair'; or fathered the equally effective change from 'traverse-rag' to 'bird-cage', and the final return to 'starve'.

If one were to have to select the two lines that best exhibit Congreve's flavour, one might do worse than choose the sentence that ushers in Millamant for the first time:

> Here she comes i' faith full sail, with her fan spread and streamers out, and a shoal of fools for tenders—Ha, no, I cry her mercy (II. 4).

The beauty of that needs no insistence; the delicate play of the vowels, the dancing rhythm, with the sharp uptake at the end attended with the entirely new sound of 'cry', sweep us away with their effect of spontaneity. And see, too, a little later in the same scene, how skilfully he can now play on one note, recurring to the same word:

> Beauty the lover's gift—Lord, what is a lover that it can give? Why one makes lovers as fast as one pleases, and they live as long as one pleases, and they die as soon as one pleases: and then, if one pleases, one makes more.

'How it chimes, and cries tink in the close, divinely!' The reiteration never gives the ear the smallest bother, because, said as they must be to gain the full meaning, the phrases only gather their weight upon 'pleases' in the last instance, the stresses otherwise playing all around it. At last the voice fatefully pounces upon the word, as a hawk, after several feints, lands upon a predestined prey.

Those extracts are from that miraculous second act, which shows a more consummate mastery than any other passage in the dramatic literature of the period. The whole rhythm of changes of swiftness from scene to scene is astoundingly beautiful and moving. The pace is made up of varying emotions, from the corrosive jealousy of Mrs. Marwood to the almost too sweet melancholy of Mirabell, and in every instance the phrasing is perfectly adapted, as well to the highest gaiety as to the gravest doubt. Nor are we at any time kept too long at the same pitch, and the succeeding scene always seems just the right one to modulate the change of our emotions. In its tuneful measure the passage between the lovers reminds one of the second act of *Le Tartufe*; and there the whole of Millamant is revealed, the wise and winning woman who knows that life is so serious that we cannot afford always to be serious about it, and wear for ever an inflexible wise face.

Yet it is not surprising that the play failed at first performance, for it does in truth 'evaporate into an essence almost too fine', and one cannot but suspect that Congreve was writing for himself alone, forgetting a little the cruder exigencies of the stage. Whence it may be said of *The Way of the World* what is often remarked of Shakespeare's plays, that it is better in the study than on the scene. With neither is this absurdity true; all it means is that intimacy of reading discloses beauties that cannot immediately be snatched, and that thoroughly to enjoy these plays in the acting we must first of all know them well. Then one awaits the delicious phrase, the thrilling movement, the breath-catching swerve of tempo, even as one expects the enunciation of a theme in a familiar Bach concerto, or revels in the arabesque of a well-known page of counterpoint. And this, perhaps, is a touchstone for the surest works of art, only to reveal their final perfection to the lover; for though, to be commended, an aspirant must declare some grace, in its most treasured, its most enriching forms, beauty is the lover's gift indeed.

CONTENTS

Mr. Congreve, to *Mr.* Dennis.

Concerning Humour in Comedy.

Dear Sir,

You write to me, that you have Entertained your self two or three days, with reading several Comedies, of several Authors; and your Observation is, that there is more of *Humour* in our English Writers, than in any of the other Comick Poets, Ancient or Modern. You desire to know my Opinion, and at the same time my Thought, of that which is generally call'd *Humour* in Comedy.

I agree with you, in an Impartial Preference of our English Writers, in that Particular. But if I tell you my Thoughts of *Humour*, I must at the same time confess, that what I take for true *Humour*, has not been so often written even by them, as is generally believed: And some who have valued themselves, and have been esteem'd by others, for that kind of Writing, have seldom touch'd upon it. To make this appear to the World, would require a long and labour'd Discourse, and such as I neither am able nor willing to undertake. But such little Remarks, as may be continued within the Compass of a Letter, and such unpremeditated Thoughts, as may be Communicated between Friend and Friend, without incurring the Censure of the World, or setting up for a *Dictator*, you shall have from me, since you have enjoyn'd it.

To Define *Humour*, perhaps, were as difficult, as to Define *Wit*; for like that, it is of infinite variety. To Enumerate the several *Humours* of Men, were a Work as endless, as to sum up their several Opinions. And in my mind the *Quot homines tot Sententiæ*, might have been more properly interpreted of *Humour* ; since there are many Men, of the same Opinion in many things, who are yet quite different in Humours. But thô we cannot certainly tell what *Wit* is, or, what *Humour* is, yet we may go near to shew something, which is not *Wit* or not *Humour* ; and yet often mistaken for both. And since I have mentioned *Wit* and *Humour* together, let me make the first Distinction between them, and observe to you that *Wit is often mistaken for Humour.*

I have observed, that when a few things have been Wittily and Pleasantly spoken by any Character in a Comedy ; it has been very usual for those, who make their Remarks on a Play, while it is acting, to say, *Such a thing is very Humorously spoken : There is a great Deal of Humour in that Part.* Thus the Character of the Person speaking, may be, Surprizingly and Pleasantly, is mistaken for a Character of *Humour*; which indeed is a Character of *Wit*. But there is a great Difference between a Comedy, wherein there are many things *Humorously*, as they call it, which is *Pleasantly* spoken ; and one, where there are several Characters of *Humour*, distinguish'd by the Particular and Different Humours, appropriated to the several Persons represented, and which naturally arise, from the different Constitutions, Complexions, and Dispositions of Men. The saying of Humorous Things, does not distinguish Characters ; For every Person in a Comedy may be allow'd to speak them. From a Witty Man they are expected ; and even a *Fool* may be permitted to stumble on 'em by chance. Thô I make a Difference betwixt *Wit* and *Humour* ; yet I do not think that Humorous Characters exclude Wit : No, but the Manner of *Wit* should be adapted to the *Humour*. As for Instance, a Character of a Splenetick and Peevish *Humour*, should have a Satyrical Wit. A Jolly and Sanguine *Humour*, should have a Facetious Wit. The Former should speak Positively ; the

Latter, Carelessly : For the former Observes, and shews things as they are ; the latter, rather overlooks Nature, and speaks things as he would have them ; and his *Wit* and *Humour* have both of them a less Alloy of Judgment than the others.

As *Wit*, so, its opposite, *Folly, is sometimes mistaken for Humour*.

When a Poet brings a *Character* on the Stage, committing a thousand Absurdities, and talking Impertinencies, roaring Aloud, and Laughing immoderately, on every, or rather upon no occasion ; this is a Character of Humour.

Is any thing more common, than to have a pretended Comedy, stuff'd with such Grotesques, Figures, and Farce Fools ? Things, that either are not in Nature, or if they are, are Monsters, and Births of Mischance ; and consequently as such, should be stifled, and huddled out of the way, like *Sooterkins* ; that Mankind may not be shock'd with an appearing Possibility of the Degeneration of a God-like *Species*. For my part, I am as willing to Laugh, as any body, and as easily diverted with an Object truly ridiculous : but at the same time, I can never care for seeing things, that force me to entertain low thoughts of my Nature. I dont know how it is with others, but I confess freely to you, I could never look long upon a Monkey, without very Mortifying Reflections ; thô I never heard any thing to the Contrary, why that Creature is not Originally of a Distinct *Species*. As I dont think *Humour* exclusive of *Wit*, neither do I think it inconsistent with *Folly* ; but I think the Follies should be only such, as Mens Humours may incline 'em to ; and not Follies intirely abstracted from both Humour and Nature.

Sometimes, *Personal Defects are misrepresented for Humours*.

I mean, sometimes Characters are barbarously exposed on the Stage, ridiculing Natural Deformities, Casual Defects in the Senses, and

Infirmities of Age. Sure the Poet must both be very Ill-natur'd himself, and think his Audience so, when he proposes by shewing a Man Deform'd, or Deaf, or Blind, to give them an agreeable Entertainment ; and hopes to raise their Mirth, by what is truly an object of Compassion. But much need not be said upon this Head to any body, especially to you, who in one of your Letters to me concerning Mr. *Johnson*'s *Fox*, have justly excepted against this Immoral part of *Ridicule* in *Corbaccio*'s Character ; and there I must agree with you to blame him, whom otherwise I cannot enough admire, for his great Mastery of true Humour in Comedy.

External Habit of Body is often mistaken for Humour.

By *External Habit*, I do not mean the Ridiculous Dress or Cloathing of a Character, thô that goes a good way in some received Characters. (But undoubtedly a Man's Humour may incline him to dress differently from other People) But I mean a Singularity of Manners, Speech, and Behaviour, peculiar to all, or most of the same Country, Trade, Profession, or Education. I cannot think, that a *Humour*, which is only a Habit, or Disposition contracted by Use or Custom ; for by a Disuse, or Complyance with other Customs, it may be worn off, or diversify'd.

Affectation is generally mistaken for Humour.

These are indeed so much alike, that at a Distance, they may be mistaken one for the other. For what is *Humour* in one, may be *Affectation* in another ; and nothing is more common, than for some to affect particular ways of saying, and doing things, peculiar to others, whom they admire and would imitate. *Humour* is the Life, *Affectation* the Picture. He that draws a Character of *Affectation*, shews *Humour* at the Second Hand ; he at best but publishes a Translation, and his Pictures are but Copies.

But as these two last distinctions are the Nicest, so it may be most proper to Explain them, by Particular Instances from some Author of Reputation. *Humour* I take, either to be born with us, and so of a Natural Growth ; or else to be grafted into us, by some accidental change in the Constitution, or revolution of the Internal Habit of Body ; by which it becomes, if I may so call it, Naturaliz'd.

Humour is from Nature, *Habit* from Custom ; and *Affectation* from Industry.

Humour, shews us as we *are*.

Habit, shews us, as we appear, under a forcible Impression.

Affectation, shews what we would be, under a Voluntary Disguise.

Thô here I would observe by the way, that a continued Affectation, may in time become a Habit.

The Character of *Morose* in the *Silent Woman*, I take to be a Character of Humour. And I choose to Instance this Character to you, from many others of the same Author, because I know it has been Condemn'd by many as Unnatural and Farce : And you have your self hinted some dislike of it, for the same Reason, in a Letter to me, concerning some of *Johnson*'s Plays.

Let us suppose *Morose* to be a Man Naturally Splenetick and Melancholly ; is there any thing more offensive to one of such a Disposition, than Noise and Clamour ? Let any Man that has the Spleen (and there are enough in *England*) be Judge. We see common Examples of this Humour in little every day. 'Tis ten to one, but three parts in four of the Company that you dine with, are Discompos'd and Startled at the Cutting of a Cork, or Scratching a Plate with a Knife : It is a Proportion of the same Humour, that makes such or any other Noise offensive to the Person that hears it ; for there are others who will not be disturb'd at all by it. Well ; But *Morose* you will say, is so Extravagant, he cannot bear any Discourse or Conversation, above a Whisper. Why, It is his excess of this Humour, that makes him become Ridiculous, and qualifies his Character for Comedy. If the Poet had given him, but a Moderate proportion of that Humour, 'tis odds but half the Audience, would have sided with the Character, and have Condemn'd the Author, for Exposing a Humour which was neither Remarkable nor Ridiculous. Besides, the distance of the Stage requires the Figure represented, to be something larger than the Life; and sure a Picture may have Features larger in Proportion, and yet be very like the Original. If this Exactness of Quantity, were to be observed in Wit, as some would have it in Humour; what would become of those Characters that are design'd for Men of Wit? I believe if a Poet should steal a Dialogue of any length, from the *Extempore* Discourse of the two Wittiest Men upon Earth, he would find the Scene but coldly receiv'd by the Town. But to the purpose.

The Character of Sir *John Daw* in the same Play, is a Character of Affectation. He every where discovers an Affectation of Learning; when he is not only Conscious to himself, but the Audience also plainly perceives that he is Ignorant. Of this kind are the Characters of *Thraso* in the Eunuch of *Terence*, and *Pyrgopolinices* in the *Miles Gloriosus* of *Plautus*. They affect to be thought Valiant, when both themselves and the Audience know they are not. Now such a boasting of Valour in Men who were really Valiant, would undoubtedly be a *Humour*; for a Fiery Disposition might naturally throw a Man into the same Extravagance, which is only affected in the Characters I have mentioned.

The Character of *Cob* in *Every Man in his Humour*, and most of the under Characters in *Bartholomew-Fair*, discover only a Singularity of Manners, appropriated to the several Educations and Professions of the Persons represented. They are not Humours but Habits contracted by Custom. Under this Head may be ranged all Country-Clowns, Sailers, Tradesmen, Jockeys, Gamesters and such like, who make use of *Cants* or peculiar *Dialects* in their several Arts and Vocations. One may almost give a Receipt for the Composition of such a Character: For the Poet has nothing to do, but to collect a few proper Phrases and terms of Art, and to make the Person apply them by ridiculous Metaphors in his Conversation, with Characters of different Natures. Some late Characters of this kind have been very successful; but in my mind they may be Painted without much Art or Labour; since they require little more, than a good Memory and Superficial Observation. But true *Humour* cannot be shewn, without a Dissection of Nature, and a Narrow Search, to discover the first Seeds, from whence it has its Root and growth.

If I were to write to the World, I should be obliged to dwell longer, upon each of these Distinctions and Examples; for I know that they would not be plain enough to all Readers. But a bare hint is sufficient to inform you of the Notions which I have on this Subject: And I hope by this time you are of my Opinion, that Humour is neither Wit, nor Folly, nor Personal defect; nor Affectation, nor Habit; and yet, that each, and all of these, have been both written and received for Humour.

I should be unwilling to venture even on a bare Description of Humour, much more, to make a Definition of it, but now my hand is in, Ile tell you what serves me instead of either. I take it to be, *A singular and unavoidable manner of doing, or saying any thing, Peculiar and Natural to one Man only; by which his Speech and Actions are distinguish'd from those of other Men.*

Our *Humour* has relation to us, and to what proceeds from us, as the Accidents have to a

Substance ; it is a Colour, Taste, and Smell, Diffused through all ; thô our Actions are never so many, and different in Form, they are all Splinters of the same Wood, and have Naturally one Complexion ; which thô it may be disguised by Art, yet cannot be wholly changed : We may Paint it with other Colours, but we cannot change the Grain. So the Natural sound of an Instrument will be distinguish'd, thô the Notes expressed by it, are never so various, and the Divisions never so many. Dissimulation may, by Degrees, become more easy to our practice ; but it can never absolutely Transubstantiate us into what we would seem : It will always be in some proportion a Violence upon Nature.

A Man may change his Opinion, but I believe he will find it a Difficulty, to part with his *Humour*, and there is nothing more provoking, than the being made sensible of that difficulty. Sometimes, one shall meet with those, who perhaps, Innocently enough, but at the same time impertinently, will ask the Question ; *Why are you not Merry* ? *Why are you not Gay*, *Pleasant*, *and Cheerful* ? then instead of answering, could I ask such one ; *Why are you not handsome ? Why have you not Black Eyes*, *and a better Complexion* ? Nature abhors to be forced.

The two Famous Philosophers of *Ephesus* and *Abdera*, have their different Sects at this day. Some Weep, and others Laugh at one and the same thing.

I dont doubt, but you have observed several Men Laugh when they are Angry ; others who are Silent ; some that are Loud : Yet I cannot suppose that it is the passion of *Anger* which is in it self different, or more or less in one than t'other ; but that it is the *Humour* of the Man that is Predominant, and urges him to express it in that manner. Demonstrations of pleasure are as Various ; one Man has a Humour of retiring from all Company, when any thing has happen'd to please him beyond expectation; he hugs himself alone, and thinks it an Addition to the pleasure to keep it Secret. Another is upon Thorns till he has made Proclamation of it; and must make other people sensible of his happiness, before he can be so himself. So it is in Grief, and other Passions. Demonstrations of Love and the Effects of that Passion upon several Humours, are infinitely different; but here the Ladies who abound in Servants are the best Judges. Talking of the Ladies, methinks something should be observed of the Humour of the Fair Sex; since they are sometimes so kind as to furnish out a Character for Comedy. But I must confess I have never made any observation of what I Apprehend to be true Humour in Women. Perhaps Passions are too powerful in that Sex, to let Humour have its Course; or may be by Reason of their Natural Coldness, Humour cannot Exert it self to that extravagant Degree, which it often does in the Male Sex. For if ever any thing does appear Comical or Ridiculous in a Woman, I think it is little more than an acquir'd Folly, or an Affectation. We may call them the weaker Sex, but I think the true Reason is, because our Follies are Stronger, and our Faults are more prevailing.

One might think that the Diversity of Humour, which must be allowed to be diffused throughout Mankind, might afford endless matter, for the support of Comedies. But when we come closely to consider that point, and nicely to distinguish the Difference of Humours, I believe we shall find the contrary. For thô we allow every Man something of his own, and a peculiar Humour; yet every Man has it not in quantity, to become Remarkable by it: Or, if many do become Remarkable by their Humours; yet all those Humours may not be Diverting. Nor is it only requisite to distinguish what Humour will be diverting, but also how much of it, what part of it to shew in Light, and what to cast in Shades ; how to set it off by preparatory Scenes, and by opposing other humours to it in the same Scene. Thrô a wrong Judgment, sometimes, Mens Humours may be opposed when there is really no specific Difference between them ; only a greater proportion of the same, in one than t'other ; occasion'd by his having more Flegm, or Choller, or whatever the Constitution is, from whence their Humours derive their Source.

There is infinitely more to be said on this Subject ; thô perhaps I have already said too much ; but I have said it to a Friend, who I am sure will not expose it, if he does not approve of it. I believe the Subject is intirely new, and was never touch'd upon before ; and if I would have any one to see this private Essay, it should be some one, who might be provoked by my Errors in it, to Publish a more Judicious Treatise on the Subject. Indeed I wish it were done, that the World being a little acquainted with the scarcity of true Humour, and the difficulty of finding and shewing it, might look a little more favourably on the Labours of them, who endeavour to search into Nature for it, and lay it open to the Publick View.

I dont say but that very entertaining and useful Characters, and proper for Comedy, may be drawn from Affectations, and those other Qualities, which I have endeavoured to distinguish from Humour : but I would not have such imposed on the World, for Humour, nor esteem'd of Equal value with it. It were perhaps, the Work of a long Life to make one Comedy true in all its Parts, and to give every Character in it a True and Distinct Humour. Therefore, every Poet must be beholding to other helps, to make out his Number of ridiculous Characters. But I think such a One deserves to be broke, who makes all false Musters ; who does not shew one true Humour in a Comedy, but entertains his Audience to the end of the Play with every thing out of Nature.

I will make but one Observation to you more, and have done; and that is grounded upon an Observation of your own, and which I mention'd at the beginning of my Letter, *viz*, That there is more of Humour in our English Comick Writers than in any others. I do not at all wonder at it, for I look upon Humour to be almost of English Growth; at least, it does not seem to have found such Encrease on any other Soil. And what appears to me to be the reason of it, is the great Freedom, Privilege, and Liberty which the Common People of *England* enjoy. Any Man that has a Humour, is under no restraint, or fear of giving it Vent; they have a Proverb among them, which, may be, will shew the Bent and Genius of the People, as well as a longer Discourse: *He that will have a May-pole, shall have a May-pole.* This is a Maxim with them, and their Practice is agreeable to it. I believe something Considerable too may be ascribed to their feeding so much on Flesh, and the Grossness of their Diet in general. But I have done, let the Physicians agree that. Thus you have my Thoughts of *Humour*, to my Power of Expressing them in so little Time and Compass. You will be kind to shew me wherein I have Err'd; and as you are very Capable of giving me Instruction, so, I think I have a very Just title to demand it from you; being without Reserve,

July 10. 1695.

Your real Friend,

and humble Servant,

W. Congreve.

THE

OLD BATCHELOR.

A

COMEDY.

Quem tulit ad Scenam ventoso gloria Curru,
Exanimat lentus Spectator; sedulus inflat.
Sic leve, sic parvum est, animum quod laudis avarum
Subruit, aut reficit——

Horat. Epist. I. Lib. II.

Printed in the Year 1710.

To the Right Honourable

CHARLES *Lord* Clifford,

OF

LANESBOROUGH, &c.

My Lord,

It is with a great deal of Pleasure, that I lay hold on this first Occasion, which, the Accidents of my Life have given me of writing to your Lordship: For since at the same time, I write to all the World, it will be a means of publishing (what I would have every Body know) the Respect and Duty which I owe and pay to you. I have so much inclination to be yours, that I need no other Engagement: But the particular Ties, by which I am bound to your Lordship and Family, have put it out of my Power to make you any Compliment; since all Offers of my self, will amount to no more than an honest Acknowledgment, and only shew a willingness in me to be grateful.

I am very near wishing, That it were not so much my Interest to be your Lordship's Servant, that it might be more my Merit; not that I would avoid being obliged to you, but I would have my own Choice to run me into the Debt; that I might have it to boast, I had distinguished a Man, to whom I would be glad to be obliged, even without the Hopes of having it in my Power, ever to make him a return.

Lanesborough, &c.] Charles Boyle, of the elder branch, which besides the Earldoms of Cork and Burlington, held the Barony of Clifford of Lanesborough, the first Lord Burlington having married the heiress of Henry Lord Clifford, Earl of Cumberland.

It is impossible for me to come near your Lordship, in any kind, and not to receive some Favour; and while in appearance I am only making an Acknowledgment (with the usual under-hand dealing of the World) I am at the same time, insinuating my own Interest. I cannot give your Lordship your due, without tacking a Bill of my own Privileges. 'Tis true, if a Man never committed a Folly, he would never stand in need of a Protection: But then Power would have nothing to do, and good Nature no Occasion to shew it self; and where those Qualities are, 'tis pity they should want Objects to shine upon. I must confess this is no reason, why a Man should do an idle thing, nor indeed any good Excuse for it, when done; yet it reconciles the uses of such Authority and Goodness, to the necessities of our Follies; and it is a sort of Poetical Logick, which, at this Time I would make use of, to argue your Lordship into a Protection of this Play. It is the first Offence I have committed in this kind, or indeed, in any kind of Poetry, tho' not the first made publick; and, therefore, I hope will the more easily be pardoned: But had it been Acted, when it was first written, more might have been said in its behalf; Ignorance of the Town and Stage, would then have been Excuses in a young Writer, which now, almost four Years Experience, will scarce allow of. Yet I must declare my self sensible of the good Nature of the Town, in receiving this Play so kindly, with all its Faults, which I must own were, for the most part, very industriously covered by the care of the Players; for, I think, scarce a Character but receiv'd all the Advantage it would admit of, from the justness of the Action.

As for the Criticks, my Lord, I have nothing to say, to, or against, any of them of any kind; from those who make just Exceptions, to those who find fault in the wrong place. I will only make this general Answer in behalf of my Play (an Answer, which Epictetus *advises every Man to make for himself, to his Censurers) viz.* That if they who find some Faults in it, were as intimate with it as I am, they would find a great many more. *This is a Confession, which I needed not to have made; but however, I can draw this use from it, to my own Advantage, that I think there are no Faults in it, but what I do know; which, as I take it, is the first step to an Amendment.*

Thus I may live in hopes (some time or other) of making the Town amends; but, you, my Lord, I never can, tho' I am ever

Your LORDSHIP's

most Obedient, and

most Humble Servant,

Will Congreve.

TO

Mr. *CONGREVE.*

WHEN Virtue in pursuit of Fame appears,
And forward shoots the Growth beyond the Years,
We timely court the rising Hero's Cause;
And on his side, the Poet wisely draws;
Bespeaking him hereafter, by Applause.
The Days will come, when we shall all receive
Returning Interest, from what now we give:
Instructed, and supported by that Praise,
And Reputation, which we strive to raise.
Nature so coy, so hardly to be woo'd,
Flies, like a Mistress, but to be pursu'd.
O *Congreve*! boldly follow on the Chase;
She looks behind, and wants thy strong Embrace:
She yields, she yields, surrenders all her Charms,
Do you but force her gently to your Arms:
Such Nerves, such Graces, in your Lines appear,
As you were made to be her Ravisher.
Dryden has long extended his Command,
By Right Divine, quite through the Muses Land,
Absolute Lord; and holding now from none,
But great *Apollo*, his undoubted Crown:
(That Empire settled, and grown old in Pow'r)
Can wish for nothing, but a Successor:
Not to enlarge his Limits, but maintain
Those Provinces, which he alone could gain.
His eldest *Wicherly*, in wise Retreat,
Thought it not worth his Quiet to be Great.
Loose, wandring, *Etherege*, in wild Pleasures tost,
And foreign Int'rests, to his Hopes long lost:
Poor *Lee* and *Otway* dead! *Congreve* appears,
The Darling, and last Comfort of his Years:
May'st thou live long in thy great Master's Smiles,
And growing under him, adorn these Isles:

But when—when part of him (be that but late)
His Body yielding must submit to Fate,
Leaving his deathless Works, and Thee behind,
(The natural Successor of his Mind)
Then may'st thou finish what he has begun:
Heir to his Merit, be in Fame his Son.
What thou hast done, shews all is in thy Pow'r;
And to write better, only must write more.
'Tis something to be willing to commend;
But my best Praise, is, that I am your Friend,

THO. SOUTHERNE.

TO

Mr. CONGREVE.

The Danger's great in these censorious Days,
When Criticks are so rife, to venture Praise:
When the infectious and ill-natur'd Brood
Behold, and damn the Work, because 'tis good;
And with a proud, ungenerous Spirit, try
To pass an Ostracism on Poetry.
But you, my Friend, your Worth does safely bear
Above their Spleen; you have no Cause for Fear;
Like a well-mettled Hawk, you took your Flight
Quite out of Reach, and almost out of Sight.
As the strong Sun, in a fair Summer's Day,
You rise, and drive the Mists and Clouds away,
The Owls and Bats, and all the Birds of Prey.
Each Line of yours, like polish'd Steel's so hard,
In Beauty safe, it wants no other Guard.
Nature her self's beholden to your Dress,
Which tho' still like, much fairer you express.
Some vainly striving Honour to obtain,
Leave to their Heirs the Traffick of their Brain,
Like China *under Ground, the ripening Ware,*
In a long time, perhaps grows worth our Care:

But you now reap the Fame, so well you've sown ;
The Planter tastes his Fruit to Ripeness grown.
As a fair Orange-tree at once is seen,
Big with what's ripe, yet springing still with green
So at one time, my worthy Friend appears,
With all the sap of Youth, and weight of Years.
Accept my pious Love, as forward Zeal,
Which tho' it ruins me I can't conceal :
Expos'd to Censure for my weak Applause,
I'm pleas'd to suffer in so just a Cause :
And tho' my Offering may unworthy prove,
Take, as a Friend, the Wishes of my Love.

J. MARSH.

To Mr. CONGREVE, *on his Play called* The Old Batchelor.

WIT, like true Gold, refin'd from all Allay,
Immortal is, and never can decay :
'Tis in all Times and Languages the same ;
Nor can an ill Translation quench the Flame :
For, tho' the Form and Fashion don't remain,
Th'intrinsick Value still it will retain.
Then let each studied Scene be writ with Art ;
And Judgment sweat to form the labour'd Part :
Each Character be just, and Nature seem ; 9
Without th'Ingredient, Wit, 'tis all but Phlegm :
For that's the Soul, which all the Mass must move,
And wake our Passions into Grief, or Love.
But you, too Bounteous, sow your Wit so thick,
We are surpriz'd, and know not where to pick :
And while with Clapping, we are just to you,
Our selves we injure, and lose something new.
What mayn't we then, great Youth, of thee presage,
Whose Art and Wit so much transcend thy Age ?

How wilt thou shine at thy Meridian height?
Who, at thy Rising, giv'st so vast a Light.
When *Dryden* dying, shall the World deceive,
Whom we Immortal, as his Works, believe;
Thou shalt succeed, the Glory of the Stage,
Adorn and entertain the coming Age.

BEVIL HIGGONS.

PROLOGUE *intended for The* OLD BATCHELOR.

Written by the Lord *FALKLAND.*

Most Authors on the Stage at first appear
Like Widows Bridegrooms, full of Doubt and Fear:
They judge, from the Experience of the Dame,
How hard a Task it is to quench her Flame:
And who falls short of furnishing a Course,
Up to his brawny Predecessor's Force;
With utmost Rage from her Embraces thrown,
Remains convicted, as an empty Drone.
Thus often, to his Shame, a pert Beginner
Proves in the end, a miserable Sinner.
As for our Youngster, I am apt to doubt him:
With all the Vigour of his Youth about him:
But he, more Sanguine, trusts in one and twenty,
And impudently hopes he shall content you:
For tho' his Batchelor be worn and cold,
He thinks the Young may club to help the Old:
And what alone can be atchiev'd by neither,
Is often brought about by both together.
The briskest of you all have felt Alarms,
Finding the Fair one prostitute her Charms
With broken Sighs, in her old Fumbler's Arms.
But for our Spark, he swears he'll ne'er be jealous
Of any Rivals, but young lusty Fellows.

Faith let him try his Chance, and if the Slave,
After his Bragging, prove a washy Knave,
May he be banish'd to some lonely Den,
And never more have leave to dip his Pen:
But if he be the Champion he pretends,
Both Sexes sure will join to be his Friends;
For all agree, where all can have their ends.
And you must own him for a Man of Might,
If he holds out to please you the third Night.

PROLOGUE,

Spoken by Mrs. Bracegirdle.

How this vile World is chang'd! In former Days,
Prologues, were serious Speeches, before Plays;
Grave solemn Things, as Graces are to Feasts;
Where Poets begg'd a Blessing from their Guests.
But now, no more like Suppliants we come;
A Play makes War, and Prologue is the Drum:
Arm'd with keen Satire, and with pointed Wit,
We threaten you who do for Judges sit,
To save our Plays, or else we'll damn your Pit.
But for your Comfort, it falls out to day,
We've a young Author and his first born Play;
So, standing only on his good Behaviour,
He's very civil, and entreats your Favour.
Not but the Man has Malice, would he show it,
But on my Conscience he's a bashful Poet;
You think that strange—no matter, he'll out-
grow it.
Well, I'm his Advocate—by me he prays you,
(I don't know whether I shall speak to please you)
He prays—O bless me! what shall I do now!
Hang me if I know what he prays, or how!
And 'twas the prettiest Prologue as he wrote it!
Well, the deuce take me, if I han't forgot it.

O Lord, for Heavens sake excuse the Play,
Because, you know, if it be damn'd to day,
I shall be hang'd for wanting what to say.
For my sake then—but I'm in such Confusion,
I cannot stay to hear your Resolution.

[*Runs off.*

Dramatis Personæ.

MEN.

Heartwell, a surly old Batchelor, pretending to slight Women, secretly in Love with *Silvia*,	Mr. *Betterton.*
Bellmour, in Love with *Belinda*,	Mr. *Powel.*
Vainlove, capricious in his Love; in Love with *Araminta*,	Mr. *Williams.*
Sharper,	Mr. *Verbruggen.*
Sir *Joseph Wittol*,	Mr. *Bowen.*
Captain *Bluffe*,	Mr. *Haines.*
Fondlewife, a Banker,	Mr. *Dogget.*
Setter, a Pimp,	Mr. *Underhill.*
Servant to *Fondlewife.*	

WOMEN.

Araminta, in Love with *Vainlove*,	Mrs. *Bracegirdle.*
Belinda, her Cousin, an affected Lady, in Love with *Bellmour*,	Mrs. *Mountfort.*
Lætitia, Wife to *Fondlewife*,	Mrs. *Barry.*
Sylvia, *Vainlove*'s forsaken Mistress,	Mrs. *Bowman.*
Lucy, her Maid,	Mrs. *Leigh.*
Betty.	
Boy and Footmen.	

SCENE, *LONDON.*

THE
OLD BATCHELOR.

ACT I. SCENE I.

SCENE, *The Street.*

Bellmour *and* Vainlove *meeting.*

BELLMOUR.

Vainlove, and abroad so early! good Morrow; I thought a Contemplative Lover could no more have parted with his Bed in a Morning, than he could have slept in't.

Vain. Bellmour, good Morrow—Why truth on't is, these early Sallies are not usual to me; but Business, as you see, Sir——[*Shewing Letters.*] And Business must be follow'd, or be lost.

Bell. Business!—And so must Time, my Friend, be close pursued, or lost. Business is the rub of Life, perverts our Aim, casts off the Bias, and leaves us wide and short of the intended Mark.

Vain. Pleasure, I guess you mean.

Bell. Ay, what else has meaning?

Vain. Oh the Wise will tell you——

Bell. More than they believe——Or understand.

Vain. How, how, *Ned*, a wise Man say more than he understands?

Bell. Ay, ay, Wisdom's nothing but a pretending to know and believe more than we really do. You read of but one wise Man, and all that he knew was, that he knew nothing. Come, come, leave

Business to Idlers, and Wisdom to Fools; they have need of 'em: Wit, be my Faculty, and Pleasure, my Occupation; and let Father Time shake his Glass. Let low and earthly Souls grovel 'till they have work'd themselves six Foot deep into a Grave——Business is not my Element——I rowl in a higher Orb, and dwell——

Vain. In Castles ith' Air of thy own building: That's thy Element, *Ned*—Well as high a Flyer as you are, I have a Lure may make you stoop. [*Flings a Letter.*

Bell. I marry Sir, I have a Hawks Eye at a Womans hand—There's more Elegancy in the false Spelling of this Superscription [*Takes up the Letter*] than in all *Cicero*—Let me see—How now! *Dear perfidious* Vainlove. [*Reads.*

Vain. Hold, hold, 'slife that's the wrong.

Bell. Nay let's see the Name (*Sylvia*!) how can'st thou be ungrateful to that Creature? She's extreamly pretty and loves thee intirely——I have heard her breath such Raptures about thee——

Vain. Ay, or any Body that she's about——

Bell. No faith *Frank* you wrong her; she has been just to you.

Vain. That's pleasant, by my troth from thee, who hast had her.

Bell. Never——Her Affections: 'Tis true by Heav'n, she own'd it to my Face; and blushing like the Virgin Morn when it disclos'd the Cheat, which that trusty Bawd of Nature, Night, had hid, confess'd her Soul was true to you; tho' I by Treachery had stoll'n the Bliss—

Vain. So was true as Turtle——in imagination, *Ned*, ha? Preach this Doctrine to Husbands, and the married Women will adore thee.

Bell. Why faith I think it will do well enough—If the Husband be out of the way, for the Wife to shew her Fondness and Impatience of his Absence,

33 Lure] A term in falconry; a dead pigeon or artificial bird, used for calling long-winged hawks, especially when young.

by chusing a Lover as like him as she can, and what is unlike, she may help out with her own Fancy.

Vain. But is it not an Abuse to the Lover to be made a Blind of?

Bell. As you say the Abuse is to the Lover, not the Husband: For 'tis an Argument of her great Zeal towards him, that she will enjoy him in Effigie.

Vain. It must be a very superstitious Country, where such Zeal passes for true Devotion. I doubt it will be damn'd by all our Protestant Husbands for flat Idolatry——But if you can make Alderman *Fondlewife* of your Perswasion, this Letter will be needless.

Bell. What, the old Banker with the handsom Wife?

Vain. Ay.

Bell. Let me see, *Lætitia*! Oh 'tis a delicious Morsel. Dear *Frank* thou art the truest Friend in the World.

Vain. Ay, am I not? To be continually starting of Hares for you to course. We were certainly cut out for one another; for my Temper quits an Amour, just where thine takes it up——But read that, it is an Appointment for me, this Evening; when *Fondlewife* will be gone out of Town, to meet the Master of a Ship, about the return of a Venture which he's in danger of losing. Read, read.

Bell. reads. Hum, Hum——*Out of Town this Evening, and talks of sending for Mr.* Spintext *to keep me Company; but I'll take care, he shall not be at home.* Good! *Spintext*! Oh the Fanatick one-ey'd Parson!

Vain. Ay.

Bell. reads. Hum, Hum——*That your Conversation will be much more agreeable, if you can counterfeit his Habit to blind the Servants.* Very good! Then I must be disguised——With all my Heart——It adds a Gusto to an Amour; gives it

92 Fanatick] Puritan, Nonconformist.

the greater resemblance of Theft; and among us lewd Mortals, the deeper the Sin the sweeter. *Frank* I'm amaz'd at thy good Nature——

Vain. Faith I hate Love when 'tis forc'd upon a Man, as I do Wine——And this Business is none of my seeking; I only hapned to be once or twice, where *Lœtitia* was the handsomest Woman in Company, so consequently apply'd my self to her—And it seems she has taken me at my Word——Had you been there, or any Body, 'thad been the same.

Bell. I wish I may succeed as the same.

Vain. Never doubt it; for if the Spirit of Cuckoldom be once raised up in a Woman, the Devil can't lay it, 'till she has don't.

Bell. Prithee, what sort of Fellow is *Fondlewife*?

Vain. A kind of Mongrel Zealot, sometimes very precise and peevish: But I have seen him pleasant enough in his way; much addicted to Jealousie, but more to Fondness: So that as he is often Jealous without a Cause, he's as often satisfied without Reason.

Bell. A very even Temper, and fit for my purpose. I must get your Man *Setter* to provide my Disguise.

Vain. Ay, you may take him for good and all if you will, for you have made him fit for no body else——Well——

Bell. You're going to visit in return of *Sylvia*'s Letter——Poor Rogue. Any Hour of the Day or Night will serve her——But do you know nothing of a new Rival there?

Vain. Yes, *Heartwell*, that surly, old, pretended Woman-Hater, thinks her Vertuous; that's one Reason why I fail her: I would have her fret her self out of Conceit with me, that she may entertain some Thoughts of him. I know he visits her ev'ry Day.

120 Fondness]. Fond still implied doting.

Bell. Yet rails on still, and thinks his Love unknown to us ; a little time will swell him so, he must be forc'd to give it birth ; and the Discovery must needs be very pleasant from himself ; to see what Pains he will take, and how he will strain to be deliver'd of a Secret, when he has miscarried of it already.

Vain. Well, good Morrow, let's dine together ; I'll meet at the old Place.

Bell. With all my Heart ; it lies convenient for us to pay our Afternoon Services to our Mistresses ; I find I am damnably in Love, I'm so uneasie for not having seen *Belinda* yesterday. 151

Vain. But I saw my *Araminta*, yet am as impatient.

SCENE II.

BELLMOUR *alone.*

Bell. Why what a Cormorant in Love am I ! who, not contented with the slavery of honourable Love in one Place, and the Pleasure of enjoying some half a score Mistresses of my own acquiring ; must yet take *Vainlove*'s Business upon my Hands, because it lay too heavy upon his ; So am not only forc'd to lie with other Mens Wives for 'em, but must also undertake the harder Task of obliging their Mistresses——I must take up, or I shall never hold out ; Flesh and Blood cannot bear it always. 11

SCENE III.

[*To him*] SHARPER.

Sharp. I'm sorry to see this, *Ned ;* Once a Man comes to his Soliloquys I give him for gone.

Bell. *Sharper*, I'm glad to see thee.

1 Cormorant] Cormorants were used to catch fish, thus doing other people's business for them.

Sharp. What, is *Belinda* cruel, that you are so thoughtful?

Bell. No faith, not for that——But there's a Business of Consequence fall'n out to Day, that requires some Consideration.

Sharp. Prithee what mighty Business of Consequence canst thou have? 10

Bell. Why you must know, 'tis a piece of Work toward the finishing of an Alderman; it seems I must put the last hand to it, and dub him Cuckold, that he may be of equal Dignity with the rest of his Brethren: So I must beg *Belinda*'s Pardon.—

Sharp. Faith e'en give her over for good-and-all; you can have no hopes of getting her for a Mistress; and she is too proud, too inconstant, too affected and too witty, and too handsome for a Wife. 21

Bell. But she can't have too much Mony——There's twelve thousand Pound, *Tom*.——'Tis true she is excessively foppish and affected, but in my Conscience I believe the Baggage loves me: For she never speaks well of me her self, nor suffers any Body else to rail at me. Then, as I told you, there's twelve thousand Pound——Hum——Why faith upon second Thoughts, she does not appear to be so very affected neither——Give her her due, I think the Womans a Woman, and that's all. As such I'm sure I shall like her; for the Devil take me if I don't love all the Sex. 33

Sharp. And here comes one who swears as heartily he hates all the Sex.

SCENE IV.

[*To them*] HEARTWELL.

Bell. Who *Heartwell!* Ay, but he knows better things——How now *George*, where hast thou been snarling odious Truths, and entertaining Company, like a Physician, with discourse of their Diseases and Infirmities? What fine Lady hast thou been putting out of Conceit with her self, and perswading that the Face she had been making all the Morning, was none of her own? for I know thou art as unmannerly and as unwelcome to a Woman, as a Looking-Glass after the Small-Pox.

Heart. I confess I have not been sneering fulsom Lyes and nauseous Flattery, fawning upon a little tawdry Whore, that will fawn upon me again, and entertain any Puppy that comes, like a Tumbler, with the same Tricks over and over. For such I guess may have been your late Employment.

Bell. Would thou hadst come a little sooner, *Vainlove* would have wrought thy Conversion, and been a Champion for the Cause.

Heart. What, has he been here? that's one of Love's *April*-Fools, is always upon some Errand that's to no purpose, ever embarking in Adventures, yet never comes to Harbour.

Sharp. That's because he always sets out in foul Weather, loves to buffet with the Winds, meet the Tide, and fail in the Teeth of Opposition.

Heart. What, has he not dropt Anchor at *Araminta*?

Bell. Truth on't is she fits his Temper best, is a kind of floating Island; sometimes seems in reach, then vanishes and keeps him busied in the search.

Sharp. She had need have a good share of Sense to manage so *Capricious* a Lover.

Bell. Faith I don't know, he's of a Temper the most easie to himself in the World; he takes as much always of an Amour as he cares for, and quits it when it grows stale or unpleasant.

Sharp. An Argument of very little Passion, very good Understanding, and very ill Nature.

Heart. And proves that *Vainlove* plays the Fool with Discretion.

Sharp. You *Bellmour* are bound in Gratitude to

stickle for him ; you with Pleasure reap that Fruit, which he takes Pains to sow : he does the Drudgery in the Mine, and you stamp your image on the Gold.

Bell. He's of another Opinion, and says I do the Drudgery in the Mine. Well, we have each our share of Sport, and each that which he likes best ; 'tis his Diversion to Set, 'tis mine to Cover the Partridge. 52

Heart. And it should be mine to let 'em go again.

Sharp. Not till you had Mouth'd a little *George*, I think that's all thou art fit for now.

Heart. Good Mr. Young-Fellow, you're mistaken ; as able as your self, and as nimble too, tho' I mayn't have so much Mercury in my Limbs ; 'tis true indeed, I don't force Appetite, but wait the natural Call of my Lust, and think it time enough to be lewd, after I have had the Temptation. 63

Bell. Time enough, ay too soon, I should rather have expected, from a Person of your Gravity.

Heart. Yet it is oftentimes too late with some of you young, termagant flashy Sinners—you have all the Guilt of the Intention, and none of the Pleasure of the Practice—'tis true you are so eager in Pursuit of the Temptation, that you save the Devil the trouble of leading you into it : Nor is it out of Discretion, that you don't swallow that very Hook your selves have baited, but you are cloy'd with the Preparative, and what you mean for a Whet, turns the Edge of your puny Stomachs. Your Love is like your Courage, which you shew for the first Year or two upon all Occasions ; 'till in a little time, being disabled or disarmed, you abate of your Vigour ; and that daring Blade which was so often drawn, is bound to the Peace for ever after. 81

Bell. Thou art an old Fornicator of a singular good Principle indeed ! and art for encouraging

Youth, that they may be as wicked as thou art at thy Years.

Heart. I am for having every body be what they pretend to be ; a Whoremaster be a Whoremaster ; and not like *Vainlove*, kiss a Lap-Dog with Passion, when it would disgust him from the Lady's own Lips.

Bell. That only happens sometimes, where the Dog has the sweeter Breath, for the more cleanly conveyance. But *George*, you must not quarrel with little Gallantries of this nature : Women are often won by 'em. Who would refuse to kiss a Lap-Dog, if it were preliminary to the Lips of his Lady ?

Sharp. Or omit playing with her Fan, and cooling her if she were hot, when it might intitle him to the Office of warming her when she should be cold ?

Bell. What is it to read a Play in a rainy Day ? Though you should be now and then interrupted in a witty Scene, and she perhaps preserve her Laughter, till the Jest were over ; even, that, may be born with, considering the Reward in Prospect.

Heart. I confess you that are Womens Asses bear greater Burdens : Are forced to undergo Dressing, Dancing, Singing, Sighing, Whining, Rhyming, Flattering, Lying, Grinning, Cringing, and the drudgery of Loving to boot.

Bell. O Brute, the drudgery of Loving !

Heart. Ay, why to come to Love through all these Incumbrances, is like coming to an Estate overcharg'd with Debts ; which by the time you have pay'd, yields no further profit than what the bare tillage and manuring of the Land will produce at the Expence of your own Sweat.

Bell. Prithee how dost thou love ?

Sharp. He ! he hates the Sex.

Heart. So I hate Physick too——yet I may love to take it for my Health.

Bell. Well come off, *George,* if at any time you should be taken straying.

Sharp. He has need of such an Excuse, considering the present state of his Body.

Heart. How d'ye mean?

Sharp. Why if whoring be purging (as you call it) then, I may say, Marriage, is entering into a Course of Physick.

Bell. How, *George,* does the Wind blow there?

Heart. It will as soon blow *North* and by *South*—marry, quotha! I hope in Heaven I have a greater Portion of Grace, and I think I have baited too many of those Traps, to be caught in one my self.

Bell. Who the Devil would have thee? unless 'twere an Oyster-Woman, to propagate young Fry for *Billingsgate*——thy Talent will never recommend thee to any things of better Quality.

Heart. My Talent is chiefly that of speaking Truth, which I don't expect should ever recommend me to People of Quality—I thank Heav'n, I have very honestly purchas'd the Hatred of all the great Families in Town.

Sharp. And you in return of Spleen hate them: But could you hope to be receiv'd into the Alliance of a noble Family——

Heart. No, I hope I shall never merit that Affliction—to be punish'd with a Wife of Birth——be a Stag of the first Head and bear my Horns aloft, like one of the Supporters of my Wifes Coat. S'death I would not be a Cuckold to e'er an illustrious Whore in *England.*

Bell. What not to make your Family Man! and provide for your Children?

Sharp. For her Children you mean.

Heart. Ay there you've nick't it——there's the Devil upon Devil——O the Pride and Joy of Heart 'twou'd be to me, to have my Son and Heir resemble such a Duke——to have a fleering Coxcomb scoff and cry, Mr. your Son's mighty like his Grace, has just his Smile and Air of's Face.

Then replies another——methinks he has more of the Marquess of such a Place, about his Nose and Eyes; though he has my Lord what-d'ye-calls Mouth to a tittle——Then, I, to put it off as unconcern'd, come chuck the Infant under the Chin, force a Smile and cry, ay, the Boy takes after his Mothers Relations——when the Devil and she knows, 'tis a little Compound of the whole Body of Nobility.

Bell.
Sharp. } Ha, ha, ha.

Bell. Well but *George* I have one Question to ask you——

Heart. Pshaw, I have pratled away my Time ——I hope you are in no haste for an Answer—— for I shan't stay now. [*Looking on his Watch.*

Bell. Nay prithee *George*——

Heart. No, besides my Business, I see a Fool coming this way. Adieu.

SCENE V

Sharper, Bellmour.

Bell. What does he mean? Oh, 'tis Sir *Joseph Wittoll* with his Friend; but I see he has turn'd the Corner, and goes another way.

Sharp. What in the name of wonder is it?

Bell. Why a Fool.

Sharp. 'Tis a tawdry Outside.

Bell. And a very beggarly Lining——yet he may be worth your Acquaintance—a little of thy Chymistry *Tom*, may extract Gold from that Dirt.

Sharp. Say you so? 'faith I am as poor as a Chymist, and would be as industrious. But what was he that follow'd him? is not he a Dragon that watches those Golden Pippins?

Bell. Hang him, no, he a Dragon! if he be 'tis a very peaceful one, I can ensure his Anger dormant; or should he seem to rouse, 'tis but well lashing him, and he will sleep like a Top.

Sharp. Ay, is he of that Kidney?

Bell. Yet is ador'd by that Biggot Sir *Joseph Wittoll*, as the Image of Valour: He calls him his Back, and indeed they are never asunder——yet last Night, I know not by what Mischance, the Knight was alone, and had fallen into the Hands of some Night-walkers, who I suppose would have pillaged him: But I chanc'd to come by, and rescued him: though I believe he was heartily frightned, for as soon as ever he was loose, he ran away, without staying to see who had help'd him.

Sharp. Is that Bully of his in the Army?

Bell. No, but is a Pretender, and wears the Habit of a Soldier; which now-a'days as often cloaks Cowardice, as a black Gown does Atheism—You must know he has been abroad——went purely to run away from a Campaign; enrich'd himself with the Plunder of a few Oaths——and here vents 'em against the General, who slighting Men of Merit, and preferring only those of Interest, has made him quit the service.

Sharp. Wherein no doubt he magnifies his own Performance.

Bell. Speaks Miracles, is the Drum to his own Praise—the only Implement of a Soldier he resembles, like that, being full of blustring Noise and Emptiness——

Sharp. And like that, of no use but to be beaten.

Bell. Right; but, then, the Comparison breaks, for he will take a drubbing with as little Noise as a Pulpit Cushion.

Sharp. His name, and I have done?

Bell. Why that, to pass it current too, he has gilded with a Title; he is call'd, Capt. *Bluffe.*

Sharp. Well, I'll endeavour his acquaintance—you steer another Course, are bound,

For Love's Island: I, for the golden Coast.
May each succeed in what he wishes most.

ACT II. SCENE I.

Sir Joseph Wittoll, Sharper *following*.

SHARPER.

Sure that's he, and alone.

Sir *Jo*. Um—Ay this, this is the very damn'd Place; the inhumane Canibals, the bloody-minded Villains would have butcher'd me last Night: No doubt, they would have flea'd me alive, have sold my Skin, and devour'd, *&c.*

Sharp. How's this!

Sir *Jo*. An it hadn't been for a civil Gentleman as came by and frighted 'em away—but agad I durst not stay to give him Thanks.

Sharp. This must be *Bellmour* he means——ha! I have a Thought——

Sir *Jo*. Zooks, would the Captain would come; the very Remembrance makes me quake; agad I shall never be reconciled to this Place heartily.

Sharp. 'Tis but trying, and being where I am at worst, now luck!——curs'd Fortune! this must be the Place, this damn'd unlucky Place——

Sir *Jo*. Agad and so 'tis——why here has been more Mischief done I perceive.

Sharp. No, 'tis gone, 'tis lost——ten thousand Devils on that Chance which drew me hither; ay here, just here, this Spot to me is Hell; nothing to be found, but the Despair of what I've lost. [*Looking about as in search.*

Sir *Jo*. Poor Gentleman——by the Lord *Harry* I'll stay no longer, for I have found too——

Sharp. Ha! who's that has found? What have you found? restore it quickly, or by——

Sir *Jo*. Not I, Sir, not I, as I've a Soul to be sav'd, I have found nothing but what has been to my loss, as I may say. and as you were saying, Sir.

Sharp. O your Servant, Sir, you are safe then it

seems ; 'tis an ill Wind that blows no body good : Well, you may rejoice over my ill Fortune, since it pay'd the Price of your Ransome.

Sir *Jo.* I rejoice ! agad not I, Sir : I'm very sorry for your Loss, with all my Heart, Blood and Guts, Sir ; and if you did but know me, you'd ne'er say I were so ill natur'd.

Sharp. Know you ; why can you be so ungrateful, to forget me !

Sir *Jo.* O Lord forget him ! No, no Sir, I don't forget you——because I never saw your Face before, agad. Ha, ha, ha.

Sharp. How ! [*Angrily.*

Sir *Jo.* Stay, stay Sir, let me recollect——he's a damn'd angry Fellow——I believe I had better remember him, 'till I can get out of his sight ; but out o'sight out o'mind agad. [*Aside.*

Sharp. Methought the Service I did you last Night, Sir, in preserving you from those Ruffians, might have taken better Root in your shallow Memory.

Sir *Jo.* Gads-Daggers-Belts-Blades and Scabbards, this is the very Gentleman ! How shall I make him a Return suitable to the Greatness of his Merit—I had a pretty thing to that purpose, if he han't frighted it out of my Memory. Hem ! hem ! Sir, I most submissively implore your Pardon for my Transgression of Ingratitude and Omission ; having my intire Dependance, Sir, upon the superfluity of your Goodness, which, like an Inundation will, I hope, totally immerge the recollection of my Error, and leave me floating in your Sight, upon the full blown Bladders of Repentance—by the help of which, I shall once more hope to swim into your Favour. [*Bows.*

Sharp. So-h, O Sir I am easily pacify'd, the Acknowledgment of a Gentleman——

Sir *Jo.* Acknowledgment ! Sir I am all over Acknowledgment, and will not stick to shew it in the greatest Extremity, by Night, or by Day, in

Sickness, or in Health, Winter, or Summer, all Seasons and Occasions shall testifie the Reality and Gratitude of your superabundant humble Servant Sir *Joseph Wittoll* Knight. Hem! hem!

Sharp. Sir *Joseph Wittoll.*

Sir *Jo*. The same Sir, of *Wittoll Hall* in *Comitatu Bucks.*

Sharp. Is it possible! Then, I am happy, to have obliged the Mirrour of Knighthood and Pink of Courtesie in the Age: let me embrace you.

Sir *Jo*. O Lord, Sir!

Sharp. My loss, I esteem as a Trifle repay'd with Interest, since it has purchas'd me the Friendship and Acquaintance of the Person in the World, whose Character I admire.

Sir *Jo*. You are only pleas'd to say so, Sir—— But pray if I may be so bold, what is that Loss you mention?

Sharp. O term it no longer so, Sir. In the Scuffle, last Night, I only dropt a Bill of a hundred Pound, which I confess, I came half despairing to recover; but thanks to my better Fortune——

Sir *Jo*. You have found it Sir then it seems; I profess I'm heartily glad——

Sharp. Sir your humble Servant——I don't question but you are; that you have so cheap an Opportunity of expressing your Gratitude and Generosity. Since the paying so trivial a Sum, will wholly acquit you and doubly engage me.

Sir *Jo*. What a dickens does he mean by a trivial Sum? [*Aside.*] But han't you found it, Sir!

Sharp. No otherwise I vow to Gad but in my Hopes in you, Sir.

Sir *Jo*. Humph.

Sharp. But that's sufficient——'Twere Injustice to doubt the Honour of Sir *Joseph Wittoll.*

Sir *Jo*. O Lord, Sir.

Sharp. You are above (I'm sure) a Thought so low, to suffer me to lose what was ventur'd in your

Service; Nay 'twas in a manner——paid down for your deliverance; 'twas so much lent you——And you scorn, I'll say that for you——

Sir *Jo.* Nay I'll say that for my self (with your leave, Sir,) I do scorn a dirty thing. But agad I'm a little out of Pocket at present.

Sharp. Pshaw you can't want a hundred Pound. Your Word is sufficient any where: 'Tis but borrowing so much Dirt, you have large Acres and can soon repay it—Money is but Dirt Sir *Joseph*—Meer Dirt.

Sir *Jo.* But I profess, 'tis a Dirt I have washed my Hands of at present; I have laid it all out upon my Back.

Sharp. Are you so extravagant in Cloaths, Sir *Joseph*?

Sir *Jo.* Ha, ha, ha, a very good Jest I profess, ha, ha, ha, a very good Jest, and I did not know that I had said it, and that's a better Jest than t'other. 'Tis a sign you and I ha'n't been long acquainted; you have lost a good Jest for want of knowing me—I only mean a Friend of mine whom I call my Back; he sticks as close to me, and follows me through all Dangers——he is indeed Back, Breast and Headpiece as it were to me——agad he's a brave Fellow—Pauh, I am quite another thing, when I am with him: I don't fear the Devil (bless us) almost if he be by. Ah——had he been with me last Night—

Sharp. If he had, Sir, what then? he could have done no more, nor perhaps have suffer'd so much—had he a hundred Pound to lose? [*Angrily.*

Sir *Jo.* O Lord Sir by no means (but I might have sav'd a hundred Pound) I meant innocently, as I hope to be saved Sir (a damn'd hot Fellow) only as I was saying, I let him have all my ready Mony to redeem his great Sword from Limbo—But Sir I have a Letter of Credit to Alderman *Fondlewife*, as far as two hundred Pound, and this Afternoon

150 Limbo] Pawn.

you shall see I am a Person, such a one as you would wish to have met with——

Sharp. That you are I'll be sworn [*Aside*.] Why that's great and like your self. 156

SCENE II.

[*To them*] *Captain* BLUFFE.

Sir *Jo*. O Here a'comes—Ay my *Hector* of *Troy*, welcome my Bully, my Back; agad my Heart has gone apit pat for thee.

Bluff. How now, my young Knight? Not for Fear I hope; he that knows me must be a Stranger to Fear.

Sir *Jo*. Nay agad I hate Fear ever since I had like to have dy'd of a Fright—But— 8

Bluff. But? Look you here Boy, here's your Antidote, here's your Jesuites Powder for a shaking Fit——But who hast thou got with thee, is he of Mettle? [*Laying his Hand upon his Sword*.

Sir *Jo*. Ay, Bully, a Devilish smart Fellow: 'a will fight like a Cock.

Bluff. Say you so? then I honour him——But has he been abroad? for every Cock will fight upon his own Dunghil.

Sir *Jo*. I don't know, but I'll present you——

Bluff. I'll recommend my self—Sir I honour you; I understand you love fighting, I reverence a Man that loves fighting, Sir I kiss your Hilts. 21

Sharp. Sir your Servant, but you are misinform'd, for unless it be to serve my particular Friend, as Sir *Joseph* here, my Country, or my Religion, or in some very justifiable Cause, I'm not for it.

Bluff. O Lord I beg your Pardon, Sir, I find you are not of my Pallat, you can't relish a Dish of fighting without sweet Sawce. Now I think——

10 Jesuites Powder] Quinine. A Jesuit having been cured of ague in South America by means of the Cinchona bark, the Society disseminated a knowledge of it throughout Europe.

fighting, for fighting sake's sufficient Cause; fighting, to me's Religion and the Laws. 31

Sir *Jo*. Ah, well said my *Hero*; was not that great Sir? by the Lord *Harry* he says true; fighting, is Meat, Drink and Cloth to him. But Back, this Gentleman is one of the best Friends I have in the World, and saved my Life last Night——You know I told you.

Bluff. Ay! Then I honour him again——Sir may I crave your Name?

Sharp. Ay, Sir, my Name's *Sharper*. 40

Sir *Jo*. Pray Mr. *Sharper* embrace my Back—very well——by the Lord *Harry* Mr. *Sharper* he's a brave a Fellow as *Cannibal*, are not you Bully-Back?

Sharp. *Hannibal* I believe you mean, Sir *Joseph*.

Bluff. Undoubtedly he did Sir; faith *Hannibal* was a very pretty Fellow——but Sir *Joseph*, Comparisons are odious—*Hannibal* was a very pretty Fellow in those Days, it must be granted—but alas Sir! were he alive now, he would be nothing, nothing in the Earth. 52

Sharp. How Sir! I make a doubt, if there be at this Day a greater General breathing.

Bluff. Oh excuse me Sir; have you serv'd abroad, Sir?

Sharp. Not I really, Sir.

Bluff. Oh I thought so——Why then you can know nothing, Sir: I am afraid you scarce know the History of the late War in *Flanders*, with all its particulars. 61

Sharp. Not I, Sir, no more than publick Letters, or *Gazettes* tell us.

Bluff. Gazette! Why there again now——Why, Sir, there are not three Words of Truth, the Year round, put into the Gazette——I'll tell you a strange thing now as to that——You must know, Sir, I was resident in *Flanders* the last Campaign,

68 Campaign] i.e. of 1692, which included Steinkirk.

had a small Post there; but no matter for that——Perhaps, Sir, there was scarce any thing of moment done but an humble Servant of yours, that shall be nameless, was an Eye Witness of——I won't say had the greatest share in't. Tho' I might say that too, since I name no Body you know——Well, Mr. *Sharper*, would you think it? In all this time——as I hope for a Truncheon—this rascally Gazette-writer never so much as once mention'd me—Not once by the Wars——Took no more notice, than as if *Nol. Bluffe* had not been in the Land of the Living.

Sharp. Strange!

Sir *Jo*. Yet by the Lord *Harry* 'tis true Mr. *Sharper*, for I went every Day to Coffee-Houses to read the Gazette my self.

Bluff. Ay, ay, no matter——You see Mr. *Sharper* after all I am content to retire——Live a private Person——*Scipio* and others have done it.

Sharp. Impudent Rogue. [*Aside*.

Sir *Jo*. Ay, this damn'd Modesty of yours——Agad if he would put in for't he might be made General himself yet.

Bluff. Oh fie, no Sir *Joseph*——You know I hate this.

Sir *Jo*. Let me but tell Mr. *Sharper* a little, how you eat Fire once out of the Mouth of a Cannon—agad he did; those impenetrable Whiskers of his have confronted Flames——

Bluff. Death, what do you mean Sir *Joseph*?

Sir *Jo*. Look you know, I tell you he's so modest he'll own nothing.

Bluff. Pish you have put me out, I have forgot what I was about. Pray hold your Tongue, and give me leave. [*Angrily*.

Sir *Jo*. I am dumb.

Bluff. This Sword I think I was telling you of Mr. *Sharper*——This Sword I'll maintain to be the best Divine, Anatomist, Lawyer or Casuist in

Europe; it shall decide a Controversie or split a Cause——

Sir *Jo*. Nay, now I must speak; it will split a Hair, by the Lord *Harry*, I have seen it.

Bluff. Zouns Sir, it's a Lie, you have not seen it, nor shan't see it; Sir I say you can't see; what d'ye say to that now?

Sir *Jo*. I am blind.

Bluff. Death, had any other Man interrupted me——

Sir *Jo*. Good Mr. *Sharper* speak to him; I dare not look that way.

Sharp. Sir *Joseph*'s penitent.

Bluff. Oh I am calm Sir, calm as a discharged Culverin——But 'twas indiscreet, when you know what will provoke me—Nay come Sir *Joseph*, you know my Heat's soon over.

Sir *Jo*. Well I am a Fool sometimes—But I'm sorry.

Bluff. Enough.

Sir *Jo*. Come we'll go take a Glass to drown Animosities. Mr. *Sharper* will you partake?

Sharp. I wait on you Sir; nay, pray Captain—You are Sir *Joseph*'s Back.

SCENE III.

Araminta, Belinda, Betty *waiting*, *in* Araminta's *Apartment*.

Belin. Ah! Nay, Dear——prithee good, dear sweet Cousin no more, oh Gad, I swear you'd make one sick to hear you.

Aram. Bless me! what have I said to move you thus?

Belin. Oh you have raved, talked idly, and all in Commendation of that filthy, awkward, two-leg'd Creature, Man—you don't know what you've said, your Fever has transported you.

Aram. If Love be the Fever which you mean,

kind Heav'n avert the Cure: Let me have Oil to feed that Flame and never let it be extinct, 'till I my self am Ashes.

Belin. There was a Whine!——O Gad I hate your horrid Fancy——This Love is the Devil, and sure to be in Love is to be possess'd——'Tis in the Head, the Heart, the Blood, the——All over——O Gad you are quite spoil'd——I shall loath the sight of Mankind for your sake. 19

Aram. Fie, this is gross Affectation—A little of *Bellmour*'s Company would change the Scene.

Belin. Filthy Fellow! I wonder Cousin—

Aram. I wonder, Cousin, you should imagine, I don't perceive you love him.

Belin. Oh I love your hideous Fancy! Ha, ha, ha, love a Man!

Aram. Love a Man! yes, you would not love a Beast. 28

Belin. Of all Beasts not an Ass——Which is so like your *Vainlove*——Lard I have seen an Ass look so Chagrin, Ha, ha, ha, (you must pardon me I can't help laughing) that an absolute Lover would have concluded the poor Creature to have had Darts, and Flames, and Altars, and all that in his Breast. *Araminta,* come I'll talk seriously to you now; could you but see with my Eyes, the buffoonry of one Scene of Address, a Lover, set out with all his Equipage and Appurtenances; O Gad! sure you would——But you play the Game, and consequently can't see the Miscarriages obvious to every stander by. 41

Aram. Yes, yes, I can see something near it when you and *Bellmour* meet. You don't know that you dreamt of *Bellmour* last Night, and call'd him aloud in your Sleep.

Belin. Pish, I can't help dreaming of the Devil sometimes; would you from thence infer I love him? 48

Aram. But that's not all; you caught me in your Arms when you named him, and press'd me to your Bosom——Sure if I had not pinch'd you 'till you wak'd you had stifled me with Kisses.

Belin. O barbarous Aspersion!

Aram. No Aspersions, Cousin, we are alone——Nay I can tell you more.

Belin. I deny it all.

Aram. What before you hear it?

Belin. My Denial is premeditated like your Malice——Lard, Cousin, you talk odly——What ever the Matter is, O my Sol, I'm afraid you'll follow evil Courses.

Aram. Ha, ha, ha, this is pleasant.

Belin. You may laugh, but——

Aram. Ha, ha, ha.

Belin. You think the malicious Grinn becomes you——The Devil take *Bellmour*——Why do you tell me of him?

Aram. Oh is it come out——now you are angry, I am sure you love him. I tell no body else, Cousin——I have not betray'd you yet.

Belin. Prithee tell it all the World, it's false.

Aram. Come then, kiss and Friends.

Belin. Pish.

Aram. Prithee don't be so Peevish.

Belin. Prithee don't be so impertinent. *Betty.*

Aram. Ha, ha, ha.

Betty. Did your Ladyship call, Madam?

Belin. Get my Hoods and Tippet, and bid the Footman call a Chair.

Aram. I hope you are not going out in dudgeon, Cousin.

SCENE IV.

[*To them*] FOOTMAN.

Foot. Madam, there are——

Belin. Is there a Chair?

Foot. No, Madam, there are Mr. *Bellmour* and Mr. *Vainlove* to wait upon your Ladyship.

Aram. Are they below?

Foot. No, Madam, they sent before, to know if you were at home.

Belin. The Visit's to you, Cousin, I suppose I am at my Liberty.

Aram. Be ready to shew 'em up.

SCENE V.

[*To them*] BETTY *with Hoods and Looking-Glass.*

I can't tell, Cousin, I believe we are equally concern'd : But if you continue your Humour, it won't be very entertaining——(I know she'd fain be persuaded to stay. [*Aside.*

Belin. I shall oblige you, in leaving you to the full and free Enjoyment of that Conversation you admire.

Belin. Let me see ; hold the Glass—Lard I look wretchedly to Day !

Aram. Betty, why don't you help my Cousin ? 9

[*Putting on her Hoods.*

Belin. Hold off your Fists, and see that he gets a Chair with a high Roof, or a very low Seat—Stay, come back here you Mrs. Fidget—you are so ready to go to the Footman——Here, take 'em all again, my Mind's chang'd, I won't go.

SCENE VI.

ARAMINTA, BELINDA.

Aram. So, this I expected——You won't oblige me then, Cousin, and let me have all the Company to my self ?

Belin. No ; upon consideration, I have too much Charity to trust you to your self. The Devil watches all Opportunities ; and in this favourable Disposition of your Mind, Heav'n knows how far you may be tempted : I am tender of your Reputation.

Aram. I am oblig'd to you—But who's malicious now, *Belinda.*

Belin. Not I; witness my Heart, I stay out of pure Affection.

Aram. In my Conscience I believe you.

SCENE VII.

[*To them*] VAINLOVE, BELLMOUR. FOOTMAN.

Bell. So, Fortune be prais'd! To find you both within, Ladies, is——

Aram. No Miracle, I hope.

Bell. Not o'your side, Madam, I confess——But my Tyrant there and I, are two Buckets that can never come together.

Belin. Nor are ever like——Yet we often meet and clash.

Bell. How never like! marry *Hymen* forbid. But this it is to run so extravagantly in Debt; I have laid out such a World of Love in your Service, that you think you can never be able to pay me all: So shun me for the same Reason that you would a Dun.

Belin. Ay, on my Conscience, and the most impertinent and troublesome of Duns—a Dun for Mony will be quiet, when he sees his Debtor has not wherewithal—But a Dun for Love is an eternal Torment that never rests——

Bell. 'Till he has created Love where there was none, and then gets it for his Pains. For Importunity in Love, like Importunity at Court; first creates its own Interest, and then pursues it for the Favour.

Aram. Favours that are got by Impudence and Importunity, are like Discoveries from the Rack, when the afflicted Person, for his ease, sometimes confesses Secrets his Heart knows nothing of.

Vain. I should rather think Favours, so gain'd, to be due Rewards to indefatigable Devotion——

For as Love is a Deity, he must be serv'd by Prayer.

Belin. O Gad, would you would all pray to Love then, and let us alone.

Vain. You are the Temples of Love, and 'tis through you, our Devotion must be convey'd.

Aram. Rather poor silly Idols of your own making, which, upon the least Displeasure you forsake, and set up new—Every Man, now, changes his Mistress and his Religion, as His Humour varies or his Interest.

Vain. O Madam——

Aram. Nay come, I find we are growing serious, and then we are in great Danger of being dull—If my Musick-Master be not gone, I'll entertain you with a new Song, which comes pretty near my own Opinion of Love and your Sex—Who's there? Is Mr. *Gavot* gone? [*Calls.*

Foot. Only to the next Door, Madam; I'll call him.

SCENE VIII.

ARAMINTA, BELINDA, VAINLOVE, *and* BELLMOUR.

Bell. Why, you won't hear me with Patience.

Aram. What's the Matter, Cousin?

Bell. Nothing, Madam, only——

Belin. Prithee hold thy Tongue——Lard, he has so pester'd me with Flames and Stuff——I think I shan't endure the sight of a Fire this Twelve-month.

Bell. Yet all can't melt that cruel frozen Heart.

Belin. O Gad I hate your hideous Fancy—you said that once before——if you must talk impertinently, for Heavens sake let it be with Variety; don't come always, like the Devil, wrapt in Flames——I'll not hear a Sentence more, that begins with an, *I burn*——Or an, *I beseech you, Madam.*

Bell. But tell me how you would be ador'd—— I am very tractable.

Belin. Then know, I would be ador'd in Silence.

Bell. Humph, I thought so, that you might have all the talk to your self——you had better let me speak; for if my Thoughts fly to any Pitch, I shall make Villainous Signs. 22

Belin. What will you get by that? to make such Signs as I won't understand.

Bell. Ay, but if I'm Tongue-ty'd, I must have all my Actions free to——Quicken your Apprehension—and I-gad let me tell you, my most prevailing Argument is express'd in dumb shew.

SCENE IX.

[*To them*] MUSICK-MASTER.

Aram. O I am glad we shall have a Song to divert the Discourse——Pray oblige us witn the last new Song.

SONG

I.

Thus to a ripe, consenting Maid,
Poor, old, repenting Delia *said,*
Would you long preserve your Lover?
  Would you still his Goddess reign?
Never let him all discover,
  Never let him much obtain.

II.

Men will admire, adore and die,
While wishing at your Feet they lye
But admitting their Embraces,
  Wakes 'em from the Golden Dream;
Nothing's new besides our Faces,
  Every Woman is the same.

Aram. So, how de'e like the Song, Gentlemen?

Bell. O very well perform'd——but I don't much admire the Words.

Aram. I expected it—there's too much Truth in 'em: If Mr. *Gavot* will walk with us in the Garden, we'll have it once again—you may like it better at second hearing. You'll bring my Cousin.

Bell. Faith Madam, I dare not speak to her, but I'll make Signs.

[*Addresses* Belinda *in dumb shew.*

Belin. O foh, your dumb Rhetorick is more ridiculous, than your talking Impertinence; as an Ape is a much more troublesome Animal than a Parrot.

Aram. Ay, Cousin, and 'tis a sign the Creatures mimick Nature well; for there are few Men, but do more silly things than they say.

Bell. Well, I find my Apishness has paid the Ransome for my Speech, and set it at Liberty—— tho, I confess, I could be well enough pleas'd to drive on a Love-Bargain, in that silent manner—'twould save a Man a world of Lying and Swearing at the Years end. Besides I have had a little Experience, that brings to Mind—

When Wit and Reason, both have fail'd, to move;
Kind Looks and Actions (from Success) do prove,
Ev'n Silence may be Eloquent in Love.

End of the Second Act.

ACT III. SCENE I.

SCENE, *The Street.*

Silvia *and* Lucy.

SILVIA.

Will he not come then?

Lucy. Yes, yes, come, I warrant him, if you will go in and be ready to receive him.

Silv. Why did you not tell me?——Whom mean you?

Lucy. Whom you should mean, *Heartwell.*

Silv. Senseless Creature, I meant my *Vainlove.*

Lucy. You may as soon hope, to recover your own Maidenhead, as his Love. Therefore e'en set your Heart at rest, and in the Name of Opportunity mind your own Business. Strike *Heartwell* home, before the Bait's worn off the Hook. Age will come. He nibbled fairly yesterday, and no doubt will be eager enough to Day, to swallow the Temptation.

Silv. Well, since there's no Remedy—Yet tell me——for I would know, though to the Anguish of my Soul; how did he refuse? Tell me—how did he receive my Letter, in Anger or in Scorn?

Lucy. Neither; but what was ten times worse, with damn'd, senseless Indifference. By this Light I could have spit in his Face——Receive it! Why he receiv'd it, as I would one of your Lovers that should come empty-handed; as a Court Lord does his Mercers Bill, or a begging Dedication:——he receiv'd it as if't had been a Letter from his Wife.

Silv. What, did he not read it?

Lucy. Hum'd it over, gave you his Respects, and said, he would take time to peruse it——but then he was in haste.

Silv. Respects, and peruse it! He's gone, and *Araminta* has bewitch'd him from me—Oh how the Name of Rival fires my Blood—I could curse 'em both; eternal Jealousie attend her Love, and Disappointment meet his. Oh that I could revenge the Torment he has caus'd——methinks I feel the Woman strong within me, and Vengeance kindles in the room of Love.

Lucy. I have that in my Head may make Mischief.

Silv. How, dear *Lucy.*

Lucy. You know *Araminta*'s dissembled Coyness has won, and keeps him hers——

Silv. Could we perswade him, that she loves another——

Lucy. No, you're out; could we perswade him, that she doats on him, himself——Contrive a kind Letter as from her, 'twould disgust his Nicety, and take away his Stomach.

Silv. Impossible, 'twill never take.

Lucy. Trouble not your Head. Let me alone ——I will inform my self of what past between 'em to Day, and about it streight—Hold, I'm mistaken, or that's *Heartwell*, who stands talking at the Corner——'tis he——go get you in Madam, receive him pleasantly, dress up your Face in Innocence and Smiles; and dissemble the very want of Dissimulation——You know what will take him.

Silv. 'Tis hard to counterfeit Love, as it is to conceal it: but I'll do my weak endeavour, though I fear I have not Art.

Lucy. Hang Art, Madam, and trust to Nature for dissembling.

Man, was by Nature Womans Cully made:
We, never are but by our selves betray'd.

SCENE II.

HEARTWELL, VAINLOVE *and* BELLMOUR *following.*

Bell. Hist, hist, is not that *Heartwell* going to *Silvia*?

Vain. He's talking to himself, I think; prithee let's try if we can hear him.

Heart. Why whither in the Devil's Name am I a going now? Hum—let me think—Is not this *Silvia*'s House, the Cave of that Enchantress, and which consequently I ought to shun as I would Infection? To enter here, is to put on the envenom'd Shirt, to run into the Embraces of a Fever, and in some raving Fit, be led to plunge my self into that more consuming Fire, a Woman's Arms. Ha! well recollected, I will recover my Reason, and be gone.

Bell. Now *Venus* forbid!

Vain. Hush——

Heart. Well, why do you not move? Feet do your Office—not one Inch; no, foregad I'm caught——There stands my North, and thither my Needle points—Now could I curse my self, yet cannot repent. O thou delicious, damn'd, dear, destructive Woman! S'death how the young Fellows will hoot me! I shall be the Jest of the Town: Nay in two Days, I expect to be Chronicled in Ditty, and sung in woeful Ballad, to the Tune of the superannuated Maidens Comfort, or the Batchelors Fall; and upon the third, I shall be hang'd in Effigie, pasted up for the exemplary Ornament of necessary Houses, and Coblers Stalls —Death, I can't think on't—I'll run into the Danger to lose the Apprehension.

SCENE III.

BELLMOUR, VAINLOVE.

Bell. A very certain Remedy, *probatum est*—— Ha, ha, ha, poor *George*, thou art i'th' right, thou hast sold thy self to Laughter; the ill-natur'd Town will find the Jest just where thou hast lost it. Ha, ha, how a' strugled, like an old Lawyer between two Fees.

Vain. Or a young Wench, between Pleasure and Reputation.

Bell. Or as you did to Day, when half afraid you snatch'd a Kiss from *Araminta.*

Vain. She has made a Quarrel on't.

Bell. Pauh, Women are only angry at such Offences, to have the Pleasure of forgiving 'em.

Vain. And I love to have the Pleasure of making my Peace——I should not esteem a Pardon if too easily won.

Bell. Thou dost not know what thou would'st be at; whether thou would'st have her angry or pleas'd. Could'st thou be content to marry *Araminta*?

Vain. Could you be content to go to Heav'n?

Bell. Hum, not immediately, in my Conscience not heartily? I'd do a little more good in my Generation first, in order to deserve it.

Vain. Nor I to marry *Araminta* 'till I merit her.

Bell. But how the Devil dost thou expect to get her if she never yield?

Vain. That's true; but I would——

Bell. Marry her without her Consent; thou'rt a Riddle beyond Woman——

SCENE IV.

[*To them*] SETTER.

Trusty *Setter* what Tidings? How goes the Project?

Setter. As all lewd Projects do, Sir, where the Devil prevents our Endeavours with Success.

Bell. A good hearing, *Setter*.

Vain. Well, I'll leave you with your Engineer.

Bell. And hast thou provided Necessaries?

Setter. All, all, Sir; the large sanctified Hat, and the little precise Band, with a swinging long spiritual Cloak, to cover carnal Knavery—not forgetting the black Patch, which Tribulation *Spintext* wears, as I'm inform'd, upon one Eye, as a penal Mourning for the ogling Offences of his Youth; and some say, with that Eye, he first discover'd the frailty of his Wife.

Bell. Well, in this fanatick Fathers Habit, will I confess *Lætitia*.

Setter. Rather prepare her for Confession, Sir, by helping her to Sin.

4 prevents] Anticipates, goes before. Cf. 'Prevent us, O Lord, in all our doings.'

Bell. Be at your Masters Lodging, in the Evening, I shall use the Robes.

SCENE V.

SETTER *alone.*

Setter. I shall Sir——I wonder to which of these two Gentlemen I do most properly appertain——the one uses me as his Attendant; the other (being the better acquainted with my Parts) employs me as a Pimp; why that's much the more honourable Employment—by all means——I follow one as my Master, t'other follows me as his Conductor.

SCENE VI.

[*To him*] LUCY.

Lucy. There's the Hang-Dog his Man——I had a Power over him in the Reign of my Mistress; but he is too true a *Valet de Chambre* not to affect his Master's Faults; and consequently is revolted from his Allegiance.

Setter. Undoubtedly 'tis impossible to be a Pimp and not a Man of Parts. That is without being politick, diligent, secret, wary, and so forth——And to all this valiant as *Hercules*—That is, passively valiant and actively obedient. Ah! *Setter* what a Treasure is here lost for want of being known.

Lucy. Here's some Villany a-foot he's so thoughtful; may be I may discover something in my Mask—Worthy Sir, a Word with you.

[*Puts on her Mask.*

Setter. Why if I were known, I might come to be a great Man——

Lucy. Not to interrupt your Meditation—

Setter. And I should not be the first that has procur'd his Greatness by Pimping.

Lucy. Now Poverty and the Pox light upon thee, for a Contemplative Pimp.

Setter. Ha! what art, who thus maliciously hast awaken'd me, from my Dream of Glory? Speak thou vile Disturber——

Lucy. Of thy most vile Cogitations—thou poor, conceited Wretch, how wert thou valuing thy self, upon thy Masters Employment. For he's the Head Pimp to Mr. *Bellmour*. 29

Setter. Good Words, Damsel, or I shall——But how dost thou know my Master or me?

Lucy. Yes I know both Master and Man to be——

Setter. To be Men perhaps; nay faith like enough; I often march in the Rear of my Master, and enter into the Breaches which he has made.

Lucy. Ay, the Breach of Faith, which he has begun: Thou Traitor to thy lawful Princess.

Setter. Why how now! prithee who art? Lay by that worldly Face and produce your natural Vizor. 41

Lucy. No Sirrah, I'll keep it on to abuse thee and leave thee without Hopes of Revenge.

Setter. Oh! I begin to smoak ye: thou art some forsaken Abigail, we have dallied with heretofore—and art come to tickle thy Imagination with Remembrance of Iniquity past.

Lucy. No thou pitiful Flatterer of thy Masters Imperfections; thou Maukin made up of the Shreds and Pairings of his superfluous Fopperies.

Setter. Thou art thy Mistress's foul self, composed of her sullied Iniquities and Cloathing. 52

Lucy. Hang thee—Beggars Curr—Thy Master is but a Mumper in Love, lies canting at the Gate; but never dares presume to enter the House.

Setter. Thou art the Wicket to thy Mistresses Gate, to be opened for all Comers. In fine thou art the high Road to thy Mistress.

Lucy. Beast, filthy Toad, I can hold no longer, look and tremble. [*Unmasks*.

Setter. How, Mrs. *Lucy*! 61

44 smoak ye] Find you out.

Lucy. I wonder thou hast the Impudence to look me in the Face.

Setter. Adsbud who's in fault, Mistress of mine? who flung the first Stone? Who undervalued my Function? and who the Devil could know you by Instinct?

Lucy. You could know my Office by Instinct, and be hang'd, which you have slander'd most abominably. It vexes me not what you said of my Person; but that my innocent Calling should be expos'd and scandaliz'd—I cannot bear it.

Setter. Nay faith *Lucy* I'm sorry, I'll own my self to blame, though we were both in fault as to our Offices.——Come I'll make you any Reparation.

Lucy. Swear.

Setter. I do swear to the utmost of my Power.

Lucy. To be brief then; what is the Reason your Master did not appear to Day according to the Summons I brought him?

Setter. To answer you as briefly——He has a Cause to be tried in another Court.

Lucy. Come tell me in plain Terms, how forward he is with *Araminta*.

Setter. Too forward to be turn'd back—Though he's a little in Disgrace at present about a Kiss which he forced. You and I can kiss *Lucy*, without all that.

Lucy. Stand off——He's a precious Jewel.

Setter. And therefore you'd have him to set in your Lady's Locket.

Lucy. Where is he now?

Setter. He'll be in the *Piazza* presently.

Lucy. Remember to Days Behaviour——Let me see you with a penitent Face.

Setter. What no Token of Amity *Lucy*? you and I don't use to part with dry Lips.

95 *Piazza*] In Covent Garden, whose arcaded sides, designed by Inigo Jones, made it a popular resort.

Lucy. No, no, avaunt—I'll not be slabber'd and kiss'd now——I'm not i'th' humour.

Setter. I'll not quit you so——I'll follow and put you into the Humour.

SCENE VII.

Sir JOSEPH WITTOLL, BLUFFE.

Bluff. And so out of your unwonted generosity——

Sir *Jo.* And good Nature, Back; I am good natur'd and I can't help it.

Bluff. You have given him a Note upon *Fondlewife* for a hundred Pound.

Sir *Jo.* Ay, ay, poor Fellow, he ventur'd fair for't.

Bluff. You have disoblig'd me in it—for I have occasion for the Mony, and if you would look me in the Face again and live, go, and force him to redeliver you the Note—go—and bring it me hither I'll stay here for you.

Sir *Jo.* You may stay 'till the Day of Judgment then, by the Lord *Harry.* I know better things than to be run through the Guts for a hundred Pound——Why I gave that hundred Pound for being saved, an d'ee think, an there were no Danger, I'll be so ungrateful to take it from the Gentleman again?

Bluff. Well, go to him from me——Tell him, I say, he must refund——or Bilbo's the Word, and Slaughter will ensue——if he refuse, tell him—but whisper that——tell him——I'll pink his Soul——but whisper that softly to him.

Sir *Jo.* So softly, that he shall never hear on't I warrant you—why, what a Devil's the matter, Bully, are you mad? Or de'e think I'm mad? Agad for my part, I don't love to be the Messenger of ill News; 'tis an ungrateful Office—So tell him your self.

22 Bilbo's] Bilbao sword.

Bluff. By these Hilts I believe he frightned you into this Composition : I believe you gave it him out of Fear, pure paultry Fear—confess.

Sir *Jo*. No, no, hang't I was not afraid neither—tho' I confess he did in a manner snap me up—yet I can't say that it was altogether out of Fear, but partly to prevent Mischief—for he was a devilish cholerick Fellow : And if my Choler had been up too, agad there would have been Mischief done, that's flat. And yet I believe if you had been by, I would as soon have let him a'had a hundred of my Teeth. Adsheart if he should come just now when I'm angry, I'd tell him——Mum.

SCENE VIII.

[*To them*] BELLMOUR, SHARPER.

Bell. Thou'rt a lucky Rogue ; there's your Benefactor, you ought to return him Thanks now you have receiv'd the Favour.

Sharp. Sir *Joseph*——Your Note was accepted, and the Mony paid at Sight : I'm come to return my Thanks——

Sir *Jo*. They won't be accepted so readily as the Bill, Sir.

Bell. I doubt the Knight repents, *Tom*—He looks like the Knight of the sorrowful Face. 10

Sharp. This is a double Generosity—Do me a Kindness and refuse my Thanks—But I hope you are not offended that I offer'd 'em.

Sir *Jo*. May be I am, Sir, may be I am not, Sir, may be I am both, Sir ; what then ? I hope I may be offended, without any Offence to you, Sir.

Sharp. Hey day ! Captain, what's the Matter ? You can tell. 19

Bluff. Mr. *Sharper*, the Matter is plain—Sir *Joseph* has found out your Trick, and does not care to be put upon ; being a Man of Honour.

Sharp. Trick, Sir ?

Sir *Jo.* Ay Trick, Sir, and won't be put upon, Sir, being a Man of Honour, Sir, and so, Sir——

Sharp. Harkee, Sir *Joseph*, a Word with ye——in Consideration of some Favours lately received; I would not have you draw your self into a Premunire, by trusting to that Sign of a Man there——That Pot-Gun charged with Wind.

Sir *Jo.* O Lord, O Lord, Captain, come justifie your self——I'll give him the Lie if you stand to it.

Sharp. Nay then I'll be beforehand with you, take that—Oafe. [*Cuffs him.*

Sir *Jo.* Captain, will you see this? Won't you pink his Soul?

Bluff. Husht, 'tis not so convenient now—I shall find a time.

Sharp. What do you mutter about a Time, Rascal—You were the Incendiary——There's to put you in Mind of your Time——A Memorandum. [*Kicks him.*

Bluff. Oh this is your Time, Sir, you had best make use on't.

Sharp. I Gad and so I will: There's again for you. [*Kicks him.*

Bluff. You are obliging, Sir, but this is too publick a Place to thank you in: But in your Ear, you are to be seen again.

Sharp. Ay thou inimitable Coward, and to be felt—as for Example. [*Kicks him.*

Bell. Ha, ha, ha, prithee come away, 'tis scandalous to kick this Puppy unless a Man were cold, and had no other way to get himself a heat.

SCENE IX.

Sir JOSEPH, BLUFFE.

Bluff. Very well——very fine——But 'tis no matter——Is not this fine, Sir *Joseph*?

Sir *Jo.* Indifferent, agad in my Opinion very

28 Premunire] i. e. be called upon to answer a challenge.

indifferent—I'd rather go plain all my Life, than wear such Finery.

Bluff. Death and Hell to be affronted thus! I'll die before I'll suffer it. [*Draws*.

Sir *Jo*. O Lord, his Anger was not raised before—nay, dear Captain, don't be in Passion now he's gone—Put up, put up, dear Back, 'tis your Sir *Joseph* begs, come let me kiss thee; so, so, put up, put up. 12

Bluff. By Heav'n 'tis not to be put up.

Sir *Jo*. What, Bully?

Bluff. The Affront.

Sir *Jo*. No agad no more 'tis, for that's put up all already, thy Sword I mean.

Bluff. Well, Sir *Joseph*, at your Entreaty—— But were not you, my Friend, abus'd, and cufft, and kickt? [*Putting up his Sword*.

Sir *Jo*. Ay, ay, so were you too; no matter, 'tis past. 22

Bluff. By the immortal Thunder of great Guns, 'tis false—he sucks not vital Air who dares affirm it to this Face. [*Looks big*.

Sir *Jo*. To that Face I grant you Captain—No, no, I grant you—Not to that Face, by the Lord *Harry*—If you had put on your fighting Face before, you had done his Business—he durst as soon have kist you, as kickt you to your Face——But a Man can no more help what's done behind his Back, than what's said——Come we'll think no more of what's past. 33

Bluff. I'll call a Council of War within to consider of my Revenge to come.

SCENE X.

HEARTWELL, SILVIA. Silvia's *Apartment*.

SONG.

As Amoret *and* Thyrsis *lay*
Melting the Hours in gentle Play;

Joining Faces, mingling Kisses,
And exchanging harmless Blisses:
He trembling cry'd, with eager haste,
O let me feed as well as taste,
I die, if I'm not wholly blest.

After the Song, a Dance of Anticks.

Silv. Indeed it is very fine——I could look upon 'em all Day.

Heart. Well has this prevail'd for me, and will you look upon me?

Silv. If you could Sing and Dance so, I should love to look upon you too.

Heart. Why 'twas I sung and danc'd; I gave Musick to the Voice, and Life to their Measures—Look you here *Silvia*,

[*Pulling out a Purse and chinking it.*

here are Songs and Dances, Poetry and Musick——hark! how sweetly one Guinea rhymes to another—and how they dance to the Musick of their own Chink. This buys all the t'other—and this thou shalt have; this, and all that I am worth for the purchase of thy Love——Say, is it mine then, ha? Speak Syren—Oons why do I look on her! Yet I must—Speak dear Angel, Devil, Saint, Witch do not rack me with Suspence.

Silv. Nay don't stare at me so—You make me blush—I cannot look.

Heart. Oh Manhood, where art thou! What am I come to? A Woman's Toy; at these Years! Death, a bearded Baby for a Girl to dandle. O Dotage, Dotage! That ever that noble Passion, *Lust*, should ebb to this degree——No reflux of vigorous Blood: But milky Love, supplies the empty Channels; and prompts me to the Softness of a Child—a meer Infant and would suck. Can you love me *Silvia*? speak.

Silv. I dare not speak 'till I believe you, and indeed I'm afraid to believe you yet.

6 Anticks] Dancers in fancy dress. 31 Baby] Doll.

Heart. Death, how her Innocence torments and pleases me! Lying, Child, is indeed the Art of Love; and Men are generally Masters in it: But I'm so newly entred, you cannot distrust me of any Skill in the treacherous Mystery—Now by my Soul I cannot lye, though it were to serve a Friend or gain a Mistress.

Silv. Must you lye then, if you say you love me?

Heart. No, no, dear Ignorance, thou beauteous Changeling——I tell thee I do love thee, and tell it for a Truth, a naked Truth, which I'm ashamed to discover.

Silv. But Love, they say, is a tender thing, that will smooth Frowns, and make calm an angry Face; will soften a rugged Temper, and make ill humoured People good: You look ready to fright one, and talk as if your Passion were not Love, but Anger.

Heart. 'Tis both; for I am angry with my self when I am pleased with you——And a Pox upon me for loving thee so well—yet I must on——'Tis a bearded Arrow, and will more easily be thrust forward than drawn back.

Silv. Indeed if I were well assur'd you lov'd; but how can I be well assur'd?

Heart. Take the Symptoms—and ask all the Tyrants of thy Sex, if their Fools are not known by this Party-coloured Livery—I am Melancholick, when thou art absent; look like an Ass, when thou art present; wake for thee, when I should sleep; and even dream of thee, when I am awake; sigh much, drink little, eat less, court Solitude, am grown very entertaining to my self, and (as I am informed) very troublesome to every body else. If this be not Love, it is Madness, and then it is pardonable—Nay yet a more certain sign than all this; I give thee my Mony.

Silv. Ay, but that is no sign; for they say, Gentlemen will give Mony to any naughty Woman to come to Bed to them——O *Gemini*, I hope you don't mean so——for I won't be a Whore.

Heart. The more is the pity. [*Aside*.

Silv. Nay, if you would marry me, you should not come to bed to me—you have such a Beard, and would so prickle one. But do you intend to marry me?

Heart. That a Fool should ask such a malicious Question! Death, I shall be drawn in, before I know where I am—However, I find I am pretty sure of her Consent, if I am put to it. [*Aside*.] Marry you? no, no, I'll love you.

Silv. Nay, but if you love me, you must marry me; what don't I know my Father lov'd my Mother, and was married to her?

Heart. Ay, ay, in old Days People married where they lov'd; but that Fashion is chang'd, Child.

Silv. Never tell me that, I know it is not chang'd by my self; for I love you, and would marry you.

Heart. I'll have my Beard shav'd, it shan't hurt thee, and we'll go to Bed—

Silv. No, no, I'm not such a Fool neither but I can't keep my self honest;——Here, I won't keep any thing that's yours, I hate you now, [*Throws the Purse*] and I'll never see you again, 'cause you'd have me be naught. [*Going*.

Heart. Damn her let her go, and a good riddance —Yet so much Tenderness and Beauty—and Honesty together is a Jewel——Stay *Silvia*—— But then to marry——Why every Man plays the Fool once in his Life: But to marry is playing the Fool all ones Life long.

Silv. What did you call me for?

Heart. I'll give thee all I have: And thou shalt live with me in every thing so like my Wife, the World shall believe it; Nay, thou shalt think so thy self——Only let me not think so.

Silv. No, I'll die before I'll be your Whore—— as well as I love you.

Heart. [*Aside.*] A Woman, and ignorant, may be honest, when 'tis out of Obstinacy and Contradiction——But S'death it is but a may be, and upon scurvy Terms——Well, farewel then——if I can get out of Sight I may get the better of my self.

Silv. Well——good buy. [*Turns and Weeps.*

Heart. Ha! Nay come, we'll kiss at parting [*Kisses her.*] By Heav'n her Kiss is sweeter than Liberty——I will marry thee——There thou hast don't. All my Resolves melted in that Kiss—one more.

Silv. But when?

Heart. I'm impatient 'till it be done; I will not give my self Liberty to think, lest I should cool—I will about a Licence straight—in the Evening expect me——One Kiss more to confirm me mad; so.

Silv. Ha, ha, ha, an old Fox trapt—

SCENE XI.

[*To her*] LUCY

Bless me! you frighted me, I thought he had been come again, and had heard me.

Lucy. Lord, Madam, I met your Lover in as much haste, as if he had been going for a Midwife.

Silv. He's going for a Parson, Girl, the forerunner of a Midwife, some nine Months hence——Well, I find dissembling to our Sex is as natural as swimming to a *Negro*; we may depend upon our skill to save us at a plunge, tho' till then we never make the experiment——But how hast thou succeeded?

Lucy. As you would wish——Since there is no reclaiming *Vainlove.* I have found out a pique she has taken at him; and have fram'd a Letter that makes her sue for Reconciliation first. I know that will do——walk in and I'll shew it you. Come

Madam, you're like to have a happy time on't, both your Love and Anger satisfied!—All that can charm our Sex conspire to please you.

That Woman sure enjoys a blessed Night,
Whom Love and Vengeance both, at once delight.

End of the Third Act.

ACT IV. SCENE I.

SCENE, *The Street.*

Bellmour *in Fanatick Habit,* Setter.

BELLMOUR.

'Tis pretty near the Hour. [*Looking on his Watch*] Well and how *Setter* hæ, does my Hypocrisie fit me hæ? Does it sit easie on me?

Set. O most religiously well, Sir.

Bell. I wonder why all our young Fellows should glory in an Opinion of Atheism; when they may be so much more conveniently lewd under the Coverlet of Religion. 8

Set. S'bud, Sir, away quickly, there's *Fondlewife* just turn'd the Corner, and's coming this way.

Bell. Gads so, there he is, he must not see me.

SCENE II.

FONDLEWIFE, BARNABY.

Fond. I say, I will tarry at home.

Bar. But, Sir.

Fond. Good lack! I profess the Spirit of Contradiction hath possest the Lad—I say I will tarry at home——*Varlet.*

Bar. I have done, Sir, then farewel 500 Pound.

Fond. Ha, how's that? Stay, stay, did you leave Word say you with his Wife? With *Comfort* her self.

9

Bar. I did; and *Comfort* will send *Tribulation* hither as soon as ever he comes home——I could have brought young Mr. *Prig*, to have kept my Mistress Company in the mean time: But you say——

Fond. How, how, say *Varlet*! I say let him not come near my Doors. I say, he is a wanton young *Levite*, and pampereth himself up with Dainties, that he may look lovely in the Eyes of Women——Sincerely I am afraid he hath already defiled the Tabernacle of our Sister *Comfort*; while her good Husband is deluded by his Godly Appearance——I say, that even Lust doth sparkle in his Eyes, and glow upon his Cheeks, and that I would as soon trust my Wife with a Lord's high-fed Chaplain.

Bar. Sir, the Hour draws nigh——and nothing will be done there 'till you come.

Fond. And nothing can be done here 'till I go—So that I'll tarry, d'ee see.

Bar. And run the Hazard to lose your Affair, Sir!

Fond. Good lack, good lack——I profess it is a very sufficient Vexation, for a Man to have a handsome Wife.

Bar. Never, Sir, but when the Man is an insufficient Husband. 'Tis then indeed, like the Vanity of taking a fine House, and yet be forced to let Lodgings, to help pay the Rent.

Fond. I profess a very apt Comparison, *Varlet*. Go and bid my Cocky come out to me, I will give her some Instructions, I will reason with her before I go.

SCENE III.

FONDLEWIFE *alone*.

And in the mean time, I will reason with my self——Tell me *Isaac*, why art thee jealous? Why art thee distrustful of the Wife of thy Bosom?——

17 Levite] Private chaplain.

Because she is young and vigorous, and I am old and impotent——Then why didst thee marry, *Isaac* ?——Because she was beautiful and tempting, and because I was obstinate and doating ; so that my Inclination was (and is still) greater than my Power——And will not that which tempted thee, also tempt others, who will tempt her, *Isaac* ?——I fear it much——But does not thy Wife love thee, nay doat upon thee ?—Yes—Why then !—Ay, but to say truth, she's fonder of me, than she has reason to be ; and in the way of Trade, we still suspect the smoothest Dealers of the deepest Designs——And that she has some Designs deeper than thou canst reach, th'hast experimented, *Isaac*—But Mum.

SCENE IV.

FONDLEWIFE, LÆTITIA.

Læt. I hope my dearest Jewel is not going to leave me—are you *Nykin* ?

Fond. Wife——Have you throughly consider'd how detestable, how heinous, and how crying a Sin, the Sin of Adultery is ? have you weigh'd it I say ? For it is a very weighty Sin ; and although it may lie heavy upon thee, yet thy Husband must also bear his Part : For thy Iniquity will fall upon his Head.

Læt. Bless me, what means my Dear !

Fond. Aside.) I profess she has an alluring Eye ; I am doubtful, whether I shall trust her, even with *Tribulation* himself—Speak, I say, have you considered, what it is to cuckold your Husband ?

Læt. Aside.) I'm amazed : Sure he has discovered nothing—Who has wrong'd me to my Dearest ? I hope my Jewel does not think, that ever I had any such thing in my Head, or ever will have.

Fond. No, no, I tell you I shall have it in my Head—

Læt. Aside.) I know not what to think. But I'm resolv'd to find the meaning of it——Unkind Dear! Was it for this you sent to call me? is it not Affliction enough that you are to leave me, but you must study to encrease it by unjust Suspicions? [*Crying*] Well—Well—you know my Fondness, and you love to Tyrannize—Go on cruel Man, do, Triumph over my poor Heart, while it holds; which cannot be long, with this Usage of yours——But that's what you want——Well You will have your Ends soon——You will—You will——Yes it will break to oblige you. [*Sighs.*

Fond. Verily I fear I have carried the Jest too far—Nay, look you now if she does not weep——'tis the fondest Fool—Nay, Cocky, Cocky, nay, dear Cocky, don't cry, I was but in jest, I was not ifeck.

Læt. Aside.) Oh then all's safe. I was terribly frighted—My Affliction is always your Jest, barbarous Man! Oh that I should love to this degree! yet——

Fond. Nay, Cocky.

Læt. No, no, you are weary of me, that's it—that's all, you would get another Wife—another fond Fool, to break her Heart——well, be as cruel as you can to me, I'll pray for you; and when I am dead with Grief, may you have one that will love you as well as I have done: I shall be contented to lye at Peace in my cold Grave—since it will please you. [*Sighs.*

Fond. Good lack, good lack, she would melt a Heart of Oak—I profess I can hold no longer——Nay dear Cocky—Ifeck you'll break my Heart—Ifeck you will——See you have made me weep——made poor *Nykin* weep——Nay come kiss, buss poor *Nykin*——and I won't leave thee——I'll lose all first.

Læt. Aside.) How! Heav'n forbid: that will be carrying the Jest too far indeed.

Fond. Won't you kiss *Nykin*?

Læt. Go naughty *Nykin*, you don't love me.

Fond. Kiss, kiss, ifeck I do.

Læt. No you don't. [*She kisses him.*

Fond. What not love Cocky!

Læt. No—h. [*Sighs.*

Fond. I profess, I do love thee better than 500 Pound—and so thou shalt say, for I'll leave it to stay with thee.

Læt. No you shan't neglect your Business for me—No indeed you sant *Nykin*——If you don't go, I'll think you been dealous of me still.

Fond. He, he, he, wilt thou poor Fool? Then I will go, I won't be dealous——Poor Cocky, kiss *Nykin*, kiss *Nykin*, ee, ee, ee——Here will be the good Man anon, to talk to Cocky and teach her how a Wife ought to behave her self.

Læt. Aside.) I hope to have one that will shew me how a Husband ought to behave himself——I shall be glad to learn, to please my Jewel. [*Kiss.*

Fond. That's my good Dear—Come kiss *Nykin* once more, and then get you in——So——Get you in, get you in. By, by.

Læt. By *Nykin*.

Fond. By Cocky.

Læt. By *Nykin*.

Fond. By Cocky, by, by.

SCENE V.

VAINLOVE, SHARPER.

Sharp. How! *Araminta* lost!

Vain. To confirm what I have said, read this—— [*Gives a Letter.*

Sharp. Reads) *Hum, hum—And what then appear'd a Fault, upon Reflection, seems only an effect of a too powerful Passion. I'm afraid I give too great a Proof of my own at this time——I am in Disorder for what I have written. But something*

I know not what, forced me. I only beg a favourable Censure of this and your Araminta.

Sharp. Lost! Pray Heav'n thou hast not lost thy Wits. Here, here, she's thy own Man, sign'd and seal'd too——To her Man——a delicious Mellon pure and consenting ripe, and only waits thy cutting up——She has been breeding Love to thee all this while, and just now she's deliver'd of it.

Vain. 'Tis an untimely Fruit, and she has miscarried of her Love.

Sharp. Never leave this damn'd, illnatur'd whimsey, *Frank*? Thou hast a sickly peevish Appetite; only chew Love and cannot digest it.

Vain. Yes, when I feed my self—But I hate to be cramm'd—By Heav'n there's not a Woman, will give a Man the Pleasure of a Chase: My Sport is always balkt or cut short——I stumble over the Game I would pursue——'Tis dull and unnatural to have a Hare run full in the Hounds Mouth; and would distaste the keenest Hunter——I would have overtaken, not have met my Game.

Sharp. However I hope you don't mean to forsake it; that will be but a kind of a Mungril Curs Trick. Well, are you for the Mall?

Vain. No, she will be there this Evening——Yes, I will go too——and she shall see her Error in——

Sharp. In her choice I gad—But thou canst not be so great a Brute as to slight her.

Vain. I should disappoint her if I did not—By her Management I should think she expects it.

All Naturally fly what does pursue:
'Tis fit Men should be coy, when Women woe.

10 Censure] Judgment.

SCENE VI.

A Room in Fondlewife's *House.*

A SERVANT *introducing* BELLMOUR *in Fanatick-Habit, with a Patch upon one Eye, and a Book in his Hand.*

Serv. Here's a Chair, Sir, if you please to repose your self. My Mistress is coming, Sir.

Bell. Secure in my Disguise, I have out-fac'd Suspicion, and even dar'd Discovery——This Cloak my Sanctity, and trusty *Scarron*'s Novels my Prayer-Book——Methinks I am the very Picture of *Montufar* in the *Hypocrites*——Oh! she comes.

SCENE VII.

BELLMOUR, LÆTITIA.

So breaks Aurora *through the Veil of Night,*
Thus fly the Clouds, divided by her Light,
And ev'ry Eye receives a new-born Sight.

[*Throwing off his Cloak, Patch, &c.*

Læt. Thus strew'd with Blushes, like
—Ah! Heav'n defend me! Who's this?

[*Discovering him, starts.*

Bell. Your Lover.

Læt. *Vainlove*'s Friend! I know his Face, and he has betray'd me to him. [*Aside.*

Bell. You are surprized. Did you not expect a Lover, Madam? Those Eyes shone kindly on my first Appearance, tho' now they are o'er-cast.

Læt. I may well be surpriz'd at your Person and Impudence; they are both new to me——You are not what your first Appearance promised: The Piety of your Habit was welcome, but not the Hypocrisy.

7 *Hypocrites*] Scarron was the author of *Le Roman Comique*, &c. In the second novella of *The Hypocrites* Montufar clothes himself in a cassock to further his designs.

Bell. Rather the Hypocrisy was welcome, but not the Hypocrite.

Læt. Who are you, Sir? You have mistaken the House sure.

Bell. I have Directions in my Pocket, which agree with every thing but your Unkindness. [*Pulls out the Letter.*

Læt. My Letter! Base *Vainlove*! Then 'tis too late to dissemble. [*Aside.*] 'Tis plain then you have mistaken the Person. [*Going.*

Bell. If we part so I'm mistaken——Hold, hold, Madam——I confess I have run into an Error——I beg your Pardon a thousand times——What an eternal Blockhead am I! Can you forgive me the Disorder I have put you into——But it is a Mistake which any Body might have made.

Læt. What can this mean! 'Tis impossible he should be mistaken after all this—A handsome Fellow if he had not surpriz'd me: Methinks, now I look on him again, I would not have him mistaken. [*Aside.*] We are all liable to Mistakes, Sir: If you own it to be so, there needs no farther Apology.

Bell. Nay 'Faith, Madam, 'tis a pleasant one; and worth your hearing. Expecting a Friend, last Night, at his Lodgings, 'till 'twas late; my Intimacy with him gave me the freedom of his Bed: He not coming home all Night, a Letter was deliver'd to me by a Servant, in the Morning: Upon the perusal I found the Contents so charming, that I could think of nothing all Day, but putting 'em in practice——'till just now, (the first time I ever look'd upon the Superscription) I am the most surpriz'd in the World to find it directed to Mr. *Vainlove*. Gad, Madam, I ask you a Million of Pardons, and will make you any Satisfaction.

Læt. I am discover'd——And either *Vainlove* is not guilty, or he has handsomely excus'd him. [*Aside.*

Bell. You appear concern'd, Madam.

Lœt. I hope you are a Gentleman;—and since you are privy to a weak Woman's Failing, won't turn it to the Prejudice of her Reputation. You look as if you had more Honour——

Bell. And more Love; or my Face is a false Witness, and deserves to be pillory'd.——No, by Heav'n, I swear—

Lœt. Nay, don't swear if you'd have me believe you; but promise——

Bell. Well, I promise—A Promise is so cold—Give me leave to swear—by those Eyes, those killing Eyes; by those healing Lips.——Oh! press the soft Charm close to mine,—and seal 'em up for ever.

Lœt. Upon that Condition. [*He kisses her.*

Bell. Eternity was in that Moment—One more, upon any Condition.

Lœt. Nay now——I never saw any thing so agreeably impudent. [*Aside.*] Won't you censure me for this, now?—but 'tis to buy your Silence. [*Kiss.*] Oh, but what am I doing!

Bell. Doing! No Tongue can express it——not thy own; nor any thing, but thy Lips. I am faint with the Excess of Bliss:——Oh, for Love-sake, lead me any whither, where I may lye down;——quickly, for I'm afraid I shall have a Fit.

Lœt. Bless me! What Fit?

Bell. Oh, a Convulsion——I feel the Symptoms.

Lœt. Does it hold you long? I'm afraid to carry you into my Chamber.

Bell. Oh, no: Let me lye down upon the Bed;——the Fit will be soon over.

SCENE VIII.

SCENE, *St.* James's *Park.*

ARAMINTA *and* BELINDA *meeting.*

Belin. Lard, my Dear: I am glad I have met you——I have been at the *Exchange* since, and am so tir'd—

Aram. Why, what's the Matter?

Belin. Oh the most inhumane, barbarous Hackney-Coach! I am jolted to a Jelly—Am I not horridly touz'd? [*Pulls out a Pocket-Glass.*

Aram. Your Head's a little out of order.

Belin. A little! O frightful! What a furious Phyz I have! O most rueful! Ha, ha, ha: O Gad, I hope no body will come this way, 'till I have put my self a little in repair—Ah! my Dear—I have seen such unhewn Creatures since—Ha, ha, ha, I can't for my Soul help thinking that I look just like one of 'em—Good Dear, pin this, and I'll tell you—Very well—So, thank you my Dear——But as I was telling you——Pish, this is the untoward'st Lock——So, as I was telling you——How d'ye like me now? Hideous, ha? Frightful still? Or how?

Aram. No, no; you're very well as can be.

Belin. And so—But where did I leave off, my Dear? I was telling you—

Aram. You were about to tell me something, Child——but you left off before you began.

Belin. Oh; a most comical Sight: A Country Squire, with the Equipage of a Wife and two Daughters, came to Mrs. *Snipwel*'s Shop while I was there—But, oh Gad! Two such unlick'd Cubs!

Aram. I warrant, plump, Cherry-cheek'd Country Girls.

Belin. Ay, O my Conscience, fat as Barn-Door Fowl: But so bedeck'd, you would have taken 'em for *Friezland* Hens, with their Feathers growing the wrong way——O such Out-landish Creatures! Such *Tramontanæ*, and Foreigners to the Fashion, or any thing in Practice! I had not Patience to behold——I undertook the modelling of one of their Fronts, the more modern Structure——

Aram. Bless me, Cousin; why would you affront any Body so? They might be Gentlewomen of a very good Family——

Belin. Of a very ancient one, I dare swear, by their Dress——Affront! Pshaw, how you're mistaken! The poor Creature, I warrant, was as full of Curtsies, as if I had been her Godmother: The Truth on't is, I did endeavour to make her look like a Christian—and she was sensible of it; for she thank'd me, and gave me two Apples, piping hot, out of her Under-Petticoat Pocket—Ha, ha, ha: And t'other did so stare and gape—I fansied her like the Front of her Father's Hall; her Eyes were the two Jut-Windows, and her Mouth the great Door, most hospitably kept open, for the Entertainment of travelling Flies.

Aram. So then; you have been diverted. What did they buy?

Belin. Why, the Father bought a Powder-Horn, and an Almanack, and a Comb-Case; the Mother, a great Fruz-Towr, and a fat Amber-Necklace; the Daughters only tore two Pair of Kid-leather Gloves, with trying 'em on——Oh Gad, here comes the Fool that din'd at my Lady *Freelove*'s t'other Day.

SCENE IX.

[*To them*] *Sir* JOSEPH *and* BLUFFE.

Aram. May be he may not know us again.

Belin. We'll put on our Masks to secure his Ignorance. [*They put on their Masks.*

Sir *Jo.* Nay, Gad, I'll pick up; I'm resolv'd to make a Night on't—I'll go to Alderman *Fondlewife* by and by, and get 50 Pieces more from him. Adslidikins, *Bully*, we'll wallow in Wine and Women. Why, this same *Madera*-Wine has made me as light as a Grasshopper—Hist, hist, Bully, dost thou see those Tearers? [*Sings.*] *Look you what here is—Look you what here is——Toll—loll—dera—toll—loll*—A Gad, t'other Glass of *Madera*

61 Fruz-Towr] The toure was a head-dress of hair.

and I durst have attack'd 'em in my own proper Person, without your help.

Bluff. Come on then, Knight——But d'ye know what to say to 'em ?

Sir *Jo*. Say : Pooh, Pox, I've enough to say—— never fear it——that is, if I can but think on't : Truth is, I have but a treacherous Memory. 19

Belin. O frightful ! Cousin, What shall we do ? These things come towards us.

Aram. No matter—I see *Vainlove* coming this Way——and, to confess my Failing, I am willing to give him an Opportunity of making his Peace with me—and to rid me of these Coxcombs, when I seem opprest with 'em, will be a fair one.

Bluff. Ladies, by these Hilts you are well met.

Aram. We are afraid not. 28

Bluff. What says my pretty little Knapsack Carrier. [*To* Belinda.

Belin. O monstrous filthy Fellow ! Good slovenly Captain *Huffe*, *Bluffe*, (what is your hideous Name ?) be gone : You stink of Brandy and Tobacco, most Soldier-like. Foh. [*Spits*.

Sir *Jo*. Now am I slap-dash down in the Mouth, and have not one Word to say ! [*Aside*.

Aram. I hope my Fool has not Confidence enough to be troublesome. [*Aside*.

Sir *Jo*. Hem ! Pray, Madam, which way's the Wind ? 4

Aram. A pithy Question—Have you sent your Wits for a Venture, Sir, that you enquire ?

Sir *Jo*. Nay, now I'm in—I can prattle like a Magpye. [*Aside*.

SCENE X.

[*To them*] SHARPER *and* VAINLOVE *at some distance*.

Belin. Dear *Araminta*, I'm tir'd.

Aram. 'Tis but pulling off our Masks, and obliging *Vainlove* to know us. I'll be rid of my

Fool by fair Means——Well, Sir *Joseph*, you shall see my Face——but, be gone immediately——I see one that will be jealous, to find me in Discourse with you——Be discreet—No Reply ; but away. [*Unmasks.*

Sir *Jo*. The great Fortune, that dined at my Lady *Freelove*'s ! Sir *Joseph*, thou art a made Man. Agad, I'm in Love up to the Ears. But I'll be discreet, and husht. [*Aside.*

Bluff. Nay, by the World, I'll see your Face.

Belin. You shall. [*Unmasks.*

Sharp. Ladies, your humble Servant——We were afraid, you would not have given us leave to know you.

Aram. We thought to have been private——But we find Fools have the same Advantage over a Face in a Mask, that a Coward has, while the Sword is in the Scabbard——So were forced to draw in our own Defence. 21

Bluff. My Blood rises at that Fellow : I can't stay where he is ; and I must not draw in the Park. [*To Sir* Joseph.

Sir *Jo*. I wish I durst stay to let her know my Lodging——

SCENE XI.

ARAMINTA, BELINDA, VAINLOVE, SHARPER.

Sharp. There is in true Beauty, as in Courage, somewhat, which narrow Souls cannot dare to admire——And see, the Owls are fled, as at the break of Day.

Belin. Very courtly——I believe, Mr. *Vainlove* has not rubb'd his Eyes, since break of Day neither, he looks as if he durst not approach—Nay, come Cousin, be Friends with him——I swear he looks so very simply, ha, ha, ha,——Well, a Lover in the State of Separation from his Mistress, is like a Body without a Soul. Mr. *Vainlove*, shall I be bound for your good Behaviour for the future?

Vain. Now must I pretend Ignorance equal to hers, of what she knows as well as I. [*Aside.*] Men are apt to offend ('tis true) where they find most Goodness to forgive——But, Madam, I hope I shall prove of a Temper, not to abuse Mercy, by committing new Offences.

Aram. So cold! [*Aside.*

Belin. I have broken the Ice for you, Mr. *Vainlove*, and so I leave you. Come, Mr. *Sharper*, you and I will take a Turn, and laugh at the Vulgar—Both the great Vulgar and the small—Oh Gad! I have a great Passion for *Cowley*——Don't you admire him?

Sharp. Oh Madam! He was our *English Horace.*

Belin. Ah so fine! So extreamly fine! So every thing in the World that I like—Oh Lord, walk this Way—I see a Couple, I'll give you their History.

SCENE XII.

ARAMINTA, VAINLOVE.

Vain. I Find, Madam, the Formality of the Law must be observ'd, tho' the Penalty of it be dispens'd with; and an Offender must plead to his Araignment, though he has his Pardon in his Pocket.

Aram. I'm amaz'd! This Insolence exceeds t'other;—whoever has encourag'd you to this Assurance—presuming upon the easiness of my Temper, has much deceiv'd you, and so you shall find.

Vain. Hey day! Which way now? Here's fine doubling. [*Aside.*

Aram. Base Man! Was it not enough to affront me with your sawcy Passion?

Vain. You have given that Passion a much kinder Epithet than sawcy, in another Place.

23 great Vulgar] Horace, Book iii, Ode 1, tr. Cowley.

Aram. Another Place! Some villainous Design to blast my Honour—But tho' thou hadst all the Treachery and Malice of thy Sex, thou canst not lay a Blemish on my Fame——No, I have not err'd in one favourable Thought of Mankind—How Time might have deceiv'd me in you, I know not; my Opinion was but young, and your early Baseness has prevented its growing to a wrong Belief—Unworthy, and ungrateful! Be gone, and never see me more.

Vain. Did I dream? Or do I dream? Shall I believe my Eyes, or Ears? The Vision is here still——Your Passion, Madam, will admit of no farther reasoning——But here's a silent Witness of your Acquaintance.

[*Takes out the Letter, and offers it: She snatches it, and throws it away.*

Aram. There's Poison in every thing you touch—Blisters will follow——

Vain. That Tongue, which denies what the Hands have done.

Aram. Still mystically senseless, and impudent—I find I must leave the Place.

Vain. No, Madam, I'm gone—She knows her Name's to it, which she will be unwilling to expose to the Censure of the first Finder.

Aram. Woman's Obstinacy made me blind, to what Woman's Curiosity now tempts me to see.

[*Takes up the Letter.*

SCENE XIII.

Belinda, Sharper.

Belin. Nay, we have spared no Body, I swear. Mr. *Sharper*, you're a pure Man; where did you get this excellent Talent of Railing?

Sharp. Faith, Madam, the Talent was born with me:—I confess, I have taken care to improve it; to qualifie me for the Society of Ladies.

Belin. Nay, sure Railing is the best Qualification in a Woman's Man.

SCENE XIV.

[*To them*] FOOTMAN.

Sharp. The second best,——indeed I think.

Belin. How now, *Pace*? Where's my Cousin?

Foot. She's not very well, Madam, and has sent to know, if your Ladyship would have the Coach come again for you?

Belin. O Lord, no, I'll go along with her. Come, Mr. *Sharper*.

SCENE XV.

SCENE, *A Chamber in* Fondlewife's *House*.

LÆTITIA *and* BELLMOUR, *his Cloak, Hat, &c. lying loose about the Chamber*.

Bell. Here's no Body, nor no Noise——'twas nothing but your Fears.

Læt. I durst have sworn, I had heard my Monster's Voice——I swear, I was heartily frightned——Feel how my Heart beats.

Bell. 'Tis an Alarm to Love—Come in again, and let us——

Fond. Without.) Cocky, Cocky, where are you Cocky? I'm come home.

Læt. Ah! There he is. Make haste, gather up your things. 11

Fond. Cocky, Cocky, open the Door.

Bell. Pox choak him, would his Horns were in his Throat. My Patch, my Patch.

[*Looking about, and gathering up his Things*.

Læt. My Jewel, art thou there? No matter for your Patch—You s'an't tum in, *Nykin*——Run into my Chamber, quickly, quickly. You s'an't tum in. 18

Fond. Nay, prithee, Dear, ifeck I'm in haste.

Læt. Then I'll let you in. [*Opens the Door*.

SCENE XVI.

LÆTITIA, FONDLEWIFE, *Sir* JOSEPH.

Fond. Kiss, Dear——I met the Master of the Ship by the way—And I must have my Papers of Accounts out of your Cabinet.

Læt. Oh, I'm undone. [*Aside.*

Sir *Jo.* Pray, first let me have 50*l.* good Alderman, for I'm in haste.

Fond. A hundred has already been paid, by your Order. Fifty? I have the Sum ready in Gold, in my Closet.

SCENE XVII.

LÆTITIA, *Sir* JOSEPH.

Sir *Jo.* Agad, it's a curious, fine, pretty Rogue; I'll speak to her—Pray, Madam, what News d'ye hear?

Læt. Sir, I seldom stir abroad.

[*Walks about in Disorder.*

Sir *Jo.* I wonder at that, Madam, for 'tis most curious fine Weather.

Læt. Methinks 'thas been very ill Weather.

Sir *Jo.* As you say, Madam, 'tis pretty bad Weather, and has been so a great while.

SCENE XVIII.

[*To them*] FONDLEWIFE.

Fond. Here are fifty Pieces in this Purse, Sir *Joseph*—If you will tarry a Moment, 'till I fetch my Papers, I'll wait upon you down Stairs.

Læt. Ruin'd, past Redemption! What shall I do—Ha! this Fool may be of use (*Aside.*) [*As* Fondlewife *is going into the Chamber, she runs to Sir* Joseph, *almost pushes him down, and cries out.*] Stand off, rude Ruffian. Help me, my Dear—— O bless me! Why will you leave me alone with such a Satyr.

Fond. Bless us! What's the Matter? What's the Matter?

Læt. Your Back was no sooner turn'd; but like a Lion, he came open Mouth'd upon me, and would have ravished a Kiss from me by main Force.

Sir *Jo.* O Lord! Oh terrible! Ha, ha, ha, is your Wife mad, Alderman?

Læt. Oh! I'm sick with the Fright; won't you take him out of my Sight?

Fond. Oh Traitor! I'm astonished. Oh bloody-minded Traitor!

Sir *Jo.* Hey-day! Traitor your self—By the Lord *Harry*, I was in most Danger of being ravish'd, if you go to that.

Fond. Oh, how the blasphemous Wretch swears! Out of my House, thou Son of the Whore of *Babylon*; Off-spring of *Bell* and the *Dragon*——Bless us! Ravish my Wife! my *Dinah*! Oh *Shechemite*! Be gone I say.

Sir *Jo.* Why, the Devil's in the People, I think.

SCENE XIX.

Lætitia, Fondlewife.

Læt. Oh! won't you follow, and see him out of Doors, my Dear?

Fond. I'll shut this Door, to secure him from coming back—Give me the Key of your Cabinet, Cocky—Ravish my Wife before my Face! I warrant he's a Papist in his Heart, at least, if not a *French*-Man.

Læt. What can I do now! (*Aside.*) Oh! my Dear, I have been in such a fright, that I forgot to tell you, poor Mr. *Spintext* has a sad Fit of the Cholick, and is forced to lye down upon our Bed ——You'll disturb him; I can tread softlier. 12

Fond. Alack poor Man—no, no——you don't know the Papers—I won't disturb him; Give me the Key.

[*She gives him the Key, goes to the Chamber Door, and speaks aloud.*

Læt. 'Tis no Body but Mr. *Fondlewife*, Mr. *Spintext*, lye still on your Stomach; lying on your Stomach, will ease you of the Cholick.

Fond. Ay, ay, lie still, lie still; don't let me disturb you.

SCENE XX.

LÆTITIA, *alone.*

Læt. Sure, when he does not see his Face, he won't discover him. Dear Fortune, help me but this once, and I'll never run in thy Debt again—But this Opportunity is the Devil.

SCENE XXI.

FONDLEWIFE *returns with Papers.*

Fond. Good lack! good lack!——I profess, the poor Man is in great Torment, he lies as flat——Dear, you should heat a Trencher, or a Napkin—Where's *Deborah*? Let her clap some warm thing to his Stomach, or chafe it with a warm Hand, rather than fail. What Book's this?

[*Sees the Book that* Bellmour *forgot.*

Læt. Mr. *Spintext*'s Prayer-Book, Dear——Pray Heav'n it be a Prayer-Book. [*Aside.*

Fond. Good Man! I warrant he dropped it on purpose, that you might take it up, and read some of the pious Ejaculations [*Taking up the Book.*] O bless me! O monstrous! A Prayer-Book? Ay, this is the Devil's *Pater-Noster*. Hold, let me see; *The Innocent Adultery.*

Læt. Misfortune! now all's ruin'd again.

[*Aside.*

Bell. [*Peeping.*] Damn'd Chance! If I had gone a whoring with the *Practice of Piety* in my Pocket, I had never been discover'd.

Fond. Adultery, and innocent! O Lord! Here's Doctrine! Ay, here's Discipline!

Læt. Dear Husband, I'm amaz'd:——Sure it is a good Book, and only tends to the Speculation of Sin.

Fond. Speculation! No, no; something went farther than Speculation when I was not to be let in——Where is this Apocryphal Elder? I'll ferret him.

Læt. I'm so distracted, I can't think of a Lie. [*Aside.*

SCENE XXII.

LÆTITIA, *and* FONDLEWIFE *haling out* BELLMOUR.

Fond. Come out here, thou *Ananias* incarnate——Who, how now! Who have we here?

Læt. Ha! [*Shrieks, as surpriz'd.*

Fond. Oh, thou salacious Woman! Am I then brutified? Ay, I feel it here; I sprout, I bud, I blossom, I am ripe-horn-mad. But who in the Devil's Name are you? Mercy on me for swearing. But—

Læt. Oh, Goodness keep us! Who's this? Who are you? What are you?

Bell. Soh.

Læt. In the Name of the—O! Good, my Dear, don't come near it, I'm afraid 'tis the Devil; indeed it has Hoofs, Dear.

Fond. Indeed, and I have Horns, Dear. The Devil, no, I am afraid, 'tis the Flesh, thou Harlot. Dear, with the Pox. Come *Syren*, speak, confess, who is this reverend, brawny Pastor?

Læt. Indeed, and indeed now my dear *Nykin*——I never saw this wicked Man before.

Fond. Oh, it is a Man then, it seems.

Læt. Rather, sure it is a Wolf in the cloathing of a Sheep.

Fond. Thou art a Devil in his proper Cloathing,

Womans Flesh. What, you know nothing of him, but his Fleece here !—You don't love Mutton ?—you *Magdalen* unconverted.

Bell. Well, now, I know my Cue——That is, very honourably to excuse her, and very impudently accuse my self. [*Aside.*

Læt. Why then, I wish I may never enter into the Heav'n of your Embraces again, my Dear, if ever I saw his Face before.

Fond. O Lord ! O strange ! I am in admiration of your Impudence Look at him a little better ; he is more modest, I warrant you, than to deny it. Come, were you two never Face to Face before ? Speak.

Bell. Since all Artifice is vain—And I think my self obliged to speak the Truth in justice to your Wife——No.

Fond. Humph.

Læt. No, indeed Dear.

Fond. Nay I find you are both in a Story ; that I must confess. But, what——not to be cured of the Cholick ? Don't you know your Patient, Mrs. *Quack* ? Oh, lye upon your Stomach ; lying upon your Stomach will cure you of the Cholick. Ah ! Answer me, *Jezabel* ?

Læt. Let the wicked Man answer for himself ; does he think that I have nothing to do but excuse him ; 'tis enough, if I can clear my own Innocence to my own Dear.

Bell. By my troth, and so 'tis——I have been a little too backward, that's the truth on't.

Fond. Come, Sir, who are you, in the first Place ? And what are you ?

Bell. A Whore-master.

Fond. Very Concise.

Læt. A beastly, impudent Creature.

Fond. Well Sir, and what came you hither for ?

Bell. To lye with your Wife.

Fond. Good again—A very civil Person this, and I believe speaks Truth.

Læt. Oh, insupportable Impudence!

Fond. Well, Sir,——Pray be cover'd——and you have—Heh! You have finish'd the Matter, heh? And I am, as I should be, a sort of a civil Perquisite to a Whore-master, call'd a *Cuckold*, heh. Is it not so? Come, I'm inclining to believe every Word you say. 71

Bell. Why, Faith I must confess, so I design'd you——But, you were a little unlucky in coming so soon, and hindred the making of your own Fortune.

Fond. Humph. Nay, if you mince the Matter once, and go back of your Word; you are not the Person I took you for. Come, come, go on boldly ——What, don't be asham'd of your Profession ——Confess, confess, I shall love thee the better for't——I shall, Ifeck——What, dost think I don't know how to behave my self in the Employment of a Cuckold, and have been three Years Apprentice to Matrimony? Come, come, Plain-dealing is a Jewel.

Bell. Well, since I see thou art a good honest Fellow, I'll confess the whole Matter to thee. 87

Fond. Oh, I am a very honest Fellow——You never lay with an honester Man's Wife in your Life.

Læt. How my Heart akes! All my Comfort lies in his Impudence, and Heaven be prais'd, he has a considerable Portion. [*Aside.*

Bell. In short then, I was inform'd of the Opportunity of your Absence, by my Spy, (for faith, honest *Isaac*, I have a long time design'd thee this Favour) I knew *Spintext* was to come by your Direction.——But I laid a Trap for him, and procured his Habit; in which, I pass'd upon your Servants, and was conducted hither. I pretended a Fit of the Cholick, to excuse my lying down upon your Bed; hoping that when she heard of it, her good Nature would bring her to administer Remedies for my Distemper.——You know what might have follow'd.——But like an uncivil

Person, you knock'd at the Door, before your Wife was come to me.

Fond. Ha! This is Apocryphal; I may chuse whether I will believe it or no.

Bell. That you may, faith, and I hope you won't believe a Word on't—But I can't help telling the Truth, for my Life.

Fond. How! wou'd not you have me believe you, say you?

Bell. No; for then you must of consequence part with your Wife, and there will be some Hopes of having her upon the Publick; then the Encouragement of a separate Maintenance——

Fond. No, no; for that matter,——when she and I part, she'll carry her separate Maintenance about her.

Læt. Ah, cruel Dear, how can you be so barbarous? You'll break my Heart, if you talk of parting. [*Cries.*

Fond. Ah, dissembling Vermin!

Bell. How can'st thou be so cruel, *Isaac*? Thou hast the Heart of a Mountain-Tyger. By the Faith of a sincere Sinner, she's innocent for me. Go to him, Madam, fling your Snowy Arms about his stubborn Neck; bath his relentless Face in your salt trickling Tears.—

[*She goes and hangs upon his Neck, and kisses him.* Bellmour *kisses her Hand behind* Fondlewife'*s Back.*

So, a few soft Words, and a Kiss, and the good Man melts. See how kind Nature works, and boils-over in him.

Læt. Indeed, my Dear, I was but just come down Stairs, when you knock'd at the Door; and the Maid told me Mr. *Spintext* was ill of the Cholick, upon our Bed. And won't you speak to me, cruel *Nykin*? Indeed, I'll die, if you don't.

Fond. Ah! No, no, I cannot speak, my Heart's so full——I have been a tender Husband, a tender Yoke-Fellow; you know I have——But thou hast been a faithless *Dalilah*, and the *Philistines*—Heh! Art thou not vile and unclean, Heh? Speak. [*Weeping.*

Læt. No-h. [*Sighing.*

Fond. Oh, that I could believe thee!

Læt. Oh, my Heart will break. [*Seeming to faint.*

Fond. Heh, how! No, stay, stay, I will believe thee, I will.——Pray bend her forward, Sir.

Læt. Oh! Oh! Where is my Dear?

Fond. Here, here; I do believe thee.——I won't believe my own Eyes.

Bell. For my part, I am so charm'd with the Love of your Turtle to you, that I'll go and sollicit Matrimony with all my might and main.

Fond. Well, well, Sir; as long as I believe it, 'tis well enough. No Thanks to you, Sir, for her Vertue.—But, I'll show you the way out of my House, if you please. Come, my Dear. Nay, I will believe thee, I do, I'feck.

Bell. See the great Blessing of an easie Faith; Opinion cannot err.

No Husband, by his Wife, can be deceiv'd;
She still is vertuous, if she's so believ'd.

End of the Fourth Act.

ACT V. SCENE I.

SCENE, *The Street.*

Bellmour *in Fanatick Habit*, Setter, Heartwell, Lucy.

BELLMOUR.

Setter! Well encounter'd.

Set. Joy of your Return, Sir. Have you made a good Voyage? or have you brought your own Lading back?

Bell. No, I have brought nothing but Ballast back—made a delicious Voyage, *Setter*; and might have rode at Anchor in the Port 'till this time, but the Enemy surpriz'd us—I would unrig.

Setter. I attend you, Sir. 9

Bell. Ha! Is not that *Heartwell* at *Sylvia*'s Door? Be gone quickly, I'll follow you:—I would not be known. Pox take 'em, they stand just in my way.

SCENE II.

BELLMOUR, HEARTWELL, LUCY.

Heart. I'm impatient 'till it be done.

Lucy. That may be, without troubling your self to go again for your Brother's Chaplain. Don't you see that stalking Form of Godliness?

Heart. O ay; he's a Fanatick.

Lucy. An Executioner qualified to do your Business. He has been lawfully ordain'd.

Heart. I'll pay him well, if you'll break the Matter to him. 9

Lucy. I warrant you—Do you go and prepare your Bride.

SCENE III.

BELLMOUR, LUCY.

Bell. Humph, sits the Wind there?—What a lucky Rogue am I! Oh, what Sport will be here, if I can persuade this Wench to Secresie?

Lucy. Sir: Reverend Sir.

Bell. Madam. [*Discovers himself.*

Lucy. Now, Goodness have Mercy upon me! Mr. *Bellmour*! is it you?

Bell. Even I. What dost think? 8

Lucy. Think! That I shou'd not believe my Eyes, and that you are not what you seem to be.

Bell. True. But to convince thee who I am, thou know'st my old Token. [*Kisses her.*

Lucy. Nay, Mr. *Bellmour*: O Lard! I believe you are a Parson in good earnest, you kiss so devoutly.

Bell. Well, your Business with me, *Lucy*?

Lucy. I had none, but through Mistake.

Bell. Which Mistake you must go thorough with, *Lucy*——Come, I know the intrigue between *Heartwell* and your Mistress; and you mistook me for *Tribulation Spintext*, to marry 'em—Ha? Are Matters in this Posture?—Confess:——Come, I'll be faithful; I will i'faith.——What, Diffide in me, *Lucy*?

Lucy. Alas-a-day! You and Mr. *Vainlove*, between you, have ruin'd my poor Mistress: You have made a Gap in her Reputation; and can you blame her if she make it up with a Husband?

Bell. Well, is it as I say?

Lucy. Well, it is then: But you'll be secret?

Bell. Phuh, Secret, ay:——And to be out of thy Debt, I'll trust thee with another Secret. Your Mistress must not marry *Heartwell*, *Lucy*.

Lucy. How! O Lord!——

Bell. Nay, don't be in Passion, *Lucy*:——I'll provide a fitter Husband for her.——Come, here's Earnest of my good Intentions for thee too; let this mollifie.——[*Gives her Mony*.] Look you, *Heartwell* is my Friend; and tho' he be blind, I must not see him fall into the Snare, and unwittingly marry a Whore.

Lucy. Whore! I'd have you to know my Mistress scorns——

Bell. Nay, nay: Look you, *Lucy*; there are Whores of as good Quality.—But to the purpose, if you will give me leave to acquaint you with it. ——Do you carry on the Mistake of me: I'll marry 'em.—Nay, don't pause;——If you do, I'll spoil all.——I have some private Reasons for what I do, which I'll tell you within.—In the mean time, I promise,——and rely upon me,——to help your

23 Diffide in me] Not confide, mistrust.

Mistress to a Husband: Nay, and thee too, *Lucy.* —Here's my Hand, I will; with a fresh Assurance. [*Gives her more Mony.*

Lucy. Ah, the Devil is not so cunning.——You know my easie Nature.——Well, for once I'll venture to serve you; but if you do deceive me, the Curse of all kind, tender-hearted Women light upon you.

Bell. That's as much as to say, *The Pox take me.*—Well, lead on.

SCENE IV.

VAINLOVE, SHARPER, *and* SETTER.

Sharp. Just now, say you, gone in with *Lucy*?

Set. I saw him, Sir, and stood at the Corner where you found me, and overheard all they said: Mr. *Bellmour* is to marry 'em.

Sharp. Ha, ha; 'twill be a pleasant Cheat,—I'll plague *Heartwell* when I see him. Prithee *Frank*, let's teaze him; make him fret 'till he foam at the Mouth, and disgorge his Matrimonial Oath with Interest——Come, thou'rt musty——

Set. [*To* Sharper.] Sir, a Word with you. [*Whispers him.*

Vain. Sharper swears she has forsworn the Letter—I'm sure he tells me Truth;—but I am not sure she told him Truth:——Yet she was unaffectedly concern'd, he says; and often blush'd with Anger and Surprize:——And so I remember in the Park.——She had Reason, if I wrong her—I begin to doubt.

Sharp. Say'st thou so!

Setter. This Afternoon, Sir, about an Hour before my Master receiv'd the Letter.

Sharp. In my Conscience, like enough.

Setter. Ay, I know her, Sir; at least, I'm sure I can fish it out of her: She's the very Sluce to her

16 Reason] She was right. An almost universal gallicism in that century, from Jonson onward.

Lady's Secrets :——'Tis but setting her Mill a going, and I can drein her of 'em all.

Sharp. Here, *Frank*, your Blood-Hound has made out the Fault : This Letter, that so sticks in thy Maw, is counterfeit ; only a Trick of *Sylvia* in Revenge, contriv'd by *Lucy*.

Vain. Ha ! It has a Colour——But how do you know it, Sirrah ?

Setter. I do suspect as much ;—because why, Sir,——She was pumping me about how your Worship's Affairs stood towards Madam *Araminta* ; as, when you had seen her last ? when you were to see her next ? and, where you were to be found at that time ? and such like.

Vain. And where did you tell her ?

Setter. In the *Piazza.*

Vain. There I receiv'd the Letter——It must be so——And why did you not find me out, to tell me this before, Sot ?

Setter. Sir, I was Pimping for Mr. *Bellmour.*

Sharp. You were well employ'd :——I think there is no Objection to the Excuse.

Vain. Pox o'my sawcy Credulity——If I have lost her, I deserve it. But if Confession and Repentance be of force, I'll win her, or weary her into a Forgiveness.

Sharp. Methinks I long to see *Bellmour* come forth.

SCENE V.

SHARPER, BELLMOUR, SETTER.

Setter. Talk of the Devil——See where he comes.

Sharp. Hugging himself in his prosperous Mischief——No real Fanatick can look better pleas'd after a successful Sermon of Sedition.

Bell. Sharper ! Fortifie thy Spleen : Such a Jest ! Speak when thou art ready.

Sharp. Now, were I ill-natur'd, would I utterly disappoint thy Mirth : Hear thee tell thy mighty Jest, with as much Gravity as a Bishop hears

Venereal Causes in the Spiritual Court: Not so much as wrinkle my Face with one Smile; but let thee look simply, and laugh by thy self.

Bell. P'shaw, no; I have a better Opinion of thy Wit—Gad, I defie thee.—

Sharp. Were it not loss of Time, you should make the Experiment. But honest *Setter*, here, over-heard you with *Lucy*, and has told me all.

Bell. Nay then, I thank thee for not putting me out of Countenance. But, to tell you something you don't know—I got an Opportunity (after I had marry'd 'em) of discovering the Cheat to *Sylvia*. She took it at first, as another Woman would the like Disappointment; but my Promise to make her amends quickly with another Husband, somewhat pacify'd her.

Sharp. But how the Devil do you think to acquit your self of your Promise? Will you marry her your self?

Bell. I have no such Intentions at present—— Prithee, wilt thou think a little for me? I am sure the ingenious Mr. *Setter* will assist.

Setter. O Lord, Sir!

Bell. I'll leave him with you, and go shift my Habit.

SCENE VI.

SHARPER, SETTER, *Sir* JOSEPH, *and* BLUFFE.

Sharp. Heh! Sure, Fortune has sent this Fool hither on purpose. *Setter*, stand close; seem not to observe 'em; and, hark-ye—— [*Whispers.*

Bluff. Fear him not——I am prepar'd for him now; and he shall find he might have safer rouz'd a sleeping Lion.

Sir *Jo.* Hush, hush: Don't you see him?

Bluff. Shew him to me.——Where is he?

Sir *Jo.* Nay, don't speak so loud——I don't jest, as I did a little while ago——Look yonder—A-gad, if he should hear the Lion roar, he'd cudgel him into an Ass, and his primitive Braying. Don't you remember the Story in *Æsop's Fables*, Bully? A-gad, there are good Morals to be pick'd out of *Æsop's Fables*, let me tell you that; and *Reynard the Fox* too.

Bluff. Damn your Morals.

Sir *Jo*. Prithee, don't speak so loud.

Bluff. Damn your Morals; I must revenge th'Affront done to my Honour. [*In a low Voice.*

Sir *Jo*. Ay; do, do, Captain, if you think fitting—You may dispose of your own Flesh as you think fitting, d'ye see:——But by the Lord *Harry*, I'll leave you. [*Stealing away upon his Tip-toes.*

Bluff. Prodigious! What, will you forsake your Friend in Extremity! You can't in Honour refuse to carry him a Challenge.

[*Almost whispering, and treading softly after him.*

Sir *Jo*. Prithee, what do you see in my Face, that looks as if I would carry a Challenge? Honour is your Province, Captain; take it——All the World know me to be a Knight, and a Man of Worship.

Setter. I warrant you, Sir, I'm instructed.

Sharp. Impossible! *Araminta*, take a liking to a Fool! [*Aloud.*

Setter. Her Head runs on nothing else, nor she can talk of nothing else.

Sharp. I know she commended him all the while we were in the Park; but I thought it had been only to make *Vainlove* jealous.——

Sir *Jo*. How's this! Good Bully, hold your Breath, and let's hearken. A-gad, this must be I.——

Sharp. Death, it can't be.—An Oaf, an Ideot, a Wittal.

15 *Reynard the Fox*] The famous beast-epic, of which Caxton's translation from the Flemish prose version *Die historie van reynaert de vos* (1479) was then popular.

'*Bayes* . . . Take it from me, *Mr. Smith*, there is as good *Morality*, and as sound Precepts in the *delectable History of Reynard the Fox*, as in any book I know, except *Seneca*.'—*The Country Mouse and the City Mouse*.

Sir *Jo*. Ay, now it's out; 'tis I, my own individual Person.

Sharp. A Wretch, that has flown for Shelter to the lowest Shrub of Mankind, and seeks Protection from a blasted Coward.

Sir *Jo*. That's you, *Bully*, Back.

[Bluffe *frowns upon Sir* Joseph.

Sharp. She has given *Vainlove* her Promise, to marry him before to Morrow Morning.——Has she not? [*To* Setter.

Setter. She has, Sir;——And I have it in Charge to attend her all this Evening, in order to conduct her to the Place appointed.

Sharp. Well, I'll go and inform your Master; and do you press her to make all the haste imaginable.

SCENE VII.

SETTER, *Sir* JOSEPH, BLUFFE.

Setter. Were I a Rogue now, what a noble Prize could I dispose of! A goodly Pinnace, richly laden, and to launch forth under my auspicious Convoy. Twelve thousand Pounds, and all her Rigging; besides what lies conceal'd under Hatches.—Ha! All this committed to my Care!—Avaunt Temptation.——*Setter*, shew thy self a Person of Worth; be true to thy Trust, and be reputed honest. Reputed honest! Hum: Is that all? Ay: For to be honest is nothing; the Reputation of it is all. Reputation! what have such poor Rogues as I to do with Reputation? 'tis above us; and for Men of Quality, they are above it; so that Reputation is e'en as foolish a thing as Honesty. And for my part, if I meet Sir *Joseph* with a Purse of Gold in his Hand, I'll dispose of mine to the best Advantage.

Sir *Jo*. Heh, heh, heh: Here 'tis for you, i'faith, Mr. *Setter*. Nay, I'll take you at your Word.

[*Chinking a purse*.

Setter. Sir *Joseph* and the Captain too! undone, undone! I'm undone, my Master's undone, my Lady's undone, and all the Business is undone.

Sir *Jo*. No, no, never fear, Man, the Lady's Business shall be done. What—Come, Mr. *Setter*, I have over-heard all, and to speak, is but loss of time; but if there be occasion, let these worthy Gentlemen intercede for me. [*Gives him Gold.*

Setter. O Lord, Sir, what d'ye mean? Corrupt my Honesty.——They have indeed very persuading Faces. But——

Sir *Jo*. 'Tis too little, there's more, Man. There, take all——Now——

Setter. Well, Sir *Joseph*, you have such a winning way with you——

Sir *Jo*. And how, and how, good *Setter*, did the little Rogue look, when she talk'd of Sir *Joseph*? Did not her Eyes twinkle, and her Mouth water? Did not she pull up her little Bubbies? And——A-gad, I'm so overjoy'd—And stroke down her Belly? and then step aside to tie her Garter, when she was thinking of her Love? Heh, *Setter*!

Setter. Oh, yes, Sir.

Sir *Jo*. How now, *Bully*? What, melancholy, because I'm in the Lady's Favour?—No matter, I'll make your Peace——I know they were a little smart upon you—But I warrant, I'll bring you into the Lady's good Graces.

Bluff. P'shaw, I have Petitions to show, from other-guess Toys than she. Look here; These were sent me this Morning——There, read, [*Shows Letters.*] That——That's a Scrawl of Quality. Here, here's from a Countess too. Hum—No, hold—that's from a Knight's Wife, she sent it me by her Husband——But here, both these are from Persons of great Quality.

Sir *Jo*. They are either from Persons of great Quality, or no Quality at all, 'tis such a damn'd ugly Hand.

While Sir Joseph *reads,* Bluffe *whispers* Setter.

Setter. Captain, I would do any thing to serve you; but this is so difficult——

Bluff. Not at all. Don't I know him?

Setter. You'll remember the Conditions?——

Bluff. I'll give't you under my Hand—In the mean time, here's Earnest. [*Gives him Mony.*] Come Knight,——I'm capitulating with Mr *Setter* for you.

Sir *Jo*. Ah, honest *Setter*;——Sirrah, I'll give thee any thing but a Night's Lodging.

SCENE VIII.

SHARPER *tugging in* HEARTWELL.

Sharp. Nay, prithee leave Railing, and come along with me: May be she mayn't be within. 'Tis but to yond' Corner-House.

Heart. Whither? Whither? Which Corner-House?

Sharp. Why, there: The two white Posts.

Heart. And who would you visit there, say you? (O'ons, how my Heart akes.)

Sharp. P'shaw, thou'rt so troublesome and inquisitive——Why, I'll tell you; 'Tis a young Creature that *Vainlove* debauch'd, and has forsaken. Did you never hear *Bellmour* chide him about *Sylvia*?

Heart. Death, and Hell, and Marriage! My Wife! [*Aside*.

Sharp. Why thou art as musty as a new marry'd Man, that had found his Wife Knowing the first Night.

Heart. Hell, and the Devil! Does he know it? But, hold——If he should not, I were a Fool to discover it——I'll dissemble, and try him. [*Aside.*] Ha, ha, ha. Why, *Tom*. Is that such an Occasion of Melancholy? Is it such an uncommon Mischief?

Sharp. No, faith; I believe not.——Few

Women, but have their Year of Probation, before they are cloister'd in the narrow Joys of Wedlock. But, prithee come along with me, or I'll go and have the Lady to my self. B'w'y *George*. [*Going.*

Heart. O Torture! How he racks and tears me!——Death! Shall I own my Shame, or wittingly let him go and whore my Wife? No, that's insupportable——Oh, *Sharper*!

Sharp. How now?

Heart. Oh, I am—marry'd.

Sharp. (Now hold Spleen.) Marry'd!

Heart. Certainly, irrecoverably marry'd.

Sharp. Heav'n forbid, Man! How long?

Heart. Oh, an Age, an Age! I have been marry'd these two Hours.

Sharp. My old Batchelor marry'd! That were a Jest. Ha, ha, ha.

Heart. Death! D'ye mock me? Heark ye, if either you esteem my Friendship, or your own Safety—Come not near that House——that Corner-House—that hot Brothel. Ask no Questions.

Sharp. Mad, by this Light.
Thus Grief still treads upon the Heels of Pleasure:
Marry'd in haste, we may repent at Leisure.

SCENE IX.

SHARPER, SETTER.

Setter. Some by Experience find those Words misplac'd:
At Leisure marry'd, they repent in haste.
As I suppose my Master *Heartwell*.

Sharp. Here again, my *Mercury!*

Setter. Sublimate, if you please, Sir: I think my Atchievements do deserve the Epithet—*Mercury* was a Pimp too, but, though I blush to own it, at this time, I must confess I am somewhat fall'n from the Dignity of my Function, and do condescend to be scandalously imploy'd in the Promotion of vulgar Matrimony. 12

Sharper. As how, dear dexterous Pimp?

Setter. Why, to be brief, for I have weighty Affairs depending—Our Stratagem succeeded as you intended—*Bluffe* turns errant Traitor; bribes me, to make a private Conveyance of the Lady to him, and put a Shame-Settlement upon Sir *Joseph*.

Sharper. O Rogue! Well, but I hope— 19

Setter. No, no; never fear me, Sir—I privately inform'd the Knight of the Treachery; who has agreed, seemingly to be cheated, that the Captain may be so in reality.

Sharp. Where's the Bride?

Setter. Shifting Cloaths for the Purpose, at a Friend's House of mine. Here's Company coming; if you'll walk this way, Sir, I'll tell you.

SCENE X.

BELLMOUR, BELINDA, ARAMINTA, *and* VAINLOVE.

Vain. Oh, 'twas Frenzy all: Cannot you forgive it?—Men in Madness have a Title to your Pity. [*To* Araminta.

Aram.——Which they forfeit, when they are restor'd to their Senses.

Vain. I am not presuming beyond a Pardon.

Aram. You who cou'd reproach me with one Counterfeit, how insolent would a real Pardon make you! But there's no need to forgive what is not worth my Anger. 9

Belin. O my Conscience, I cou'd find in my Heart to marry thee, purely to be rid of thee——At least, thou art so troublesome a Lover, there's Hopes thou'lt make a more than ordinary quiet Husband. [*To* BELLMOUR.

Bell. Say you so?——Is that a Maxim among ye?

Belin. Yes: You fluttering Men of the Mode have made Marriage a meer *French* Dish.

Bell. I hope there's no *French* Sawce. [*Aside.*

Belin. You are so curious in the Preparation, that is, your Courtship, one wou'd think you meant a noble Entertainment——But when we come to feed, 'tis all Froth, and poor, but in show. Nay, often, only Remains, which have been I know not how many times warm'd for other Company, and at last serv'd up cold to the Wife.

Bell. That were a miserable Wretch indeed, who could not afford one warm Dish for the Wife of his Bosom——But you timorous Virgins form a dreadful Chimæra of a Husband, as of a Creature contrary to that soft, humble, pliant, easie thing, a Lover; so guess at Plagues in Matrimony, in Opposition to the Pleasures of Courtship. Alas! Courtship to Marriage, is but as the Musick in the Play-House, 'till the Curtain's drawn; but that once up, then opens the Scene of Pleasure.

Belin. Oh, foh—no: Rather, Courtship to Marriage, as a very witty Prologue to a very dull Play.

SCENE XI.

[*To them*] SHARPER.

Sharper. Hist,—*Bellmour*: If you'll bring the Ladies, make haste to *Sylvia's* Lodgings, before *Heartwell* has fretted himself out of Breath.——

Bell. You have an Opportunity now, Madam, to revenge your self upon *Heartwell*, for affronting your Squirrel. [*To* Belinda.

Belin. O the filthy rude Beast.

Aram. 'Tis a lasting Quarrel: I think he has never been at our House since.

Bell. But give your selves the trouble to walk to that Corner-House, and I'll tell you by the way what may divert and surprize you.

SCENE XII.

SCENE, Sylvia's *Lodgings.*

HEARTWELL *and Boy.*

Heart. Gone forth, say you, with her Maid!

Boy. There was a Man too that fetch'd 'em out—*Setter*, I think they call'd him.

Heart. So-h——That precious Pimp too—Damn'd, damn'd Strumpet? Cou'd she not contain her self on her Wedding Day! Not hold out 'till Night! O cursed State! How wide we err, when apprehensive of the Load of Life!

——We hope to find
That help which Nature meant in Woman-kind,
To Man that Supplemental Self design'd;
But proves a burning Caustick when apply'd,
And Adam, *sure, cou'd with more Ease abide*
The Bone when broken, than when made A Bride.

SCENE XIII.

[*To him*] BELLMOUR, BELINDA, VAINLOVE, ARAMINTA.

Bell. Now *George*, what Rhyming! I thought the Chimes of Verse were past, when once the doleful Marriage Knell was rung.

Heart. Shame and Confusion. I am exposed.

[Vainlove *and* Araminta *talk a-part.*

Belin. Joy, Joy Mr. *Bridegroom*; I give you Joy Sir.

Heart. 'Tis not in thy Nature to give me Joy—A Woman can as soon give Immortality.

Belin. Ha, ha, ha, O Gad, Men grow such Clowns when they are marry'd.

Bell. That they are fit for no Company but their Wives.

Belin. Nor for them neither, in a little time——I swear, at the Month's end, you shall hardly find a marry'd Man, that will do a civil thing to his

Wife, or say a civil thing to any Body else. How he looks already. Ha, ha, ha.

Bell. Ha, ha, ha.

Heart. Death, Am I made your laughing-Stock? For you, Sir, I shall find a time; but take off your Wasp here, or the Clown may grow boistrous, I have a Fly-Flap.

Belin. You have occasion for't, your Wife has been blown upon.

Bell. That's home.

Heart. Not Fiends or Furies could have added to my Vexation, or any thing, but another Woman ——You've rack'd my Patience; be gone, or by——

Bell. Hold, hold. What the Devil, thou wilt not draw upon a Woman!

Vain. What's the Matter?

Aram. Bless me! What have you done to him?

Belin. Only touch'd a gall'd-Beast 'till he winch'd.

Vain. *Bellmour*, give it over; you vex him too much? 'tis all serious to him.

Belin. Nay, I swear, I begin to pity him, my self.

Heart. Damn your Pity—But let me be calm a little——How have I deserv'd this of you? Any of ye? Sir, have I impair'd the Honour of your House, promis'd your Sister Marriage, and whor'd her? Wherein have I injur'd you? Did I bring a Physician to your Father when he lay expiring, and endeavour to prolong his Life, and you one and twenty? Madam, have I had an Opportunity with you and bauk'd it? Did you ever offer me the Favour that I refus'd it? Or——

Belin. Oh foh! What does the filthy Fellow mean? Lard, let me be gone.

Aram. Hang me, if I pity you; you are right enough serv'd.

Bell. This is a little scurrilous tho'.

Vain. Nay, 'tis a Sore of your own scratching—Well *George*,—

Heart. You are the principal Cause of all my present Ills. If *Sylvia* had not been your Mistress, my Wife might have been honest.

Vain. And if *Sylvia* had not been your Wife, my Mistress might have been just—There, we are even——But have a good Heart, I heard of your Misfortune, and come to your Relief.

Heart. When Execution's over, you offer a Reprieve.

Vain. What would you give?

Heart. Oh! Any thing, every thing, a Leg or two, or an Arm; nay, I would be divorced from my Virility, to be divorced from my Wife.

SCENE XIV.

[*To them*] SHARPER.

Vain. Faith, that's a sure way—But here's one can sell you Freedom better cheap.

Sharp. *Vainlove*, I have been a kind of a Godfather to you, yonder. I have promised and vow'd some things in your Name, which I think you are bound to perform.

Vain. No signing to a Blank, Friend.

Sharp. No, I'll deal fairly with you—'Tis a full and free Discharge to Sir *Joseph Wittal* and Captain *Bluffe*; for all Injuries whatsoever, done unto you by them, until the present Date hereof——How say you?

Vain. Agreed.

Sharp. Then, let me beg these Ladies to wear their Masks, a Moment. Come in Gentlemen and Ladies.

Heart. What the Devil's all this to me?

Vain. Patience.

SCENE *The Last.*

[*To them*] *Sir* JOSEPH, BLUFFE, SYLVIA, LUCY, SETTER.

Bluff. All injuries whatsoever, Mr. *Sharper*.

Sir *Jo*. Ay, ay, whatsoever, Captain, stick to that; whatsoever.

Sharp. 'Tis done, these Gentlemen are Witnesses to the general Release.

Vain. Ay, ay, to this instant Moment——I have pass'd an Act of Oblivion.

Bluff. 'Tis very generous, Sir, since I needs must own——

Sir *Jo*. No, no, Captain, you need not own, heh, heh, heh. 'Tis I must own—

Bluff.——That you are over-reach'd too, ha, ha, ha, only a little Art military used——only undermined, or so, as shall appear by the fair *Araminta*, my Wife's Permission. Oh, the Devil, cheated at last! [Lucy *unmasks*.

Sir *Jo*. Only a little Art-military Trick, Captain, only countermin'd, or so——Mr. *Vainlove*, I suppose you know whom I have got——now, but all's forgiven.

Vain. I know whom you have not got; pray Ladies convince him. [Aram. *and* Belin. *unmask*.

Sir *Jo*. Ah! O Lord, my Heart akes——Ah! *Setter*, a Rogue of all sides.

Sharp. Sir *Joseph*, you had better have preengag'd this Gentleman's Pardon: For though *Vainlove* be so generous to forgive the loss of his Mistress—I know not how *Heartwell* may take the loss of his Wife. [Sylvia *unmasks*.

Heart. My Wife! By this Light 'tis she, the very Cockatrice—Oh *Sharper*! Let me embrace thee——But art thou sure she is really marry'd to him?

Setter. Really and lawfully marry'd, I am Witness.

Sharp. *Bellmour* will unriddle to you.

[Heartwell *goes to* Bellmour.

Sir *Jo*. Pray, Madam, who are you? For I find, you and I are like to be better acquainted.

Sylv. The worst of me, is, that I am your Wife——

Sharp. Come, Sir *Joseph*; your Fortune is not so bad as you fear——A fine Lady, and a Lady of very good Quality.

Sir *Jo*. Thanks to my Knight-hood, she's a Lady——

Vain.—That deserves a Fool with a better Title ——Pray use her as my Relation, or you shall hear on't.

Bluff. What, are you a Woman of Quality too, Spouse?

Setter. And my Relation; pray let her be respected accordingly—Well, honest *Lucy*, fare thee well——I think, you and I have been Play-fellows off and on, any time this seven Years.

Lucy. Hold your prating—I'm thinking what Vocation I shall follow while my Spouse is planting Lawrels in the Wars.

Bluff. No more Wars, Spouse, no more Wars—— While I plant Lawrels for my Head abroad, I may find the Branches sprout at home.

Heart. *Bellmour*, I approve thy Mirth, and thank thee——And I cannot in Gratitude (for I see which way thou art going) see thee fall into the same Snare, out of which thou hast deliver'd me.

Bell. I thank thee, *George*, for thy good Intention——But there is a Fatality in Marriage—— For I find I'm resolute.

Heart. Then good Counsel will be thrown away upon you——For my part, I have once escap'd—— And when I wed again, may she be——Ugly, as an old Bawd.

Vain.——Ill-natur'd, as an old Maid—

Bell. Wanton as a young Widow——

Sharp. And jealous as a barren Wife.

Heart. Agreed.

Bell. Well; 'Midst of these dreadful Denunciations, and notwithstanding the Warning and Example before me, I commit my self to lasting Durance. 79

Belin. Prisoner, make much of your Fetters.
[*Giving her Hand*.

Bell. *Frank*, Will you keep us in Countenance?

Vain. May I presume to hope so great a Blessing?

Aram. We had better take the Advantage of a little of our Friends Experience first.

Bell. O my Conscience she dares not consent, for fear he shou'd recant. [*Aside*.] Well, we shall have your Company to Church in the Morning—— May be it may get you an Appetite to see us fall to before ye. *Setter*, did not you tell me?——

Setter. They're at the Door: I'll call 'em in. 91

A DANCE.

Bell. Now set we forward on a Journey for Life——Come take your Fellow-Travellers. Old *George*, I'm sorry to see thee still plod on alone.

Heart. With gaudy Plumes and gingling Bells made proud,
The youthful Beast sets forth, and neighs aloud.
A Morning-Sun his Tinsell'd Harness gilds,
And the first Stage a Down-Hill Green-sword yields. 101
But, Oh——
What rugged Ways attend the Noon of Life!
(Our Sun declines,) and with what anxious Strife,
What Pain we tug that galling Load, a Wife;
All Coursers the first Heat with Vigour run;
But 'tis with Whip and Spur the Race is won.

Exeunt Omnes.

EPILOGUE.

Spoken by Mrs. *Barry*.

As a rash Girl, who will all Hazards run,
And be enjoy'd, tho' sure to be undone ;
Soon as her Curiosity is over,
Would give the World she could her Toy recover :
So fares it with our Poet ; and I'm sent
To tell you, he already does repent
Would you were all as forward, to keep Lent.
Now the Deed's done, the Giddy-thing has Leisure
To think o'th' Sting, that's in the Tail of Pleasure.
Methinks I hear him in Consideration !
What will the World say ? Where's my Reputation ?
Now that's at stake—No Fool, 'tis out o' Fashion.
If loss of that should follow want of Wit,
How many Undone Men were in the Pit !
Why that's some Comfort, to an Author's Fears,
If he's an Ass, he will be Try'd by's Peers.
But hold—I am exceeding my Commission ;
My Business here, was humbly to Petition :
But we're so us'd to rail on these Occasions,
I could not help one Trial of your Patience :
For 'tis our way (you know) for fear o'th' worst,
To be before-hand still, and cry Fool first.
How say you, Sparks ? How do you stand affected ?
I swear, young Bays *within, is so dejected,*
'Twou'd grieve your Hearts to see him ; shall I call him?
But then you cruel Criticks would so maul him !
Yet, may be, you'll encourage a Beginner ;
But how ?—Just as the Devil does a Sinner.
Women and Wits are us'd e'en much at one,
You gain your End, and damn 'em when you've done.

THE

DOUBLE-DEALER.

A

COMEDY.

Interdum tamen, & vocem Comœdia tollit.

Hor. Ar. Po.

Huic equidem Consilio palmam do: hic me magnifice effero, qui vim tantam in me & potestatem habeam tantæ astutiæ, vera dicendo ut eos ambos fallam. Syr. in Terent. Heaut.

Printed in the YEAR 1710.

To the Right Honourable

Charles Montague,

One of the

Lords of the Treasury.

SIR,

I Heartily wish this Play were as perfect as I intended it, that it might be more worthy your Acceptance; and that my Dedication of it to you, might be more becoming that Honour and Esteem which I, with every Body, who is so fortunate as to know you, have for you. It had your Countenance when yet unknown; and now it is made publick, it wants your Protection.

I would not have any Body imagine, that I think this Play without its Faults, for I am Conscious of several. I confess I design'd (whatever Vanity or Ambition occasion'd that Design) to have written a true and regular Comedy: but I found it an Undertaking which put me in mind of——*Sudet multum, frustraque laboret ausus idem.* And now to make Amends for the Vanity of such a Design, I do confess both the Attempt, and the imperfect Performance. Yet I must take the Boldness to say, I have not miscarry'd in the whole; for the Mechanical part of it is regular. That I may say with as little Vanity, as a Builder may say he has built a House according to the

Montague] Afterwards for a short time, First Lord, i. e. Prime Minister. This brilliant financier was afterwards created Earl of Halifax. He is the Bufo of Pope's *Prologue to the Satires*. His literary reputation was founded chiefly upon the *Country Mouse and the City Mouse*, a parody of the *Hind and Panther*, which he wrote in collaboration with Prior. He 'claimed the station to be Maecenas to the nation'.

Model laid down before him; or a Gardner that he has set his Flowers in a Knot of such or such a Figure. I design'd the Moral first, and to that Moral I invented the Fable, and do not know that I have borrow'd one Hint of it any where. I made the Plot as strong as I could, because it was single, and I made it single, because I would avoid Confusion, and was resolved to preserve the three Unities of the Drama. Sir, this Discourse is very impertinent to you, whose Judgement much better can discern the Faults, than I can excuse them; and whose good Nature, like that of a Lover, will find out those hidden Beauties (if there are any such) which it wou'd be great Immodesty for me to discover. I think I don't speak improperly when I call you a *Lover* of Poetry; for it is very well known she has been a very kind Mistress to you; she has not deny'd you the last Favour; and she has been fruitful to you in a most beautiful Issue——If I break off abruptly here, I hope every Body will understand that it is to avoid a Commendation, which, as it is your Due, would be most easie for me to pay, and too troublesome for you to receive.

I have, since the Acting of this Play, harken'd after the Objections which have been made to it; for I was Conscious where a true Critick might have put me upon my Defence. I was prepared for the Attack; and am pretty confident I could have vindicated some Parts, and excused others; and where there were any plain Miscarriages, I would most ingenuously have confess'd 'em. But I have not heard any thing said sufficient to provoke an Answer. That which looks most like an Objection, does not relate in particular to this Play, but to all or most that ever have been written; and that is Soliloquy. Therefore I will answer it, not only for my own sake, but to save others the Trouble, to whom it may hereafter be Objected.

I grant, that for a Man to Talk to himself,

appears absurd and unnatural; and indeed it is so in most Cases; but the Circumstances which may attend the Occasion, make great Alteration. It oftentimes happens to a Man, to have Designs which require him to himself, and in their Nature cannot admit of a Confident. Such, for certain, is all Villany; and other less mischievous Intentions may be very improper to be Communicated to a second Person. In such a Case therefore the Audience must observe, whether the Person upon the Stage takes any notice of them at all, or no. For if he supposes any one to be by, when he talks to himself, it is monstrous and ridiculous to the last degree. Nay, not only in this Case, but in any Part of a Play, if there is expressed any Knowledge of an Audience, it is insufferable. But otherwise, when a Man in Soliloquy reasons with himself, and *Pro*'s and *Con*'s, and weighs all his Designs: We ought not to imagine that this Man either talks to us, or to himself; he is only thinking, and thinking such Matter as were inexcusable Folly in him to speak. But because we are conceal'd Spectators of the Plot in Agitation, and the Poet finds it necessary to let us know the whole Mystery of his Contrivance, he is willing to inform us of this Person's Thoughts; and to that end is forc'd to make use of the Expedient of Speech, no other better way being yet invented for the Communication of Thought.

Another very wrong Objection has been made by some who have not taken Leisure to distinguish the Characters. The Hero of the Play, as they are pleas'd to call him, (meaning *Mellefont*) is a Gull, and made a Fool, and cheated. Is every Man a Gull and a Fool that is deceiv'd? At that rate I'm afraid the two Classes of Men will be reduc'd to one, and the Knaves themselves be at a loss to justifie their Title: But if an Open-hearted honest Man, who has an entire Confidence in one whom he takes to be his Friend, and whom he has oblig'd to be so ; and who (to confirm him in his Opinion) in all Appearance, and upon several Trials has been so : If this Man be deceiv'd by the Treachery of the other ; must he of necessity commence Fool immediately, only because the other has prov'd a Villain ? Ay, but there was Caution given to *Mellefont* in the first Act by his Friend *Careless*. Of what Nature was that Caution ? Only to give the Audience some light into the Character of *Maskwell*, before his Appearance ; and not to convince *Mellefont* of his Treachery ; for that was more than *Careless* was then able to do : He never knew *Maskwell* guilty of any Villany ; he was only a sort of Man which he did not like. As for his suspecting his Familiarity with my Lady *Touchwood :* Let 'em examine the Answer that *Mellefont* makes him, and compare it with the Conduct of *Maskwell*'s Character through the Play.

I would beg 'em again to look into the Character of *Maskwell* before they accuse *Mellefont* of Weakness for being deceiv'd by him. For upon summing up the Enquiry into this Objection, it may be found they have mistaken Cunning in one Character, for Folly in another.

But there is one thing, at which I am more concerned than all the false Criticisms that are made upon me ; and that is, some of the Ladies are offended. I am heartily sorry for it, for I declare I would rather disoblige all the Criticks in the World, than one of the fair Sex. They are concerned that I have represented some Women Vicious and Affected : How can I help it ? It is the Business of a Comick Poet to paint the Vices and Follies of Human-kind ; and there are but two Sexes, Male, and Female, *Men*, and *Women*, which have a Title to humanity : And if I leave one half of them out, the Work will be imperfect. I should be very glad of an Opportunity to make my Compliment to those Ladies who are offended :

But they can no more expect it in a Comedy, than to be Tickled by a Surgeon, when he's letting 'em Blood. They who are Virtuous or Discreet, should not be offended, for such Characters as these distinguish *them*, and make their Beauties more shining and observ'd: And they who are of the other kind, may nevertheless pass for such, by seeming not to be displeas'd, or touch'd with the Satire of this *Comedy*. Thus have they also wrongfully accus'd me of doing them a Prejudice, when I have in reality done them a Service.

You will pardon me, Sir, for the Freedom I take of making Answers to other People, in an Epistle which ought wholly to be sacred to you: But since I intend the Play to be so too, I hope I may take the more Liberty of Justifying it, where it is in the Right.

I must now, Sir, declare to the World, how kind you have been to my Endeavours; for in regard of what was well meant, you have excus'd what was ill perform'd. I beg you would continue the same Method in your Acceptance of this Dedication. I know no other way of making a Return to that Humanity you shew'd, in protecting an Infant, but by enrolling it in your Service, now that it is of Age and come into the World. Therefore be pleas'd to accept of this as an Acknowledgement of the Favour you have shewn me, and an Earnest of the real Service and Gratitude of,

SIR,

Your Most Obliged,

Humble Servant,

William Congreve.

To my Dear Friend

Mr. *CONGREVE*,

On his COMEDY, call'd,

The Double-Dealer.

Well then ; the promis'd Hour is come at last ;
The present Age of Wit obscures the past :
Strong were our Syres ; and as they Fought they Writ,
Conqu'ring with Force of Arms, and Dint of Wit ;
Theirs was the Giant Race, before the Flood ;
And thus, when Charles *Return'd, our Empire stood.*
Like Janus *he the stubborn Soil manur'd,*
With rules of Husbandry the Rankness cur'd :
Tam'd us to Manners, when the Stage was rude ;
And boistrous English *Wit, with Art indu'd.*
Our Age was cultivated thus at length ;
But what we gain'd in Skill, we lost in Strength.
Our Builders were, with Want of Genius, curst ;
The second Temple was not like the First :
'Till You, the best Vitruvius, *come at length ;*
Our Beauties equal ; but excel our Strength.
Firm Dorique *Pillars found Your solid Base :*
The fair Corinthian *crowns the higher Space ;*
Thus all below is Strength, and all above is Grace.
In easie Dialogue is Fletcher's *Praise :*
He mov'd the Mind, but had no Pow'r to raise.
Great Johnson *did by Strength of Judgement please :*
Yet doubling Fletcher's *Force, he wants his Ease.*
In diff'ring Talents both adorn'd their Age ;
One for the Study, t'other for the Stage.
But both to Congreve *justly shall submit,*
One match'd in Judgement, both o'er-match'd in Wit.
In Him all Beauties of this Age we see ;
Etherege *his Courtship,* Southern's *Purity ;*
The Satire, Wit, and Strength of Manly Wicherly.
All this in blooming Youth you have Atchiev'd ;

Nor are your foil'd Contemporaries griev'd;
So much the Sweetness of your Manners move,
We cannot Envy you, because we Love.
Fabius *might joy in* Scipio, *when he saw*
A Beardless Consul made against the Law,
And join his Suffrage to the Votes of Rome;
Though he with Hannibal *was overcome.*
Thus old Romano *bow'd to* Raphael's *Fame;*
And Scholar to the Youth he taught, became.
Oh that your Brows my Lawrel had sustain'd,
Well had I been Depos'd if You had Reign'd!
The Father had descended for the Son;
For only You are lineal to the Throne.
Thus when the State one Edward *did depose;*
A Greater Edward *in his Room arose.*
But now, not I, but Poetry is curs'd;
For Tom *the Second reigns like* Tom *the First.*
But let 'em not mistake my Patron's Part;
Nor call his Charity their own Desert.
Yet this I Prophesie; Thou shalt be seen,
(Tho' with some short Parenthesis between:)
High on the Throne of Wit; and seated there,
Not mine (that's little) but thy Lawrel wear.
Thy first Attempt an early Promise made;
That early Promise this has more than paid.
So bold, yet so judiciously you dare,
That your least Praise, is to be Regular.
Time, Place, and Action, may with Pains be wrought,
But Genius must be born; and never can be taught.
This is Your Portion; this Your Native Store;
Heav'n, that but once was Prodigal before,
To Shakespear *gave as much; she cou'd not give him more.*
Maintain your Post: That's all the Fame you need;
For 'tis impossible you shou'd proceed.

48 Tom the First] Dryden's enemy, Thomas Shadwell, the Og of *Absalom and Achitophel*, already trounced in *MacFlecknoe*. He was made laureate vice Dryden at the Revolution. On his death Thomas Rymer succeeded to the post of historiographer.

Already I am worn with Cares and Age ;
And just abandoning th' Ungrateful Stage :
Unprofitably kept at Heav'ns Expence,
I live a Rent-charge on his Providence :
But You, whom ev'ry Muse and Grace adorn,
Whom I foresee to better Fortune born,
Be kind to my Remains ; and oh defend,
Against your Judgment, your departed Friend !
Let not th' insulting Foe my Fame pursue ;
But shade those Lawrels which descend to You :
And take for Tribute what these Lines express :
You merit more ; nor cou'd my Love do less.

John Dryden.

PROLOGUE,

Spoken by Mrs. *Bracegirdle.*

Moors have this Way (as Story tells) to know
Whether their Brats are truly got, or no ;
Into the Sea the New-born Babe is thrown,
There, as Instinct directs, to swim, or drown.
A barbarous Device, to try if Spouse
Has kept religiously her Nuptial Vows.

Such are the Trials, Poets make of Plays :
Only they trust to more inconstant Seas ;
So does our Author, this his Child commit
To the tempestuous Mercy of the Pit,
To know if it be truly born of Wit.

Criticks avaunt ; for you are Fish of Prey,
And feed, like Sharks, upon an Infant Play.
Be ev'ry Monster of the Deep away ;
Let's a fair Trial have and a clear Sea.

Let Nature work, and do not Damn too soon,
For Life will struggle long, e'er it sink down:
And will at least rise thrice, before it drown.
Let us consider, had it been our Fate,
Thus hardly to be prov'd Legitimate!
I will not say, we'd all in Danger been,
Were each to suffer for his Mother's Sin:
But by my Troth I cannot avoid thinking,
How nearly some good Men might have 'scap'd sinking.
But, Heav'n be prais'd, this Custom is confin'd
Alone to th' Offspring of the Muses kind:
Our Christian Cuckolds are more bent to Pity;
I know not one Moor-*Husband in the City.*
I'th' good Man's Arms the Chopping Bastard thrives,
For he thinks all his own, that is his Wives.

Whatever Fate is for this Play design'd,
The Poet's sure he shall some Comfort find:
For if his Muse has play'd him false, the worst
That can befal him, is, to be divorc'd;
You Husbands Judge, if that, be to be Curs'd.

Dramatis Personæ.

MEN.

Maskwell, A Villain ; pretended Friend to *Mellefont*, Gallant to Lady *Touchwood*, and in Love with *Cynthia*.	Mr. *Betterton*.
Lord *Touchwood*, Uncle to *Mellefont*.	Mr. *Kynaston*.
Mellefont, promised to, and in Love with *Cynthia*.	Mr. *Williams*.
Careless, his Friend.	Mr. *Verbruggen*.
Lord *Froth*, A Solemn Coxcomb.	Mr. *Bowman*.
Brisk, A pert Coxcomb.	Mr. *Powell*.
Sir *Paul Plyant*, An Uxorious, Foolish, old Knight ; Brother to Lady *Touchwood*, and Father to *Cynthia*.	Mr. *Dogget*.

WOMEN.

Lady *Touchwood*, In Love with *Mellefont*.	Mrs. *Barrey*.
Cynthia, Daughter to Sir *Paul* by a former Wife, promised to *Mellefont*.	Mrs. *Bracegirdle*.
Lady *Froth*, A great Coquet ; pretender to Poetry, Wit, and Learning.	Mrs. *Mountfort*.
Lady *Plyant*, Insolent to her Husband, and easie to any Pretender.	Mrs. *Leigh*.

Chaplain, *Boy*, *Footmen*, and *Attendants*.

The SCENE, A Gallery in the Lord *Touchwood's* House. with Chambers adjoining.

THE

DOUBLE-DEALER.

ACT I. SCENE I.

A Gallery in the Lord Touchwood's *House, with Chambers adjoining.*

Enter Careless, *Crossing the Stage, with his Hat, Gloves, and Sword in his Hands ; as just risen from Table :* Mellefont *following him.*

MELLEFONT.

Ned, Ned, whither so fast ? What, turn'd Flincher ! Why, you wo' not leave us ?

Care. Where are the Women ? I'm weary of guzling, and begin to think them the better Company.

Mel. Then thy Reason staggers, and thou'rt almost Drunk.

Care. No Faith, but your Fools grow noisie—— and if a Man must endure the Noise of Words without Sense, I think the Women have more Musical Voices, and become Nonsense better.

Mel. Why, they are at the end of the Gallery ; retir'd to their Tea, and Scandal ; according to their Ancient Custom, after Dinner.——But I made a Pretence to follow you, because I had something to say to you in private, and I am not like to have many Opportunities this Evening.

Care. And here's this Coxcomb most critically come to interrupt you.

SCENE II.

[*To them*] Brisk.

Brisk. Boys, Boys, Lads, where are you? What, do you give ground? Mortgage for a Bottle, ha? *Careless*, this is your Trick; you're always spoiling Company by leaving it.

Care. And thou art always spoiling Company by coming into't.

Brisk. Pooh, ha, ha, I know you envy me. Spite, proud Spite, by the Gods! and burning Envy——I'll be judg'd by *Mellefont* here, who gives and takes Raillery better, you or I. Pshaw, Man, when I say you spoil Company by leaving it, I mean you leave no Body for the Company to laugh at. I think there I was with you, ha? *Mellefont.*

Mell. O' my Word, *Brisk*, that was a home thrust, you have silenc'd him.

Brisk. Oh, my Dear *Mellefont*, let me perish, if thou art not the Soul of Conversation, the very Essence of Wit, and Spirit of Wine,—The Deuce take me if there were three good Things said, or understood, since thy Amputation from the Body of our Society.——He, I think that's pretty and Metaphorical enough: I'Gad I could not have said it out of thy Company,——*Careless*, ha?

Care. Hum, ay, what is't?

Brisk. O, *Mon Cœur*! What is't! Nay gad I'll punish you for want of Apprehension: The Duce take me if I tell you.

Mel. No, no, hang him, he has no Taste,—— But, dear *Brisk*, excuse me, I have a little Business.

Care. Prithee get thee gone; thou see'st we are serious.

Mel. We'll come immediately, if you'll but go in, and keep up good Humour and Sense in the Company: Prithee do, they'll fall asleep else.

Brisk. I'gad so they will—Well I will, I will,

gad you shall command me from the *Zenith* to the *Nadir*.——But the duce take me if I say a good thing till you come.——But prithee dear Rogue, make haste prithee make haste, I shall burst else.——And yonder your Uncle, my Lord *Touchwood*, swears he'll disinherit you, and Sir *Paul Plyant* threatens to disclaim you for a Son-in-Law, and my Lord *Froth* won't dance at your Wedding to Morrow; nor the Duce take me, I won't write your Epithalamium—and see what a Condition you're like to be brought to.

Mel. Well, I'll speak but three Words, and follow you.

Brisk. Enough, enough, *Careless*, bring your Apprehension along with you.

SCENE III.

Mellefont, Careless.

Care. Pert Coxcomb.

Mel. Faith 'tis a good natur'd Coxcomb, and has very entertaining Follies——You must be more humane to him; at this Juncture, it will do me Service.——I'll tell you, I would have Mirth continued this Day at any rate; tho' Patience purchase Folly, and Attention be paid with Noise: There are Times when Sense may be unseasonable, as well as Truth. Prithee do thou wear none to Day; but allow *Brisk* to have Wit, that thou may'st seem a Fool.

Care. Why, how now, why this extravagant Proposition?

Mel. O, I would have no room for serious Design; for I am jealous of a Plot. I would have Noise and Impertinence keep my Lady *Touchwood*'s Head from working: For Hell is not more busie than her Brain, nor contains more Devils, than that Imaginations.

Care. I thought your Fear of her had been over——Is not to Morrow appointed for your Marriage with *Cynthia*, and her Father, Sir *Paul Plyant*, come to settle the Writings this Day, on purpose ?

Mel. True ; but you shall judge whether I have not Reason to be allarm'd. None besides you, and *Maskwell*, are acquainted with the Secret of my Aunt *Touchwood*'s violent Passion for me. Since my first Refusal of her Addresses, she has endeavour'd to do me all ill Offices with my Uncle ; yet has managed 'em with that Subtilty, that to him they have born the Face of Kindness ; while her Malice, like a dark Lanthorn, only shone upon me, where it was directed. Still it gave me less Perplexity to prevent the Success of her Displeasure, than to avoid the Importunities of her Love ; and of two Evils, I thought my self favour'd in her Aversion : But whether urg'd by her Despair, and the short Prospect of Time she saw, to accomplish her Designs ; whether the Hopes of Revenge, or of her Love, terminated in the View of this my Marriage with *Cynthia*, I know not ; but this Morning she surpriz'd me in my Bed.— 42

Care. Was there ever such a Fury ! 'tis well Nature has not put it into her Sex's Power to ravish. ——Well, bless us ! proceed. What follow'd ?

Mel. What at first amaz'd me ; for I look'd to have seen her in all the Transports of a slighted and revengeful Woman : But when I expected Thunder from her Voice, and Lightning in her Eyes ; I saw her melted into Tears, and hush'd into a Sigh. It was long before either of us spoke, Passion had ty'd her Tongue, and Amazement mine.—In short, the Consequence was thus, she omitted nothing that the most violent Love could urge, or tender Words express ; which when she saw had no effect, but still I pleaded Honour and Nearness of Blood to my Uncle ; then came the Storm I fear'd at first : For starting from my Bed-side like a Fury, she flew to my Sword, and with much ado I prevented her doing me or her self a Mischief : Having disarm'd her, in a Gust of

Passion she left me, and in a Resolution, confirm'd by a thousand Curses, not to close her Eyes, 'till they had seen my Ruin.

Care. Exquisite Woman! But what the Devil does she think, thou hast no more Sense, than to get an Heir upon her Body to disinherit thy self: for as I take it this Settlement upon you, is, with a Proviso, that your Uncle have no Children.

Mel. It is so. Well, the Service you are to do me, will be a Pleasure to your self; I must get you to engage my Lady *Plyant* all this Evening, that my pious Aunt may not work her to her Interest. And if you chance to secure her to your self, you may incline her to mine. She's handsome, and knows it; is very silly, and thinks she has Sense, and has an old fond Husband.

Care. I confess a very fair Foundation, for a Lover to build upon.

Mel. For my Lord *Froth*, he and his Wife will be sufficiently taken up, with admiring one another, and *Brisk*'s Gallantry, as they call it. I'll observe my Uncle my self; and *Jack Maskwell* has promised me, to watch my Aunt narrowly, and give me notice upon any Suspicion. As for Sir *Paul*, my wise Father-in-Law that is to be, my Dear *Cynthia* has such a share in his Fatherly Fondness, he would scarce make her a Moment uneasie, to have her happy hereafter.

Care. So, you have mann'd your Works: but I wish you may not have the weakest Guard, where the Enemy is strongest.

Mel. Maskwell, you mean; prithee why should you suspect him?

Care. Faith I cannot help it, you know I never lik'd him; I am a little superstitious in Physiognomy.

Mel. He has Obligations of Gratitude, to bind him to me; his Dependance upon my Uncle is through my Means.

Care. Upon your Aunt, you mean.

Mel. My Aunt!

Care. I'm mistaken if there be not a Familiarity between them, you do not suspect: Notwithstanding her Passion for you.

Mel. Pooh, pooh, nothing in the World but his Design to do me Service; and he endeavours to be well in her Esteem, that he may be able to effect it.

Care. Well, I shall be glad to be mistaken; but, your Aunt's Aversion in her Revenge, cannot be any way so effectually shown, as in bringing forth a Child to disinherit you. She is handsome and cunning, and naturally wanton. *Maskwell* is Flesh and Blood at best, and Opportunities between them are frequent. His Affection to you, you have confessed, is grounded upon his Interest, that you have transplanted; and should it take Root in my Lady, I don't see what you can expect from the Fruit.

Mel. I confess the Consequence is visible, were your Suspicions just.——But see, the Company is broke up, let's meet 'em.

SCENE IV.

[*To them*] *Lord* TOUCHWOOD, *Lord* FROTH, *Sir* PAUL PLYANT, *and* BRISK.

Ld. *Touch.* Out upon't, Nephew——Leave your Father-in-law, and me, to maintain our Ground against young People.

Mel. I beg your Lordship's Pardon——we were just returning.——

Sir *Paul.* Were you, Son? Gadsbud much better as it is——Good, strange! I swear I'm almost tipsie—t'other Bottle would have been too powerful for me,—as sure as can be it would.—We wanted your Company, but Mr. *Brisk*—Where is he? I swear and vow, he's a most facetious Person—and the best Company.—And, my Lord *Froth*, your Lordship is so merry a Man, he, he, he.

Ld. *Froth.* O foy, Sir *Paul*, what do you mean? Merry! O barbarous! I'd as lieve you call'd me Fool.

Sir *Paul.* Nay, I protest and vow now, 'tis true; when Mr. *Brisk* Jokes, your Lordship's Laugh does so become you, he, he, he. 19

Ld. *Froth.* Ridiculous! Sir *Paul*, you're strangely mistaken, I find Champagne is powerful. I assure you, Sir *Paul*, I laugh at no Bodies Jest but my own, or a Lady's; I assure you, Sir *Paul.*

Brisk. How? how, my Lord? what affront my Wit! Let me perish, do I never say any thing worthy to be laugh'd at? 26

Ld. *Froth.* O foy, don't misapprehend me, I don't say so, for I often smile at your Conceptions. But there is nothing more unbecoming a Man of Quality, than to Laugh; 'tis such a vulgar Expression of the Passion! every Body can laugh. Then especially to laugh at the Jest of an inferior Person, or when any body else of the same Quality does not laugh with one; ridiculous! To be pleased with what pleases the Croud! Now when I laugh, I always laugh alone.

Brisk. I suppose that's because you laugh at your own Jests, I'gad, ha, ha, ha.

Ld. *Froth.* He, he, I swear tho', your Raillery provokes me to a Smile. 40

Brisk. Ay, my Lord, it's a sign I hit you in the Teeth, if you show 'em.

Ld. *Froth.* He, he, he, I swear that's so very pretty, I can't forbear.

Care. I find a Quibble bears more sway in your Lordship's Face, than a Jest.

Ld. *Touch.* Sir *Paul*, if you please we'll retire to the Ladies, and drink a Dish of Tea, to settle our Heads. 49

Sir *Paul.* With all my Heart.——Mr. *Brisk* you'll come to us,——or call me when you joke, I'll be ready to laugh incontinently.

SCENE V.

MELLEFONT, CARELESS, *Lord* FROTH, BRISK.

Mel. But does your Lordship never see Comedies?

Ld. *Froth.* O yes, sometimes,—But I never laugh.

Mel. No?

Ld. *Froth.* Oh, no,——Never laugh indeed, Sir.

Care. No! why what d'ye go there for?

Ld. *Froth.* To distinguish my self from the Commonalty, and mortifie the Poets; the Fellows grow so conceited, when any of their foolish Wit prevails upon the Side-Boxes.—I swear,——he, he, he, I have often constrain'd my Inclinations to laugh,——he, he, he, to avoid giving them Encouragement.

Mel. You are cruel to your self, my Lord, as well as malicious to them.

Ld. *Froth.* I confess I did my self some Violence at first, but now I think I have conquer'd it.

Brisk. Let me perish, my Lord, but there is something very particular in the Humour; 'tis true, it makes against Wit, and I'm sorry for some Friends of mine that write, but——I'gad, I love to be malicious.—Nay, duce take me there's Wit in't too——And Wit must be foil'd by Wit; cut a Diamond with a Diamond; no other way, I'gad.

Ld. *Froth.* Oh, I thought you would not be long, before you found out the Wit.

Care. Wit! In what? Where the Devil's the Wit, in not laughing when a Man has a Mind to't.

Brisk. O Lord, why can't you find it out?—Why there 'tis, in the not laughing——Don't you apprehend me?—My Lord, *Careless* is a very honest Fellow, but harkee,—you understand me, somewhat heavy, a little shallow, or so.——Why I'll tell you now, suppose now you come up to me——Nay, prithee *Careless* be instructed. Suppose, as I was saying, you come up to me holding your Sides, and laughing, as if you would—Well—I look grave, and ask the Cause of this immoderate Mirth.——You laugh on still, and are not able to tell me——Still I look grave, not so much as smile.——

Care. Smile, no, what the Devil should you smile at, when you suppose I can't tell you!

Brisk. Pshaw, pshaw, prithee don't interrupt me.——But I tell you, you shall tell me—at last——But it shall be a great while first.

Care. Well, but prithee don't let it be a great while, because I long to have it over.

Brisk. Well then, you tell me some good Jest, or very witty Thing, laughing all the while as if you were ready to die——and I hear it, and look thus.—Would not you be disappointed?

Care. No; for if it were a witty Thing, I should not expect you to understand it.

Ld. *Froth.* O foy, Mr. *Careless*, all the World allows Mr. *Brisk* to have Wit; my Wife says, he has a great deal. I hope you think her a Judge.

Brisk. Pooh, my Lord, his Voice goes for nothing.——I can't tell how to make him apprehend.—Take it t'other Way. Suppose I say a witty thing to you?

Care. Then I shall be disappointed indeed.

Mel. Let him alone, *Brisk*, he is obstinately bent not to be instructed.

Brisk. I'm sorry for him, the duce take me.

Mel. Shall we go to the Ladies, my Lord?

Ld. *Froth.* With all my Heart, methinks we are a Solitude without 'em.

Mel. Or, what say you, to another Bottle of Champagne?

Ld. *Froth.* O, for the Universe, not a Drop more I beseech you. Oh Intemperate! I have a Flushing in my Face already.

[*Takes out a Pocket-Glass, and looks in it.*

Brisk. Let me see, let me see, my Lord, I broke my Glass that was in the Lid of my Snuff-Box. Hum! Duce take me, I have encourag'd a Pimple here too. [*Takes the Glass and looks.*

Ld. *Froth*. Then you must mortifie him with a Patch; my Wife shall supply you. Come, Gentlemen, *allons*, here is Company coming. 82

SCENE VI.

Lady TOUCHWOOD, *and* MASKWELL.

L. *Touch*. I'll hear no more.——Y'are false and ungrateful; come, I know you false.

Mask. I have been frail, I confess, Madam, for your Ladyship's Service.

L. *Touch*. That I should trust a Man, whom I had known betray his Friend!

Mask. What Friend have I betray'd? Or to whom?

L. *Touch*. Your fond Friend *Mellefont*, and to me; can you deny it? 10

Mask. I do not.

L. *Touch*. Have you not wrong'd my Lord, who has been a Father to you in your Wants, and given you Being? Have you not wrong'd him in the highest manner, in his Bed?

Mask. With your Ladyship's help, and for your Service, as I told you before. I can't deny that neither.——Any thing more, Madam?

L. *Touch*. More! Audacious Villain. O, what's more, is most my Shame,——Have you not dishonour'd me? 21

Mask. No, that I deny; for I never told in all my Life: So that Accusation's answer'd; on to the next.

L. *Touch*. Death, do you dally with my Passion? Insolent Devil! But have a Care,——Provoke me not; for, by the Eternal Fire, you shall not 'scape my Vengeance.——Calm Villain! How unconcern'd he stands, confessing Treachery, and

Ingratitude! Is there a Vice more black!——O I have Excuses, thousands for my Faults; Fire in my Temper, Passions in my Soul, apt to ev'ry Provocation; oppressed at once with Love, and with Despair. But a sedate, a thinking Villain, whose black Blood runs temperately bad, what Excuse can clear!

Mask. Will you be in Temper, Madam? I would not talk to be heard. I have been [*She walks about disorder'd*] a very great Rogue for your sake, and you reproach me with it; I am ready to be a Rogue still, to do you Service; and you are flinging Conscience and Honour in my Face, to rebate my Inclinations. How am I to behave my self? You know I am your Creature, my Life and Fortune in your Power; to disoblige you, brings me certain Ruin. Allow it, I would betray you, I would not be a Traitor to my self: I don't pretend to Honesty, because you know I am a Rascal: But I would convince you, from the Necessity of my being firm to you.

L. *Touch*. Necessity, Impudence! Can no Gratitude incline you, no Obligations touch you? Have not my Fortune, and my Person, been subjected to your Pleasure? Were you not in the nature of a Servant, and have not I in effect made you Lord of all, of me, and of my Lord? Where is that humble Love, the Languishing, that Adoration, which once was paid me, and everlastingly engaged?

Mask. Fixt, rooted in my Heart, whence nothing can remove 'em, yet you——

L. *Touch*. Yet, what yet?

Mask. Nay, misconceive me not, Madam, when I say I have had a Gen'rous, and a Faithful Passion, which you had never favour'd, but through Revenge and Policy.

L. *Touch*. Ha!

37 in Temper] i. e. temperate.

Mask. Look you, Madam, we are alone,——Pray contain your self, and hear me. You know you lov'd your Nephew, when I first sigh'd for you; I quickly found it; an Argument that I Lov'd; for with that Art you veil'd your Passion, 'twas imperceptible to all but Jealous Eyes. This Discovery made me bold; I confess it; for by it, I thought you in my Power. Your Nephew's Scorn of you, added to my Hopes; I watch'd the Occasion, and took you, just Repulsed by him, warm at once with Love and Indignation; your Disposition, my Arguments, and happy Opportunity, accomplish'd my Design; I prest the yielding Minute, and was blest. How I have lov'd you since, Words have not shown, then how should Words express? 83

L. *Touch*. Well mollifying Devil!——And have I not met your Love with forward Fire?

Mask. Your Zeal I grant was ardent, but misplac'd; there was Revenge in view; that Woman's Idol had defil'd the Temple of the God, and Love was made a Mock-Worship.——A Son and Heir would have edg'd young *Mellefont* upon the Brink of Ruin, and left him none but you to catch at for Prevention. 92

L. *Touch*. Again, provoke me! Do you wind me like a Larum, only to rouse my own still'd Soul for your Diversion? Confusion!

Mask. Nay, Madam, I'm gone, if you Relapse, ——What needs this? I say nothing but what you your self, in open Hours of Love, have told me. Why should you deny it? Nay, how can you? Is not all this present Heat owing to the same Fire? Do you not love him still? How have I this Day offended you, but in not breaking off his Match with *Cynthia*? Which ere to Morrow shall be done,——had you but Patience.

L. *Touch*. How, what said you *Maskwell*,——Another Caprice to unwind my Temper?

Mask. By Heav'n, no; I am your Slave, the

Slave of all your Pleasures ; and will not rest 'till I have given you Peace, would you suffer me. 109

L. *Touch*. O, *Maskwell*, in vain I do disguise me from thee, thou know'st me, knowest the very inmost Windings and Recesses of my Soul.——Oh *Mellefont* ! I burn ; married to Morrow ! Despair strikes me. Yet my Soul knows I hate him too : Let him but once be mine, and next immediate Ruin seize him.

Mask. Compose your self, you shall possess and ruin him too,——Will that please you ?

L. *Touch*. How, how ? Thou dear, thou precious Villain, how ? 120

Mask. You have already been tampering with my Lady *Plyant*.

L. *Touch*. I have : She is ready for any Impression I think fit.

Mask. She must be thoroughly persuaded, that *Mellefont* loves her.

L. *Touch*. She is so credulous that way naturally, and likes him so well, that she will believe it faster than I can persuade her. But I don't see what you can propose from such a trifling Design ; for her first conversing with *Mellefont*, will convince her of the contrary. 132

Mask. I know it——I don't depend upon it.——But it will prepare something else ; and gain us Leisure to lay a stronger Plot : If I gain a little Time, I shall not want Contrivance.

One minute, gives Invention to destroy,
What, to rebuild, will a whole Age employ.

End of the First Act.

ACT II. SCENE I.

Lady Froth *and* Cynthia.

Cynthia.

Indeed, Madam! Is it possible your Ladyship could have been so much in Love?

L. *Froth*. I could not sleep; I did not sleep one Wink for three Weeks together.

Cynt. Prodigious! I wonder, want of Sleep, and so much Love, and so much Wit as your Ladyship has, did not turn your Brain.

L. *Froth*. O my dear *Cynthia*, you must not rally your Friend,——But really, as you say, I wonder too,——But then I had a Way.——For between you and I, I had Whimsies and Vapours, but I gave them Vent.

Cynt. How pray, Madam?

L. *Froth*. O I writ, writ abundantly,——Do you never write?

Cynt. Write, what?

L. *Froth*. Songs, Elegies, Satires, Encomiums, Panegyricks, Lampoons, Plays, or Heroick Poems.

Cynt. O Lord, not I, Madam; I'm content to be a courteous Reader.

L. *Froth*. O Inconsistent! In Love, and not write! If my Lord and I had been both of your Temper, we had never come together,——O bless me! What a sad thing would that have been, if my Lord and I should never have met!

Cynt. Then neither my Lord nor you would ever have met with your Match, on my Conscience.

L. *Froth*. O'my Conscience no more we should; thou say'st right——For sure my Lord *Froth* is as fine a Gentleman, and as much a Man of Quality! Ah! Nothing at all of the common Air,—I think I may say he wants nothing, but a blue Ribbon and a Star, to make him shine, the very Phosphorus of our Hemisphere. Do you understand those two hard Words? If you don't, I'll explain 'em to you.

Cynt. Yes, yes, Madam, I'm not so Ignorant. ——At least I won't own it, to be troubled with your Instructions. [*Aside.*

L. *Froth.* Nay, I beg your Pardon; but being deriv'd from the *Greek*, I thought you might have escap'd the Etymology.——But I'm the more amaz'd, to find you a Woman of Letters, and not write! Bless me! how can *Mellefont* believe you love him?

Cynt. Why Faith, Madam, he that won't take my Word, shall never have it under my Hand.

L. *Froth.* I vow *Mellefont*'s a pretty Gentleman, but methinks he wants a Manner.

Cynt. A Manner! What's that, Madam?

L. *Froth.* Some distinguishing Quality, as for Example, the *bel air* or *Brillant* of Mr. *Brisk*; the Solemnity, yet Complaisance of my Lord, or something of his own that should look a little *Je-ne-scay-quoysh*; he is too much a Mediocrity, in my Mind.

Cynt. He does not indeed affect either Pertness or Formality; for which I like him: Here he comes.

L. *Froth.* And my Lord with him: Pray observe the Difference.

SCENE II.

[*To them*] *Lord* FROTH, MELLEFONT, *and* BRISK.

Cynt. Impertinent Creature! I could almost be angry with her now. [*Aside.*

L. *Froth.* My Lord, I have been telling *Cynthia*, how much I have been in love with you; I swear I have; I'm not asham'd to own it now; Ah! it makes my Heart leap, I vow I sigh when I think on't: My dear Lord! Ha, ha, ha, do you remember, my Lord?

[*Squeezes him by the Hand, looks kindly on him, sighs and then laughs out.*

Ld. *Froth*. Pleasant Creature! perfectly well, ah! that Look, ay, there it is; who could resist! 'twas so my Heart was made a Captive first, and ever since t'has been in Love with happy Slavery.

L. *Froth*. O that Tongue, that dear deceitful Tongue! that charming Softness in your Mien and your Expression, and then your Bow! Good my Lord, bow as you did when I gave you my Picture, here suppose this my Picture——

[*Gives him a Pocket-Glass.*

Pray mind my Lord; ah! he bows charmingly; nay, my Lord, you shan't kiss it so much; I shall grow jealous, I vow now.

[*He bows profoundly low, then kisses the Glass.*

Ld. *Froth*. I saw my self there, and kiss'd it for your sake.

L. *Froth*. Ah! Gallantry to the last Degree—— Mr. *Brisk*, you're a Judge; was ever any thing so well bred as my Lord?

Brisk. Never any thing; but your Ladyship, let me perish.

L. *Froth*. O prettily turn'd again; let me die but you have a great deal of Wit: Mr. *Mellefont*, don't you think Mr. *Brisk* has a World of Wit?

Mel. O, yes, Madam.

Brisk. O dear, Madam——

L. *Froth*. An infinite deal!

Brisk. O Heav'ns, Madam——

L. *Froth*. More Wit than any Body.

Brisk. I'm everlastingly your humble Servant, duce take me, Madam.

Ld. *Froth*. Don't you think us a happy Couple?

Cynt. I vow, my Lord, I think you the happiest Couple in the World, for you're not only happy in one another, and when you are together, but happy in your selves, and by your selves.

Ld. *Froth*. I hope *Mellefont* will make a good Husband too.

Cynt. 'Tis my Interest to believe he will, my Lord.

Ld. *Froth.* D'ye think he'll Love you as well as I do my Wife ? I'm afraid not.

Cynt. I believe he'll love me better.

Ld. *Froth.* Heav'ns ! that can never be ; but why do you think so ?

Cynt. Because he has not so much reason to be fond of himself.

Ld. *Froth.* O your humble Servant for that, dear Madam ; well, *Mellefont*, you'll be a happy Creature.

Mel. Ay, my Lord, I shall have the same Reason for my Happiness that your Lordship has, I shall think my self happy.

Ld. *Froth.* Ah, that's all.

Brisk. [*to Lady* Froth.] Your Ladyship is in the right ; but I'gad I'm wholly turn'd into Satire. I confess I write but seldom, but when I do—— keen *Iambicks* I'gad. But my Lord was telling me, your Ladyship has made an Essay toward an Heroick Poem.

L. *Froth.* Did my Lord tell you ? Yes I vow, and the Subject is my Lord's Love to me. And what do you think I call it ? I dare swear you won't guess——*The Sillabub*, ha, ha, ha.

Brisk. Because my Lord's Title's *Froth*, I'gad, ha, ha, ha, duce take me very *a Propos* and surprizing, ha, ha, ha.

L. *Froth.* He, ay, is not it ?——And then I call my Lord *Spumoso* ; and my self, what d'ye think I call my self ?

Brisk. Lactilla may be,——'gad I cannot tell.

L. *Froth. Biddy*, that's all ; just my own Name.

Brisk. Biddy ! I'gad very pretty——Duce take me if your Ladyship has not the Art of surprizing the most naturally in the World,——I hope you'll make me happy in communicating the Poem.

L. *Froth.* O, you must be my Confident, I must ask your Advice.

Brisk. I'm your humble Servant, let me perish, ——I presume your Ladyship has read *Bossu* ?

L. *Froth.* O yes, and *Rapine*, and *Dacier* upon *Aristotle* and *Horace.*——My Lord, you must not be jealous, I'm communicating all to Mr. *Brisk.*

Ld. *Froth.* No, no, I'll allow Mr. *Brisk* ; have you nothing about you to shew him, my Dear ?

L. *Froth.* Yes, I believe I have.——Mr. *Brisk,* come will you go into the next Room ? and there I'll shew you what I have.

Ld. *Froth.* I'll walk a Turn in the Garden, and come to you.

SCENE III.

MELLEFONT, CYNTHIA.

Mel. You're thoughtful, *Cynthia* ?

Cynt. I'm thinking, tho' Marriage makes Man and Wife one Flesh, it leaves 'em still two Fools ; and they become more conspicuous by setting off one another.

Mel. That's only when two Fools meet, and their Follies are oppos'd.

Cynt. Nay, I have known two Wits meet, and by the Opposition of their Wit, render themselves as ridiculous as Fools. 'Tis an odd Game we're going to Play at : What think you of drawing Stakes, and giving over in time ?

Mel. No, hang't, that's not endeavouring to win, because it's possible we may lose ; since we have shuffled and cut, let's e'en turn up Trump now.

Cynt. Then I find it's like Cards, if either of us have a good Hand it is an Accident of Fortune.

Mel. No, Marriage is rather like a Game at Bowls, Fortune indeed makes the Match, and the two nearest, and sometimes the two farthest are together, but the Game depends intirely upon Judgement.

88 Horace] René le Bossu was author of a *Traité du Poème Épique*, 1675. R. Rapin wrote *Réflections sur la Poésie d'Aristote*, 1674. André Dacier translated Aristotle and Horace, 1687, with notes and a preface.

Cynt. Still it is a Game, and consequently one of us must be a Loser.

Mel. Not at all; only a friendly Trial of Skill, and the Winnings to be laid out in an Entertainment.——What's here, the Musick!—Oh, my Lord has promised the Company a new Song, we'll get 'em to give it us by the way.

[*Musicians crossing the Stage.*

Pray let us have the Favour of you, to practise the Song, before the Company hear it.

SONG.

I.

Cynthia *frowns when-e'er I woe her,*
Yet she's vext if I give over;
Much she fears I should undo her,
But much more to lose her Lover:
Thus, in doubting, she refuses;
And not winning, thus she loses.

II.

Prithee Cynthia *look behind you,*
Age and Wrinkles will o'ertake you;
Then too late Desire will find you,
When the Power must forsake you:
Think, O think o'th' sad Condition,
To be past, yet wish Fruition.

Mel. You shall have my Thanks below.

[*To the Musick, they go out.*

SCENE IV.

[*To them*] *Sir* PAUL PLYANT *and Lady* PLYANT.

Sir *Paul.* Gads bud! I am provok'd into a Fermentation, as my Lady *Froth* says; was ever the like read of in Story?

L. *P.* Sir *Paul* have Patience, let me alone to rattle him up.

Sir *Paul*. Pray your Ladyship give me leave to be angry——I'll rattle him up I warrant you, I'll firk him with a *Certiorari*.

L. *P*. You firk him, I'll firk him my self; pray Sir *Paul* hold you contented.

Cynt. Bless me, what makes my Father in such a Passion!——I never saw him thus before.

Sir *Paul*. Hold your self contented, my Lady *Plyant*,——I find Passion coming upon me by Inflation, and I cannot submit as formerly, therefore give way.

L. *P*. How now! will you be pleased to retire, and——

Sir *Paul*. No marry will I not be pleased, I am pleased to be angry, that's my Pleasure at this time.

Mel. What can this mean!

L. *P*. Gads my Life, the Man's distracted, why how now, who are you? What am I? Slidikins can't I govern you? What did I marry you for? Am I not to be absolute and uncontrolable? Is it fit a Woman of my Spirit, and Conduct, should be contradicted in a Matter of this Concern?

Sir *Paul*. It concerns me, and only me;——Besides, I'm not to be govern'd at all times. When I am in Tranquility, my Lady *Plyant* shall command Sir *Paul*; but when I am provok'd to Fury, I cannot incorporate with Patience and Reason,—as soon may Tygers match with Tygers, Lambs with Lambs, and every Creature couple with its Foe, as the Poet says.——

L. *P*. He's hot-headed still! 'Tis in vain to talk to you; but remember I have a Curtain-Lecture for you, you disobedient, headstrong Brute.

Sir *Paul*. No, 'tis because I won't be Headstrong, because I won't be a Brute, and have my Head fortify'd, that I am thus exasperated,——

8 *Certiorari*] Beat him with a Chancery writ.

But I will protect my Honour, and yonder is the Violater of my Fame.

L. *P.* 'Tis my Honour that is concern'd, and the Violation was intended to me. Your Honour! You have none but what is in my keeping, and I can dispose of it when I please——therefore don't provoke me.

Sir *Paul.* Hum, gads-bud she says true—— Well, my Lady, march on, I will fight under you then: I am convinced, as far as Passion will permit.

[*L.* Plyant *and Sir* Paul *come up to* Mellefont.

L. *P.* Inhuman and treacherous——

Sir *Paul.* Thou Serpent and first Tempter of Womankind.—

Cynt. Bless me! Sir; Madam; what mean you?

Sir *Paul.* *Thy, Thy,* come away *Thy,* touch him not, come hither Girl, go not near him, there's nothing but Deceit about him; Snakes are in his Peruke, and the Crocodile of *Nilus* is in his Belly, he will eat thee up alive.

L. *P.* Dishonourable, impudent Creature!

Mel. For Heav'ns sake, Madam, to whom do you direct this Language!

L. *P.* Have I behav'd my self with all the Decorum and Nicety, befitting the Person of Sir *Paul*'s Wife? Have I preserv'd my Honour as it were in a Snow-House for these three Years past? Have I been white and unsully'd even by Sir *Paul* himself?

Sir *Paul.* Nay, she has been an invincible Wife, even to me, that's the truth on't.

L. *P.* Have I, I say, preserv'd my self, like a fair Sheet of Paper, for you to make a Blot upon?——

Sir *Paul.* And she shall make a Simile with any Woman in *England.*

Mel. I am so amaz'd, I know not what to say.

Sir *Paul.* Do you think my Daughter, this

pretty Creature; gads-bud she's a Wife for a Cherubin! Do you think her fit for nothing but to be a stalking Horse, to stand before you, while you take aim at my Wife; Gads-bud I was never angry before in my Life, and I'll never be appeas'd again.

Mel. Hell and Damnation! This is my Aunt; such Malice can be engendred no where else. [*Aside.*

L. *P.* Sir *Paul*, take *Cynthia* from his Sight; leave me to strike him with the Remorse of his intended Crime.

Cynt. Pray, Sir, stay, hear him, I dare affirm he's Innocent.

Sir *Paul.* Innocent! Why hark'ee, come hither *Thy*, hark'ee, I had it from his Aunt, my sister *Touchwood*,——gads-bud he does not care a Farthing for any thing of thee, but thy Portion, why he's in love with my Wife; he would have tantaliz'd thee, and made a Cuckold of thy poor Father,——and that would certainly have broke my Heart—I'm sure if ever I should have Horns, they would kill me; they would never come kindly, I should die of 'em, like a Child, that was cutting his Teeth—I should indeed, *Thy*—therefore come away; but Providence has prevented all, therefore come away, when I bid you.

Cynt. I must obey.

SCENE V.

Lady PLYANT, MELLEFONT.

L. *P.* O, such a thing! the Impiety of it startles me——to wrong so good, so fair a Creature, and one that loves you tenderly——'tis a Barbarity of Barbarities, and nothing could be guilty of it——

Mel. But the greatest Villain Imagination can form, I grant it; and next to the Villany of such a Fact, is the Villany of aspersing me with the

Guilt. How? which way was I to wrong her? For yet I understand you not.

L. *P*. Why, gads my Life, Cousin *Mellefont*, you cannot be so peremptory as to deny it; when I tax you with it to your Face; for now Sir *Paul*'s gone, you are *Corum Nobus*.

Mel. By Heav'n, I love her more than Life, or——

L. *P*. Fiddle, faddle, don't tell me of this and that, and ev'ry Thing in the World, but give me Mathemacular Demonstration, answer me directly —But I have not Patience——Oh! The Impiety of it, as I was saying, and the unparallell'd Wickedness! O merciful Father! How could you think to reverse Nature so, to make the Daughter the Means of procuring the Mother?

Mel. The Daughter to procure the Mother!

L. *P*. Ay, for tho' I am not *Cynthia*'s own Mother, I am her Father's Wife; and that's near enough to make it Incest.

Mel. Incest! O my precious Aunt, and the Devil in Conjunction. [*Aside*.

L. *P*. O reflect upon the Horror of that, and then the Guilt of deceiving every Body; marrying the Daughter, only to make a Cuckold of the Father; and then seducing me, debauching my Purity, and perverting me from the Road of Vertue, in which I have trod thus long, and never made one Trip, not one *faux pas*; O consider it, what would you have to answer for, if you should provoke me to Frailty? Alas! Humanity is feeble, Heav'n knows! very feeble, and unable to support it self.

Mel. Where am I? Is it Day? and am I awake? Madam—

L. *P*. And no Body knows how Circumstances may happen together,——To my thinking, now I could resist the strongest Temptation,—But yet I know, 'tis impossible for me to know whether I could or not, there's no certainty in the Things of this Life.

Mel. Madam, pray give me leave to ask you one Question.—

L. *P.* O Lord, ask me the Question, I'll swear I'll refuse it; I swear I'll deny it—therefore don't ask me, nay you shan't ask me, I swear I'll deny it. O Gemini, you have brought all the Blood into my Face; I warrant I am as red as a Turky-Cock; O fie, Cousin *Mellefont*!

Mel. Nay, Madam, hear me; I mean—

L. *P.* Hear you, no, no; I'll deny you first, and hear you afterwards. For one does not know how ones Mind may change upon hearing——Hearing is one of the Senses, and all the Senses are fallible; I won't trust my Honour, I assure you; my Honour is infallible and uncomatible.

Mel. For Heav'ns sake, Madam,——

L. *P.* O name it no more—Bless me, how can you talk of Heav'n! and have so much Wickedness in your Heart? May be you don't think it a Sin,—They say some of you Gentlemen don't think it a Sin,—May be it is no Sin to them that don't think it so; Indeed, if I did not think it a Sin——But still my Honour, if it were no Sin,—But then, to marry my Daughter, for the Conveniency of frequent Opportunities,—I'll never consent to that, as sure as can be, I'll break the Match.

Mel. Death and Amazement,——Madam, upon my Knees——

L. *P.* Nay, nay, rise up, come you shall see my good Nature. I know Love is powerful, and no Body can help his Passion: 'Tis not your Fault; nor I swear it is not mine,—How can I help it, if I have Charms? And how can you help it, if you are made a Captive? I swear it is pity it should be a Fault,——But my Honour,—well, but your Honour too—but the Sin!—well, but the Necessity—O Lord, here's some Body coming, I dare not stay. Well, you must consider of your Crime; and strive as much as can be against it,——strive be sure——But don't be melancholick, don't despair,—But never think that I'll grant you any thing; O Lord, no;—But be sure you lay aside all Thoughts of the Marriage, for tho' I know you don't love *Cynthia*, only as a blind for your Passion to me; yet it will make me Jealous,—O Lord, what did I say? Jealous! no, no, I can't be jealous, for I must not love you,——therefore don't hope,——But don't despair neither,——O, they're coming, I must fly. 98

SCENE VI.

MELLEFONT *alone*.

Mel. (*after a Pause.*) So then,——spight of my Care and Foresight, I am caught, caught in my Security,——Yet this was but a shallow Artifice, unworthy of my Machiavelian Aunt: There must be more behind, this is but the first Flash, the priming of her Engine; Destruction follows hard, if not most presently prevented.

SCENE VII.

[*To him*] MASKWELL.

Mel. Maskwell, welcome, thy Presence is a view of Land, appearing to my shipwrack'd Hopes: The Witch has rais'd the Storm, and her Ministers have done their Work; you see the Vessels are parted.

Mask. I know it; I met Sir *Paul* towing away *Cynthia*: Come, trouble not your Head, I'll join you together e'er to Morrow Morning, or drown between you in the Attempt.

Mel. There's Comfort in a Hand stretch'd out, to one that's sinking; tho' ne'er so far off. 11

Mask. No sinking, nor no Danger,—Come, cheer up; why you don't know, that while I plead for you, your Aunt has given me a retaining Fee; ——Nay, I am your greatest Enemy, and she does but Journey-Work under me.

Mel. Ha! How's this?

Mask. What d'ye think of my being employ'd in the Execution of all her Plots? Ha, ha, ha, by Heav'n it's true; I have undertaken to break the Match, I have undertaken to make your Uncle disinherit you, to get you turn'd out of Doors; and to——Ha, ha, ha, I can't tell you for Laughing,—Oh she has open'd her Heart to me,——I am to turn you a grazing, and to——Ha, ha, ha, marry *Cynthia* my self; there's a Plot for you. 26

Mel. Ha! O see, I see my rising Sun! Light breaks thro' Clouds upon me, and I shall live in Day——O my *Maskwell*! How shall I thank or praise thee; Thou hast out-witted Woman.——But tell me, how could'st thou thus get into her Confidence?——Ha! How? But was it her Contrivance to perswade my Lady *Plyant* to this extravagant Belief?

Mask. It was, and to tell you the Truth, I encourag'd it for your Diversion: Tho' it made you a little uneasie for the present, yet the Reflection of it must needs be entertaining,—I warrant she was very violent at first. 39

Mel. Ha, ha, ha, ay, a very Fury; but I was most afraid of her Violence at last——If you had not come as you did; I don't know what she might have attempted.

Mask. Ha, ha, ha, I know her Temper.—Well, you must know then, that all my Contrivances were but Bubbles; 'till at last I pretended to have been long secretly in love with *Cynthia*; that did my Business; that convinc'd your Aunt, I might be trusted; since it was as much my Interest as hers to break the Match: Then, she thought my Jealousie might qualifie me to assist her in her Revenge. And, in short, in that Belief, told me the Secrets of her Heart. At length we made this Agreement, if I accomplish her Designs (as I told you before) she has ingag'd to put *Cynthia* with all her Fortune into my Power. 56

Mel. She is most gracious in her Favour,—— Well, and dear *Jack*, how hast thou contrived?

Mask. I would not have you stay to hear it now; for I don't know, but she may come this Way; I am to meet her anon; after that, I'll tell you the whole Matter; be here in this Gallery an Hour hence, by that time I imagine our Consultation may be over.

Mel. I will; 'till then Success attend thee.

SCENE VIII.

Maskwell *alone.*

'Till then, Success will attend me; for when I meet you, I meet the only Obstacle to my Fortune. *Cynthia*, let thy Beauty gild my Crimes; and whatsoever I commit of Treachery or Deceit, shall be imputed to me as a Merit—— Treachery, what Treachery? Love cancels all the Bonds of Friendship, and sets Men right upon their first Foundations. 8

Duty to Kings, Piety to Parents, Gratitude to Benefactors, and Fidelity to Friends, are different and particular Ties: But the Name of Rival cuts 'em all asunder, and is a general Acquittance—— Rival is equal, and Love like Death an universal Leveller of Mankind. Ha! But is there not such a Thing as Honesty? Yes, and whosoever has it about him, bears an Enemy in his Breast: For your honest Man, as I take it, is that nice, scrupulous, conscientious Person, who will cheat no Body but himself; such another Coxcomb, as your wise Man, who is too hard for all the World, and will be made a Fool of by no Body, but himself: Ha, ha, ha. Well for Wisdom and Honesty, give me Cunning and Hypocrisie; oh, 'tis such a Pleasure, to angle for fair fac'd Fools! Then that hungry Gudgeon Credulity, will bite at any thing——Why, let me see, I have the same Face, the same Words and Accents, when I speak what I do think; and when I speak what I do not think——the very same——and dear Dissimulation is the only Art, not to be known from Nature.

Why will Mankind be Fools, and be deceiv'd?
And why are Friends and Lovers Oaths believ'd?
When, each, who searches strictly his own Mind,
May so much Fraud and Power of Baseness find.

End of the Second Act.

ACT III. SCENE I.

Lord Touchwood, *and Lady* Touchwood.

Lady TOUCHWOOD.

My Lord, can you blame my Brother *Plyant*, if he refuse his Daughter upon this Provocation? The Contract's void by this unheard of Impiety.

Ld. *T.* I don't believe it true; he has better Principles——Pho, 'tis Nonsense. Come, come, I know my Lady *Plyant* has a large Eye, and wou'd centre every Thing in her own Circle; 'tis not the first time she has mistaken Respect for Love, and made Sir *Paul* jealous of the Civility of an undesigning Person, the better to bespeak his Security in her unfeigned Pleasures.

L. *T.* You censure hardly, my Lord; my Sister's Honour is very well known.

Ld. *T.* Yes, I believe I know some that have been familiarly acquainted with it. This is a little Trick wrought by some pitiful Contriver, envious of my Nephew's Merit.

L. *T.* Nay, my Lord, it may be so, and I hope it will be found so: But that will require some time; for in such a Case as this, Demonstration is necessary.

Ld. *T.* There should have been Demonstration of the contrary too, before it had been believ'd——

L. *T*. So I suppose there was.

Ld. *T*. How? Where? When?

L. *T*. That I can't tell; nay I don't say there was—I am willing to believe as favourably of my Nephew as I can.

Ld. *T*. I don't know that. [*Half Aside*.

L. *T*. How? Don't you believe that, say you, my Lord? 31

Ld. *T*. No, I don't say so——I confess I am troubled to find you so cold in his Defence.

L. *T*. His Defence! Bless me, wou'd you have me defend an ill Thing.

Ld. *T*. You believe it then?

L. *T*. I don't know; I am very unwilling to speak my Thoughts in any thing that may be to my Cousin's Disadvantage; besides, I find, my Lord, you are prepared to receive an ill Impression from any Opinion of mine which is not consenting with your own: But since I am like to be suspected in the End, and 'tis a Pain any longer to dissemble, I own it to you; in short I do believe it, nay, and can believe any thing worse, if it were laid to his Charge—Don't ask me my Reasons, my Lord, for they are not fit to be told you. 47

Ld. *T*. I'm amazed, here must be something more than ordinary in this. [*Aside*.] Not fit to be told me, Madam? You can have no Interests, wherein I am not concern'd, and consequently the same Reasons ought to be convincing to me, which create your Satisfaction or Disquiet.

L. *T*. But those which cause my Disquiet, I am willing to have remote from your hearing. Good my Lord, don't press me.

Ld. *T*. Don't oblige me to press you.

L. *T*. Whatever it was, 'tis past: And that is better to be unknown which cannot be prevented; therefore let me beg you to rest satisfy'd— 60

Ld. *T*. When you have told me, I will—

L. *T*. You won't.

Ld. *T*. By my Life, my Dear, I will.

L. *T*. What if you can't.

Ld. *T*. How? Then I must know, nay I will: No more trifling——I charge you tell me——By all our mutual Peace to come; upon your Duty——

L. *T*. Nay, my Lord, you need say no more, to make me lay my Heart before you, but don't be thus transported; compose your self: It is not of Concern, to make you lose one Minute's Temper. 'Tis not indeed my Dear. Nay, by this Kiss you shan't be angry. O Lord, I wish I had not told you any thing.——Indeed, my Lord, you have frighted me. Nay, look pleas'd, I'll tell you.

Ld. *T*. Well, well.

L. *T*. Nay, but will you be calm——indeed it's nothing but——

Ld. *T*. But what?

L. *T*. But will you promise me not to be angry——Nay you must——Not to be angry with *Mellefont*——I dare swear he's sorry——and were it to do again, would not——

Ld. *T*. Sorry, for what? 'Death, you rack me with Delay.

L. *T*. Nay, no great Matter, only—Well I have your Promise,——Pho, why nothing, only your Nephew had a mind to amuse himself, sometimes with a little Gallantry towards me. Nay, I can't think he meant any thing seriously, but methought it look'd odly.

Ld. *T*. Confusion and Hell, what do I hear!

L. *T*. Or, may be, he thought he was not enough a-kin to me, upon your Account, and had a mind to create a nearer Relation on his own; a Lover you know, my Lord—Ha, ha, ha. Well but that's all——Now you have it; well remember your Promise, my Lord, and don't take any Notice of it to him.

Ld. *T*. No, no, no—Damnation!

L. *T*. Nay, I swear you must not——A little harmless Mirth—Only misplac'd, that's all—But if it were more, 'tis over now, and all's well. For my Part I have forgot it; and so has he, I hope—for I have not heard any thing from him these two Days. 107

Ld. *T*. These two Days! Is it so fresh? Unnatural Villain! 'Death, I'll have him stripp'd and turn'd naked out of my Doors this Moment, and let him rot and perish, incestuous Brute!

L. *T*. O for Heav'ns sake, my Lord, you'll ruin me if you take such publick Notice of it, it will be a Town-Talk: Consider your own and my Honour—nay, I told you you would not be satisfied when you knew it.

Ld. *T*. Before I've done, I will be satisfy'd. Ungrateful Monster, how long?— 118

L. *T*. Lord, I don't know: I wish my Lips had grown together when I told you—Almost a Twelvemonth—Nay, I won't tell you any more, 'till you are your self. Pray, my Lord, don't let the Company see you in this Disorder——Yet, I confess, I can't blame you; for I think I was never so surpriz'd in my Life——Who would have thought my Nephew could have so misconstrued my Kindness—But will you go into your Closet, and recover your Temper. I'll make an Excuse of sudden Business to the Company, and come to you. Pray, good dear my Lord, let me beg you do now: I'll come immediately, and tell you all; will you, my Lord? 132

Ld. *T*. I will—I am mute with Wonder.

L. *T*. Well but go now, here's some body coming.

Ld. *T*. Well I go—You won't stay, for I would hear more of this.

L. *T*. I follow instantly—So.

SCENE II.

Lady TOUCHWOOD, MASKWELL.

Mask. This was a Master-Piece, and did not need my Help—tho' I stood ready for a Cue to come in and confirm all, had there been Occasion.

L. *T*. Have you seen *Mellefont*?

Mask. I have; and am to meet him here about this time.

L. *T*. How does he bear his Disappointment?

Mask. Secure in my Assistance, he seem'd not much afflicted, but rather laugh'd at the shallow Artifice, which so little time must of necessity discover. Yet he is apprehensive of some farther Design of yours, and has engaged me to watch you. I believe he will hardly be able to prevent your Plot, yet I would have you use Caution and Expedition.

L. *T*. Expedition indeed; for all we do, must be perform'd in the remaining Part of this Ev'ning, and before the Company break up; lest my Lord should cool, and have an Opportunity to talk with him privately—My Lord must not see him again. 21

Mask. By no Means; therefore you must aggravate my Lord's Displeasure to a Degree that will admit of no Conference with him.——What think you of mentioning me?

L. *T*. How?

Mask. To my Lord, as having been privy to *Mellefont*'s Design upon you, but still using my utmost Endeavours to dissuade him: Tho' my Friendship and Love to him has made me conceal it; yet you may say, I threatned the next time he attempted any thing of that kind, to discover it to my Lord. 33

L. *T*. To what end is this?

Mask. It will confirm my Lord's Opinion of my Honour and Honesty, and create in him a new Confidence in me, which (should this Design miscarry) will be necessary to the forming another Plot that I have in my Head—To cheat you, as well as the rest. [*Aside*.

L. *T*. I'll do it—I'll tell him you hindred him once from forcing me. 42

Mask. Excellent! Your Ladyship has a most improving Fancy. You had best go to my Lord, keep him as long as you can in his Closet, and I doubt not but you will mould him to what you please; your Guests are so engaged in their own Follies and Intrigues, they'll miss neither of you.

L. T. When shall we meet?—At eight this Evening in my Chamber; there rejoice at our Success, and toy an Hour in Mirth.

Mask. I will not fail.

SCENE III.

Maskwell *alone.*

I know what she means by toying away an Hour well enough. Pox I have lost all Appetite to her; yet she's a fine Woman, and I lov'd her once. But I don't know, since I have been in a great measure kept by her, the Case is alter'd; what was my Pleasure is become my Duty: And I have as little Stomach to her now as if I were her Husband. Should she smoak my Design upon *Cynthia*, I were in a fine pickle. She has a damn'd penetrating Head, and knows how to interpret a Coldness the right Way; therefore I must dissemble Ardour and Ecstasie, that's resolv'd: How easily and pleasantly is that dissembled before Fruition! Pox on't that a Man can't drink without quenching his Thirst. Ha! yonder comes *Mellefont* thoughtful. Let me think: Meet her at eight ——hum——ha! By Heav'n I have it——If I can speak to my Lord before——Was it my Brain or Providence? No matter which——I will deceive 'em all, and yet secure my self, 'twas a lucky Thought! Well, this Double-Dealing is a Jewel. Here he comes, now for me.——

[Maskwell *pretending not to see him, walks by him, and speaks as it were to himself.*

SCENE IV.

[*To him*] Mellefont *musing*.

Mask. Mercy on us, what will the Wickedness of this World come to?

Mel. How now, *Jack*? What, so full of Contemplation that you run over!

Mask. I'm glad you're come, for I could not contain my self any longer: And was just going to give vent to a Secret, which no Body but you ought to drink down.——Your Aunt's just gone from hence.

Mel. And having trusted thee with the Secrets of her Soul, thou art villainously bent to discover 'em all to me, ha?

Mask. I'm afraid my Frailty leans that way——But I don't know whether I can in Honour discover 'em all.

Mel. All, all Man: What, you may in Honour betray her as far as she betrays her self. No tragical Design upon my Person, I hope.

Mask. No, but it's a comical Design upon mine.

Mel. What dost thou mean?

Mask. Listen and be dumb, we have been bargaining about the Rate of your Ruin——

Mel. Like any two Guardians to an Orphan Heiress——Well.

Mask. And whereas Pleasure is generally paid with Mischief, what Mischief I do is to be paid with Pleasure.

Mel. So when you've swallow'd the Potion, you sweeten your Mouth with a Plumb.

Mask. You are merry, Sir, but I shall probe your Constitution. In short, the Price of your Banishment is to be paid with the Person of——

Mel. Of *Cynthia*, and her Fortune—Why you forget you told me this before.

Mask. No, no—So far you are right; and I am,

as an earnest of that Bargain, to have full and free Possession of the Person of——your Aunt.

Mel. Ha !——Pho, you trifle. 39

Mask. By this Light, I'm serious ; all Raillery apart——I knew 'twould stun you : This Evening at eight she will receive me in her Bed-Chamber.

Mel. Hell and the Devil, is she abandon'd of all Grace——Why the Woman is possess'd——

Mask. Well, will you go in my stead ?

Mel. By Heav'n into a hot Furnace sooner.

Mask. No, you would not—It would not be so convenient, as I can order Matters.

Mel. What d'ye mean ! 49

Mask. Mean ? Not to disappoint the Lady I assure you—Ha, ha, ha, how gravely he looks—Come, come, I won't perplex you. 'Tis the only Thing that Providence could have contriv'd to make me capable of serving you, either to my Inclination or your own Necessity.

Mel. How, how, for Heav'ns sake, dear *Maskwell* ? 57

Mask. Why thus—I'll go according to Appointment ; you shall have Notice at the critical Minute to come and surprize your Aunt and me together : Counterfeit a Rage against me, and I'll make my Escape through the private Passage from her Chamber, which I'll take care to leave open : 'Twill be hard, if then you can't bring her to any Conditions. For this Discovery will disarm her of all Defence, and leave her entirely at your Mercy : Nay, she must ever after be in awe of you.

Mel. Let me adore thee, my better *Genius* ! By Heav'n I think it is not in the Power of Fate to disappoint my Hopes—My Hopes, my Certainty ! 71

Mask. Well, I'll meet you here, within a Quarter of eight, and give you Notice.

Mel. Good Fortune ever go along with thee.

SCENE V

Mellefont, Careless.

Care. Mellefont, get out o'th' Way, my Lady *Plyant*'s coming, and I shall never succeed while thou art in sight——Tho' she begins to tack about; but I made Love a great while to no purpose.

Mel. Why, what's the Matter? She's convinc'd that I don't care for her.

Care. I can't get an Answer from her, that does not begin with her Honour, or her Vertue, her Religion, or some such Cant. Then she has told me the whole History of Sir *Paul's* nine Years Courtship; how he has lain for whole Nights together upon the Stairs, before her Chamber-Door; and that the first Favour he received from her, was a Piece of an old Scarlet Petticoat for a Stomacher; which since the Day of his Marriage, he has, out of a Piece of Gallantry, converted into a Night-Cap, and wears it still with much Solemnity on his Anniversary Wedding-Night.

Mel. That I have seen, with the Ceremony thereunto belonging——For on that Night he creeps in at the Bed's Feet like a gull'd Bassa that has marry'd a Relation of the *Grand Signior*, and that Night he has his Arms at Liberty. Did not she tell you at what a Distance she keeps him. He has confess'd to me that but at certain times, that is I suppose when she apprehends being with Child, he never has the Privilege of using the Familiarity of a Husband with a Wife. He was once given to scrambling with his Hands and sprawling in his Sleep; and ever since she has him swaddled up in Blankets, and his Hands and Feet swath'd down, and so put to Bed; and there he lies with a great Beard, like a *Russian* Bear upon a drift of Snow. You are very great with him, I wonder he never told you his Grievances, he will I warrant you.

21 Bassa] Pasba.

Care. Excessively foolish!——But that which gives me most Hopes of her, is her telling me of the many Temptations she has resisted.

Mel. Nay, then you have her; for a Woman's bragging to a Man that she has overcome Temptations, is an Argument that they were weakly offer'd, and a Challenge to him to engage her more irresistibly. 'Tis only an inhancing the Price of the Commodity, by telling you how many Customers have underbid her.

Care. Nay, I don't despair—But still she has a grudging to you—I talk'd to her t'other Night at my Lord *Froth's* Masquerade, when I'm satisfy'd she knew me, and I had no Reason to complain of my Reception; but I find Women are not the same bare-faced and in Masks,—and a Vizor disguises their Inclinations as much as their Faces.

Mel. 'Tis a Mistake, for Women may most properly be said to be unmask'd when they wear Vizors; for that secures them from Blushing, and being out of Countenance, and next to being in the Dark, or alone, they are most truly themselves in a Vizor Mask. Here they come, I'll leave you. Ply her close, and by and by clap a *Billet doux* into her Hand: For a Woman never thinks a Man truly in Love with her, 'till he has been Fool enough to think of her out of her Sight, and to lose so much time as to write to her.

SCENE VI.

CARELESS, *Sir* PAUL, *and Lady* PLYANT.

Sir *Paul.* Shan't we disturb your Meditation, Mr. *Careless*: you wou'd be private?

Care. You bring that along with you, Sir *Paul*, that shall be always welcome to my Privacy.

Sir *Paul.* O, sweet Sir, you load your humble Servants, both me and my Wife, with continual Favours.

L. *P.* Sir *Paul*, what a Phrase was there? You will be making Answers, and taking that upon you, which ought to lie upon me: That you should have so little Breeding to think Mr. *Careless* did not apply himself to me. Pray what have you to entertain any Bodies Privacy? I swear and declare in the Face of the World I'm ready to blush for your Ignorance.

Sir *Paul.* I acquiesce, my Lady; but don't snub so loud. [*Aside to her.*

L. *P.* Mr. *Careless*, if a Person that is wholly illiterate might be supposed to be capable of being qualify'd to make a suitable Return to those Obligations which you are pleased to confer upon one that is wholly incapable of being qualify'd in all those Circumstances, I'm sure I shou'd rather attempt it than any thing in the World, [*Courtesies*] for I'm sure there's nothing in the World that I would rather. [*Courtesies*] But I know Mr. *Careless* is so great a Critick and so fine a Gentleman, that it is impossible for me——

Care. O Heav'ns! Madam, you confound me.

Sir *Paul.* Gads-bud, she's a fine Person——

L. *P.* O Lord! Sir, pardon me, we Women have not those Advantages: I know my own Imperfections——But at the same time you must give me leave to declare in the Face of the World that no Body is more sensible of Favours and Things; for with the Reserve of my Honour, I assure you, Mr. *Careless*, I don't know any thing in the World I would refuse to a Person so meritorious——You'll pardon my Want of Expression.——

Care. O your Ladyship is abounding in all Excellence, particularly that of Phrase.

L. *P.* You are so obliging, Sir.

Care. Your Ladyship is so charming.

Sir *Paul.* So, now, now; now, my Lady.

L. *P.* So well bred.

Care. So surprizing.

L. *P.* So well drest, so *bonne mine*, so eloquent,

so unaffected, so easie, so free, so particular, so agreeable——

Sir *Paul.* Ay, so, so, there.

Care. O Lord, I beseech you, Madam, don't——

L. *P.* So gay, so graceful, so good Teeth, so fine Shape, so fine Limbs, so fine Linnen, and I don't doubt but you have a very good Skin, Sir.

Care. For Heav'ns sake, Madam—I'm quite out of Countenance.

Sir *Paul.* And my Lady's quite out of Breath; or else you should hear—Gad's-bud, you may talk of my Lady *Froth.*

Care. O fie, fie, not to be named of a Day—My Lady *Froth* is very well in her Accomplishments——But it is when my Lady *Plyant* is not thought of——If that can ever be.

L. *P.* O you overcome me——That is so excessive.

Sir *Paul.* Nay, I swear and vow that was pretty.

Care. O Sir *Paul*, you are the happiest Man alive. Such a Lady! that is the Envy of her own Sex, and the Admiration of ours.

Sir *Paul.* Your humble Servant, I am I thank Heav'n in a fine way of living, as I may say, peacefully and happily, and I think need not envy any of my Neighbours, blessed be Providence——Ay, truly, Mr. *Careless*, my Lady is a great Blessing, a fine, discreet, well-spoken Woman as you shall see—If it becomes me to say so; and we live very comfortably together; she is a little hasty sometimes, and so am I; but mine's soon over, and then I'm so sorry—O, Mr. *Careless*, if it were not for one thing—

SCENE VII.

CARELESS, *Sir* PAUL, *Lady* PLYANT, *Boy with a Letter.*

L. *P.* How often have you been told of that, you Jackanapes?

Sir *Paul*. Gad so, gad's-bud——*Tim*. carry it to my Lady, you should have carry'd it to my Lady first.

Boy. 'Tis directed to your Worship.

Sir *Paul*. Well, well, my Lady reads all Letters first——Child, do so no more ; d'ye hear *Tim*.

Boy. No, and please you.

SCENE VIII.

CARELESS, *Sir* PAUL, *Lady* PLYANT.

Sir *Paul*. A Humour of my Wife's, you know Women have little Fancies——But as I was telling you, Mr. *Careless*, if it were not for one thing, I should think my self the happiest Man in the World ; indeed that touches me near, very near.

Care. What can that be, Sir *Paul* ? 7

Sir *Paul*. Why, I have, I thank Heaven, a very plentiful Fortune, a good Estate in the Country, some Houses in Town, and some Mony, a pretty tolerable personal Estate ; and it is a great Grief to me, indeed it is, Mr. *Careless*, that I have not a Son to inherit this—'Tis true, I have a Daughter, and a fine dutiful Child she is, though I say it, blessed be Providence I may say ; for indeed, Mr. *Careless*, I am mightily beholden to Providence——A poor unworthy Sinner——But if I had a Son, ah, that's my Affliction, and my only Affliction ; indeed I cannot refrain Tears when it comes in my Mind. [*Cries*.

Care. Why, methinks that might be easily remedied—my Lady's a fine likely Woman——

Sir *Paul*. Oh, a fine likely Woman as you shall see in a Summer's Day—Indeed she is, Mr. *Careless*, in all Respects.

Care. And I should not have taken you to have been so old—

Sir *Paul*. Alas, that's not it, Mr. *Careless* ; ah ! that's not it ; no, no, you shoot wide of the Mark a Mile ; indeed you do, that's not it, Mr. *Careless* ; no, no, that's not it.

Care. No, what can be the Matter then ?

Sir *Paul.* You'll scarcely believe me, when I shall tell you—my Lady is so Nice—It's very strange, but it's True : Too true—she's so very Nice, that I don't believe she would touch a Man for the World—At least not above once a Year ; I'm sure I have found it so ; and alas, what's once a Year to an old Man, who would do good in his Generation ? Indeed it's true, Mr. *Careless*, it breaks my Heart—I am her Husband, as I may say ; though far unworthy of that Honour, yet I am her Husband ; but alas-a-day, I have no more Familiarity with her Person—as to that Matter—than with my own Mother—no indeed.

Care. Alas-a-day, this is a lamentable Story ; my Lady must be told on't ; she must i'faith, Sir *Paul* ; 'tis an Injury to the World.

Sir *Paul.* Ah ! would to Heav'n you would, Mr. *Careless* ; you are mightily in her Favour.

Care. I warrant you ; what, we must have a Son some way or other.

Sir *Paul.* Indeed, I should be mightily bound to you, if you could bring it about, Mr. *Careless*.

L. *P.* Here, Sir *Paul*, it's from your Steward, here's a Return of 600 Pounds ; you may take fifty of it for the next half Year.

[*Gives him the Letter.*

SCENE IX.

[*To them*] *Lord* Froth, Cynthia.

Sir *Paul.* How does my Girl ? come hither to thy Father, poor Lamb, thou'rt melancholick,

Ld. *Froth.* Heav'n, Sir *Paul*, you amaze me, of all things in the World——You are never pleas'd but when we are all upon the broad Grin ; all Laugh and no Company ; ah, then 'tis such a Sight to see some Teeth—Sure you're a great

Admirer of my Lady *Whifler*, Mr. *Sneer*, and Sir *Laurence Loud*, and that Gang.

Sir *Paul*. I vow and swear she's a very merry Woman, but, I think she laughs a little too much.

Ld. *Froth*. Merry! O Lord, what a Character that is of a Woman of Quality—You have been at my Lady *Whifler*'s upon her Day, Madam?

Cynt. Yes my Lord—I must humour this Fool. [*Aside*.

Ld. *Froth*. Well and how? hee! What is your Sense of the Conversation?

Cynt. O most ridiculous, a perpetual Consort of laughing without any Harmony; for sure, my Lord, to laugh out of Time, is as disagreeable as to sing out of Time or out of Tune.

Ld. *Froth*. Hee, hee, hee, right; and then, my Lady *Whifler* is so ready——she always comes in three Bars too soon——And then, what do they laugh at? For you know laughing without a Jest is as impertinent; hee! as, as—

Cynt. As dancing without a Fiddle.

Ld. *Froth*. Just 'ifaith, that was at my Tongue's end.

Cynt. But that cannot be properly said of them, for I think they are all in good Nature with the World, and only laugh at one another; and you must allow they have all Jests in their Persons, though they have none in their Conversation.

Ld. *Froth*. True, as I'm a Person of Honour—For Heav'ns sake let us sacrifice 'em to Mirth a little. [*Enters Boy and whispers Sir* Paul.

Sir *Paul*. Gads so—Wife, Wife, my Lady *Plyant*, I have a Word.

L. *P*. I'm busie, Sir *Paul*, I wonder at your Impertinence—

Care. Sir *Paul*, harkee, I'm reasoning the Matter you know; Madam,—if your Ladyship please, we'll discourse of this in the next Room.

18 Consort] Concert.

Sir *Paul.* O ho, I wish you good Success, I wish you good Success. Boy, tell my Lady, when she has done, I would speak with her below.

SCENE X.

CYNTHIA, *Lord* FROTH, *Lady* FROTH, BRISK.

L. *Froth.* Then you think that *Episode* between *Susan*, the Dairy-Maid, and our Coach-Man is not amiss; you know, I may suppose the Dairy in Town, as well as in the Country.

Brisk. Incomparable, let me perish—But then being an Heroick Poem, had not you better call him a *Charioteer*? *Charioteer* sounds great; besides your Ladyship's Coachman having a red Face, and you comparing him to the Sun——And you know the Sun is call'd *Heav'ns Charioteer.*

L. *Froth.* Oh, infinitely better; I'm extreamly beholden to you for the Hint; stay, we'll read over those half a Score Lines again. [*Pulls out a Paper.*] Let me see here, you know what goes before—the Comparison, you know. [Reads]

For as the Sun shines ev'ry Day,
So of our Coachman I may say.

Brisk. I'm afraid that Simile won't do in wet Weather—Because you say the Sun shines ev'ry Day.

L. *Froth.* No, for the Sun it won't, but it will do for the Coach-man, for you know there's most Occasion for a Coach in wet Weather.

Brisk. Right, right, that saves all.

L. *Froth.* Then I don't say the Sun shines all the Day, but that he peeps now and then, yet he does shine all the Day too, you know, tho' we don't see him.

Brisk. Right, but the Vulgar will never comprehend that.

L. *Froth.* Well, you shall hear—Let me see. [Reads] *For as the Sun shines ev'ry Day,*
So, of our Coach-man I may say,

He shows his drunken fiery Face,
Just as the Sun does, more or less.

Brisk. That's right, all's well, all's well. *More or less.*

[L. *Froth* reads] *And when at Night his Labour's done,*
Then too, like Heav'ns Charioteer the Sun:
Ay, *Charioteer* does better.
Into the Dairy he descends
And there his Whipping and his Driving ends;
There he's secure from Danger of a Bilk,
His Fare is paid him, and he sets in Milk.
For *Susan*, you know, is *Thetis*, and so—

Brisk. Incomparable well and proper, Igad——But I have one Exception to make——Don't you think *Bilk* (I know its good Rhime) but don't you think *Bilk* and *Fare* too like a Hackney Coach-man?

L. *Froth.* I swear and vow I'm afraid so——And yet our *Jehu* was a Hackney Coach-man, when my Lord took him.

Brisk. Was he? I'm answer'd, if *Jehu* was a Hackney Coach-man——You may put that in the marginal Notes tho', to prevent Criticism——Only mark it with a small Asterism, and say,——*Jehu* was formerly a Hackney Coach-man.

L. *Froth.* I will; you'd oblige me extreamly to write Notes to the whole Poem.

Brisk. With all my Heart and Soul, and proud of the vast Honour, let me perish.

Ld. *Froth.* Hee, hee, hee, my Dear, have you done——won't you join with us, we were laughing at my Lady *Whifler*, and Mr. *Sneer*.

L. *Froth.*——Ay my Dear——Were you? Oh filthy Mr. *Sneer*; he's a nauseous Figure, a most fulsamick Fop, foh—He spent two Days together in going about *Covent-Garden* to suit the Lining of his Coach with his Complexion.

45 *Thetis*] and therefore dwelling under the sea with her sister Nereids.

Ld. *Froth.* O silly! yet his Aunt is as fond of him, as if she had brought the Ape into the World her self.

Brisk. Who, my Lady *Toothless*; O, she's a mortifying Spectacle; she's always chewing the Cud like an old *Ewe.*

Cynt. Fie, Mr. *Brisk, Eringo's* for her Cough.

L. *Froth.* I have seen her take 'em half chew'd out of her Mouth, to laugh, and then put 'em in again—Foh.

Ld. *Froth.* Foh.

L. *Froth.* Then she's always ready to laugh when *Sneer* offers to speak—And sits in Expectation of his no Jest, with her Gums bare, and her Mouth open—

Brisk. Like an Oyster at low Ebb, I'gad——Ha, ha, ha.

Cynt. (*Aside.*) Well, I find there are no Fools so inconsiderable in themselves, but they can render other People contemptible by exposing their Infirmities.

L. *Froth.* Then that t'other great strapping Lady——I can't hit of her Name; the old fat Fool that paints so exorbitantly.

Brisk. I know whom you mean——But duce take me I can't hit of her Name neither—Paints d'ye say? Why she lays it on with a Trowel——Then she has a great Beard that bristles through it, and makes her look as if she were plaister'd with Lime and Hair, let me perish.

L. *Froth.* O you made a Song upon her, Mr. *Brisk.*

Brisk. He? egad, so I did—My Lord can sing it.

Cynt. O good my Lord let's hear it.

Brisk. 'Tis not a Song neither—It's a sort of an Epigram, or rather an Epigrammatick Sonnet; I don't know what to call it, but it's Satire.——Sing it my Lord.

Lord Froth *sings.*

Ancient Phillis *has young Graces,*
'Tis a strange thing, but a true one ;
Shall I tell you how ?
She her self makes her own Faces,
And each Morning wears a new one ;
Where's the Wonder now ?

Brisk. Short, but there's Salt in't ; my way of Writing I'gad.

SCENE XI.

[*To them*] Footman.

L. *Froth.* How now ?

Foot. Your Ladyship's Chair is come.

L. *Froth.* Is Nurse and the Child in it ?

Foot. Yes, Madam.

L. *Froth.* O the dear Creature ! Let's go see it.

Ld. *Froth.* I swear, my Dear, you'll spoil that Child, with sending it to and again so often, this is the seventh time the Chair has gone for her to Day.

L. *Froth.* O-law, I swear it's but the sixth——and I han't seen her these two Hours—The poor dear Creature——I swear, my Lord, you don't love poor little *Sapho*——Come, my dear *Cynthia*, Mr. *Brisk*, we'll go see *Sapho*, tho' my Lord won't.

Cynt. I'll wait upon your Ladyship.

Brisk. Pray, Madam, how old is Lady *Sapho* ?

L. *Froth.* Three Quarters, but I swear she has a World of Wit, and can sing a Tune already. My Lord, won't you go ? Won't you ? What not to see *Saph* ? Pray, my Lord, come see little *Saph.* I knew you cou'd not stay.

SCENE XII.

Cynthia, *alone.*

Cynt. 'Tis not so hard to counterfeit Joy in the Depth of Affliction, as to dissemble Mirth in

Company of Fools——Why should I call 'em Fools? The World thinks better of 'em; for these have Quality and Education, Wit and fine Conversation, are receiv'd and admir'd by the World—If not, they like and admire themselves——And why is not that true Wisdom, for 'tis Happiness: And for ought I know, we have misapply'd the Name all this while, and mistaken the Thing: Since

If Happiness in Self-content is plac'd,
The Wise are Wretched, and Fools only Bless'd.

End of the Third Act.

ACT IV. SCENE I.

Mellefont *and* Cynthia.

Cynthia.

I heard him loud as I came by the Closet-Door, and my Lady with him, but she seem'd to moderate his Passion.

Mel. Ay, Hell thank her, as gentle Breezes moderate a Fire; but I shall counter-work her Spells, and ride the Witch in her own Bridle.

Cynt. It's impossible; she'll cast beyond you still—I'll lay my Life it will never be a Match.

Mel. What?

Cynt. Between you and me.

Mel. Why so?

Cynt. My Mind gives me it won't——because we are both willing; we each of us strive to reach the Goal, and hinder one another in the Race; I swear it never does well when the Parties are so agreed——For when People walk Hand in Hand, there's neither overtaking nor meeting: We Hunt in Couples where we both pursue the same Game, but forget one another; and 'tis because we are so near that we don't think of coming together.

Mel. Hum, 'gad I believe there's something in't;——Marriage is the Game that we hunt, and while we think that we only have it in View, I don't see but we have it in our Power.

Cynt. Within reach; for Example, give me your Hand; you have look'd through the wrong End of the Perspective all this while; for nothing has been between us but our Fears.

Mel. I don't know why we should not steal out of the House this very Moment and marry one another, without Consideration or the Fear of Repentance. Pox o'Fortune, Portion, Settlements and Jointures.

Cynt. Ay, ay, what have we to do with 'em; you know we marry for Love.

Mel. Love, Love, down-right very villainous Love.

Cynt. And he that can't live upon Love, deserves to die in a Ditch.—Here then, I give you my Promise, in spight of Duty, any Temptation of Wealth, your Inconstancy, or my own Inclination to change——

Mel. To run most wilfully and unreasonably away with me this Moment, and be married.

Cynt. Hold——Never to marry any Body else.

Mel. That's but a kind of Negative Consent—Why, you won't baulk the Frolick?

Cynt. If you had not been so assured of your own Conduct I would not——But 'tis but reasonable that since I consent to like a Man without the vile Consideration of Mony, he should give me a very evident Demonstration of his Wit: Therefore let me see you undermine my Lady *Touchwood*, as you boasted, and force her to give her Consent, and then—

Mel. I'll do it.

Cynt. And I'll do't.

Mel. This very next ensuing Hour of eight a Clock, is the last Minute of her Reign, unless the Devil assist her in *propria persona*.

Cynt. Well, if the Devil should assist her, and your Plot miscarry.——

Mel. Ay, what am I to trust to then?

Cynt. Why if you give me very clear Demonstration that it was the Devil, I'll allow for irresistible Odds. But if I find it to be only Chance, or Destiny, or unlucky Stars, or any thing but the very Devil, I'm inexorable: Only still I'll keep my Word, and live a Maid for your sake.

Mel. And you won't die one, for your own, so still there's Hope.

Cynt. Here's my Mother-in-Law, and your Friend *Careless*, I would not have 'em see us together yet.

SCENE II.

CARELESS *and Lady* PLYANT.

L. *P.* I swear, Mr. *Careless*, you are very alluring —And say so many fine Things, and nothing is so moving to me as a fine Thing. Well, I must do you this Justice, and declare in the Face of the World, never any Body gain'd so far upon me as your self; with Blushes I must own it, you have shaken, as I may say, the very Foundation of my Honour—Well, sure if I escape your Importunities, I shall value my self as long as I live, I swear.

Care. And despise me. [*Sighing.*

L. *P.* The last of any Man in the World, by my Purity; now you make me swear—O Gratitude forbid, that I should ever be wanting in a respectful Acknowledgment of an intire Resignation of all my best Wishes, for the Person and Parts of so accompish'd a Person, whose Merit challenges much more, I'm sure, than my illiterate Praises can description——

Care. (*In a whining Tone.*) Ah Heav'ns, Madam, you ruin me with Kindness; your charming Tongue pursues the Victory of your Eyes, while at your Feet your poor Adorer dies.

L. *P*. Ah! Very fine.

Care. (*Still whining*.) Ah why are you so Fair, so bewitching Fair? O let me grow to the Ground here, and feast upon that Hand; O let me press it to my Heart, my trembling Heart, the nimble Movement shall instruct your Pulse, and teach it to alarm Desire.

[*Zoons I'm almost at the end of my Cant, if she does not yield quickly*. (*Aside*.)

L. *P*. O that's so passionate and fine, I cannot hear it——I am not safe if I stay, and must leave you.

Care. And must you leave me! Rather let me languish out a wretched Life, and breath my Soul beneath your Feet.

[*I must say the same Thing over again, and can't help it*. (*Aside*.)

L. *P*. I swear I'm ready to languish too——O my Honour! Whither is it going? I protest you have given me the Palpitation of the Heart.

Care. Can you be so cruel.——

L. *P*. O rise I beseech you, say no more 'till you rise——Why did you kneel so long? I swear I was so transported, I did not see it.——Well, to shew you how far you have gain'd upon me; I assure you if Sir *Paul* should die, of all Mankind there's none I'd sooner make my second Choice.

Care. O Heav'n! I can't out-live this Night without your Favour——I feel my Spirits faint, a general Dampness over-spreads my Face, a cold deadly Dew already vents through all my Pores, and will to Morrow wash me for ever from your Sight, and drown me in my Tomb.

L. *P*. O you have conquer'd, sweet, melting, moving Sir, you have conquer'd——What Heart of Marble can refrain to weep, and yield to such sad Sayings.— [*Cries*.

Care. I thank Heav'n, they are the saddest that I ever said——Oh!

[*I shall never contain Laughter*. (*Aside*.)

L. P. Oh, I yield my self all up to your uncontroulable Embraces——Say, thou dear dying Man, when, where, and how.—Ah, there's Sir *Paul.*

Care. 'Slife, yonder's Sir *Paul,* but if he were not come, I'm so transported I cannot speak——This Note will inform you. [*Gives her a Note.*

SCENE III.

Lady Plyant, *Sir* Paul, Cynthia.

Sir *Paul.* Thou art my tender Lambkin, and shalt do what thou wilt——But endeavour to forget this *Mellefont.*

Cynt. I would obey you to my Power, Sir; but if I have not him, I have sworn never to marry.

Sir *Paul.* Never to marry! Heav'ns forbid; must I neither have Sons nor Grandsons? must the Family of the *Plyants* be utterly extinct for want of Issue Male. Oh Impiety! But did you swear, did that sweet Creature swear! ha? How durst you swear without my Consent, ah? Gads-bud, who am I? 12

Cynt. Pray don't be angry, Sir, when I swore, I had your Consent; and therefore I swore.

Sir *Paul.* Why then the revoking my Consent does annul, or make of none effect your Oath: So you may unswear it again——The Law will allow it.

Cynt. Ay, but my Conscience never will. 19

Sir *Paul.* Gads-bud no matter for that, Conscience and Law never go together; you must not expect that.

L. P. Ay, but Sir *Paul,* I conceive if she has sworn, d'ye mark me, if she has once sworn; it is most unchristian, inhuman, and obscene that she shou'd break it.——I'll make up the Match again, because Mr. *Careless* said it would oblige him. [*Aside.*

Sir *Paul.* Does your Ladyship conceive so——Why I was of that Opinion once too—Nay if your

Ladyship conceives so, I'm of that Opinion again; but I can neither find my Lord nor my Lady to know what they intend.

L. P. I'm satisfy'd that my Cousin *Mellefont* has been much wrong'd.

Cynt. (*Aside.*) I'm amaz'd to find her of our side, for I'm sure she lov'd him.

L. P. I know my Lady *Touchwood* has no Kindness for him; and besides I have been inform'd by Mr. *Careless*, that *Mellefont* had never any thing more than a profound Respect——That he has own'd himself to be my Admirer 'tis true, but he was never so presumptuous to entertain any dishonourable Notions of Things; so that if this be made plain——I don't see how my Daughter can in Conscience, or Honour, or any thing in the World——

Sir *Paul.* Indeed if this be made plain, as my Lady your Mother says, Child——

L. P. Plain! I was inform'd of it by Mr. *Careless*—And I assure you Mr. *Careless* is a Person—that has a most extraordinary Respect and Honour for you, Sir *Paul.*

Cynt. (*Aside.*) And for your Ladyship too, I believe, or else you had not chang'd Sides so soon; now I begin to find it.

Sir *Paul.* I am much obliged to Mr. *Careless* really, he is a Person that I have a great Value for, not only for that, but because he has a great Veneration for your Ladyship.

L. P. O las, no indeed, Sir *Paul*, 'tis upon your Account.

Sir *Paul.* No I protest and vow, I have no Title to his Esteem, but in having the Honour to appertain in some Measure to your Ladyship, that's all.

L. P. O law now, I swear and declare, it shan't be so, you're too modest, Sir *Paul.*

Sir *Paul.* It becomes me, when there is any Comparison made, between——

L. *P.* O fy, fy, Sir *Paul*, you'll put me out of Countenance—Your very obedient and affectionate Wife; that's all—And highly honour'd in that Title.

Sir *Paul.* Gads-bud I am transported! Give me leave to kiss your Ladyship's Hand.

Cynt. That my poor Father should be so very silly. [*Aside.*

L. *P.* My Lip indeed, Sir *Paul*, I swear you shall. [*He kisses her, and bows very low.*

Sir *Paul.* I humbly thank your Ladyship——I don't know whether I fly on Ground, or walk in Air——Gads-bud, she was never thus before——Well, I must own my self the most beholden to Mr. *Careless*——As sure as can be this is all his doing,——something that he has said; well, 'tis a rare thing to have an ingenious Friend. Well, your Ladyship is of Opinion that the Match may go forward.

L. *P.* By all means——Mr. *Careless* has satisfy'd me of the Matter. 89

Sir *Paul.* Well, why then Lamb you may keep your Oath, but have a care of making rash Vows; come hither to me, and kiss *Papa*.

L. *P.* I swear and declare, I am in such a twitter to read Mr. *Careless* his Letter, that I can't forbear any longer—But though I may read all Letters first by Prerogative, yet I'll be sure to be unsuspected this time.—Sir *Paul.*

Sir *Paul.* Did your Ladyship call? 98

L. *P.* Nay, not to interrupt you my Dear—Only lend me your Letter, which you had from your Steward to Day: I would look upon the Account again; and may be increase your Allowance.

Sir *Paul.* There it is, Madam; Do you want a Pen and Ink? [*Bows and gives the Letter.*

L. *P.* No, no, nothing else, I thank you, Sir *Paul.*—So now I can read my own Letter under the Cover of his. [*Aside.*

Sir *Paul*. He? And wilt thou bring a Grandson at nine Months end——He? A brave chopping Boy.——I'll settle a thousand Pound a Year upon the Rogue as soon as ever he looks me in the Face, I will Gads-bud. I'm overjoy'd to think I have any of my Family that will bring Children into the World. For I would fain have some Resemblance of my self in my Posterity, he *Thy*? Can't you contrive that Affair Girl? Do Gads-bud, think on thy old Father; heh? Make the young Rogue as like as you can.

Cynt. I'm glad to see you so merry, Sir.

Sir *Paul*. Merry, Gads-bud I'm serious, I'll give thee 500 *l*. for every Inch of him that resembles me; ah this Eye, this left Eye! A thousand Pound for this left Eye. This has done Execution in its time Girl; why thou hast my Leer Hussey, just thy Father's Leer.——Let it be transmitted to the young Rogue by the help of Imagination; why 'tis the Mark of our Family *Thy*; our House is distinguish'd by a languishing Eye, as the House of *Austria* is by a thick Lip.——Ah! when I was of your Age Hussey, I would have held fifty to one, I could have drawn my own Picture—Gads-bud I could have done——not so much as you neither,——but——nay, don't blush——

Cynt. I don't blush, Sir, for I vow I don't understand—

Sir *Paul*. Pshaw, Pshaw, you fib you Baggage, you do understand, and you shall understand; come don't be no nice, Gads-bud don't learn after your Mother-in-Law my Lady here: Marry Heav'n forbid that you should follow her Example, that would spoil all indeed. Bless us, if you should take a Vagarie and make a rash Resolution on your Wedding Night, to die a Maid, as she did; all were ruin'd, all my Hopes lost——My Heart would break, and my Estate would be left to the wide Word, he? I hope you are a better Christian than to think of living a Nun; he? Answer me?

Cynt. I'm all Obedience, Sir, to your Commands.

L. *P.* [*Having read the Letter.*] O dear Mr. *Careless*, I swear he writes charmingly, and he looks charmingly, and he has charm'd me, as much as I have charm'd him; and so I'll tell him in the Wardrobe when 'tis dark. O Crimine! I hope Sir *Paul* has not seen both Letters.

[*Puts the wrong Letter hastily up, and gives him her own.*

Sir *Paul*, here's your Letter, to Morrow Morning I'll settle Accounts to your Advantage.

SCENE IV.

[*To them*] BRISK.

Brisk. Sir *Paul*, Gads-bud you're an uncivil Person, let me tell you, and all that; and I did not think it had been in you.

Sir *Paul.* O Law, what's the matter now? I hope you are not angry, Mr. *Brisk.*

Brisk. Deuce take me I believe you intend to marry your Daughter your self; you're always brooding over her like an old Hen, as if she were not well hatch'd, I'gad, he?

Sir *Paul.* Good strange! Mr. *Brisk* is such a merry facetious Person, he, he, he. No, no, I have done with her, I have done with her now.

Brisk. The Fiddles have stay'd this Hour in the Hall, and my Lord *Froth* wants a Partner, we can never begin without her.

Sir *Paul.* Go, go Child, go, get you gone and dance and be merry, I'll come and look at you by and by.—Where's my Son *Mellefont*?

L. *P.* I'll send him to them, I know where he is—

Brisk. Sir *Paul*, will you send *Careless* into the Hall if you meet him.

Sir *Paul.* I will, I will, I'll go and look for him on purpose.

SCENE V

Brisk *alone.*

Brisk. So now they are all gone, and I have an Opportunity to practise.——Ah! My dear Lady *Froth*! She's a most engaging Creature, if she were not so fond of that damn'd coxcombly Lord of hers; and yet I am forced to allow him Wit too, to keep in with him——No matter, she's a Woman of Parts, and I'gad Parts will carry her. She said she would follow me into the Gallery—Now to make my Approaches——Hem hem! Ah Ma- (*Bows.*) dam!—Pox on't, why should I disparage my Parts by thinking what to say? None but dull Rogues *think*; witty Men, like rich Fellows, are always ready for all Expences; while your Blockheads, like poor needy Scoundrels, are forced to examine their Stock, and forecast the Changes of the Day. Here she comes, I'll seem not to see her, and try to win her with a new airy Invention of my own, hem!

SCENE VI.

[*To him*] *Lady* Froth.

Brisk *Sings, walking about. I'm sick with Love,* ha, ha, ha, *prithee come cure me.*

I'm sick with, &c.

O ye Pow'rs! O my Lady *Froth*, my Lady *Froth*! My Lady *Froth*! Heigho! Break heart; Gods I thank you.

[*Stands musing with his Arms a-cross.*

L. Froth. O Heav'ns, Mr. *Brisk*! What's the Matter? 8

Brisk. My Lady *Froth*! Your Ladyship's most humble Servant;—The Matter, Madam? Nothing, Madam, nothing at all I'gad. I was fallen into the most agreeable Amusement in the whole Province of Contemplation: That's all——(I'll seem to conceal my Passion, and that will look like Respect.) [*Aside.*

L. *Froth.* Bless me, why did you call out upon me so loud?—

Brisk. O Lord, I, Madam! I beseech your Ladyship—when?

L. *Froth.* Just now as I came in, bless me, why don't you know it? 21

Brisk. Not I, let me perish—But did I! Strange! I confess your Ladyship was in my Thoughts; and I was in a sort of Dream that did in a manner represent a very pleasing Object to my Imagination, but——but did I indeed?—To see how Love and Murder will out. But did I really name my Lady *Froth*? 28

L. *Froth.* Three times aloud, as I love Letters—But did you talk of Love? O *Parnassus*! Who would have thought Mr. *Brisk* could have been in Love, ha, ha, ha. O Heav'ns I thought you cou'd have no Mistress but the Nine Muses.

Brisk. No more I have I'gad, for I adore 'em all in your Ladyship——Let me perish, I don't know whether to be splenatick, or airy upon't; the Deuce take me if I can tell whether I am glad or sorry that your Ladyship has made the Discovery.

L. *Froth.* O be merry by all means—Prince *Volscius* in Love! Ha, ha, ha. 41

Brisk. O barbarous, to turn me into Ridicule! Yet, ha, ha, ha. The Deuce take me, I can't help laughing my self, ha, ha, ha; yet by Heav'ns I have a violent Passion for your Ladyship, seriously.

L. *Froth.* Seriously? Ha, ha, ha.

40 Prince *Volscius* in Love! Ha, ha, ha.] A reference to Buckingham's *Rehearsal*, III. 2:

Vols.	O inauspicious Stars! that I was born To sudden love, and to more sudden scorn.
Ama. Cloris.	How! Prince Volscius in love? Ha, ha, ha.

Brisk. Seriously, ha, ha, ha. Gad I have, for all I laugh.

L. *Froth.* Ha, ha, ha! What d'ye think I laugh at? Ha, ha, ha.

Brisk. Me I'gad, ha, ha.

L. *Froth.* No the Deuce take me if I don't laugh at my self; for hang me if I have not a violent Passion for Mr. *Brisk*, ha, ha, ha.

Brisk. Seriously?

L. *Froth.* Seriously, ha, ha, ha.

Brisk. That's well enough; let me perish, ha, ha, ha. O miraculous, what a happy Discovery. Ah my dear charming Lady *Froth*!

L. *Froth.* Oh my adored Mr. *Brisk*! [*Embrace.*

SCENE VII.

[*To them*] *Lord* FROTH.

Ld. *Froth.* The Company are all ready—How now!

Brisk. Zoons, Madam, there's my Lord. [*Softly to her.*

L. *Froth.* Take no notice——but observe me ——Now cast off, and meet me at the lower end of the Room, and then join Hands again; I could teach my Lord this Dance purely, but I vow, Mr. *Brisk*, I can't tell how to come so near any other Man. Oh here's my Lord, now you shall see me do it with him.

[*They pretend to practise part of a Country Dance.*

Ld. *Froth.*—Oh I see there's no harm yet— But I don't like this Familiarity. [*Aside.*

L. *Froth.*——Shall you and I do our close Dance, to show Mr. *Brisk*?

Ld. *Froth.* No, my Dear, do it with him.

L. *Froth.* I'll do it with him, my Lord, when you are out of the way.

Brisk. That's good I'gad, that's good. Deuce take me I can hardly hold laughing in his Face. [*Aside.*

Ld. *Froth.* Any other time, my Dear, or we'll dance it below.

L. *Froth.* With all my Heart.

Brisk. Come my Lord, I'll wait on you—My charming witty Angel! [*To her.*

L. *Froth.* We shall have whispering time enough, you know, since we are Partners.

SCENE VIII.

Lady Plyant, *and* Careless

L. *P.* O Mr. *Careless*, Mr. *Careless*, I'm ruin'd, I'm undone.

Care. What's the Matter, Madam?

L. *P.* O the unlucky'st Accident, I'm afraid I shan't live to tell it you.

Care. Heav'n forbid! What is it?

L. *P.* I'm in such a Fright; the strangest Quandary and Premunire! I'm all over in a Universal Agitation, I dare swear every Circumstance of me trembles.——O your Letter, your Letter! By an unfortunate Mistake, I have given Sir *Paul* your Letter instead of his own.

Care. That was unlucky.

L. *P.* O yonder he comes reading of it, for Heav'ns sake step in here and advise me quickly, before he sees.

SCENE IX.

Sir Paul *with the Letter.*

Sir *Paul.*—O Providence, what a Conspiracy have I discover'd——But let me see to make an an end on't.——(*Reads*) Hum—*After Supper in the Wardrobe by the Gallery. If Sir* Paul *should surprize us, I have a Commission from him to treat with you about the very Matter of Fact*—Matter of Fact! Very pretty; it seems then I am conducing to my own Cuckoldom; why this is the very traiterous Position of taking up Arms by my

Authority, against my Person! Well, let me see ——*'Till then I languish in Expectation of my adored Charmer.* 12

Dying Ned. Careless.

Gads-bud, would that were matter of Fact too. Die and be damn'd for a *Judas Maccabeus*, and *Iscariot* both. O Friendship! What art thou but a Name! Henceforward let no Man make a Friend that would not be a Cuckold: For whomsoever he receives into his Bosom, will find the Way to his Bed, and there return his Caresses with Interest to his Wife. Have I for this been pinion'd Night after Night for three Years past? Have I been swath'd in Blankets 'till I have been even depriv'd of Motion? Have I approach'd the Marriage Bed with Reverence as to a sacred Shrine, and deny'd my self the Enjoyment of lawful Domestick Pleasures to preserve its Purity, and must I now find it polluted by foreign Iniquity? O my Lady *Plyant*, you were chaste as Ice, but you are melted now, and false as Water. ——But Providence has been constant to me in discovering this Conspiracy; still I am beholden to Providence, if it were not for Providence, sure poor Sir *Paul* thy Heart would break.

SCENE X.

[*To him*] *Lady* PLYANT.

L. *P.* So, Sir, I see you have read the Letter,— Well now, Sir *Paul*, what do you think of your Friend *Careless*? Has he been treacherous, or did you give his Insolence a License to make Trial of your Wife's suspected Virtue? D'ye see here?

[*Snatches the Letter as in Anger.*

Look, read it? Gad's my Life if I thought it were so, I would this Moment renounce all Communication with you. Ungrateful Monster! He? Is it so? Ay, I see it, a Plot upon my Honour; your guilty Cheeks confess it: Oh where shall wrong'd

Virtue fly for Reparation! I'll be divorced this Instant.

Sir *Paul*. Gads-bud what shall I say? This is the strangest Surprize! Why I don't know any thing at all, nor I don't know whether there be any thing at all in the World, or no.

L. *P*. I thought I should try you, false Man. I that never dissembled in my Life: Yet to make Trial of you, pretended to like that Monster of Iniquity, *Careless*, and found out that Contrivance to let you see this Letter; which now I find was of your own inditing—I do Heathen, I do; see my Face no more; I'll be divorced presently.

Sir *Paul*. O strange, what will become of me!—I'm so amaz'd, and so overjoy'd, so afraid, and so sorry.—But did you give me this Letter on Purpose, he? Did you?

L. *P*. Did I? Do you doubt me, Turk, Sarazen? I have a Cousin that's a Proctor in the Commons, I'll go to him instantly.——

Sir *Paul*. Hold, stay, I beseech your Ladyship——I'm so overjoy'd, stay, I'll confess all.

L. *P*. What will you confess, Jew?

Sir *Paul*. Why now as I hope to be saved, I had no Hand in this Letter——Nay hear me, I beseech your Ladyship: The Devil take me now if he did not go beyond my Commission—If I desired him to do any more than speak a good Word only just for me; Gads-bud only for poor Sir *Paul*, I'm an Anabaptist, or a Jew, or what you please to call me.

L. *P*. Why is not here Matter of Fact?

Sir *Paul*. Ay, but by your own Virtue and Continency that matter of Fact is all his own doing.—I confess I had a great Desire to have some Honours conferr'd upon me, which lye all in your Ladyship's Breast, and he being a well-spoken Man, I desired him to intercede for me.——

L. *P*. Did you so, Presumption! Oh! he comes, the *Tarquin* comes; I cannot bear his Sight.

SCENE XI.

Careless, *Sir* Paul.

Care. Sir *Paul*, I'm glad I've met with you, 'gad I have said all I could, but can't prevail—— Then my Friendship to you has carry'd me a little farther in this Matter—

Sir *Paul.* Indeed——Well Sir——I'll dissemble with him a little. [*Aside.*

Care. Why faith I have in my Time known honest Gentlemen abused by a pretended Coyness in their Wives, and I had a Mind to try my Lady's Virtue—And when I could not prevail for you, 'gad I pretended to be in Love my self—but all in vain, she would not hear a Word upon that Subject: Then I writ a Letter to her; I don't know what Effects that will have, but I'll be sure to tell you when I do, tho' by this Light I believe her Virtue is impregnable.

Sir *Paul.* O Providence! Providence! What Discoveries are here made? Why, this is better and more miraculous than the rest.

Care. What do you mean?

Sir *Paul.* I can't tell you, I'm so overjoy'd; come along with me to my Lady, I can't contain my self; come my dear Friend.

Care. So, so, so, this Difficulty's over. [*Aside.*

SCENE XII.

Mellefont, Maskwell, *from different Doors.*

Mel. Maskwell! I have been looking for you—'tis within a Quarter of Eight.

Mask. My Lady is just gone into my Lord's Closet, you had best steal into her Chamber before she comes, and lye concealed there, otherwise she may lock the Door when we are together, and you not easily get in to surprize us.

Mel. He? You say true.

Mask. You had best make haste, for after she has made some Apology to the Company for her own, and my Lord's Absence all this while, she'll retire to her Chamber instantly.

Mel. I go this Moment: Now Fortune I defie thee.

SCENE XIII.

Maskwell, *alone.*

Mask. I confess you may be allow'd to be secure in your own Opinion; the Appearance is very fair, but I have an After-Game to play that shall turn the Tables, and here comes the Man that I must manage.

SCENE XIV.

[*To him*] *Lord* Touchwood.

Ld. *T. Maskwell*, you are the Man I wish'd to meet.

Mask. I am happy to be in the way of your Lordship's Commands.

Ld. *Touch.* I have always found you prudent and careful in any thing that has concern'd me or my Family.

Mask. I were a Villain else——I am bound by Duty and Gratitude, and my own Inclination, to be ever your Lordship's Servant.

Ld. *Touch.* Enough——You are my Friend; I know it: Yet there has been a thing in your Knowledge, which has concern'd me nearly, that you have conceal'd from me.

Mask. My Lord!

Ld. *Touch.* Nay, I excuse your Friendship to my unnatural Nephew thus far—But I know you have been privy to his impious Designs upon my Wife. This Ev'ning she has told me all: Her good Nature conceal'd it as long as was possible; but he perseveres so in Villany, that she has told me even you were weary of dissuading him, though you have once actually hindered him from forcing her.

Mask. I am sorry, my Lord, I can't make you an Answer; this is an Occasion in which I would not willingly be silent.

Ld. *Touch.* I know you would excuse him—— And I know as well that you can't.

Mask. Indeed I was in Hopes t'had been a youthful Heat that might have soon boil'd over; but——

Ld. *Touch.* Say on.

Mask. I have nothing more to say, my Lord—— But to express my Concern; for I think his Frenzy increases daily.

Ld. *Touch.* How! Give me but Proof of it, Ocular Proof, that I may justifie my Dealing with him to the World, and share my Fortunes.

Mask. O my Lord! consider that is hard: Besides, time may work upon him: Then, for me to do it! I have profess'd an everlasting Friendship to him.

Ld. *Touch.* He is your Friend, and what am I?

Mask. I am answered.

L. *Touch.* Fear not his Displeasure; I will put you out of his, and Fortune's Power, and for that thou art scrupulously honest, I will secure thy Fidelity to him, and give my Honour never to own any Discovery that you shall make me. Can you give me a demonstrative Proof? Speak.

Mask. I wish I could not——To be plain, my Lord, I intended this Ev'ning to have try'd all Arguments to dissuade him from a Design, which I suspect; and if I had not succeeded, to have informed your Lordship of what I knew.

Ld. *Touch.* I thank you. What is the Villain's Purpose?

Mask. He has own'd nothing to me of late, and what I mean now, is only a bare Suspicion of my own. If your Lordship will meet me a Quarter of an Hour hence there, in that Lobby by my Lady's Bed-Chamber, I shall be able to tell you more.

Ld. *Touch.* I will. 64

Mask. My Duty to your Lordship, makes me do a severe Piece of Justice.—

Ld. *Touch.* I will be secret, and reward your Honesty beyond your Hopes.

SCENE XV.

SCENE *opening shews Lady* TOUCHWOOD'S *Chamber.*

MELLEFONT *Solus.*

Mel. Pray Heav'n my Aunt keep touch with her Assignation.——Oh that her Lord were but sweating behind this Hanging, with the Expectation of what I shall see—Hist, she comes——Little does she think what a Mine is just ready to spring under her Feet. But to my Post.

[*Goes behind the Hangings.*

SCENE XVI.

Lady TOUCHWOOD.

L. *Touch.* 'Tis Eight a Clock: Methinks I should have found him here. Who does not prevent the Hour of Love, outstays the Time; for to be dully punctual, is too slow.—I was accusing you of Neglect.

SCENE XVII.

Lady TOUCHWOOD, MASKWELL, MELLEFONT *absconding.*

Mask. I Confess you do reproach me when I see you here before me; but 'tis fit I should be still behind hand, still to be more and more indebted to your Goodness.

absconding] hiding.

L. *Touch.* You can excuse a Fault too well, not to have been to blame—A ready answer shews you were prepar'd.

Mask. Guilt is ever at a Loss, and Confusion waits upon it; when Innocence and bold Truth are always ready for Expression—

L. *Touch.* Not in Love; Words are the weak Support of cold Indifference; Love has no Language to be heard.

Mask. Excess of Joy has made me stupid! Thus may my Lips be ever clos'd. (*Kisses her.*) And thus—Oh who would not lose his Speech, upon condition to have Joys above it?

L. *Touch.* Hold, let me lock the Door first.

[*Goes to the Door.*

Mask. (*Aside.*) That I believ'd; 'twas well I left the private Passage open.

L. *Touch.* So, that's safe.

Mask. And so may all your Pleasures be, and secret as this Kiss——

Mel. And may all Treachery be thus discover'd.

[*Leaps out.*

L. *Touch.* Ah! [*Shrieks.*

Mel. Villain! [*Offers to draw.*

Mask. Nay then, there's but one Way.

[*Runs out.*

SCENE XVIII.

Lady TOUCHWOOD, MELLEFONT.

Mel. Say you so, were you provided for an Escape? Hold, Madam, you have no more Holes to your Burrough, I'll stand between you and this Sally-Port.

L. *Touch.* Thunder strike thee dead for this Deceit, immediate Lightning blast thee, me and the whole World——Oh! I could rack my self, play the Vulture to my own Heart, and gnaw it piece-meal, for not boding to me this Misfortune.

Mel. Be Patient.——

L. *Touch.* Be Damn'd.

Mel. Consider I have you on the Hook; you will but flounder your self a weary, and be nevertheless my Prisoner.

L. *Touch.* I'll hold my Breath and die, but I'll be free.

Mel. O Madam, have a care of dying unprepar'd, I doubt you have some unrepented Sins that may hang heavy, and retard your Flight.

L. *Touch* O! what shall I do? say? Whither shall I turn? Has Hell no Remedy? 21

Mel. None, Hell has serv'd you ev'n as Heav'n has done, left you to your self.——You're in a kind of *Erasmus* Paradice; yet if you please you may make it a Purgatory; and with a little Penance and my Absolution all this may turn to good Account. 27

L. *Touch.* (*Aside.*) Hold in my Passion, and fall, fall a little thou swelling Heart; let me have some Intermission of this Rage, and one Minute's Coolness to dissemble. [*She weeps.*

Mel. You have been to blame.—I like those Tears, and hope they are of the purest kind——Penitential Tears.

L. *Touch.* O the Scene was shifted quick before me——I had not time to think—I was surprised to see a Monster in the Glass, and now I find 'tis my self; Can you have Mercy to forgive the Faults I have imagin'd, but never put in Practice——O consider, consider how fatal you have been to me, you have already kill'd the Quiet of this Life. The Love of you, was the first wand'ring Fire that e'er misled my Steps, and while I had only that in View, I was betray'd into unthought of Ways of Ruin.

Mel. May I believe this true? 46

L. *Touch.* O be not cruelly incredulous——

24 *Erasmus* Paradice] i. e. 'crushed between the two extremes, as they hang up Erasmus himself, betwixt Heaven and Hell'. Introduction to L'Estrange's translation of the Colloquies. (Summers.)

How can you doubt these streaming Eyes? Keep the severest Eye o'er all my future Conduct; and if I once relapse, let me not hope Forgiveness, 'twill ever be in your Power to ruin me—My Lord shall sign to your Desires; I will my self create your Happiness, and *Cynthia* shall be this Night your Bride—Do but conceal my Failings, and forgive.

Mel. Upon such Terms I will be ever yours in ev'ry honest Way.

SCENE XIX.

MASKWELL *softly introduces Lord* TOUCHWOOD, *and retires.*

Mask. I have kept my Word, he's here, but I must not be seen.

SCENE XX.

Lady TOUCHWOOD, *Lord* TOUCHWOOD, MELLEFONT.

Ld. *Touch.* Hell and Amazement, she's in Tears.

L. *Touch.* (*Kneeling*) Eternal Blessings thank you——Ha! My Lord list'ning! O Fortune has o'erpaid me all, all! all's my own! [*Aside.*

Mel. Nay, I beseech you rise.

L. *Touch.* (*Aloud.*) Never, never! I'll grow to the Ground, be buried quick beneath it, e'er I'll be consenting to so damn'd a Sin as Incest! unnatural Incest!

Mel. Ha!

L. *Touch.* O cruel Man, will you not let me go——I'll forgive all that's past—O Heav'n, you will not ravish me!

Mel. Damnation!

Ld. *Touch.* Monster, Dog! your Life shall answer this——

[*Draws and runs at* Mellefont, *is held by Lady* Touchwood.

L. *Touch.* O Heav'ns my Lord! Hold, hold for Heav'ns sake.

Mel. Confusion, my Uncle! O the damn'd Sorceress.

L. *Touch.* Moderate your Rage, good my Lord! He's Mad, alas he's mad——Indeed he is my Lord, and knows not what he does—See how wild he looks.

Mel. By Heav'n 'twere senseless not to be mad, and see such Witchcraft.

L. *Touch.* My Lord, you hear him, he talks idly.

Ld. *Touch.* Hence from my Sight, thou living Infamy to my Name; when next I see that Face, I'll write Villain in't with my Sword's Point.

Mel. Now, by my Soul, I will not go 'till I have made known my Wrongs——Nay, 'till I have made known yours, which (if possible) are greater —though she has all the Host of Hell her Servants.

L. *Touch.* Alas he raves! Talks very Poetry! For Heav'ns sake away my Lord, he'll either tempt you to Extravagance, or commit some himself.

Mel. Death and Furies, will you not hear me——Why by Heav'n she laughs, grins, points to your Back; she forks out Cuckoldom with her Fingers, and you're running Horn-mad after your Fortune. [*As she is going she turns back and smiles at him.*

Ld. *Touch.* I fear he's mad indeed——Let's send *Maskwell* to him.

Mel. Send him to her.

L. *Touch.* Come, come, good my Lord, my Heart akes so, I shall faint if I stay.

SCENE XXI.

Mellefont *alone.*

Mel. O I could curse my Stars, Fate, and Chance; all Causes and Accidents of Fortune in this Life! But to what Purpose? Yet, 'sdeath, for a Man to have the Fruit of all his Industry grow full and ripe, ready to drop into his Mouth, and just when he holds out his Hand to gather it, to have a sudden Whirlwind come, tear up Tree and all, and bear away the very Root and Foundation of his Hopes; What Temper can contain? They talk of sending *Maskwell* to me; I never had more need of him—But what can he do? Imagination cannot form a fairer and more plausible Design than this of his which has miscarried——O my precious Aunt, I shall never thrive without I deal with the Devil, or another Woman.

Women like Flames have a destroying Pow'r,
Ne'er to be quench'd, 'till they themselves devour.

SCENE *shuts.*

ACT V. SCENE I.

Lady Touchwood *and* Maskwell.

Lady TOUCHWOOD.

Was't not lucky?

Mask. Lucky! Fortune is your own, and 'tis her Interest so to be; by Heav'n I believe you can controul her Pow'r, and she fears it; though Chance brought my Lord, 'twas your own Art that turn'd it to Advantage.

L. *Touch.* 'Tis true it might have been my Ruin—But yonder's my Lord, I believe he's coming to find you, I'll not be seen.

SCENE II.

MASKWELL, *alone.*

Mask. So; I durst not own my introducing my Lord, though it succeeded well for her, for she would have suspected a Design which I should have been puzzled to excuse. My Lord is thoughtful——I'll be so too; yet he shall know my Thoughts; or think he does—

SCENE III.

[*To him*] *Lord* TOUCHWOOD.

Mask. What have I done?

Ld. *Touch.* Talking to himself!

Mask. 'Twas honest——and shall I be rewarded for it? No, 'twas honest, therefore I shan't; ——Nay, rather therefore I ought not; for it rewards it self.

L. *Touch.* Unequall'd Virtue! [*Aside.*

Mask. But should it be known! then I have lost a Friend! He was an ill Man, and I have gain'd; for half my self I lent him, and that I have recall'd; so I have served my self, and what is yet better, I have served a worthy Lord to whom I owe my self. 13

Ld. *Touch.* Excellent Man! [*Aside.*

Mask. Yet I am wretched—O there is a Secret burns within this Breast, which should it once blaze forth, would ruin all, consume my honest Character, and brand me with the Name of Villain.

Ld. *Touch.* Ha! 19

Mask. Why do I love! Yet Heav'n and my waking Conscience are my Witnesses, I never gave one working Thought a Vent; which might discover that I lov'd, nor ever must; no, let it prey upon my Heart; for I would rather die, than seem once, barely seem, dishonest:—O, should it once be known I love fair *Cynthia*, all this that I have done would look like Rival's Malice, false Friendship to my Lord, and base Self-interest. Let me perish first, and from this Hour avoid all Sight and Speech, and, if I can, all Thought of that pernicious Beauty. Ha! But what is my Distraction doing? I am wildly talking to my self, and some ill Chance might have directed malicious Ears this way.

[*Seems to start, seeing my Lord.*

Ld. *Touch.* Start not—let guilty and dishonest Souls start at the Revelation of their Thoughts, but be thou fix'd, as is thy Virtue.

Mask. I am confounded and beg your Lordship's Pardon for those free Discourses which I have had with my self.

L. *Touch.* Come, I beg your Pardon that I overheard you, and yet it shall not need—Honest *Maskwell*! thy and my good Genius led me hither——Mine, in that I have discover'd so much manly Virtue; thine, in that thou shalt have due Reward of all thy Worth. Give me thy Hand——my Nephew is the alone remaining Branch of all our ancient Family; him I thus blow away, and constitute thee in his room to be my Heir——

Mask. Now Heav'n forbid——

Ld. *Touch.* No more—I have resolv'd—The Writings are ready drawn, and wanted nothing but to be sign'd, and have his Name inserted—Yours will fill the Blank as well—I will have no Reply—Let me command this time; for 'tis the last, in which I will assume Authority—hereafter, you shall rule where I have Power.

Mask. I humbly would Petition——

Ld. *Touch.* Is't for your self?—[Mask. *pauses.*] I'll hear of nought for any Body else.

Mask. Then Witness Heav'n for me, this Wealth and Honour was not of my seeking, nor would I build my Fortune on another's Ruin: I had but one Desire—

Ld. *Touch.* Thou shalt enjoy it——If all I'm worth in Wealth or Interest can purchase *Cynthia*, she is thine.—I'm sure Sir *Paul*'s Consent will follow Fortune; I'll quickly show him which way that is going.

Mask. You oppress me with Bounty; my Gratitude is weak, and shrinks beneath the Weight, and cannot rise to thank you—What, enjoy my Love! Forgive the Transports of a Blessing so unexpected, so unhop'd for, so unthought of!

Ld. *Touch.* I will confirm it, and rejoice with thee.

SCENE IV.

MASKWELL *alone.*

Mask. This is prosp'rous indeed——Why let him find me out a Villain, settled in Possession of a fair Estate, and full Fruition of my Love, I'll bear the Railings of a losing Gamester—But shou'd he find me out before! 'tis dangerous to delay—Let me think——shou'd my Lord proceed to treat openly of my Marriage with *Cynthia*, all must be discover'd, and *Mellefont* can be no longer blinded.——It must not be; nay, shou'd my Lady know it——ay, then were fine Work indeed! Her Fury wou'd spare nothing, tho' she involv'd her self in Ruin. No, it must be by Stratagem—I must deceive *Mellefont* once more, and get my Lord to consent to my private Management. He comes opportunely—Now will I, in my old way, discover the whole and real truth of the Matter to him, that he may not suspect one Word on't.

No Mask like open Truth to cover Lies,
As to go Naked is the best Disguise.

SCENE V.

[*To him*] MELLEFONT.

Mel. O *Maskwell*, what Hopes? I am confounded in a maze of Thoughts, each leading into one another, and all ending in Perplexity. My Uncle will not see, nor hear me.

Mask. No matter, Sir, don't trouble your Head, all's in my Power.

Mel. How? For Heav'ns sake?

Mask. Little do you think that your Aunt has kept her Word,——How the Devil she wrought my Lord into this Dotage, I know not; but he's gone to Sir *Paul* about my Marriage with *Cynthia*, and has appointed me his Heir.

Mel. The Devil he has! What's to be done?

Mask. I have it, it must be by Stratagem; for it's vain to make Application to him. I think I have that in my Head that cannot fail: Where's *Cynthia*?

Mel. In the Garden.

Mask. Let us go and consult her, my Life for yours, I cheat my Lord.

SCENE VI.

Lord TOUCHWOOD, *Lady* TOUCHWOOD.

L. *Touch. Maskwell* your Heir, and marry *Cynthia*!

Ld. *Touch.* I cannot do too much, for so much Merit.

L. *Touch.* But this is a thing of too great Moment to be so suddenly resolv'd. Why *Cynthia*? Why must he be marry'd? Is there not Reward enough in raising his low Fortune, but he must mix his Blood with mine, and wed my Niece? How know you that my Brother will consent, or she? Nay, he himself perhaps may have Affections otherwhere.

Ld. *Touch.* No, I am convinc'd he loves her.

L. *Touch. Maskwell* love *Cynthia*, impossible!

Ld. *Touch.* I tell you, he confess'd it to me.

L. *Touch.* Confusion! How's this! [*Aside.*

Ld. *Touch.* His Humility long stifled his Passion: And his love of *Mellefont* would have made him still conceal it.—But by Encouragement, I wrung the Secret from him; and know he's no way to be rewarded but in her. I'll defer my farther Proceedings in it, 'till you have consider'd it; but remember how we are both indebted to him.

SCENE VII.

Lady TOUCHWOOD *alone*.

L. *Touch*. Both indebted to him! Yes, we are both indebted to him, if you knew all, Villain! Oh, I am wild with this Surprize of Treachery: It is impossible, it cannot be.——He love *Cynthia*! What have I been Bawd to his Designs, his Property only, a baiting Place! Now I see what made him false to *Mellefont*,——Shame and Distraction! I cannot bear it, oh! what Woman can bear to be a Property? To be kindled to a Flame, only to light him to another's Arms; oh! that I were Fire indeed, that I might burn the vile Traitor. What shall I do? How shall I think? I cannot think,——All my Designs are lost, my Love unsated, my Revenge unfinish'd, and fresh cause of Fury from unthought of Plagues.

SCENE VIII.

[*To her*] *Sir* PAUL.

Sir *Paul*. Madam, Sister, my Lady Sister, did you see my Lady my Wife?

L. *Touch*. Oh! Torture!

Sir *Paul*. Gads-bud, I can't find her high nor low; where can she be, think you?

L. *Touch*. Where she's serving you, as all your Sex ought to be serv'd; making you a Beast. Don't you know that you're a Fool, Brother?

Sir *Paul*. A Fool; he, he, he, you're merry—No, no, not I, I know no such Matter.

L. *Touch*. Why then you don't know half your Happiness.

6 Property] Tool. Used in the same sense by Lady Wishfort in *The Way of the World*, v. I.

Sir *Paul*. That's a Jest with all my Heart, faith and troth,——But harkee, my Lord told me something of a Revolution of things; I don't know what to make on't,——Gads-bud I must consult my Wife,—he talks of disinheriting his Nephew; and I don't know what,——Look you, Sister, I must know what my Girl has to trust to; or not a Syllable of a Wedding, Gads-bud——to shew you that I am not a Fool.

L. *Touch*. Hear me; consent to the breaking off this Marriage, and the promoting any other, without consulting me, and I'll renounce all Blood, all Relation and Concern with you for ever,—nay, I'll be your Enemy, and pursue you to Destruction, I'll tear your Eyes out, and tread you under my Feet.——

Sir *Paul*. Why, what's the Matter now? Good Lord, what's all this for? Pooh, here's a Joke indeed——Why, where's my Wife?

L. *Touch*. With *Careless*, in the close Arbour; he may want you by this time, as much as you want her.

Sir *Paul*. O, if she be with Mr. *Careless*, 'tis well enough.

L. *Touch*. Fool, Sot, insensible Ox! But remember what I said to you, or you had better eat your own Horns, by this Light you had.

Sir *Paul*. You're a passionate Woman, Gads-bud,——But to say Truth, all our Family are Cholerick; I am the only peaceable Person amongst 'em.

SCENE IX.

Mellefont, Maskwell *and* Cynthia.

Mel. I know no other Way but this he has propos'd; if you have Love enough to run the Venture.

Cynt. I don't know whether I have Love enough,—but I find I have Obstinacy enough to pursue whatever I have once resolv'd; and a true Female Courage to oppose any thing that resists my Will, tho' 'twere Reason it self.

Mask. That's right,—Well, I'll secure the Writings, and run the Hazard along with you.

Cynt. But how can the Coach and Six Horses be got ready without Suspicion?

Mask. Leave it to my Care; that shall be so far from being suspected, that it shall be got ready by my Lord's own Order.

Mel. How?

Mask. Why, I intend to tell my Lord the whole Matter of our Contrivance, that's my way.

Mel. I don't understand you.

Mask. Why, I'll tell my Lord, I laid this Plot with you, on purpose to betray you; and that which put me upon it, was, the finding it impossible to gain the Lady any other way, but in the Hopes of her marrying you.—

Mel. So—

Mask. So, why so, while you're busied in making your self ready, I'll wheedle her into the Coach; and instead of you, borrow my Lord's Chaplain, and so run away with her my self.

Mel. O I conceive you, you'll tell him so?

Mask. Tell him so! ay; why you don't think I mean to do so?

Mel. No, no; ha, ha, I dare swear thou wilt not.

Mask. Therefore for our farther Security, I would have you disguis'd like a Parson that if my Lord should have Curiosity to peep, he may not discover you in the Coach, but think the Cheat is carried on as he would have it.

Mel. Excellent *Maskwell*! thou wert certainly meant for a Statesman or a Jesuite,—but thou art too honest for one, and too pious for the other.

Mask. Well, get your selves ready, and meet me in half an Hour, yonder in my Lady's Dressing-

41 Jesuite] A reference to the Popish Plot.

Room ; go by the back Stairs, and so we may slip down without being observ'd.—I'll send the Chaplain to you with his Robes ; I have made him my own,——and ordered him to meet us to Morrow Morning at St. *Albans* ; there we will sum up this Account, to all our Satisfactions.

Mel. Should I begin to thank or praise thee, I should waste the little time we have.

SCENE X.

CYNTHIA, MASKWELL.

Mask. Madam, you will be ready ?

Cynt. I will be punctual to the Minute. [*Going.*

Mask. Stay, I have a Doubt——Upon second Thoughts, we had better meet in the Chaplain's Chamber here, the corner Chamber at this end of the Gallery, there is a back way into it, so that you need not come through this Door—and a Pair of private Stairs leading down to the Stables——It will be more convenient.

Cynt. I am guided by you,—but *Mellefont* will mistake.

Mask. No, no, I'll after him immediately, and tell him.

Cynt. I will not fail.

SCENE XI.

MASKWELL *alone.*

Mask. Why, *qui vult decipi decipiatur.*—'Tis no Fault of mine, I have told 'em in plain Terms, how easie 'tis for me to cheat 'em ; and if they will not hear the Serpent's Hiss, they must be stung into Experience, and future Caution.—Now to prepare my Lord to consent to this.——But first I must instruct my little Levite ; there is no Plot, publick or private, that can expect to prosper without one of them has a Finger in't, he promised me to be within at this Hour,——Mr. *Saygrace*, Mr. *Saygrace*.

[*Goes to the Chamber Door, and knocks.*

SCENE XII.

Maskwell, Saygrace.

Mr. *Saygrace*, (*looking out.*) Sweet Sir, I will but pen the last Line of an Acrostick, and be with you in the twinkling of an Ejaculation, in the pronouncing of an *Amen*, or before you can——

Mask. Nay, good Mr. *Saygrace* do not prolong the Time, by describing to me the Shortness of your Stay; rather if you please, defer the finishing of your Wit, and let us talk about our Business, it shall be Tithes in your way.

Sayg. (*Enters*) You shall prevail, I would break off in the middle of a Sermon to do you a Pleasure.

Mask. You could not do me a greater,—except—the Business in hand—Have you provided a Habit for *Mellefont*?

Sayg. I have, they are ready in my Chamber, together with a clean starch'd Band and Cuffs.

Mask. Good, let them be carry'd to him,——have you stitched the Gown Sleeve, that he may be puzzled, and waste time in putting it on?

Sayg. I have; the Gown will not be indued without Perplexity.

Mask. Meet me in half an Hour, here in your own Chamber. When *Cynthia* comes, let there be no Light, and do not speak, that she may not distinguish you from *Mellefont*. I'll urge haste, to excuse your Silence.

Sayg. You have no more Commands?

Mask. None, your Text is short.

Sayg. But pithy, and I will handle it with Discretion.

Mask. It will be the first you have so serv'd.

SCENE XIII.

Lord TOUCHWOOD, MASKWELL.

Ld. *Touch.* Sure I was born to be controlled by those I should command: My very Slaves will shortly give me Rules how I shall govern them.

Mask. I am concern'd to see your Lordship discompos'd.—

Ld. *Touch.* Have you seen my Wife lately, or disoblig'd her?

Mask. No my Lord. What can this mean! [*Aside.*

Ld. *Touch.* Then *Mellefont* has urg'd some Body to incense her—Something she has heard of you which carries her beyond the Bounds of Patience.

Mask. This I fear'd. (*Aside.*) Did not your Lordship tell of the Honours you design'd me?

Ld. *Touch.* Yes.

Mask. 'Tis that; you know my Lady has a high Spirit, she thinks I am unworthy.

Ld. *Touch.* Unworthy! 'Tis an ignorant Pride in her to think so——Honesty to me is true Nobility. However, 'tis my Will it shall be so, and that shou'd be convincing to her as much as Reason——By Heav'n, I'll not be Wife-Ridden; were it possible, it shou'd be done this Night.

Mask. By Heav'n he meets my Wishes. (*Aside.*) Few Things are impossible to willing Minds.

Ld. *Touch.* Instruct me how this may be done, you shall see I want no Inclination.

Mask. I had laid a small Design for to Morrow (as Love will be inventing) which I thought to communicate to your Lordship—But it may be as well done to Night.

Ld. *Touch.* Here's company—Come this way, and tell me.

SCENE XIV.

Careless *and* Cynthia.

Care. Is not that he, now gone out with my Lord?

Cynt. Yes.

Care. By Heav'n there's Treachery—The Confusion that I saw your Father in, my Lady *Touchwood*'s Passion, with what imperfectly I overheard between my Lord and her, confirm me in my Fears. Where's *Mellefont*?

Cynt. Here he comes.

SCENE XV.

[*To them*] Mellefont.

Cynt. Did *Maskwell* tell you any thing of the Chaplain's Chamber?

Mel. No; my Dear, will you get ready——the Things are all in my Chamber; I want nothing but the Habit.

Care. You are betray'd, and *Maskwell* is the Villain I always thought him.

Cynt. When you were gone, he said his Mind was chang'd, and bid me meet him in the Chaplain's Room, pretending immediately to follow you, and give you Notice. 11

Mel. How!

Care. There's *Saygrace* tripping by with a Bundle under his Arm——He cannot be ignorant that *Maskwell* means to use his Chamber; let's follow and examine him.

Mel. 'Tis loss of Time——I cannot think him false.

SCENE XVI.

Cynthia, *Lord* Touchwood.

Cynt. My Lord musing!

Ld. *Touch.* He has a quick Invention, if this

were suddenly design'd—Yet he says he had prepar'd my Chaplain already.

Cynt. How's this! Now I fear indeed.

Ld. *Touch. Cynthia* here! Alone, fair Cousin, and melancholy?

Cynt. Your Lordship was thoughtful.

Ld. *Touch*. My Thoughts were on serious Business, not worth your hearing.

Cynt. Mine were on Treachery concerning you, and may be worth your hearing.

Ld. *Touch*. Treachery concerning me! pray be plain—Hark! What Noise!

Mask. (*within*.) Will you not hear me?

L. *Touch*. (*within*.) No, Monster! Traitor! No.

Cynt. My Lady and *Maskwell*! this may be lucky——My Lord, let me intreat you to stand behind this Skreen, and listen; perhaps this Chance may give you Proof of what you ne'er could have believ'd from my Suspicions.

SCENE XVII.

Lady TOUCHWOOD *with a Dagger*, MASKWELL: CYNTHIA *and Lord* TOUCHWOOD *abscond, listning*.

L. *Touch*. You want but Leisure to invent fresh Falshood, and sooth me to a fond Belief of all your Fictions; but I will stab the Lie that's forming in your Heart, and save a Sin, in pity to your Soul.

Mask. Strike then——Since you will have it so.

L. *Touch*. Ha! A steady Villain to the last!

Mask. Come, why do you dally with me thus?

L. *Touch*. Thy stubborn Temper shocks me, and you knew it would——this is Cunning all, and not Courage; no, I know thee well: But thou shalt miss thy Aim.

Mask. Ha, ha, ha.

L. *Touch*. Ha! Do you mock my Rage? Then this shall punish your fond, rash Contempt! Again Smile! [*Goes to strike*.

And such a Smile as speaks in Ambiguity! Ten thousand Meanings lurk in each Corner of that
various Face. 19
O! That they were written in thy Heart, That I, with this, might lay thee open to my Sight! But then 'twill be too late to know— Thou hast, thou hast found the only way to turn my Rage; Too well thou know'st my jealous Soul cou'd never bear Uncertainty. Speak then, and tell me—Yet are you silent? Oh, I am wilder'd in all Passions! But thus my Anger melts. (*Weeps*) Here, take this Ponyard, for my very Spirits faint, and I want Strength to hold it, thou hast disarm'd my Soul. [*Gives the Dagger*.

Ld. *Touch*. Amazement shakes me—Where will
this end? 32

Mask. So, 'tis well——let your wild Fury have a Vent; and when you have Temper, tell me.

L. *Touch*. Now, now, now I am calm, and can hear you.

Mask. (*Aside*.) Thanks, my Invention; and now I have it for you.——First tell me what urg'd you to this Violence? For your Passion broke in such imperfect Terms, that yet I am to
learn the Cause. 41

L. *Touch*. My Lord himself surpriz'd me with the News, you were to marry *Cynthia*—— That you had own'd your Love to him, and his Indulgence would assist you to attain your Ends.

Cynt. How, my Lord!

Ld. *Touch*. Pray forbear all Resentments for a
while, and let us hear the rest. 49

Mask. I grant you in Appearance all is true; I seem'd consenting to my Lord; nay, transported with the Blessing—But could you think that I, who had been happy in your lov'd Embraces, could e'er be fond of an inferior Slavery?

Ld. *Touch*. Ha! O Poison to my Ears! What do I hear!

Cynt. Nay, good my Lord, forbear Resentment, let us hear it out.

Ld. *Touch.* Yes, I will contain, tho' I cou'd burst.

Mask. I that had wanton'd in the rich Circle of your World of Love, cou'd be confin'd within the puny Province of a Girl? No—Yet tho' I dote on each last Favour more than all the rest; though I would give a Limb for every Look you cheaply throw on any other Object of your Love; yet so far I prize your Pleasures o'er my own, that all this seeming Plot that I have laid, has been to gratifie your Taste, and cheat the World, to prove a faithful Rogue to you.

L. *Touch.* If this were true—But how can it be?

Mask. I have so contriv'd, that *Mellefont* will presently, in the Chaplain's Habit, wait for *Cynthia* in your Dressing-Room: But I have put the Change upon her, that she may be otherwise employ'd——Do you procure her Night-Gown, and with your Hoods tyed over your Face, meet him in her stead; you may go privately by the back Stairs, and, unperceiv'd, there you may propose to reinstate him in his Uncle's Favour, if he'll comply with your Desires; his Case is desperate, and I believe he'll yield to any Conditions,——If not, here take this; you may employ it better, than in the Heart of one who is nothing when not yours. [*Gives the Dagger.*

L. *Touch.* Thou can'st deceive every Body,—— Nay, thou hast deceiv'd me; but 'tis as I would wish,—Trusty Villain! I could worship thee.——

Mask. No more.——it wants but a few Minutes of the time; and *Mellefont*'s Love will carry him there before his Hour.

L. *Touch.* I go, I fly, incomparable *Maskwell*!

SCENE XVIII.

MASKWELL, CYNTHIA, *Lord* TOUCHWOOD.

Mask. So, this was a Pinch indeed, my Invention was upon the Rack; and made Discovery of her last Plot: I hope *Cynthia* and my Chaplain will be ready, I'll prepare for the Expedition.

SCENE XIX.

CYNTHIA *and Lord* TOUCHWOOD.

Cynt. Now, my Lord?

Ld. *Touch.* Astonishment binds up my Rage! Villany upon Villany! Heav'ns, what a long Track of dark Deceit has this discover'd! I am confounded when I look back, and want a Clue to guide me through the various Mazes of unheard of Treachery. My Wife! Damnation! my Hell!

Cynt. My Lord, have Patience, and be sensible how great our Happiness is, that this Discovery was not made too late. 11

Ld. *Touch.* I thank you, yet it may be still too late, if we don't presently prevent the Execution of their Plots;—Ha, I'll do't. Where's *Mellefont*, my poor injur'd Nephew,————How shall I make him ample Satisfaction?——

Cynt. I dare answer for him. 17

Ld. *Touch.* I do him fresh Wrong to question his Forgiveness; for I know him to be all Goodness,——Yet my Wife! Damn her,——She'll think to meet him in that Dressing-Room;——Was't not so? And *Maskwell* will expect you in the Chaplain's Chamber,—For once, I'll add my Plot too,—let us haste to find out, and inform my Nephew; and do you, quickly as you can, bring all the Company into this Gallery.——I'll expose the Strumpet, and the Villain. 27

SCENE XX.

Lord FROTH *and Sir* PAUL.

Ld. *Froth*. By Heav'ns I have slept an Age,—— Sir *Paul*, what a Clock is't? Past Eight, on my Conscience, my Lady's is the most inviting Couch; and a Slumber there, is the prettiest Amusement! But where's all the Company?—

Sir *Paul*. The Company, gads-bud, I don't know, my Lord, but here's the strangest Revolution, all turn'd topsie turvy; as I hope for Providence.

Ld. *Froth*. O Heav'ns, what's the matter? Where's my Wife?

Sir *Paul*. All turn'd topsie turvy as sure as a Gun.

Ld. *Froth*. How do you mean? My Wife!

Sir *Paul*. The strangest Posture of Affairs!

Ld. *Froth*. What, my Wife?

Sir *Paul*. No, no, I mean the Family,——Your Lady's Affairs may be in a very good Posture; I saw her go into the Garden with Mr. *Brisk*.

Ld. *Froth*. How? where, when, what to do?

Sir *Paul*. I suppose they have been laying their Heads together.

Ld. *Froth*. How?

Sir *Paul*. Nay, only about Poetry, I suppose, my Lord; making Couplets.

Ld. *Froth*. Couplets!

Sir *Paul*. O, here they come.

SCENE XXI.

[*To them*] *Lady* FROTH, BRISK.

Brisk. My Lord, your humble Servant; Sir *Paul* yours,——the finest Night!

L. *Froth*. My Dear, Mr. *Brisk* and I have been Star-gazing, I don't know how long.

Sir *Paul*. Does it not tire your Ladyship? are you not weary with looking up?

L. *Froth*. Oh, no, I love it violently,——My Dear, you're melancholly.

Ld. *Froth*. No, my Dear; I'm but just awake.—

L. *Froth*. Snuff some of my Spirit of Hartshorn.

Ld. *Froth*. I've some of my own, thank you, my Dear. 12

L. *Froth*. Well, I swear, Mr. *Brisk*, you understood Astronomy like an old *Egyptian*.

Brisk. Not comparably to your Ladyship; you are the very *Cynthia* of the Skies, and Queen of Stars.

L. *Froth*. That's because I have no Light, but what's by Reflection from you, who are the Sun.

Brisk. Madam, you have Eclips'd me quite, let me perish,——I can't answer that. 21

L. *Froth*. No matter,——Hark'ee, shall you and I make an Almanack together?

Brisk. With all my Soul,—Your Ladyship has made me the Man in't already, I'm so full of the Wounds which you have given.

L. *Froth*. O finely taken! I swear now you are even with me, O *Parnassus*, you have an infinite deal of Wit.

Sir *Paul*. So he has, Gads-bud, and so has your Ladyship. 31

SCENE XXII.

[*To them*] *Lady* PLYANT, CARELESS, CYNTHIA.

L. *P*. You tell me most surprizing things; bless me, who would ever trust a Man? O my Heart akes for fear they should be all deceitful alike.

Care. You need not fear, Madam, you have Charms to fix Inconstancy it self.

L. *P*. O dear, you make me blush.

Ld. *Froth*. Come, my Dear, shall we take leave of my Lord and Lady?

Cynt. They'll wait upon your Lordship presently.

L. *Froth.* Mr. *Brisk,* my Coach shall set you down. 11

All. What's the matter?

[*A great Shriek from the Corner of the Stage.*

SCENE XXIII.

[*To them*] *Lady* TOUCHWOOD *runs out affrighted, my Lord after her, like a Parson.*

L. *Touch.* O I'm betray'd.——Save me, help me.

Ld. *Touch.* Now what Evasion, Strumpet?

L. *Touch.* Stand off, let me go.

Ld. *Touch.* Go, and thy own Infamy pursue thee.—You stare as you were all amazed,—I don't wonder at it,——but too soon you'll know mine, and that Woman's Shame.

SCENE *The Last.*

Lord TOUCHWOOD, *Lord* FROTH, *Lady* FROTH, *Lady* PLYANT, *Sir* PAUL, CYNTHIA, MELLEFONT, MASKWELL; MELLEFONT *disguised in a Parson's Habit and pulling in* MASKWELL.

Mel. Nay, by Heav'n you shall be seen.—*Careless,* your Hand;—Do you hold down your Head? Yes, I am your Chaplain, look in the Face of your injur'd Friend; thou Wonder of all Falshood.

Ld. *Touch.* Are you silent, Monster?

Mel. Good Heav'ns! How I believ'd and lov'd this Man!—Take him hence, for he's a Disease to my Sight.

Ld. *Touch.* Secure that manifold Villain.

[*Servants seize him.*

Care. Miracle of Ingratitude!

Brisk. This is all very surprizing, let me perish.

L. *Froth.* You know I told you *Saturn* look'd a little more angry than usual.

Ld. *Touch.* We'll think of Punishment at Leisure, but let me hasten to do Justice, in rewarding Virtue and wrong'd Innocence.——Nephew, I hope I have your Pardon, and *Cynthia*'s.

Mel. We are your Lordship's Creatures.

Ld. *Touch.* And be each other's Comfort ;——Let me join your Hands:——Unwearied Nights, and wishing Days attend you both ; mutual Love, lasting Health, and circling Joys, tread round each happy Year of your long Lives.

Let secret Villany from hence be warn'd ;
Howe'er in private Mischiefs are conceiv'd,
Torture and Shame attend their open Birth ;
Like Vipers in the Womb, base Treachery lies,
Still gnawing that, whence first it did arise ;
No sooner born, but the Vile Parent dies.

[*Exeunt Omnes.*

30 *dies*] Alluding to the Vulgar Error that 'Vipers force their way through the bowels of their dam'. (*Browne*, Book III, Chap. xvi.)

EPILOGUE,

Spoken by Mrs. *Mountford.*

Cou'd Poets but foresee how Plays would take,
Then they cou'd tell what Epilogues to make;
Whether to thank or blame their Audience most:
But that late Knowledge does much Hazard cost,
Till Dice are thrown, there's nothing won, nor lost.
So 'till the Thief has stoll'n, he cannot know
Whether he shall escape the Law, or no.
But Poets run much greater Hazards far,
Than they who stand their Trials at the Barr;
The Law provides a Curb for it's own Fury,
And suffers Judges to direct the Jury.
But in this Court, what Diff'rence does appear!
For every one's both Judge and Jury here;
Nay, and what's worse, an Executioner.
All have a Right and Title to some Part,
Each chusing that in which he has most Art.
The dreadful Men of Learning all Confound,
Unless the Fable's good, and Moral sound.
The Vizor-Masks, that are in Pit and Gallery,
Approve, or Damn, the Repartee and Rallery.
The Lady Criticks, who are better read,
Enquire if Characters are nicely bred;
If the soft things are penn'd and spoke with Grace:
They Judge of Action too, and Time, and Place;
In which we do not doubt but they're discerning,
For that's a kind of Assignation Learning.
Beaus judge of Dress; the Witlings judge of Songs;
The Cuckoldom, of Ancient Right, to Cits belongs.
Thus poor Poets, the Favour are deny'd,
Even to make Exceptions, when they're Try'd.
'Tis hard that they must ev'ry one admit:
Methinks I see some Faces in the Pit,
Which must of Consequence be Foes to Wit.
You who can Judge, to Sentence may proceed;
But tho' he cannot Write, let him be freed
At least from their Contempt, who cannot Read.

LOVE for *LOVE*:

A

COMEDY.

Nudus agris, nudus nummis paternis,
Insanire parat certa ratione modoque. Hor.

Printed in the YEAR, 1710.

To the Right Honourable

CHARLES

EARL of

Dorset and *Middlesex*,

Lord Chamberlain of His Majesty's Houshold, and Knight of the Most Noble Order of the Garter, &c.

MY LORD,

A Young Poet, is liable to the same Vanity and Indiscretion with a Young Lover; and the Great Man who smiles upon one, and the Fine Woman who looks kindly upon t'other, are both of 'em in Danger of having the Favour publish'd with the first Opportunity.

But there may be a different Motive, which will a little distinguish the Offenders. For tho' one shou'd have a Vanity in ruining another's Reputation, yet the other may only have an Ambition to advance his own. And I beg Leave, my Lord, that I may plead the latter, both as the Cause and Excuse of this Dedication.

Whoever is King, is also the Father of his Country; and as no body can dispute Your Lordship's *Monarchy* in *Poetry*; so all that are concern'd, ought to acknowledge Your Universal Patronage: And it is only presuming on the

Dedication] *Middlesex.* 'The grace of courts, the Muses' pride', a descendant of Sackville, the *great* poet of Induction to *The Mirror for Magistrates*. As Buckhurst he wrote the famous ballad 'To all you ladies now at land'. As Lord Chamberlain he was instrumental in licensing the Lincoln's Inn Fields theatre, which opened its career with this play. 'Universal patronage' was no idle compliment to the man who aided such enemies as Dryden and Shadwell.

Privilege of a Loyal Subject, that I have ventur'd to make this my Address of Thanks, to Your Lordship; which at the same Time, Includes a Prayer for Your Protection.

I am not Ignorant of the Common Form of Poetical Dedications, which are generally made up of Panegyricks, where the Authors endeavour to distinguish their Patrons, by the shining Characters they give them, above other Men. But that, my Lord, is not my Business at this time, nor is Your Lordship *now* to be distinguish'd. I am contented with the Honour I do my self in this Epistle; without the Vanity of attempting to add to, or explain Your Lordship's Character.

I confess it is not without some strugling, that I behave my self in this Case, as I ought: For it is very hard to be pleased with a Subject, and yet forbear it. But I chuse rather to follow *Pliny*'s Precept, than his Example, when in his Panegyrick to the Emperor *Trajan*, he says,

Nec minus considerabo quid aures ejus pati possint,
Quam quid virtutibus debeatur.

I hope I may be excus'd the Pedantry of a Quotation, when it is so justly apply'd. Here are some Lines in the Print, (and which your Lordship read before this Play was Acted) that were omitted on the Stage; and particularly one whole Scene in the Third Act, which not only helps the Design forward with less Precipitation, but also heightens the ridiculous Character of *Foresight*, which indeed seems to be maim'd without it. But I found my self in great Danger of a long Play, and was glad to help it where I could. Tho' not withstanding my Care, and the kind Reception it had from the Town; I could heartily wish it yet shorter: But the Number of Different Characters represented in it, would have been too much crowded in less room.

This Reflection on Prolixity, (a Fault, for which

scarce any one Beauty will atone) warns me not to be tedious now, and detain Your Lordhip any longer with the Trifles of,

MY LORD,

Your Lordship's Most

Obedient and Most

Humble Servant,

William Congreve.

PROLOGUE.

Spoken at the Opening of the New House, By Mr. *Betterton.*

The husbandman in vain renews his Toil,
To cultivate each Year a hungry Soil;
And fondly hopes for rich and generous Fruit,
When what should feed the Tree, devours the Root:
Th' unladen Boughs, he sees, bode certain Dearth,
Unless transplanted to more kindly Earth.
So, the poor Husbands of the Stage, who found
Their Labours lost upon ungrateful Ground,
This last and only Remedy have prov'd;
And hope new Fruit from ancient Stocks remov'd.
Well may they hope, when you so kindly aid,
Well plant a Soil which you so rich have made.
As Nature gave the World to Man's first Age,
So from your Bounty, we receive this Stage;
The Freedom Man was born to, you've restor'd,
And to our World, such Plenty you afford,
It seems like Eden, *fruitful of its own accord.*
But since in Paradise *frail Flesh gave way,*
And when but two were made, both went astray

Forbear your Wonder, and the Fault forgive,
If in our larger Family we grieve
One falling Adam, *and one tempted* Eve.
We who remain, would gratefully repay
What our Endeavours can, and bring, this Day,
The First-fruit Offering, of a Virgin Play.
We hope there's something that may please each Taste,
And tho' of Homely Fare we make the Feast,
Yet you will find Variety at least.
There's Humour, which for chearful Friends we got,
And for the thinking Party there's a Plot.
We've something too, to gratifie ill Nature,
(If there be any here) and that is Satire.
Tho' Satire scarce dares grin, 'tis grown so mild
Or only shews its Teeth, as if it smil'd.
As Asses Thistles, Poets mumble Wit,
And dare not bite, for fear of being bit.
They hold their Pens, as Swords are held by Fools,
And are afraid to use their own Edge-Tools.
Since the Plain-Dealer's *Scenes of Manly Rage,*
Not one has dar'd to lash this Crying Age.
This time, the Poet owns the bold Essay,
Yet hopes there's no Ill-manners in his Play :
And he declares by me, he has design'd
Affront to none, but frankly speaks his Mind.
And shou'd th' ensuing Scenes not chance to hit,
He offers but this one Excuse, 'twas writ
Before your late Encouragement of Wit.

39 Plain-Dealer's . . . *Manly*] A reference to Wycherley's play, and its hero, Manly, 1671.

Dramatis Personae.

MEN.

Sir *Sampson Legend*, Father to *Valentine* and *Ben*.	Mr. *Underhill*.
Valentine, Fallen under his Father's Displeasure by his expensive way of living, in Love with *Angelica*.	Mr. *Betterton*.
Scandal, His Friend, a free Speaker.	Mr. *Smith*.
Tattle, A half-witted Beau, vain of his Amours, yet valuing himself for Secresie.	Mr. *Boman*.
Ben, Sir *Sampson*'s younger Son, half home bred, and half Sea bred, design'd to marry Miss *Prue*.	Mr. *Dogget*.
Foresight, An illiterate old Fellow, peevish and positive, superstitious, and pretending to understand Astrology, Palmistry, Phisiognomy, Omens, Dreams, *&c.* Uncle to *Angelica*.	Mr. *Sanford*.
Jeremy, Servant to *Valentine*.	Mr. *Bowen*.
Trapland, A Scrivener.	Mr. *Triffusis*.
Buckram, A Lawyer.	Mr. *Freeman*.

WOMEN.

Angelica, Niece to *Foresight*, of a considerable Fortune in her own Hands.	Mrs. *Bracegirdle*.
Mrs. *Foresight*, Second Wife to *Foresight*.	Mrs. *Bowman*.
Mrs. *Frail*, Sister to Mrs. *Foresight*, a Woman of the Town.	Mrs. *Barry*.
Miss *Prue*, Daughter to *Foresight* by a former Wife, a silly awkward Country Girl.	Mrs. *Ayliff*.
Nurse to Miss.	Mrs. *Leigh*.
Jenny.	Mrs. *Lawson*.

A Steward, Officers, Sailers, and several Servants.

The SCENE *in* LONDON.

L O V E for *L O V E.*

ACT I. SCENE I.

Valentine *in his Chamber Reading.* Jeremy *waiting.*

Several Books upon the Table.

VALENTINE.

Jeremy.

Jere. Sir.

Val. Here, take away; I'll walk a turn, and digest what I have read——

Jere. You'll grow devilish fat upon this Paper Diet. [*Aside, and taking away the Books.*

Val. And d'ye hear, go you to Breakfast——There's a Page doubled down in *Epictetus*, that is a Feast for an Emperor.

Jere. Was *Epictetus* a real Cook, or did he only write Receipts?

Val. Read, read, Sirrah, and refine your Appetite; learn to live upon Instruction; feast your Mind, and mortifie your Flesh; Read, and take your Nourishment in at your Eyes; shut up your Mouth, and chew the Cud of Understanding. So *Epictetus* advises.

Jere. O Lord! I have heard much of him, when I waited upon a Gentleman at *Cambridge*: Pray what was that *Epictetus*?

Val. A very rich Man,—Not worth a Groat.

Jere. Humph, and so he has made a very fine Feast, where there is nothing to be eaten.

Val. Yes.

Jere. Sir, you're a Gentleman, and probably understand this fine feeding: But if you please,

I had rather be at Board-Wages. Does your *Epictetus*, or your *Seneca* here, or any of these poor rich Rogues, teach you how to pay your Debts without Mony? Will they shut up the Mouths of your Creditors? Will *Plato* be Bail for you? Or *Diogenes*, because he understands Confinement, and liv'd in a Tub, go to Prison for you? 'Slife, Sir, what do you mean, to mew your self up here with three or four musty Books, in Commendation of Starving and Poverty?

Val. Why, Sirrah, I have no Mony, you know it; and therefore resolve to rail at all that have: And in that I but follow the Examples of the wisest and wittiest Men in all Ages; these Poets and Philosophers whom you naturally hate, for just such another Reason; because they abound in Sense, and you are a Fool.

Jere. Ay, Sir, I am a Fool, I know it: And yet, Heav'n help me, I'm poor enough to be a Wit—— But I was always a Fool, when I told you what your Expenses would bring you to; your Coaches and your Liveries; your Treats and your Balls; your being in Love with a Lady, that did not care a Farthing for you in your Prosperity; and keeping Company with Wits, that car'd for nothing but your Prosperity; and now when you are poor, hate you as much as they do one another.

Val. Well; and now I am poor, I have an Opportunity to be reveng'd on them all; I'll pursue *Angelica* with more Love than ever, and appear more notoriously her Admirer in this Restraint, than when I openly rival'd the rich Fops, that made Court to her; so shall my Poverty be a Mortification to her Pride, and perhaps, make her compassionate the Love, which has principally reduc'd me to this Lowness of Fortune. And for the Wits, I'm sure I am in a Condition to be even with them——

Jere. Nay, your Condition is pretty even with theirs, that's the truth on't.

Val. I'll take some of their Trade out of their Hands.

Jere. Now Heav'n of Mercy continue the Tax upon Paper; you don't mean to write!

Val. Yes, I do; I'll write a Play.

Jere. Hem!——Sir, if you please to give me a small Certificate of three Lines——only to certifie those whom it may concern; That the Bearer hereof, *Jeremy Fetch* by Name, has for the Space of sev'n Years truly and faithfully serv'd *Valentine Legend*, Esq; and that he is not now turn'd away for any Misdemeanour; but does voluntarily dismiss his Master from any future Authority over him—

Val. No, Sirrah, you shall live with me still.

Jere. Sir, it's impossible—I may die with you, starve with you, or be damn'd with your Works: But to live, even three Days, the Life of a Play, I no more expect it, than to be canoniz'd for a Muse, after my Decease.

Val. You are witty, you Rogue, I shall want your Help;——I'll have you learn to make Couplets, to tag the ends of Acts: D'ye hear, get the Maids to Crambo in an Evening, and learn the knack of Rhiming, you may arrive at the height of a Song, sent by an unknown Hand, or a Chocolate-House Lampoon.

Jere. But Sir, is this the way to recover your Father's Favour? Why Sir *Sampson* will be irreconcilable. If your younger Brother shou'd come from Sea, he'd never look upon you again. You're undone, Sir; you're ruin'd; you won't have a Friend left in the World, if you turn Poet. ——Ah Pox confound that *Will*'s Coffee-House, it

84 Play] The third day was the author's benefit; thus even the worst play would be made to last out that length, if anyways possible.

100 *Will*'s] Where Dryden reigned. It 'was situated at No. 1 Bow Street, at the corner of Russell Street, and was called after its proprietor, William Urwin. It was frequented at this date by gamblers as well as wits' (Ewald).

has ruin'd more young Men than the *Royal Oak* Lottery—Nothing thrives that belongs to't. The Man of the House would have been an Alderman by this time with half the Trade, if he had set up in the City——For my part, I never sit at the Door, that I don't get double the Stomach that I do at a Horse Race. The Air upon *Banstead-Downs* is nothing to it for a Whetter; yet I never see it, but the Spirit of Famine appears to me, sometimes like a decay'd Porter, worn out with Pimping, and carrying *Billet doux* and Songs; not like other Porters for Hire, but for the Jests sake. Now like a thin Chairman, melted down to half his Proportion, with carrying a Poet upon Tick, to visit some great Fortune; and his Fare to be paid him like the Wages of Sin, either at the Day of Marriage, or the Day of Death.

Val. Very well, Sir; can you proceed?

Jere. Sometimes like a bilk'd Bookseller, with a meagre terrify'd Countenance, that looks as if he had written for himself, or were resolv'd to turn Author, and bring the rest of his Brethren into the same Condition. And lastly, in the Form of a worn-out Punk, with Verses in her Hand, which her Vanity had prefer'd to Settlementts, without a whole Tatter to her Tail, but as ragged as one of the Muses; or as if she were carrying her Linnen to the Paper-Mill, to be converted into Folio Books, of Warning to all young Maids, not to prefer Poetry to good Sense; or lying in the Arms of a needy Wit, before the Embraces of a wealthy Fool.

101 *Royal Oak* Lottery] the only one not afterwards prohibited by the law of 1698. It was for the benefit of the Royal Fishing Company.

107 *Banstead-Downs*] In the close neighbourhood of Epsom Downs.

SCENE II.

VALENTINE, SCANDAL, JEREMY.

Scan. What, *Jeremy* holding forth?

Val. The Rogue has (with all the Wit he could muster up) been declaiming against Wit.

Scan. Ay? Why then I'm afraid *Jeremy* has Wit: For where-ever it is, it's always contriving its own Ruin.

Jere. Why so I have been telling my Master, Sir: Mr. *Scandal*, for Heav'ns sake, Sir, try if you can disswade him from turning Poet.

Scan. Poet! He shall turn Soldier first, and rather depend upon the Out-side of his Head, than the Lining. Why, what the Devil has not your Poverty made you Enemies enough? Must you needs shew your Wit to get more?

Jere. Ay, more indeed: for who cares for any Body that has more Wit than himself?

Scan. Jeremy speaks like an Oracle. Don't you see how worthless great Men, and dull rich Rogues, avoid a witty Man of small Fortune? Why, he looks like a Writ of Enquiry into their Titles and Estates; and seems Commission'd by Heaven to seize the better half.

Val. Therefore I would rail in my Writings, and be reveng'd.

Scan. Rail? At whom? the whole World? Impotent and vain! Who would die a Martyr to Sense in a Country where the Religion is Folly? You may stand at Bay for a while; but when the full Cry is against you, you shan't have fair play for your Life. If you can't be fairly run down by the Hounds, you will be treacherously shot by the Huntsmen.—No, turn Pimp, Flatterer, Quack, Lawyer, Parson, be Chaplain to an Atheist, or Stallion to an old Woman, any thing but Poet; a Modern Poet is worse, more servile, timorous, and fawning, than any I have nam'd: Without you could retrieve the Ancient Honours of the Name, recall the Stage of *Athens*, and be allow'd the Force of open honest Satire.

Val. You are as inveterate against our Poets, as if your Character had been lately expos'd upon the Stage.——Nay, I am not violently bent upon the Trade.——[*One Knocks.*] *Jeremy*, see who's there. [Jer. *goes to the Door.*] But tell me what you would have me do?——What do the World say of me, and my forc'd Confinement?

Scan. The World behaves it self, as it uses to do on such Occasions; some pity you, and condemn your Father: Others excuse him, and blame you; only the Ladies are merciful, and wish you well: since Love and Pleasurable Expence, have been your greatest Faults.

Val. How now?

Jere. Nothing new, Sir; I have dispatch'd some half a Dozen Duns with as much Dexterity, as a hungry Judge does Causes at Dinner-time.

Val. What Answer have you giv'n 'em?

Scan. Patience, I suppose, the old Receipt.

Jere. No, faith Sir; I have put 'em off so long with Patience and Forbearance, and other fair Words; that I was forc'd now to tell 'em in plain downright *English*——

Val. What?

Jere. That they should be paid.

Val. When?

Jere. To Morrow.

Val. And how the Devil do you mean to keep your Word?

Jere. Keep it? Not at all; it has been so very much stretch'd, that I reckon it will break of course by to Morrow, and no body be surpriz'd at the Matter—— [*Knocking.*]—Again! Sir, if you don't like my Negotiation, will you be pleas'd to answer these your self.

Val. See who they are.

SCENE III.

VALENTINE, SCANDAL.

By this, *Scandal*, you may see what it is to be great; Secretaries of State, Presidents of the Council, and Generals of an Army lead just such a Life as I do; have just such Crowds of Visitants in a Morning, all soliciting of past Promises; which are but a civiller sort of Duns, that lay claim to voluntary Debts.

Scan. And you, like a true great Man, having engaged their Attendance, and promis'd more than ever you intended to perform; are more perplex'd to find Evasions, than you would be to invent the honest Means of keeping your Word, and gratifying your Creditors.

Val. Scandal, learn to spare your Friends, and do not provoke your Enemies; this Liberty of your Tongue, will one Day bring a Confinement on your Body, my Friend.

SCENE IV.

VALENTINE, SCANDAL, JEREMY.

Jere. O Sir, there's *Trapland*, the Scrivener, with two suspicious Fellows like lawful Pads, that would knock a Man down with Pocket-Tipstaves,—And there's your Father's Steward, and the Nurse with one of your Children from *Twitnam*.

Val. Pox on her, cou'd she find no other time to fling my Sins in my Face: Here, give her this, [*Gives Mony*.] and bid her trouble me no more; a thoughtless two handed Whore, she knows my Condition well enough, and might have overlaid the Child a Fortnight ago, if she had had any forecast in her.

Scan. What, is it bouncing *Margery*, with my Godson?

5 *Twitnam*] Twickenham.

Jere. Yes, Sir.

Scan. My blessing to the Boy, with this Token [*Gives Mony.*] of my Love. And d'ye hear, bid *Margery* put more Flocks in her Bed, shift twice a Week, and not work so hard, that she may not smell so vigorously.——I shall take the Air shortly.

Val. *Scandal*, don't spoil my Boy's Milk :—— Bid *Trapland* come in. If I can give that *Cerberus* a Sop, I shall be at rest for one Day.

SCENE V.

VALENTINE, SCANDAL, TRAPLAND, JEREMY.

Val. O Mr. *Trapland*! my old Friend! Welcome. *Jeremy*, a Chair quickly : A Bottle of Sack and a Toast—fly—a Chair first.

Trap. A good Morning to you Mr. *Valentine*, and to you Mr. *Scandal*.

Scan. The Morning's a very good Morning, if you don't spoil it.

Val. Come sit you down, you know his way.

Trap. sits.] There is a Debt, Mr. *Valentine*, of 1500*l*. of pretty long standing——

Val. I cannot talk about Business with a thirsty Palate.——Sirrah, the Sack.

Trap. And I desire to know what Course you have taken for the Payment ?

Val. Faith and Troth, I am heartily glad to see you,——my Service to you,—fill, fill, to honest Mr. *Trapland*, fuller.

Trap. Hold, Sweet-heart.——This is not to our Business :——my Service to you Mr. *Scandal*— [*Drinks*]—I have forborn as long—

Val. T'other Glass, and then we'll talk. Fill, *Jeremy*.

Trap. No more, in truth.—I have forborn, I say—

Val. Sirrah, fill when I bid you.——And how

does your handsome Daughter ?——Come, a good Husband to her. [*Drinks.*

Trap. Thank you——I have been out of this Mony——

Val. Drink first. *Scandal*, why do you not drink ? [*They drink.*

Trap. And in short, I can be put off no longer.

Val. I was much oblig'd to you for your Supply : It did me Signal Service in my Necessity. But you delight in doing good.—*Scandal*, drink to me, my Friend *Trapland*'s Health. An honester Man lives not, nor one more ready to serve his Friend in Distress : Tho' I say it to his Face. Come, fill each Man his Glass.

Scan. What, I know *Trapland* has been a Whoremaster, and loves a Wench still. You never knew a Whoremaster, that was not an honest Fellow.

Trap. Fie, Mr. *Scandal*, you never knew——

Scan. What don't I know ?——I know the Buxom black Widow in the *Poultry*——800*l.* a Year Jointure, and 20000*l.* in Mony. Ahah ! Old *Trap*.

Val. Say you so, i'faith : Come, we'll remember the Widow : I know whereabouts you are ; Come, to the Widow—

Trap. No more indeed.

Val. What, the Widow's Health ; give it him—off with it : [*They drink.* A lovely Girl, I'faith, black sparkling Eyes, soft pouting Ruby-Lips ? better sealing there, than a Bond for a Million, hah !

Trap. No, no, there's no such thing, we'd better mind our Business—You're a Wag.

Val. No faith, we'll mind the Widow's Business, fill again——Pretty round heaving Breasts,—a *Barbary* Shape, and a Jut with her Bum, would stir an *Anchoret* : And the prettiest Foot ! Oh if a Man could but fasten his Eyes to her Feet, as they steal in and out, and play at Bo-peep under her Petticoats, ah ! Mr. *Trapland* ?

Trap. Verily, give me a Glass,—you're a Wag, ——and here's to the Widow. [*Drinks*.

Scan. He begins to Chuckle;——ply him close, or he'll relapse into a Dun.

SCENE VI.

[*To them*] OFFICER.

Offi. By your Leave, Gentlemen,——Mr. *Trapland*, if we must do our Office, tell us.—We have half a dozen Gentlemen to arrest in *Pall-Mall* and *Covent-Garden*; and if we don't make haste, the Chairmen will be abroad, and block up the Chocolate-Houses, and then our Labour's lost.

Trap. Udso that's true, Mr. *Valentine* I love Mirth, but Business must be done, are you ready to——

Jere. Sir, your Father's Steward says he comes to make Proposals concerning your Debts.

Val. Bid him come in: Mr. *Trapland*, send away your Officer, you shall have an Answer presently.

Trap. Mr. *Snap* stay within Call.

SCENE VII.

VALENTINE, SCANDAL, TRAPLAND, JEREMY, STEWARD *who whispers* VALENTINE.

Scan. Here's a Dog now, a Traitor in his Wine, Sirrah refund the Sack: *Jeremy* fetch him some warm Water, or I'll rip up his Stomach, and go the shortest way to his Conscience.

Trap. Mr. *Scandal*, you are uncivil; I did not value your Sack; but you cannot expect it again, when I have drunk it.

Scan. And how do you expect to have your Mony again, when a Gentleman has spent it?

Val. You need say no more, I understand the Conditions; they are very hard, but my Necessity is very pressing: I agree to 'em. Take Mr. *Trapland* with you, and let him draw the Writing— Mr. *Trapland*, you know this Man, he shall satisfie you.

Trap. Sincerely, I am loth to be thus pressing, but my Necessity—

Val. No Apology, good Mr. Scrivener, you shall be paid.

Trap. I hope you forgive me, my Business requires— 21

SCENE VIII.

Valentine, Scandal.

Scan. He begs Pardon like a Hangman at an Execution.

Val. But I have got a Reprieve.

Scan. I am surpriz'd; what does your Father relent?

Val. No; He has sent me the hardest Conditions in the World: You have heard of a Booby-Brother of mine, that was sent to Sea three Years ago? This Brother, my Father hears is landed; whereupon he very affectionately sends me Word; If I will make a Deed of Conveyance of my Right to his Estate after his Death, to my younger Brother, he will immediately furnish me with four thousand Pound to pay my Debts, and make my Fortune. This was once propos'd before, and I refus'd it; but the present Impatience of my Creditors for their Mony, and my own Impatience of Confinement, and Absence from *Angelica*, force me to consent. 19

Scan. A very desperate Demonstration of your Love to *Angelica*: And I think she has never given you any Assurance of hers.

Val. You know her Temper; she never gave me any great Reason either for Hope or Despair.

Scan. Women of her airy Temper, as they seldom think before they act, so they rarely give us any Light to guess at what they mean: But you have little Reason to believe that a Woman of this Age, who has had an Indifference for you in your Prosperity, will fall in Love with your ill Fortune; besides, *Angelica* has a great Fortune of her own; and great Fortunes either expect another great Fortune, or a Fool. 33

SCENE IX.

[*To them*] JEREMY.

Jere. More Misfortunes, Sir.

Val. What, another Dun?

Jere. No, Sir, but Mr. *Tattle* is come to wait upon you.

Val. Well, I can't help it,—you must bring him up; he knows I don't go abroad.

SCENE X.

VALENTINE, SCANDAL.

Scan. Pox on him, I'll be gone.

Val. No, prithee stay: *Tattle* and you should never be asunder; you are Light and Shadow, and shew one another; he is perfectly thy Reverse both in Humour and Understanding; and as you set up for Defamation, he is a mender of Reputations. 7

Scan. A mender of Reputations! ay, just as he is a keeper of Secrets, another Virtue that he sets up for in the same manner. For the Rogue will speak aloud in the Posture of a Whisper; and deny a Woman's Name, while he gives you the Marks of her Person: He will forswear receiving a Letter from her, and at the same time, shew you her Hand in the Superscription: And yet perhaps he has counterfeited the Hand too, and sworn to a Truth; but he hopes not to be believ'd; and refuses the Reputation of a Lady's Favour, as a Doctor says, No, to a Bishoprick, only that it may be granted him.—In short, he is a publick Professor of Secresie, and makes Proclamation that he holds private Intelligence——He's here.

SCENE XI.

[*To them*] TATTLE.

Tatt. Valentine good Morrow, *Scandal* I am Yours,——That is, when you speak well of me.

Scan. That is, when I am yours; for while I am my own, or any Body's else, that will never happen.

Tatt. How Inhuman!

Val. Why *Tattle*, you need not be much concern'd at anything that he says; For to converse with *Scandal*, is to play at *Losing Loadum*; you must lose a good Name to him, before you can win it for your self.

Tatt. But how barbarous that is, and how unfortunate for him, that the World shall think the better of any Person for his Calumniation! ——I thank Heav'n, it has always been a part of my Character, to handle the Reputations of others very tenderly indeed.

Scan. Ay, such rotten Reputations as you have to deal with, are to be handl'd tenderly indeed.

Tatt. Nay, but why rotten? Why should you say rotten, when you know not the Persons of whom you speak? How cruel that is?

Scan. Not know 'em? Why, thou never hadst to do with any body that did not stink to all the Town.

Tatt. Ha, ha, ha; nay, now you make a Jest of it indeed. For there is nothing more known, than that no body knows any thing of that Nature of me: As I hope to be sav'd, *Valentine*, I never expos'd a Woman, since I knew what Woman was.

Val. And yet you have convers'd with several.

Tatt. To be free with you, I have—I don't care if I own that——Nay more (I'm going to say a bold Word now) I never could meddle with a Woman, that had to do with any Body else.

Scan. How!

Val. Nay faith, I'm apt to believe him——Except her Husband, *Tattle.*

Tatt. Oh that——

Scan. What think you of that Noble Commoner, Mrs. *Drab*?

Tatt. Pooh, I know Madam *Drab* has made her Brags in three or four Places, that I said this and that, and writ to her, and did I know not what——But, upon my Reputation, she did me wrong——Well, well, that was Malice——But I know the bottom of it. She was brib'd to that by one we all know—A Man too. Only to bring me into Disgrace with a certain Woman of Quality—

Scan. Whom we all know.

Tatt. No matter for that—Yes, yes, every body knows——No doubt on't, every body knows my Secrets——But I soon satisfy'd the Lady of my Innocence; for I told her——Madam, says I, there are some Persons, who make it their Business to tell Stories, and say this and that of one and t'other, and every thing in the World; and, says I, if your Grace—

Scan. Grace!

Tatt. O Lord, what have I said? My unlucky Tongue!

Val. Ha, ha, ha.

Scan. Why, *Tattle*, thou hast more Impudence than one can in Reason expect: I shall have an Esteem for thee, well, and ha, ha, ha, well, go on, and what did you say to her Grace?

Val. I confess this is something extraordinary.

Tatt. Not a Word, as I hope to be sav'd; an errant *Lapsus Linguæ*—Come, let's talk of something else.

Val. Well, but how did you acquit your self?

Tatt. Pooh, pooh, nothing at all, I only rally'd with you—a Woman of ordinary Rank was a little jealous of me, and I told her something or other, faith——I know not what——Come, let's talk of something else.

[*Hums a Song.*

Scan. Hang him, let him alone, he has a Mind we should enquire.

Tatt. *Valentine*, I Supp'd last Night with your Mistress, and her Uncle Old *Foresight*: I think your Father lies at *Foresight*'s.

Val. Yes.

Tatt. Upon my Soul *Angelica*'s a fine Woman—And so is Mrs. *Foresight*, and her Sister Mrs. *Frail*.

Scan. Yes, Mrs. *Frail* is a very fine Woman, we all know her.

Tatt. Oh that is not fair.

Scan. What?

Tatt. To tell.

Scan. To tell what? Why, what do you know of Mrs. *Frail*?

Tatt. Who I? Upon Honour I don't know whether she be Man or Woman; but by the Smoothness of her Chin, and Roundness of her Hips.

Scan. No!

Tatt. No.

Scan. She says otherwise.

Tatt. Impossible!

Scan. Yes Faith. Ask *Valentine* else.

Tatt. Why then, as I hope to be sav'd, I believe a Woman only obliges a Man to Secresie, that she may have the Pleasure of telling her self.

Scan. No doubt on't. Well, but has she done you Wrong, or no? You have had her? Ha?

Tatt. Tho' I have more Honour than to tell first; I have more Manners than to contradict what a Lady has declar'd.

Scan. Well, you own it?

Tatt. I am strangely surpriz'd! Yes, yes, I can't deny't, if she taxes me with it.

Scan. She'll be here by and by, she sees *Valentine* every Morning.

Tatt. How!

Val. She does me the Favour——I mean of a Visit sometimes.

I did not think she had granted more to any body.

Scan. Nor I faith——But *Tattle* does not use to bely a Lady; it is contrary to his Character——How one may be deceiv'd in a Woman, *Valentine*?

Tatt. Nay, what do you mean, Gentlemen?

Scan. I'm resolv'd I'll ask her.

Tatt. O barbarous! Why did you not tell me——

Scan. No, you told us.

Tatt. And bid me ask *Valentine*?

Val. What did I say? I hope you won't bring me to confess an Answer, when you never ask'd me the Question?

Tatt. But, Gentlemen, this is the most inhuman Proceeding——

Val. Nay, if you have known *Scandal* thus long, and cannot avoid such a palpable Decoy as this was; the Ladies have a fine time, whose Reputations are in your keeping.

SCENE XII.

[*To them*] JEREMY.

Jere. Sir, Mrs. *Frail* has sent to know if you are stirring.

Val. Shew her up when she comes.

SCENE XIII.

VALENTINE, SCANDAL, TATTLE.

Tatt. I'll be gone.

Val. You'll meet her.

Tatt. Is there not a back way?

Val. If there were, you have more Discretion, than to give *Scandal* such an Advantage; why, your running away will prove all that he can tell her.

Tatt. Scandal, you will not be so ungenerous—— O, I shall lose my Reputation of Secresie for ever ——I shall never be receiv'd but upon Publick Days; and my Visits will never be admitted beyond a drawing-Room: I shall never see a Bed-Chamber again, never be lock'd in a Closet, nor run behind a Screen, or under a Table; never be distinguish'd among the Waiting-Women by the Name of Trusty Mr. *Tattle* more——You will not be so cruel.

Val. Scandal, have pity on him; he'll yield to any Conditions.

Tatt. Any, any Terms.

Scan. Come then, sacrifice half a Dozen Women of good Reputation to me presently——Come, where are you familiar?——And see that they are Women of Quality too, the first Quality—

Tatt. 'Tis very hard——Won't a Baronet's Lady pass?

Scan. No, nothing under a Right Honourable.

Tatt. O inhuman! You don't expect their Names.

Scan. No, their Titles shall serve.

Tatt. Alas, that's the same thing: Pray spare me their Titles; I'll describe their Persons.

Scan. Well, begin then: But take notice, if you are so ill a Painter, that I cannot know the Person by your Picture of her, you must be condemn'd, like other bad Painters, to write the Name at the Bottom.

Tatt. Well, first then——

SCENE XIV.

[*To them*] *Mrs.* FRAIL.

Tatt. O unfortunate! she's come already; will you have Patience 'till another time——I'll double the Number.

Scan. Well, on that Condition—Take heed you don't fail me.

Mrs. *Frail.* I shall get a fine Reputation, by coming to see Fellows in a Morning. *Scandal*, you Devil, are you here too? Oh Mr. *Tattle*, every thing is safe with you, we know.

Scan. Tattle.

Tatt. Mum——O Madam, you do me too much Honour.

Val. Well Lady Galloper, how does *Angelica*?

Mrs. *Frail. Angelica*? Manners!

Val. What, you will allow an absent Lover——

Mrs. *Frail.* No, I'll allow a Lover present with his Mistress to be particular—But otherwise I think his Passion ought to give place to his Manners.

Val. But what if he has more Passion than Manners?

Mrs. *Frail.* Then let him marry and reform.

Val. Marriage indeed may qualifie the Fury of his Passion, but it very rarely mends a Man's Manners.

Mrs. *Frail.* You are the most mistaken in the World; there is no Creature perfectly civil, but a Husband. For in a little time he grows only rude to his Wife, and that is the highest good Breeding, for it begets his Civility to other People. Well, I'll tell you News; but I suppose you hear your Brother *Benjamin* is landed. And my Brother *Foresight*'s Daughter is come out of the Country——I assure you, there's a Match talk'd of by the old People——Well, if he be but as great a Sea-Beast, as she is a Land-Monster, we shall have a most amphibious Breed——The Progeny will be all Otters: He has been bred at Sea, and she has never been out of the Country.

Val. Pox take 'em, their Conjunction bodes me no good, I'm sure. 41

Mrs. *Frail.* Now you talk of Conjunction, my Brother *Foresight* has cast both their Nativities, and Prognosticates an Admiral and an eminent Justice of the Peace to be the Issue-Male of their two Bodies; 'tis the most superstitious old Fool! He would have perswaded me, that this was an unlucky Day, and wou'd not let me come abroad: But I invented a Dream, and sent him to *Artimedorus* for Interpretation, and so stole out to see you. Well, and what will you give me now? Come, I must have something. 52

Val. Step into the next Room——and I'll give you something.

Scan. Ay, we'll all give you something.

Mrs. *Frail.* Well, what will you all give me?

Val. Mine's a Secret.

Mrs. *Frail.* I thought you would give me something, that would be a Trouble to you to keep.

Val. And *Scandal* shall give you a good Name.

Mrs. *Frail.* That's more than he has for himself. And what will you give me, Mr. *Tattle*? 62

Tatt. I? My Soul, Madam.

Mrs. *Frail.* Pooh, No I thank you, I have enough to do to take care of my own. Well; but I'll come and see you one of these Mornings: I hear you have a great many Pictures.

Tatt. I have a pretty good Collection at your Service, some Originals. 69

Scan. Hang him, he has nothing but the *Seasons* and the *Twelve Cæsars*, paultry Copies; and the *Five Senses*, as ill represented as they are in himself; and he himself is the only Original you will see there.

Mrs. *Frail.* Ay, but I hear he has a Closet of Beauties.

Scan. Yes, all that have done him Favours, if you will believe him.

Mrs. *Frail.* Ay, let me see those, Mr. *Tattle.*

Tatt. Oh Madam, those are sacred to Love and Contemplation. No Man but the Painter and my self was ever blest with the Sight.

Mrs. *Frail.* Well, but a Woman——

Tatt. Nor Woman, 'till she consented to have her Picture there too——for then she's oblig'd to keep the Secret.

Scan. No, no; come to me if you'd see Pictures.

Mrs. *Frail.* You?

Scan. Yes Faith, I can shew you your own Picture, and most of your Acquaintance to the Life, and as like as at *Kneller*'s.

Mrs. *Frail.* O lying Creature—*Valentine*, does not he lye?——I can't believe a Word he says.

Val. No indeed, he speaks truth now: For as *Tattle* has Pictures of all that have granted him Favours, he has the Pictures of all that have refus'd him: If Satires, Descriptions, Characters, and Lampoons are Pictures.

Scan. Yes, mine are most in black and white.—And yet there are some set out in their true Colours, both Men and Women. I can shew you Pride, Folly, Affectation, Wantonness, Inconstancy, Covetousness, Dissimulation, Malice and Ignorance, all in one Piece. Then I can shew you Lying, Foppery, Vanity, Cowardice, Bragging, Lechery, Impotence and Ugliness in another Piece; and yet one of these is a celebrated Beauty, and t'other a profest Beau. I have Paintings too, some pleasant enough.

Mrs. *Frail.* Come, let's hear 'em.

Scan. Why, I have a Beau in a Bagnio, Cupping for a Complexion, and sweating for a Shape.

Mrs. *Frail.* So.

Scan. Then I have a Lady burning Brandy in a Cellar with a Hackney Coachman.

Mrs. *Frail.* O Devil! Well, but that Story is not true.

Scan. I have some Hieroglyphicks too; I have a Lawyer with a hundred Hands, two Heads, and but one Face; a Divine with two Faces, and one Head; and I have a Soldier with his Brains in his Belly, and his Heart where his Head shou'd be.

Mrs. *Frail*. And no Head?

Scan. No Head.

Mrs. *Frail*. Pooh, this is all Invention. Have you ne'er a Poet?

Scan. Yes, I have a Poet weighing Words, and selling Praise for Praise, and a Critick picking his Pocket. I have another large Piece too, representing a School; where there are huge Proportion'd Criticks, with long Wiggs, Lac'd Coats, *Steinkirk* Cravats, and terrible Faces; with Cat-calls in their Hands, and Horn-Books about their Necks. I have many more of this kind, very well painted, as you shall see.

Mrs. *Frail*. Well, I'll come, if it be but to disprove you.

SCENE XV.

[*To them*] JEREMY.

Jere. Sir, here's the Steward again from your Father.

Val. I'll come to him——will you give me Leave, I'll wait on you again presently.

Mrs. *Frail*. No, I'll be gone. Come, who Squires me to the *Exchange*, I must call my Sister *Foresight* there?

Scan. I will: I have a Mind to your Sister.

Mrs. *Frail*. Civil!

Tatt. I will; because I have a Tendre for your Ladyship.

6 *Exchange*] The New Exchange, which replaced the old one burned by the fire of London. It had galleries with shops above them, and was a favourite, not very fashionable promenade. It was in its turn destroyed by fire in 1838.

Mrs. *Frail*. That's somewhat the better Reason, to my Opinion.

Scan. Well, if *Tattle* entertains you, I have the better Opportunity to engage your Sister.

Val. Tell *Angelica*, I am about making hard Conditions to come abroad, and be at Liberty to see her.

Scan. I'll give an Account of you, and your Proceedings. If Indiscretion be a Sign of Love, you are the most a Lover of any Body that I know: You fancy that parting with your Estate, will help you to your Mistress——In my Mind he is a Thoughtless Adventurer,

Who hopes to purchase Wealth, by selling Land;
Or win a Mistress, with a losing Hand.

End of the First Act.

ACT II. SCENE I.

A Room in Foresight's *House.*

FORESIGHT *and* SERVANT.

FORESIGHT.

Hey day! What, are all the Women of my Family abroad? Is not my Wife come home? Nor my Sister, nor my Daughter?

Serv. No, Sir.

Fore. Mercy on us, what can be the meaning of it? Sure the Moon is in all her Fortitudes; Is my Neice *Angelica* at home?

Serv. Yes, Sir.

Fore. I believe you lie, Sir.

Serv. Sir?

Fore. I say you lie, Sir. It is impossible that any thing should be as I wou'd have it; for

I was born, Sir, when the Crab was ascending, and all my Affairs go backward.

Serv. I can't tell indeed, Sir.

Fore. No, I know you can't, Sir: But I can tell, and foretell, Sir.

SCENE II.

[*To them*] NURSE.

Fore. Nurse, where's your young Mistress?

Nurse. Wee'st heart, I know not, they're none of 'em come home yet: Poor Child, I warrant she's fond o' seeing the Town—Marry, pray Heav'n they ha' given her any Dinner——Good lack-a-day, ha, ha, ha, O strange; I'll vow and swear now, ha, ha, ha, marry and did you ever see the like!

Fore. Why how now, what's the Matter?

Nurse. Pray Heav'n send your Worship good Luck, Marry and Amen with all my Heart, for you have put on one Stocking with the wrong side outward.

Fore. Ha, how? Faith and troth I'm glad of it, and so I have, that may be good Luck in troth, in troth it may, very good Luck: Nay I have had some Omens: I got out of Bed backwards too this Morning, without Premeditation; pretty good that too; but then I stumbled coming down Stairs, and met a Weasel; bad Omens those: Some bad, some good, our Lives are checquer'd: Mirth and Sorrow, Want and Plenty, Night and Day, make up our Time——But in troth I am pleas'd at my Stocking; very well pleas'd at my Stocking——Oh here's my Neice!——Sirrah, go tell Sir *Sampson Legend* I'll wait on him if he's at leisure,——'tis now three a Clock, a very good Hour for Business, *Mercury* governs this Hour.

SCENE III.

ANGELICA, FORESIGHT, NURSE.

Ang. Is it not a good Hour for Pleasure too, Uncle? pray lend me your Coach, mine's out of Order.

Fore. What, wou'd you be gadding too? Sure all Females are mad to day—It is of evil Portent, and bodes Mischief to the Master of a Family—— I remember an old Prophesie written by *Messahalah* the *Arabian*, and thus translated by a Reverend *Buckinghamshire* Bard.

When Housewifes all the House forsake,
And leave good Man to Brew and Bake,
Withouten Guile, then be it said,
That House doth stond upon its Head;
And when the Head is set in Grond,
Ne marl, if it be fruitful fond.

Fruitful, the Head fruitful, that bodes Horns; the Fruit of the Head is Horns——Dear Neice, stay at home——For by the Head of the House is meant the Husband; the Prophecy needs no Explanation.

Ang. Well, but I can neither make you a Cuckold, Uncle, by going abroad; nor secure you from being one, by staying at home.

Fore. Yes, yes; while there's one Woman left, the Prophecy is not in full Force.

Ang. But my Inclinations are in force; I have a mind to go abroad; and if you won't lend me your Coach, I'll take a Hackney, or a Chair, and leave you to erect a Scheme, and find who's in Conjunction with your Wife. Why don't you keep her at home, if you're Jealous of her when she's abroad? You know my Aunt is a little Retrograde (as you call it) in her Nature. Uncle, I'm afraid you are not Lord of the Ascendant, ha, ha, ha.

Fore. Well, Jill-flirt, you are very pert——and always ridiculing that Celestial Science. 37

Ang. Nay Uncle, don't be angry——If you are, I'll reap up all your false Prophecies, ridiculous Dreams, and idle Divinations. I'll swear you are a Nusance to the Neighbourhood——What a Bustle did you keep against the last invisible Eclipse, laying in Provision as 'twere for a Siege? What a world of Fire and Candle, Matches and Tinderboxes did you purchase! One would have thought we were ever after to live under Ground, or at least making a Voyage to *Greenland*, to inhabit there all the dark Season.

Fore. Why, you malapert Slut—— 49

Ang. Will you lend me your Coach, or I'll go on——Nay, I'll declare how you prophecy'd Popery was coming, only because the Butler had mis-laid some of the Apostle Spoons, and thought they were lost. Away went Religion and Spoon-meat together——Indeed, Uncle, I'll indite you for a Wizard.

Fore. How Hussy! was there ever such a provoking Minx?

Nurse. O merciful Father, how she talks! 59

Ang. Yes, I can make Oath of your unlawful Midnight Practices; you and the Old Nurse there——

Nurse. Marry Heav'n defend——I at Midnight Practices——O Lord, what's here to do?—I in unlawful Doings with my Master's Worship——Why, did you ever hear the like now——Sir, did ever I do any thing of your Midnight Concerns——but warm your Bed, and tuck you up, and set the Candle and your Tobacco-Box, and your Urinal by you, and now and then rub the Soles of your Feet?——O Lord, I!—— 71

Ang. Yes, I saw you together, thro' the Key-hole of the Closet, one Night, like *Saul* and the Witch of *Endor*, turning the Sieve and Sheers, and pricking your Thumbs, to write poor innocent

Servants Names in Blood, about a little Nutmeg Grater, which she had forgot in the Caudle-Cup——Nay, I know something worse, if I would speak of it——

Fore. I defie you, Hussy; but I'll remember this, I'll be reveng'd on you, Cockatrice; I'll hamper you——You have your Fortune in your own Hands—but I'll find a way to make your Lover, your Prodigal Spendthrift Gallant, *Valentine*, pay for all, I will.

Ang. Will you? I care not, but all shall out then——Look to't, Nurse; I can bring Witness that you have a great unnatural Teat under your left Arm, and he another; and that you suckle a young Devil in the Shape of a Tabby-Cat, by turns, I can.

Nurse. A Teat, a Teat, I an unnatural Teat! O the false slanderous thing; feel, feel here, if I have any thing but like another Christian. [*Crying.*

Fore. I will have Patience, since it is the Will of the Stars I should be thus tormented——This is the Effect of the malicious Conjunctions and Oppositions in the third House of my Nativity; there the Curse of Kindred was foretold——But I will have my Doors lock'd up——I'll punish you, not a Man shall enter my House.

Ang. Do Uncle, lock 'em up quickly before my Aunt come home——You'll have a Letter for Alimony to Morrow Morning——But let me be gone first, and then let no Mankind come near the House, but converse with Spirits and the Celestial Signs, the Bull, and the Ram, and the Goat. Bless me! there are a great many horn'd Beasts among the twelve Signs, Uncle. But Cuckolds go to Heav'n.

Fore. But there's but one Virgin among the Twelve Signs, Spitfire, but one Virgin.

Ang. Nor there had not been that one, if she had had to do with any thing but Astrologers, Uncle. That makes my Aunt go abroad.

Fore. How? How? Is that the Reason? Come, you know something; tell me, and I'll forgive you; do, good Neice—Come, you shall have my Coach and Horses,——Faith and troth you shall——Does my Wife complain? Come, I know Women tell one another—She is young and sanguine, has a wanton Hazle Eye, and was born under *Gemini*, which may incline her to Society; she has a Mole upon her Lip, with a moist Palm, and an open Liberality on the Mount of *Venus*.

Ang. Ha, ha, ha.

Fore. Do you laugh?——Well Gentlewoman, I'll——But come, be a good Girl, don't perplex your poor Uncle, tell me——won't you speak? Odd I'll——

SCENE IV.

[*To them*] SERVANT.

Serv. Sir *Sampson* is coming down to wait upon you—

Ang. Good bu'y Uncle——Call me a Chair——I'll find out my Aunt, and tell her, she must not come home.

Fore. I'm so perplex'd and vex'd, I am not fit to receive him; I shall scarce recover my self before the Hour be past: Go Nurse, tell Sir *Sampson* I'm ready to wait on him.

Nurse. Yes, Sir.

Fore. Well—Why, if I was born to be a Cuckold, there's no more to be said—he's here already.

SCENE V.

FORESIGHT, *and Sir* SAMPSON LEGEND *with a Paper*.

Sir *Samp*. Nor no more to be done, old Boy; that's plain—here 'tis, I have it in my Hand, old *Ptolomee*; I'll make the ungracious Prodigal know who begat him; I will, old *Nostrodamus*. What, I warrant my Son thought nothing belong'd to a Father, but Forgiveness and Affection; no Authority, no Correction, no Arbitrary Power; nothing to be done, but for him to offend and me to pardon. I warrant you, if he danc'd till Doomsday, he thought I was to pay the Piper. Well, but here it is under black and white, *Signatum, Sigillatum*. and *Deliberatum*; that as soon as my Son *Benjamin* is arriv'd, he is to make over to him his Right of Inheritance. Where's my Daughter that is to be——hah! old *Merlin*! body o'me, I'm so glad I'm reveng'd on this undutiful Rogue.

Fore. Odso, let me see; Let me see the Paper—Ay, faith and troth, here 'tis, if it will but hold——I wish things were done, and the Conveyance made——When was this sign'd, what Hour? Odso, you should have consulted me for the time. Well, but we'll make haste——

Sir *Samp*. Haste, ay, ay; haste enough, my Son *Ben* will be in Town to Night—I have order'd my Lawyer to draw up Writings of Settlement and Jointure——All shall be done to Night—No matter for the time; prithee, Brother *Foresight*, leave Superstition——Pox o'th' time; there's no time but the time present, there's no more to be said of what's past, and all that is to come will happen. If the Sun shine by Day, and the Stars by Night, why, we shall know one another's Faces without the help of a Candle, and that's all the Stars are good for.

Fore. How, how? Sir *Sampson*, that all? Give me leave to contradict you, and tell you, you are ignorant.

Sir *Samp*. I tell you I am wise; and *sapiens dominabitur astris*; there's Latin for you to prove

4 *Nostrodamus*] Nostradamus: Michel de Notredame, 1503–66, the famous French astrologer. He is buried at Salons, not far from Marseilles.

it, and an Argument to confound your *Ephemeris* ——Ignorant!——I tell you, I have travell'd old *Fircu*, and know the Globe. I have seen the *Antipodes*, where the Sun rises at Midnight, and sets at Noon-Day.

Fore. But I tell you, I have travell'd, and travell'd in the Cœlestial *Spheres*, known the *Signs* and the *Planets*, and their Houses. Can judge of Motions Direct and Retrograde, of *Sextiles*, *Quadrates*, *Trines* and *Oppositions*, Fiery *Trigons* and Aquatical *Trigons*. Know whether Life shall be long or short, Happy or Unhappy, whether Diseases are Curable or Incurable. If Journeys shall be prosperous, Undertakings successful; or Goods stoll'n recover'd, I know——

Sir *Samp*. I know the length of the Emperor of *China*'s Foot; have kiss'd the *Great Mogul*'s Slipper, and rid a Hunting upon an Elephant with the Cham of *Tartary*,——Body o'me, I have made a Cuckold of a King, and the present Majesty of *Bantam* is the Issue of these Loins.

Fore. I know when Travellers lye or speak Truth, when they don't know it themselves.

Sir *Samp*. I have known an Astrologer made a Cuckold in the Twinkling of a Star; and seen a Conjurer, that cou'd not keep the Devil out of his Wife's Circle.

Fore. What, does he twit me with my Wife too? I must be better inform'd of this,—[*Aside*.] ——Do you mean my Wife, Sir *Sampson*? Tho' you made a Cuckold of the King of *Bantam*, yet by the Body of the Sun——

Sir *Samp*. By the Horns of the Moon, you wou'd say, Brother *Capricorn*.

Fore. *Capricorn* in your Teeth, thou Modern *Mandevil*; *Ferdinand Mendez Pinto* was but a

76 *Mandevil . . . Pinto*] Sir John Mandeville, author of the famous Travels, *c*. 1360. Pinto was a Portuguese adventurer, who published his Peregrination in 1614. He was by no means such a liar as Foresight believed.

Type of thee, thou Liar of the first Magnitude. Take back your Paper of Inheritance; send your Son to Sea again. I'll wed my Daughter to an *Egyptian* Mummy, e'er she shall Incorporate with a Contemner of Sciences, and a Defamer of Virtue.

Sir *Samp*. Body o'me, I have gone too far;—— I must not provoke honest *Albumazar*,——an *Egyptian* Mummy is an Illustrious Creature, my trusty Hieroglyphick; and may have Significations of Futurity about him; Odsbud, I would my Son were an *Egyptian* Mummy for thy sake. What, thou art not angry for a Jest, my good *Haly*——I reverence the Sun, Moon and Stars with all my Heart.—What, I'll make thee a Present of a Mummy: Now I think on't, Body o'me, I have a Shoulder of an *Egyptian* King, that I purloin'd from one of the Pyramids, powder'd with Hieroglyphicks, thou shalt have it brought home to thy House, and make an Entertainment for all the *Philomaths*, and Students in Physick and Astrology in and about *London*.

Fore. But what do you know of my Wife, Sir *Sampson*? 99

Sir *Samp*. Thy Wife is a Constellation of Virtues; she's the Moon, and thou art the Man in the Moon: Nay, she is more Illustrious than the Moon; for she has her Chastity without her Inconstancy, s'bud I was but in Jest.

SCENE VI.

[*To them*] JEREMY.

Sir *Samp*. How now, who sent for you? Ha! What wou'd you have?

Fore. Nay, if you were but in jest——Who's that Fellow? I don't like his Physiognomy.

83 *Albumazar*] a Persian astrologer, popularized by Tomkis's play, revived 1668.

89 *Haly*] Either Halley, the calculator of his famous comet, or a Persian astronomer of the ninth century.

Sir *Samp*. My son, Sir; what Son, Sir? My Son *Benjamin*, hoh?

Jere. No, Sir, Mr. *Valentine*, my Master,—'tis the first time he has been abroad since his Confinement, and he comes to pay his Duty to you.

Sir *Samp*. Well, Sir.

SCENE VII.

FORESIGHT, *Sir* SAMPSON, VALENTINE, JEREMY.

Jere. He is here, Sir.

Val. Your Blessing, Sir.

Sir *Samp*. You've had it already, Sir, I think I sent it you to Day in a Bill of Four thousand Pound: A great deal of Mony, Brother *Foresight*.

Fore. Ay indeed, Sir *Sampson*, a great deal of Mony for a young Man, I wonder what he can do with it!

Sir *Samp*. Body o'me, so do I.——Hark ye, *Valentine*, if there be too much, refund the Superfluity; Do'st hear Boy?

Val. Superfluity, Sir, it will scarce pay my Debts,—I hope you will have more Indulgence, than to oblige me to those hard Conditions, which my Necessity sign'd to.

Sir *Samp*. Sir, how, I beseech you, what were you pleas'd to intimate, concerning Indulgence?

Val. Why, Sir, that you wou'd not go to the extremity of the Conditions, but release me at least from some Part.——

Sir *Samp*. Oh Sir, I understand you—that's all, ha?

Val. Yes, Sir, all that I presume to ask.—But what you, out of Fatherly Fondness, will be pleas'd to add, shall be doubly welcome.

Sir *Samp*. No doubt of it, sweet Sir, but your filial Piety, and my fatherly Fondness wou'd fit like two Tallies.——Here's a Rogue, Brother

Foresight, makes a Bargain under Hand and Seal in the Morning, and would be releas'd from it in the Afternoon; here's a Rogue, Dog, here's Conscience and Honesty; this is your Wit now, this is the Morality of your Wits! You are a Wit, and have been a Beau, and may be a——Why Sirrah, is it not here under Hand and Seal——Can you deny it?

Val. Sir, I don't deny it.——

Sir *Samp.* Sirrah, you'll be hang'd; I shall live to see you go up *Holborn-Hill*—Has he not a Rogue's Face?——Speak, Brother, you understand Physiognomy, a hanging Look to me——of all my Boys the most unlike me; he has a damn'd *Tyburn*-Face, without the Benefit o'the Clergy.

Fore. Hum—truly I don't care to discourage a young Man,——he has a violent Death in his Face; but I hope no Danger of Hanging.

Val. Sir, is this Usage for your Son?—for that old Weather-headed Fool, I know how to laugh at him; but you, Sir——

Sir *Samp.* You, Sir; and you, Sir:—Why, who are you, Sir?

Val. Your Son, Sir.

Sir *Samp.* That's more than I know, Sir, and I believe not.

Val. Faith, I hope not.

Sir *Samp.* What, wou'd you have your Mother a Whore! Did you ever hear the like! Did you ever hear the like! Body o'me——

Val. I would have an Excuse for your Barbarity and unnatural Usage.

Sir *Samp.* Excuse! Impudence! Why, Sirrah, mayn't I do what I please? Are not you my Slave? Did not I beget you? And might not I have chosen whether I would have begot you or no? 'Oons who are you? Whence came you? What brought you into the World? How came you here, Sir? Here, to stand here, upon those

39 *Holborn-Hill*] i. e. on the way to Tyburn (Ewald).

two Legs, and look erect with that audacious Face, hah? Answer me that? Did you come a Volunteer into the World? Or did I, with the lawful Authority of a Parent, press you to the Service?

Val. I know no more why I came, than you do why you call'd me. But here I am, and if you don't mean to provide for me, I desire you would leave me as you found me.

Sir *Samp.* With all my Heart: Come, uncase, strip, and go naked out of the World, as you came into't.

Val. My Cloaths are soon put off:——But you must also divest me of Reason, Thought, Passions, Inclinations, Affections, Appetites, Senses, and the huge Train of Attendants that you begot along with me.

Sir *Samp.* Body o'me, what a many-headed Monster have I propagated!

Val. I am of my self, a plain easie simple Creature; and to be kept at small Expence; but the Retinue that you gave me are craving and invincible; they are so many Devils that you have rais'd, and will have Employment.

Sir *Samp.* 'Oons, what had I to do to get Children,——can't a private Man be born without all these Followers?——Why nothing under an Emperor should be born with Appetites,——Why at this rate a Fellow that has but a Groat in his Pocket, may have a Stomach capable of a Ten Shilling Ordinary.

Jere. Nay that's as clear as the Sun; I'll make Oath of it before any Justice in *Middlesex.*

Sir *Samp.* Here's a Cormorant too,—'S'heart this Fellow was not born with you?——I did not beget him, did I?—

Jere. By the Provision that's made for me, you might have begot me too:—Nay, and to tell your Worship another Truth, I believe you did, for I find I was born with those same Whoreson Appetites too, that my Master speaks of.

Sir *Samp*. Why look you there now,——I'll maintain it, that by the Rule of right Reason, this Fellow ought to have been born without a Palate. 'S'heart, what shou'd he do with a distinguishing Taste ?—I warrant now he'd rather eat a Pheasant, than a Piece of poor *John* ; and smell, now, why I warrant he can smell, and loves Perfumes above a Stink.——Why there's it ; and Musick, don't you love Musick, Scoundrel ?

Jere. Yes, I have a reasonable good Ear, Sir, as to Jiggs and Country Dances ; and the like ; I don't much matter your *Solo's* or *Sonata's*, they give me the Spleen.

Sir *Samp*. The Spleen, ha, ha, ha, a Pox confound you—*Solo's* or *Sonata's* ? 'Oons whose Son are you ? How were you engendred, Muckworm ?

Jere. I am by my Father, the Son of a Chairman ; my Mother sold Oisters in Winter, and Cucumbers in Summer ; and I came up Stairs into the World ; for I was born in a Cellar.

Fore. By your Looks, you shou'd go up Stairs out of the World too, Friend.

Sir *Samp*. And if this Rogue were Anatomiz'd now, and dissected, he has his Vessels of Digestion and Concoction, and so forth, large enough for the inside of a Cardinal, this Son of a Cucumber.——These things are unaccountable and unreasonable, —Body o'me, why was not I a Bear ? that my Cubs might have liv'd upon sucking their Paws ; Nature has been provident only to Bears and Spiders ; the one has its Nutriment in his own Hands ; and t'other spins his Habitation out of his own Entrails.

Val. Fortune was provident enough to supply all the Necessities of my Nature ; if I had my right of Inheritance.

Sir *Samp*. Again ! 'Oons han't you four thousand Pound——if I had it again, I wou'd not

113 poor *John*] salted hake (a type of poor fare)—C. T. ONIONS, *Shakespeare Glossary*.

give thee a Groat,——What, would'st thou have me turn Pelican, and feed thee out of my own Vitals ?—'S'heart, live by your Wits,——You were always fond of the Wits,—Now let's see, if you have Wit enough to keep your self——Your Brother will be in Town to Night, or to Morrow Morning, and then look you perform Covenants, and so your Friend and Servant.——Come Brother *Foresight*.

SCENE VIII.

VALENTINE, JEREMY.

Jere. I told you what your Visit wou'd come to.

Val. 'Tis as much as I expected—I did not come to see him : I came to *Angelica* : But since she was gone abroad, it was easily turn'd another way ; and at least look'd well on my side : What's here ? Mrs. *Foresight* and Mrs. *Frail*, they are earnest,——I'll avoid 'em,—Come this way, and go and enquire when *Angelica* will return.

SCENE IX.

Mrs. FORESIGHT, *and Mrs.* FRAIL.

Mrs. *Frail.* What have you to do to watch me ? 'S'life I'll do what I please.

Mrs. *Fore.* You will ?

Mrs. *Frail.* Yes marry will I——A great Piece of Business to go to *Covent Garden Square* in a Hackney-Coach, and take a turn with one's Friend.

Mrs. *Fore.* Nay, two or three Turns, I'll take my Oath. 9

Mrs. *Frail.* Well, what if I took twenty——I warrant if you had been there, it had been only innocent Recreation,—Lord, where's the Comfort of this Life, if we can't have the Happiness of conversing where we like ?

Mrs. *Fore.* But can't you converse at home ?——

I own it, I think there's no Happiness like conversing with an agreeable Man; I don't quarrel at that, nor I don't think but your Conversation was very innocent; but the Place is publick, and to be seen with a Man in a Hackney-Coach is scandalous: What if any Body else shou'd have seen you alite, as I did?——How can any Body be happy, while they're in perpetual Fear of being seen and censur'd?—Besides it wou'd not only reflect upon you, Sister, but me.

Mrs. *Frail.* Pooh, here's a Clutter—Why shou'd it reflect upon you?—I don't doubt but you have thought your self happy in a Hackney-Coach before now.—If I had gone to *Knight's-Bridge*, or to *Chelsey*, or to *Spring-Garden*, or *Barn-Elms* with a Man alone——something might have been said.

Mrs. *Fore.* Why, was I ever in any of those Places? What do you mean, Sister?

Mrs. *Frail.* Was I? What do you mean?

Mrs. *Fore.* You have been at a worse Place.

Mrs. *Frail.* I at a worse Place, and with a Man!

Mrs. *Fore.* I suppose you would not go alone to the *World's-End.*

Mrs. *Frail.* The *World's-End*! What, do you mean to banter me?

Mrs. *Fore.* Poor Innocent! You don't know that there's a Place call'd the *World's-End*? I'll swear you can keep your Countenance purely, you'd make an admirable Player.

Mrs. *Frail.* I'll swear you have a great deal of Confidence, and in my Mind too much for the Stage.

39 *World's-End*] In Chelsea. Knightsbridge contained The Swan, a similar place of resort. Barn Elms, at Hampstead, where Jacob Tonson afterwards built the Kit-Cat room. Spring Gardens was on the site of the present Admiralty Arch, and was 'a kind of Mahommedan paradise' (*Spectator*, 383). The character of these places is obvious from the context.

Mrs. *Fore.* Very well, that will appear who has most, you never were at the *World's-End*?

Mrs. *Frail.* No.

Mrs. *Fore.* You deny it positively to my Face.

Mrs. *Frail.* Your Face, what's your Face?

Mrs. *Fore.* No matter for that, it's as good a Face as yours.

Mrs. *Frail.* Not by a Dozen Years wearing.——But I do deny it positively to your Face then.

Mrs. *Fore.* I'll allow you now to find fault with my Face;——for I'll swear your Impudence has put me out of Countenance:——But look you here now,—where did you lose this Gold Bodkin?——Oh Sister, Sister!

Mrs. *Frail.* My Bodkin!

Mrs. *Fore.* Nay, 'tis yours, look at it.

Mrs. *Frail.* Well, if you go to that, where did you find this Bodkin?——Oh Sister, Sister!—Sister every way.

Mrs. *Fore.* O Devil on't, that I cou'd not discover her, without betraying my self. [*Aside.*

Mrs. *Frail.* I have heard Gentlemen say, Sister; that one shou'd take great Care, when one makes a Thrust in Fencing, not to lye open ones self.

Mrs. *Fore.* It's very true, Sister: Well, since all's out, and as you say, since we are both wounded, let us do what is often done in Duels, take care of one another, and grow better Friends than before.

Mrs. *Frail.* With all my Heart, ours are but slight flesh Wounds, and if we keep 'em from Air, not at all dangerous: Well, give me your Hand in Token of Sisterly Secresie and Affection.

Mrs. *Fore.* Here 'tis with all my Heart.

Mrs. *Frail.* Well, as an Earnest of Friendship and Confidence: I'll acquaint you with a Design that I have: To tell Truth, and speak openly one to another: I'm afraid the World have observ'd us more than we have observ'd one another. You have a rich Husband, and are provided for, I am at a Loss, and have no great Stock either of Fortune or Reputation; and therefore must look sharply about me. Sir *Sampson* has a Son that is expected to Night; and by the Account I have heard of his Education, can be no Conjurer: The Estate you know is to be made over to him: Now if I cou'd wheedle him, Sister, ha? You understand me? 97

Mrs. *Fore.* I do; and will help you to the utmost of my Power—And I can tell you one thing that falls out luckily enough; my awkward Daughter-in-Law, who you know is design'd to be his Wife, is grown fond of Mr. *Tattle*; now if we can improve that, and make her have an Aversion for the Booby, it may go a great way towards his liking you. Here they come together; and let us contrive some way or other to leave 'em together.

SCENE X.

[*To them*] Tattle *and Miss* Prue.

Miss. Mother, Mother, Mother, look you here.

Mrs. *Fore.* Fie, fie, Miss, how you bawl——Besides, I have told you, you must not call me Mother.

Miss. What must I call you then, are you not my Father's Wife?

Mrs. *Fore.* Madam; you must say Madam——By my Soul, I shall fancy my self old indeed, to have this great Girl call me Mother——Well, but Miss, what are you so over-joy'd at?

Miss. Look you here, Madam then, what Mr. *Tattle* has giv'n me——Look you here Cousin, here's a Snuff-Box; nay, there's Snuff in't;—here, will you have any——Oh good! how sweet it is—Mr. *Tattle* is all over sweet, his Perruke is sweet, and his Gloves are sweet,——and his Handkerchief is sweet, pure sweet, sweeter than

Roses—Smell him Mother, Madam, I mean—He gave me this Ring for a Kiss.

Tatt. O fie Miss, you must not kiss and tell.

Miss. Yes ; I may tell my Mother——And he says he'll give me something to make me smell so ——Oh pray lend me your Handkerchief—Smell, Cousin ; he says, he'll give me something that will make my Smocks smell this way——Is not it pure ?——It's better than Lavender mun—I'm resolv'd I won't let Nurse put any more Lavender among my Smocks—ha, Cousin ?

Mrs. *Frail.* Fie, Miss ; amongst your Linnen, you must say—You must never say Smock.

Miss. Why, it is not bawdy, is it, Cousin ?

Tatt. Oh Madam ; you are too severe upon Miss ; you must not find fault with her pretty Simplicity, it becomes her strangely——pretty Miss, don't let 'em perswade you out of your Innocency.

Mrs. *Fore.* Oh, demm you Toad——I wish you don't perswade her out of her Innocency.

Tatt. Who I, Madam ?——Oh Lord how can your Ladyship have such a Thought—sure you don't know me ?

Mrs. *Frail.* Ah Devil, sly Devil——He's as close, Sister, as a Confessor——He thinks we don't observe him.

Mrs. *Fore.* A cunning Cur, how soon he cou'd find out a fresh harmless Creature ; and left us, Sister, presently.

Tatt. Upon Reputation.——

Mrs. *Fore.* They're all so, Sister, these Men—they love to have the spoiling of a young thing, they are as fond of it, as of being first in the Fashion, or of seeing a new Play the first Day,——I warrant it would break Mr. *Tattle*'s Heart, to think that any Body else shou'd be beforehand with him.

Tatt. Oh Lord, I swear I wou'd not for the World——

Mrs. *Frail.* O hang you; who'll believe you?—You'd be hang'd before you'd confess—we know you—she's very pretty!—Lord, what pure red and white!—she looks so wholsome;—ne'er stir, I don't know, but I fancy, if I were a Man—

Miss. How you love to jeer one, Cousin.

Mrs. *Fore.* Hark'ee, Sister,—by my Soul the Girl is spoil'd already—d'ee think she'll ever endure a great lubberly Tarpawlin—Gad I warrant you, she won't let him come near her, after Mr. *Tattle.*

Mrs. *Frail.* O'my Soul, I'm afraid not—eh!—filthy Creature, that smells all of Pitch and Tarr——Devil take you, you confounded Toad——why did you see her, before she was married?

Mrs. *Fore.* Nay, why did we let him——my Husband will hang us——He'll think we brought 'em acquainted.

Mrs. *Frail.* Come, Faith let us be gone——If my Brother *Foresight* shou'd find us with them;——He'd think so, sure enough.

Mrs. *Fore.* So he wou'd——but then leaving 'em together is as bad——And he's such a sly Devil, he'll never miss an Opportunity.

Mrs. *Frail.* I don't care; I won't be seen in't.

Mrs. *Fore.* Well, if you should, Mr. *Tattle*, you'll have a World to answer for, remember I wash my Hands of it, I'm throughly Innocent.

SCENE XI.

TATTLE, *Miss* PRUE.

Miss. What makes 'em go away, Mr. *Tattle*? What do they mean, do you know?

Tatt. Yes, my Dear——I think I can guess—But hang me if I know the Reason of it.

Miss. Come, must not we go too?

Tatt. No, no, they don't mean that.

Miss. No! What then? What shall you and I do together?

Tatt. I must make Love to you, pretty Miss; will you let me make Love to you?

Miss. Yes, if you please.

Tatt. Frank, I Gad, at least. What a Pox does Mrs. *Foresight* mean by this Civility? Is it to make a Fool of me? or does she leave us together out of good Morality, and do as she would be done by——Gad I'll understand it so. [*Aside.*

Miss. Well; and how will you make Love to me——Come, I long to have you begin——must I make Love too? You must tell me how.

Tatt. You must let me speak Miss, you must not speak first; I must ask you Questions, and you must answer.

Miss. What, is it like the Catechism?——Come then ask me.

Tatt. D'ye think you can love me?

Miss. Yes.

Tatt. Pooh, Pox, you must not say yes already; I shan't care a Farthing for you then in a twinkling.

Miss. What must I say then?

Tatt. Why you must say no, or you believe not, or you can't tell——

Miss. Why, must I tell a Lie then?

Tatt. Yes, if you'd be well bred. All well-bred Persons Lie——Besides, you are a Woman, you must never speak what you think: Your Words must contradict your Thoughts; but your Actions may contradict your Words. So, when I ask you, if you can love me, you must say no, but you must love me too—If I tell you you are handsome, you must deny it, and say I flatter you——But you must think your self more charming than I speak you:—And like me, for the Beauty which I say you have, as much as if I had it my self—If I ask you to kiss me, you must be angry, but you must not refuse me. If I ask you for more, you must be more angry,—but more complying; and as soon as ever I make you say you'll cry out, you must be sure to hold your Tongue.

Miss. O Lord, I swear this is pure,—I like it better than our old fashion'd Country way of speaking one's Mind;—and must not you lie too?

Tatt. Hum——Yes—But you must believe I speak Truth.

Miss. O *Gemini*! Well, I always had a great Mind to tell Lies——but they frighted me, and said it was a Sin.

Tatt. Well, my pretty Creature; will you make me happy by giving me a Kiss?

Miss. No, indeed; I'm angry at you.— 59
[*Runs and kisses him.*

Tatt. Hold, hold, that's pretty well—but you should not have given it me, but have suffer'd me to have taken it.

Miss. Well, we'll do it again.

Tatt. With all my Heart——Now then my little Angel. [*Kisses her.*

Miss. Pish.

Tatt. That's right,——again my Charmer.
[*Kisses again.*

Miss. O fie, nay, now I can't abide you. 68

Tatt. Admirable! That was as well as if you had been born and bred in *Covent-Garden*,—And won't you shew me, pretty Miss, where your Bed-Chamber is?

Miss. No, indeed won't I: but I'll run there, and hide my self from you behind the Curtains.

Tatt. I'll follow you.

Miss. Ah, but I'll hold the Door with both Hands, and be angry;—and you shall push me down before you come in.

Tatt. No, I'll come in first, and push you down afterwards. 80

Miss. Will you? then I'll be more angry, and more complying.

Tatt. Then I'll make you cry out.

Miss. Oh but you shan't, for I'll hold my Tongue—

Tatt. Oh my dear apt Scholar.

Miss. Well, now I'll run and make more haste than you.

Tatt. You shall not fly so fast, as I'll pursue.

End of the Second Act.

ACT III. SCENE I.

Nurse alone.

Nurse.

Miss, Miss, Miss *Prue*—Mercy on me, marry and Amen. Why, what's become of the Child?——Why Miss, Miss *Foresight*—Sure she has lockt her self up in her Chamber, and gone to sleep, or to Prayers: Miss, Miss, I hear her——Come to your Father, Child: Open the Door——Open the Door, Miss——I hear you cry husht——O Lord, who's there? [*peeps*] What's here to do?——O the Father! a Man with her!——Why, Miss I say; God's my Life, here's fine doings towards——O Lord, we're all undone——O you young Harlotry [*knocks.*] Od's my Life, won't you open the Door? I'll come in the back way.

SCENE II.

Tattle, *Miss* Prue.

Miss. O Lord, she's coming—and she'll tell my Father, what shall I do now?

Tatt. Pox take her; if she had staid two Minutes longer, I shou'd have wish'd for her coming.

Miss. O Dear, what shall I say? Tell me, Mr. *Tattle*, tell me a Lie.

Tatt. There's no occasion for a Lie; I cou'd never tell a Lie to no purpose——But since we have done nothing, we must say nothing, I think. I hear her——I'll leave you together, and come off as you can. [*Thrusts her in, and shuts the Door,*

SCENE III.

TATTLE, VALENTINE, SCANDAL, ANGELICA.

Ang. You can't accuse me of Inconstancy; I never told you that I lov'd you.

Val. But I can accuse you of Uncertainty, for not telling me whether you did or not.

Ang. You mistake Indifference for Uncertainty; I never had Concern enough to ask my self the Question.

Scan. Nor good Nature enough to answer him that did ask you: I'll say that for you, Madam.

Ang. What, are you setting up for good Nature?

Scan. Only for the Affectation of it, as the Women do for ill Nature.

Ang. Perswade your Friend, that it is all Affectation.

Scan. I shall receive no Benefit from the Opinion: For I know no effectual Difference between continued Affectation and Reality.

Tatt. [*coming up.*] *Scandal*, are you in private Discourse, any thing of Secresie? [*Aside to* Scandal.

Scan. Yes, but I dare trust you; we were talking of *Angelica*'s Love to *Valentine*; you won't speak of it.

Tatt. No, no, not a Syllable—I know that's a Secret, for it's whisper'd every where.

Scan. Ha, ha, ha.

Ang. What is, Mr. *Tattle*? I heard you say something was whisper'd every where.

Scan. Your Love of *Valentine*.

Ang. How!

Tatt. No, Madam, his Love for your Ladiship——Gad take me, I beg your Pardon——for I never heard a Word of your Ladiship's Passion, 'till this instant.

Ang. My Passion! And who told you of my Passion, pray Sir?

Scan. Why, is the Devil in you? Did not I tell it you for a Secret?

Tatt. Gadso; but I thought she might have been trusted with her own Affairs.

Scan. Is that your Discretion? trust a Woman with her self?

Tatt. You say true, I beg your Pardon;—I'll bring all off—it was impossible, Madam, for me to imagine, that a Person of your Ladiship's Wit and Gallantry, could have so long receiv'd the passionate Addresses of the accomplish'd *Valentine*, and yet remain insensible; therefore you will pardon me, if from a just weight of his Merit, with your Ladiship's good Judgment, I form'd the Ballance of a reciprocal Affection.

Val. O the Devil, what damn'd Costive Poet has given thee this Lesson of Fustian to get by Rote?

Ang. I dare swear you wrong him, it is his own—And Mr. *Tattle* only judges of the Success of others, from the Effects of his own Merit. For certainly Mr. *Tattle* was never deny'd any thing in his Life.

Tatt. O Lord! yes indeed, Madam, several times.

Ang. I swear I don't think 'tis possible.

Tatt. Yes, I vow and swear I have: Lord, Madam, I'm the most unfortunate Man in the World, and the most cruelly us'd by the Ladies.

Ang. Nay, now you're ungrateful.

Tatt. No, I hope not——'tis as much Ingratitude to own some Favours, as to conceal others.

Val. There, now it's out.

Ang. I don't understand you now. I thought you had never ask'd any thing, but what a Lady might modestly grant, and you confess.

Scan. So faith, your Business is done here; now you may go brag somewhere else.

Tatt. Brag! O Heav'ns! Why, did I name any body?

Ang. No; I suppose that is not in your Power; but you wou'd if you cou'd, no doubt on't.

Tatt. Not in my Power, Madam! What does your Ladiship mean, that I have no Woman's Reputation in my Power?

Scan. 'Oons, why you won't own it, will you? [*Aside.*

Tatt. Faith, Madam, you're in the right; no more I have, as I hope to be sav'd; I never had it in my Power to say any thing to a Lady's Prejudice in my Life——For as I was telling you, Madam, I have been the most unsuccessful Creature living, in things of that Nature; and never had the good Fortune to be trusted once with a Lady's Secret, not once.

Ang. No.

Val. Not once, I dare answer for him.

Scan. And I'll answer for him; for I'm sure if he had, he wou'd have told me; I find, Madam, you don't know Mr. *Tattle*.

Tatt. No indeed, Madam, you don't know me at all, I find. For sure my intimate Friends wou'd have known——

Ang. Then it seems you would have told, if you had been trusted.

Tatt. O Pox, *Scandal*, that was too far put——Never have told particulars, Madam. Perhaps I might have talk'd as of a third Person—or have introduc'd an Amour of my own, in Conversation, by way of Novel: But never have explain'd Particulars.

Ang. But whence comes the Reputation of Mr. *Tattle*'s Secresie, if he was never trusted?

Scan. Why thence it arises——The thing is proverbially spoken; but may be apply'd to him——As if we should say in general Terms, he only is secret who never was trusted; a Satirical Proverb upon our Sex——There's another upon yours——As she is chaste, who was never ask'd the Question. That's all.

Val. A couple of very civil Proverbs, truly: 'Tis hard to tell whether the Lady or Mr. *Tattle* be the more oblig'd to you. For you found her Virtue upon the Backwardness of the Men; and his Secresie upon the Mistrust of the Women.

Tatt. Gad, it's very true, Madam, I think we are oblig'd to acquit our selves——And for my part——But your Ladyship is to speak first—

Ang. Am I? Well, I freely confess I have resisted a great deal of Temptation.

Tatt. And I Gad, I have given some Temptation that has not been resisted.

Val. Good.

Ang. I cite *Valentine* here, to declare to the Court, how fruitless he has found his Endeavours, and to confess all his Sollicitations and my Denials.

Val. I am ready to plead, Not guilty for you; and Guilty, for my self.

Scan. So, why this is fair, here's Demonstration with a Witness.

Tatt. Well, my Witnesses are not present——But I confess I have had Favours from Persons——But as the Favours are numberless, so the Persons are nameless.

Scan. Pooh, this proves nothing.

Tatt. No? I can shew Letters, Lockets, Pictures, and Rings; and if there be Occasion for Witnesses, I can summon the Maids at the Chocolate-Houses, all the Porters at *Pall-Mall* and *Covent-Garden*, the Door-Keepers at the Play-House, the Drawers at *Locket*'s, *Pontack*'s, the *Rummer*, *Spring-Garden*; my own Landlady and *Valet de Chambre*; all who shall make Oath, that I receive more Letters than the Secretary's Office; and that I have more Vizor-Masks to enquire for me, than ever went to see the Hermaphrodite, or the naked Prince. And it is notorious, that in

146 *Spring-Garden*] Pontack's and Locket's were famous ordinaries. The Rummer was where Matt Prior served his uncle as pot-boy.

a Country Church, once, an Enquiry being made, who I was, it was answer'd, I was the famous *Tattle*, who had ruin'd so many Women.

Val. It was there, I suppose, you got the Nick-Name of the *Great Turk*.

Tatt. True; I was call'd *Turk-Tattle* all over the Parish——The next *Sunday* all the old Women kept their Daughters at home, and the Parson had not half his Congregation. He wou'd have brought me into the Spiritual Court, but I was reveng'd upon him, for he had a handsome Daughter whom I initiated into the Science. But I repented it afterwards, for it was talk'd of in Town——And a Lady of Quality that shall be nameless, in a raging Fit of Jealousie, came down in her Coach and six horses, and expos'd her self upon my Account; Gad I was sorry for it with all my Heart——You know whom I mean—You know where we raffl'd——

Scan. Mum, *Tattle*.

Val. 'Sdeath, are not you asham'd?

Ang. O barbarous! I never heard so insolent a Piece of Vanity—Fie, Mr. *Tattle*—I'll swear I could not have believ'd it——Is this your Secresie?

Tatt. Gad so, the Heat of my Story carry'd me beyond my Discretion, as the Heat of the Lady's Passion hurry'd her beyond her Reputation—But I hope you don't know whom I mean; for there was a great many Ladies raffled—Pox on't, now could I bite off my Tongue.

Scan. No don't; for then you'll tell us no more——Come, I'll recommend a Song to you upon the Hint of my two Proverbs, and I see one in the next Room that will sing it.

[*Goes to the Door.*

Tatt. For Heav'ns sake, if you do guess, say nothing; Gad, I'm very unfortunate.

Scan. Pray sing the first Song in the last new Play.

SONG.

Set by Mr. *John Eccles.*

I.

A Nymph and a Swain to Apollo *once pray'd,*
The Swain had been jilted, the Nymph been betray'd:
Their Intent was to try if his Oracle knew
E'er a Nymph that was Chaste, or a Swain that was true.

II.

Apollo *was mute, and had like t'have been pos'd,*
But sagely at length he this Secret disclos'd:
He alone won't betray in whom none will Confide;
And the Nymph may be Chaste that has never been try'd.

SCENE IV.

[*To them*] *Sir* Sampson, *Mrs.* Frail, *Miss* Prue, *and Servant.*

Sir *Samp.* Is *Ben* come? Odso, my Son *Ben* come? Odd, I'm glad on't: Where is he? I long to see him. Now, Mrs. *Frail*, you shall see my Son *Ben*——Body o'me, he's the Hopes of my Family—I han't seen him these three Years——I warrant he's grown——Call him in, bid him make haste——I'm ready to cry for Joy.

Mrs. *Frail*. Now Miss you shall see your Husband.

Miss. Pish, he shall be none of my Husband. 9
[*Aside to* Frail.

Mrs. *Frail*. Hush: Well he shan't, leave that to me—I'll beckon Mr. *Tattle* to us.

Ang. Won't you stay and see your Brother?

Val. We are the Twin-Stars, and cannot shine in one Sphere; when he rises I must set——

Eccles] The most considerable of the immediate successors of Purcell. He set Congreve's *Judgment of Paris*

Besides, if I shou'd stay, I don't know but my Father in good Nature may press me to the immediate signing the Deed of Conveyance of my Estate; and I'll defer it as long as I can——Well, you'll come to a Resolution.

Ang. I can't. Resolution must come to me, or I shall never have one.

Scan. Come, *Valentine*, I'll go with you; I've something in my Head to communicate to you.

SCENE V.

ANGELICA, *Sir* SAMPSON, TATTLE, *Mrs.* FRAIL, *Miss* PRUE.

Sir *Samp.* What, is my Son *Valentine* gone? What, is he sneak'd off, and would not see his Brother? There's an unnatural Whelp! There's an ill-natur'd Dog! What, were you here too, Madam, and could not keep him! Cou'd neither Love, nor Duty, nor natural Affection oblige him. Odsbud, Madam, have no more to say to him; he is not worth your Consideration. The Rogue has not a Drachm of generous Love about him: All Interest, all Interest; he's an undone Scoundrel, and courts your Estate: Body o'me, he does not care a Doit for your Person.

Ang. I'm pretty even with him, Sir *Sampson*; for if ever I cou'd have lik'd any thing in him, it shou'd have been his Estate too: But since that's gone, the Bait's off, and the naked Hook appears.

Sir *Samp.* Odsbud, well spoken; and you are a wiser Woman than I thought you were: For most young Women now a-days are to be tempted with a naked Hook.

Ang. If I marry, Sir *Sampson*, I'm for a good Estate with any Man, and for any Man with a good Estate: Therefore if I were oblig'd to make a Choice, I declare I'd rather have you than your Son.

Sir *Samp*. Faith and Troth you're a wise Woman, and I'm glad to hear you say so; I was afraid you were in Love with the Reprobate; Odd, I was sorry for you with all my Heart: Hang him, Mungrel; cast him off; you shall see the Rogue shew himself, and make Love to some desponding *Cadua* of fourscore for Sustenance. Odd, I love to see a young Spendthrift forc'd to cling to an old Woman for Support, like Ivy round a dead Oak: Faith I do; I love to see 'em hug and cotten together, like Down upon a Thistle.

SCENE VI.

[*To them*] Ben. Legend, *and Servant.*

Ben. Where's Father?

Serv. There, Sir, his Back's towards you.

Sir *Samp.* My Son *Ben*! Bless thee my dear Boy; body o'me, thou art heartily welcome.

Ben. Thank you Father, and I'm glad to see you.

Sir *Samp.* Odsbud, and I'm glad to see thee, kiss me Boy, kiss me again and again, dear *Ben*. [*Kisses him.*

Ben. So, so, enough Father——Mess, I'd rather kiss these Gentlewomen.

Sir *Samp.* And so thou shalt—Mrs. *Angelica*, my Son *Ben*.

Ben. Forsooth if you please——[*Salutes her.*] Nay, Mistress, I'm not for dropping Anchor here; about Ship I faith—[*Kisses* Frail.] Nay, and you too, my little Cock-Boat——so——[*Kisses Miss.*

Tatt. Sir, you're welcome a-shoar.

Ben. Thank you, thank you, Friend.

Sir *Samp.* Thou hast been many a weary League *Ben*, since I saw thee.

Ben. Ey, ey, been! Been far enough, an that be all——Well Father, and how do all at home? How does Brother *Dick*, and Brother *Val*?

Sir *Samp*. *Dick*, body o'me, *Dick* has been dead these two Years ; I writ you Word, when you were at *Legorne*.

Ben. Mess, that's true : Marry I had forgot. *Dick's* dead as you say—Well, and how ? I have a many Questions to ask you ; well, you ben't marry'd again, Father, be you ?

Sir *Samp*. No, I intend you shall marry, *Ben* ; I would not marry for thy sake.

Ben. Nay, what does that signifie ?——an you marry again——Why then, I'll go to Sea again, so there's one for t'other, an that be all——Pray don't let me be your Hindrance ; e'en marry a God's Name an the Wind sit that way. As for my part, may-hap I have no Mind to marry.

Frail. That wou'd be pity, such a handsome young Gentleman.

Ben. Handsome ! he, he, he, nay Forsooth, an you be for joking, I'll joke with you, for I love my Jest, an the Ship were sinking, as we sayn at Sea. But I'll tell you why I don't much stand towards Matrimony. I love to roam about from Port to Port, and from Land to Land : I could never abide to be Port-bound, as we call it : Now a Man that is marry'd, has as it were, d'ye see, his Feet in the Bilboes, and may-hap mayn't get 'em out again when he wou'd.

Sir *Samp*. *Ben's* a Wagg.

Ben. A Man that is marry'd, d'ye see, is no more like another Man, than a Gally-Slave is like one of us free Sailors, he is chain'd to an Oar all his Life ; and may-hap forc'd to tug a leaky Vessel into the Bargain.

Sir *Samp*. A very Wag, *Ben*'s a very Wag ; only a little tough, he wants a little polishing.

Mrs. *Frail*. Not at all ; I like his Humour mightily, it's plain and honest, I shou'd like such a Humour in a Husband extreamly.

Ben. Say'n you so Forsooth ? Marry and

49 Bilboes] Ships' irons, stocks.

I shou'd like such a handsome Gentlewoman for a Bed-fellow hugely; how say you, Mistress, wou'd you like going to Sea? Mess, you're a tight Vessel, and well rigg'd, an you were but as well mann'd.

Mrs. *Frail.* I shou'd not doubt that, if you were Master of me.

Ben. But I'll tell you one thing, an you come to Sea in a high Wind, or that Lady——You mayn't carry so much Sail o'your Head——Top and top gallant, by the Mess.

Mrs. *Frail.* No, why so?

Ben. Why an you do, you may run the risk to be over-set, and then you'll carry your Keels above Water, he, he, he.

Ang. I swear, Mr. *Benjamin* is the veriest Wag in Nature; an absolute Sea-Wit.

Sir *Samp.* Nay, *Ben* has Parts, but as I told you before, they want a little Polishing: You must not take any thing ill, Madam.

Ben. No, I hope the Gentlewoman is not angry; I mean all in good part: For if I give a Jest, I'll take a Jest: And so Forsooth you may be as free with me.

Ang. I thank you, Sir, I am not at all offended; —But methinks Sir *Sampson*, you shou'd leave him alone with his Mistress. Mr. *Tattle*, we must not hinder Lovers.

Tatt. Well, *Miss*, I have your Promise.

[*Aside to* Miss.

Sir *Samp.* Body o'me, Madam, you say true: ——Look you *Ben*; this is your Mistress,——Come Miss, you must not be shame-fac'd we'll leave you together.

Miss. I can't abide to be left alone, mayn't my Cousin stay with me?

Sir *Samp.* No, no. Come, let's away.

Ben. Look you, Father, may-hap the young Woman mayn't take a liking to me.——

Sir *Samp.* I warrant thee Boy, come, come, we'll be gone; I'll venture that.

SCENE VII.

Ben, *and* Miss Prue.

Ben. Come Mistress, will you please to sit down? for an you stand a stern a that'n, we shall never grapple together,—Come, I'll haule a Chair; there, an you please to sit, I'll sit by you.

Miss. You need not sit so near me, if you have any thing to say, I can hear you farther off, I an't deaf.

Ben. Why that's true, as you say, nor I an't dumb, I can hear as far as another,—I'll heave off, to please you. [*Sits farther off.*] An we were a League asunder, I'd undertake to hold Discourse with you, an 'twere not a main high Wind indeed, and full in my teeth. Look you Forsooth, I am as it were, bound for the Land of Matrimony; 'tis a Voyage d'ye see, that was none of my seeking, I was commanded by Father, and if you like of it, may-hap I may steer into your Harbour. How say you, Mistress? The short of the thing is, that if you like me, and I like you, we may chance to swing in a Hammock together.

Miss. I don't know what to say to you, nor I don't care to speak with you at all.

Ben. No, I'm sorry for that.——But pray why are you so scornful?

Miss. As long as one must not speak one's Mind, one had better not speak at all, I think, and truly I won't tell a Lie for the Matter.

Ben. Nay, you say true in that, it's but a Folly to lie: For to speak one thing, and to think just the contrary Way; is as it were, to look one way, and to row another. Now, for my part d'ye see, I'm for carrying things above Board, I'm not for keeping any thing under Hatches,—so that if you ben't as willing as I, say so a God's Name, there's no harm done; may-hap you may be shame-fac'd, some Maidens thof' they love a Man well enough yet they don't care to tell'n so to's Face: If that's the Case, why Silence gives Consent. 38

Miss. But I'm sure it is not so, for I'll speak sooner than you should believe that; and I'll speak Truth, tho' one should always tell a Lie to a Man; and I don't care, let my Father do what he will; I'm too big to be whipt, so I'll tell you plainly, I don't like you, nor love you at all, nor ever will, that's more: So, there's your Answer for you; and don't trouble me no more, you ugly thing. 47

Ben. Look you, young Woman, you may learn to give good Words however. I spoke you fair, d'ye see, and civil.——As for your Love or your liking, I don't value it of a Rope's End;——And may-hap I like you as little as you do me:——What I said was in Obedience to Father; Gad I fear a Whipping no more than you do. But I tell you one thing, if you shou'd give such Language at Sea, you'd have a Cat o' Nine Tails laid cross your Shoulders. Flesh! who are you? You heard t'other handsome young Woman speak civilly to me, of her own Accord: Whatever you think of your self, Gad I don't think you are any more to compare to her, than a Can of small-Beer to a Bowl of Punch. 62

Miss. Well, and there's a handsome Gentleman, and a fine Gentleman, and a sweet Gentleman, that was here that loves me, and I love him; and if he sees you speak to me any more, he'll thrash your Jacket for you, he will, you great Sea-Calf.

Ben. What, do you mean that fair-Weather Spark that was here just now? Will he thrash my Jacket?—Let'n,——let'n,——But an he comes near me, may-hap I may giv'n a salt Eel for's Supper, for all that. What does Father mean to leave me alone as soon as I come home, with such a dirty dowdy.——Sea-Calf? I an't Calf enough to lick your chalk'd Face, you Cheese-Curd you,——marry thee! Oons I'll marry a *Lapland*

Witch as soon, and live upon selling contrary Winds, and wreck'd Vessels. 78

Miss. I won't be call'd Names, nor I won't be abus'd thus, so I won't.—If I were a Man——[*Cryes*.]——you durst not talk at this rate——No you durst not, you stinking Tar-Barrel.

SCENE VIII.

[*To them*] *Mrs.* FORESIGHT *and Mrs.* FRAIL.

Mrs. *Fore*. They have quarrel'd just as we cou'd wish.

Ben. Tar-Barrel? Let your Sweet-Heart there call me so, if he'll take your Part, your *Tom Essence*, and I'll say something to him; Gad I'll lace his Musk-Doublet for him, I'll make him stink; he shall smell more like a Weasel than a Civet-Cat, afore I ha' done with 'en.

Mrs. *Fore*. Bless me, what's the Matter, Miss? What, does she cry?——Mr. *Benjamin*, what have you done to her? 11

Ben. Let her cry: The more she cries, the less she'll——she has been gathering foul Weather in her Mouth, and now it rains out at her Eyes.

Mrs. *Fore*. Come, Miss, come along with me, and tell me, poor Child.

Mrs. *Frail*. Lord, what shall we do, there's my Brother *Foresight*, and Sir *Sampson* coming. Sister, do you take Miss down into the Parlour, and I'll carry Mr. *Benjamin* into my Chamber, for they must not know that they are fall'n out.—Come, Sir, will you venture your self with me? 22

[*Looking kindly on him.*

Ben. Venture, Mess, and that I will, tho' 'twere to Sea in a Storm.

SCENE IX.

Sir Sampson *and* Foresight.

Sir *Samp.* I left 'em together here; what are they gone? *Ben*'s a brisk Boy: He has got her into a Corner, Father's own Son, faith, he'll touzle her, and mouzle her: The Rogue's sharp set, coming from Sea; if he should not stay for saying Grace, old *Foresight*, but fall to without the help of a Parson, ha? Odd if he shou'd I cou'd not be angry with him; 'twould be but like me, *A Chip of the old Block.* Ha! thou'rt melancholick, old Prognostication; as melancholick as if thou hadst spilt the Salt, or par'd thy Nails on a Sunday:——Come, cheer up, look about thee Look up old Star-Gazer. Now is he poring upon the Ground for a crooked Pin, or an old Horse-Nail, with the Head towards him.

Fore. Sir *Sampson*, we'll have the Wedding to Morrow Morning.

Sir *Samp.* With all my Heart.

Fore. At ten a Clock, punctually at ten. 19

Sir *Samp.* To a Minute, to a Second; thou shall set thy Watch, and the Bridegroom shall observe its Motions; they shall be marry'd to a Minute, go to Bed to a Minute; and when the Alarm strikes, they shall keep time like the Figures of St. *Dunstan*'s Clock, and *Consummatum est* shall ring all over the Parish——

SCENE X.

[*To them*] Scandal.

Scan. Sir *Sampson*, sad News.

Fore. Bless us!

Sir *Samp.* Why, what's the Matter?

Scan. Can't you guess at what ought to afflict you and him, and all of us, more than any thing else?

Sir *Samp*. Body o'me, I don't know any Universal Grievance, but a new Tax, or the loss of the Canary Fleet. Unless Popery shou'd be landed in the *West*, or the *French* Fleet were at Anchor at *Blackwall*.

Scan. No. Undoubtedly, Mr. *Foresight* knew all this, and might have prevented it.

Fore. 'Tis no Earthquake!

Scan. No, not yet; nor Whirlwind. But we don't know what it may come to——
But it has had a Consequence already that touches us all.

Sir *Samp*. Why, body o'me, out with't.

Scan. Something has appear'd to your Son *Valentine*——He's gone to Bed upon't, and very ill——He speaks little, yet he says he has a World to say. Asks for his Father and the wise *Foresight*; talks of *Raymond Lully*, and the Ghost of *Lilly*. He has Secrets to impart I suppose to you two. I can get nothing out of him but Sighs. He desires he may see you in the Morning, but would not be disturb'd to Night, because he has some Business to do in a Dream.

Sir *Samp*. Hoity toity, what have I to do with his Dreams or his Divination—Body o'me, this is a Trick to defer signing the Conveyance. I warrant the Devil will tell him in a Dream, that he must not part with his Estate. But I'll bring him a Parson to tell him, that the Devil's a Liar——
Or if that won't do, I'll bring a Lawyer that shall out-lie the Devil. And so I'll try whether my Black-Guard or his shall get the better of the Day.

SCENE XI.

SCANDAL, FORESIGHT.

Scan. Alas, Mr. *Foresight*, I'm afraid all is not

9 Popery] James II.
24 *Lilly*] The English astrologer, at one time very popular.

right——You are a Wise Man, and a Conscientious Man; a Searcher into Obscurity and Futurity; and if you commit an Error, it is with a great deal of Consideration, and Discretion, and Caution——

Fore. Ah, good Mr. *Scandal*—— 6

Scan. Nay, nay, 'tis manifest; I do not flatter you——But Sir *Sampson* is hasty, very hasty;——I'm afraid he is not scrupulous enough, Mr. *Foresight*——He has been wicked, and Heav'n grant he may mean well in his Affair with you——But my Mind gives me, these things cannot be wholly insignificant. You are wise, and shou'd not be over-reach'd, methinks you shou'd not——

Fore. Alas, Mr. *Scandal*,—*Humanum est errare.*

Scan. You say true, Man will err; meer Man will err—but you are something more——There have been wise Men; but they were such as you—Men who consulted the Stars, and were Observers of Omens——*Salomon* was wise, but how?—by his Judgment in Astrology—So says *Pineda* in his Third Book and Eighth Chapter—— 22

Fore. You are learn'd, Mr. *Scandal*—

Scan. A Trifler—but a Lover of Art——And the Wise Men of the *East* ow'd their Instruction to a Star, which is rightly observ'd by *Gregory* the Great in Favour of Astrology! And *Albertus Magnus* makes it the most valuable Science, Because, says he, it teaches us to consider the Causation of Causes, in the Causes of things. 30

Fore. I protest I honour you, Mr. *Scandal*——I did not think you had been read in these matters——Few Young Men are inclin'd——

Scan. I thank my Stars that have inclined me——But I fear this Marriage and making over this Estate, this transferring of a rightful Inheritance, will bring Judgments upon us. I prophesie it, and I wou'd not have the Fate of *Cassandra*, not to be believ'd. *Valentine* is disturb'd, what can be the Cause of that? and Sir *Sampson* is hurry'd on by an unusual Violence——I fear he does not act wholly from himself; methinks he does not look as he used to do.

Fore. He was always of an impetuous Nature ——But as to this Marriage I have consulted the Stars; and all Appearances are prosperous——

Scan. Come, come, Mr. *Foresight*, let not the Prospect of worldly Lucre carry you beyond your Judgment, nor against your Conscience——You are not satisfy'd that you act justly.

Fore. How!

Scan. You are not satisfy'd, I say——I am loth to discourage you——But it is palpable that you are not satisfy'd.

Fore. How does it appear, Mr. *Scandal*? I think I am very well satisfy'd.

Scan. Either you suffer your self to deceive your self; or you do not know your self.

Fore. Pray explain your self.

Scan. Do you sleep well o'nights?

Fore. Very well.

Scan. Are you certain? You do not look so.

Fore. I am in Health, I think.

Scan. So was *Valentine* this Morning; and look'd just so.

Fore. How! Am I alter'd any way? I don't perceive it.

Scan. That may be, but your Beard is longer than it was two Hours ago.

Fore. Indeed! bless me.

SCENE XII.

[*To them*] *Mrs.* FORESIGHT.

Mrs. *Fore.* Husband, will you go to Bed? It's ten a Clock. Mr. *Scandal*, your Servant.

Scan. Pox on her, she has interrupted my Design——but I must work her into the Project. You keep early Hours, Madam.

Mrs. *Fore.* Mr. *Foresight* is punctual, we sit up after him.

Fore. My Dear, pray lend me your Glass, your little Looking-glass.

Scan. Pray lend it him, Madam——I'll tell you the Reason. [*She gives him the Glass*: Scandal *and she whisper.*] My Passion for you is grown so violent——that I am no longer Master of my self—I was interrupted in the Morning, when you had Charity enough to give me your Attention, and I had Hopes of finding another Opportunity of explaining my self to you——but was disappointed all this Day; and the Uneasiness that has attended me ever since, brings me now hither at this unseasonable Hour.——

Mrs. *Fore.* Was there ever such Impudence, to make Love to me before my Husband's Face? I'll swear I'll tell him.

Scan. Do, I'll die a Martyr, rather than disclaim my Passion. But come a little farther this way, and I'll tell you what Project I had to get him out of the way; that I might have an Opportunity of waiting upon you. [*Whisper.*

[Foresight *looking in the Glass.*

Fore. I do not see any Revolution here;——Methinks I look with a serene and benign aspect——pale, a little pale——but the Roses of these Cheeks have been gather'd many Years;——ha! I do not like that sudden Flushing—Gone already!—hem, hem, hem! faintish. My Heart is pretty good; yet it beats; and my Pulses, ha!——I have none——Mercy on me——hum—Yes, here they are——Gallop, gallop, gallop, gallop, gallop, gallop, hey! Whither will they hurry me?—Now they're gone again—And now I'm faint again; and pale again, and hem! and my hem!—breath, hem!—grows short; hem! hem! he, he, hem!

Scan. It takes, pursue it in the Name of Love and Pleasure.

Mrs. *Fore.* How do you do, Mr. *Foresight*?

Fore. Hum, not so well as I thought I was. Lend me your Hand.

Scan. Look you there now——Your Lady says, your Sleep has been unquiet of late.

Fore. Very likely.

Mrs. *Fore.* O mighty restless, but I was afraid to tell him so,——He has been subject to Talking and Starting.

Scan. And did not use to be so.

Mrs. *Fore.* Never, never; 'till within these three Nights; I cannot say, that he has once broken my Rest, since we have been marry'd.

Fore. I will go to Bed.

Scan. Do so, Mr. *Foresight*, and say your Pray'rs——He looks better than he did.

Mrs. *Fore.* Nurse, Nurse!

Fore. Do you think so, Mr. *Scandal*?

Scan. Yes, yes, I hope this will be gone by Morning, taking it in time.——

Fore. I hope so.

SCENE XIII.

[*To them*] Nurse.

Mrs. *Fore.* Nurse; your Master is not well; put him to Bed.

Scan. I hope you will be able to see *Valentine* in the Morning,——you had best take a little Diacodion and Cowslip-Water, and lye upon your Back, may be you may dream.

Fore. I thank you Mr. *Scandal*, I will——Nurse, let me have a Watch-Light, and lay the Crums of Comfort by me.—

Nurse. Yes, Sir.

Fore. And——hem, hem! I am very faint.——

Scan. No, no, you look much better.

Fore. Do I? And d'ye hear——bring me, let me see——within a Quarter of Twelve—hem—he, hem!—just upon the turning of the Tide, bring me the Urinal;——And I hope, neither the Lord of my Ascendant, nor the Moon will be combust; and then I may do well.

Scan. I hope so——Leave that to me; I will erect a Scheme; and I hope I shall find both *Sol* and *Venus* in the sixth House.

Fore. I thank you, Mr. *Scandal*, indeed that wou'd be a great Comfort to me. Hem, hem! good Night.

SCENE XIV.

SCANDAL, *Mrs.* FORESIGHT.

Scan. Good Night, good Mr. *Foresight*;——and I hope *Mars* and *Venus* will be in Conjunction;——while your Wife and I are together.

Mrs. *Fore.* Well; and what use do you hope to make of this Project? You don't think, that you are ever like to succeed in your Design upon me.

Scan. Yes, Faith I do; I have a better Opinion both of you and my self, than to despair.

Mrs. *Fore.* Did you ever hear such a Toad—hark'ee Devil; do you think any Woman honest?

Scan. Yes, several, very honest;——they'll cheat a little at Cards, sometimes, but that's nothing.

Mrs. *Fore.* Pshaw! but virtuous I mean.

Scan. Yes, Faith, I believe some Women are virtuous too; but 'tis as I believe some Men are Valiant, thro' Fear——For why shou'd a Man court Danger, or a Woman shun Pleasure.

Mrs. *Fore.* O monstrous! What are Conscience and Honour?

Scan. Why, Honour is a publick Enemy; and Conscience a Domestick Thief; and he that wou'd secure his Pleasure, must pay a Tribute to one, and go halves with t'other. As for Honour, that you have secur'd, for you have purchas'd a perpetual Opportunity for Pleasure.

Mrs. *Fore.* An Opportunity for Pleasure!

Scan. Ay, your Husband, a Husband is an Opportunity for Pleasure, so you have taken care of Honour, and 'tis the least I can do to take care of Conscience.

Mrs. *Fore.* And so you think we are free for one another?

Scan. Yes Faith, I think so; I love to speak my Mind.

Mrs. *Fore.* Why then I'll speak my Mind. Now as to this Affair between you and me. Here you make love to me; why, I'll confess it does not displease me. Your Person is well enough, and your Understanding is not amiss.

Scan. I have no great Opinion of my self; but I think, I'm neither deform'd, nor a Fool.

Mrs. *Fore.* But you have a villainous Character; you are a Libertine in Speech, as well as Practice.

Scan. Come, I know what you wou'd say,—— you think it more dangerous to be seen in Conversation with me, than to allow some other Men the last Favour; you mistake, the Liberty I take in talking, is purely affected, for the Service of your Sex. He that first cries out stop Thief, is often he that has stol'n the Treasure. I am a Jugler, that act by Confederacy; and if you please, we'll put a Trick upon the World.

Mrs. *Fore.* Ay; but you are such a universal Jugler,——that I'm afraid you have a great many Confederates.

Scan. Faith, I'm sound.

Mrs. *Fore.* O, fie——I'll swear you're impudent.

Scan. I'll swear you're handsome.

Mrs. *Fore.* Pish, you'd tell me so, tho' you did not think so.

Scan. And you'd think so, tho' I shou'd not tell you so: And now I think we know one another pretty well.

Mrs. *Fore.* O Lord, who's here?

SCENE XV.

[*To them*] Mrs. FRAIL *and* BEN.

Ben. Mess, I love to speak my Mind——Father has nothing to do with me—Nay, I can't say that neither; he has something to do with me. But what does that signifie? If so be, that I ben't minded to be steer'd by him; 'tis as tho'f he should strive against Wind and Tide.

Mrs. *Frail.* Ay, but my Dear, we must keep it secret, 'till the Estate be settled; for you know, marrying without an Estate, is like sailing in a Ship without Ballast.

Ben. He, he, he; why that's true; just so for all the World it is indeed, as like as two Cable Ropes.

Mrs. *Frail.* And tho' I have a good Portion; you know one wou'd not venture all in one Bottom.

Ben. Why that's true again; for may-hap one Bottom may spring a Leak. You have hit it indeed, Mess, you've nick'd the Channel.

Mrs. *Frail.* Well, but if you shou'd forsake me after all, you'd break my Heart.

Ben. Break your Heart? I'd rather the *Marygold* shou'd break her Cable in a Storm, as well as I love her. Flesh, you don't think I'm false-hearted, like a Land-Man. A Sailor will be honest, tho'f may-hap he has never a Penny of Mony in his Pocket——May-hap I may not have so fair a Face, as a Citizen or a Courtier; but for all that, I've as good Blood in my Veins, and a Heart as sound as a Bisket.

Mrs. *Frail.* And will you love me always?

Ben. Nay, an I love once, I'll stick like Pitch; I'll tell you what. Come, I'll sing you a Song of a Sailor.

Mrs. *Frail.* Hold, there's my Sister, I'll call her to hear it.

Mrs. *Fore.* Well; I won't go to Bed to my Husband to Night; because I'll retire to my own Chamber, and think of what you have said.

Scan. Well; you'll give me Leave to wait upon you to your Chamber Door; and leave you my last Instructions?

Mrs. *Fore.* Hold, here's my Sister coming towards us.

Mrs. *Frail.* If it won't interrupt you, I'll entertain you with a Song.

Ben. The Song was made upon one of our Ships-Crew's Wife; our Boat-swain made the Song, may-hap you may know her, Sir. Before she was marry'd, she was call'd Buxom *Joan* of *Deptford.*

Scan. I have heard of her. [Ben *sings.*

BALLAD.

Set by Mr. *John Eccles.*

I.

A Soldier and a Sailor,
A Tinker, and a Tailor,
Had once a doubtful Strife, Sir,
To make a Maid a Wife, Sir,
Whose Name was Buxom Joan.
For now the time was ended,
When she no more intended,
To lick her Lips at Men, Sir.
And gnaw the Sheets in vain, Sir,
And lye o'Nights alone.

II.

The Soldier swore like Thunder,
He lov'd her more than Plunder;
And shew'd her many a Scar, Sir,
That he had brought from far, Sir,
With fighting for her Sake.
The Tailor thought to please her,
With off'ring her his Measure.
The Tinker too with Mettle,
Said he could mend her Kettle,
And stop up ev'ry Leak.

III.

But while these three were prating,
The Sailor slily waiting,
Thought if it came about, Sir,
That they should all fall out, Sir:
He then might play his Part.
And just e'en as he meant, Sir,
To loggerheads they went, Sir,
And then he let fly at her,
A shot 'twixt Wind and Water,
That won this fair Maid's Heart.

Ben. If some of our Crew that came to see me, are not gone; you shall see, that we Sailors can dance sometimes, as well as other Folks. [*Whistles.*] I warrant that brings 'em, an they be within hearing.

Enter Seamen.

Oh here they be——And Fiddles along with 'em; come, my Lads, let's have a Round, and I'll make one. [*Dance.*

Ben. We're merry Folks, we Sailors, we han't much to care for. Thus we live at Sea; eat Bisket, and drink Flip; put on a clean Shirt once a Quarter——Come home, and lye with our Landladies once a Year, get rid of a little Mony; and then put off with the next fair Wind. How d'ye like us?

Mrs. *Frail.* O'you are the happiest, merriest Men alive.

Mrs. *Fore.* We're beholden to Mr. *Benjamin* for this Entertainment.
I believe it's late.

Ben. Why, forsooth, an you think so, you had best go to Bed. For my Part, I mean to toss a Can, and remember my Sweet-Heart, a-fore I turn in; may-hap I may dream of her.

Mrs. *Fore.* Mr. *Scandal*, you had best go to Bed and dream too.

Scan. Why Faith, I have a good lively Imagination; and can dream as much to the Purpose as another, if I set about it: But dreaming is the poor Retreat of a lazy, hopeless, and imperfect Lover; 'tis the last Glimpse of Love to worn-out Sinners, and the faint dawning of a Bliss to wishing Girls, and growing Boys.

There's nought but willing, waking Love, that can
Make blest the Ripen'd Maid and finish'd Man.

End of the Third Act.

ACT IV. SCENE I.

Valentine's *Lodging.*

SCANDAL *and* JEREMY.

SCANDAL.

Well, is your Master ready; does he look madly, and talk madly?

Jere. Yes Sir; you need make no great doubt of that; he that was so near turning Poet yesterday Morning, can't be much to seek in playing the Madman to Day.

Scan. Would he have *Angelica* acquainted with
the Reason of his Design? 8

Jere. No, Sir, not yet;——He has a Mind to try, whether his playing the Madman, won't make her play the Fool, and fall in Love with him; or at least own, that she has lov'd him all this while, and conceal'd it.

Scan. I saw her take Coach just now with her Maid; and think I heard her bid the Coachman drive hither.

Jere. Like enough, Sir, for I told her Maid this Morning, my Master was run stark mad only for Love of her Mistress; I hear a Coach stop; if it should be she, Sir, I believe he would not see her, till he hears how she takes it.

Scan. Well, I'll try her——'tis she, here she comes.

SCENE II.

[*To them*] ANGELICA *with* JENNY.

Ang. Mr. *Scandal*, I suppose you don't think it a Novelty, to see a Woman visit a Man at his own Lodgings in a Morning?

Scan. Not upon a kind Occasion, Madam. But when a Lady comes tyrannically to insult a ruin'd Lover, and make manifest the cruel Triumphs of her Beauty; the Barbarity of it something surprizes me.

Ang. I don't like Raillery from a serious Face——pray tell me what is the Matter?

Jere. No strange Matter, Madam; my Master's mad, that's all: I suppose your Ladyship has thought him so a great while.

Ang. How d'ye mean, mad?

Jere. Why faith, Madam, he's mad for want of his Wits, just as he was poor for want of Mony; his Head is e'en as light as his Pockets; and any Body that has a Mind to a bad Bargain, can't do better than to beg him for his Estate.

Ang. If you speak Truth, your endeavouring at Wit is very unseasonable——

Scan. She's concern'd, and loves him. [*Aside.*

Ang. Mr. *Scandal*, you can't think me guilty of so much Inhumanity, as not to be concern'd for a Man I must own my self oblig'd to—pray tell me Truth.

Scan. Faith, Madam, I wish telling a Lie would mend the Matter. But this is no new Effect of an unsuccessful Passion.

Ang. [*Aside.*] I know not what to think——Yet I shou'd be vext to have a Trick put upon me——May I not see him?

Scan. I'm afraid the Physician is not willing you shou'd see him yet—*Jeremy*, go in and enquire.

SCENE III.

Scandal, Angelica, Jenny.

Ang. Ha! I saw him wink and smile—I fancy 'tis a Trick—I'll try—I would disguise to all the World a Failing, which I must own to you——I fear my Happiness depends upon the Recovery of *Valentine*. Therefore I conjure you, as you are his Friend, and as you have Compassion upon one fearful of Affliction, to tell me what I am to hope for——I cannot speak——But you may tell me, tell me, for you know what I wou'd ask?

Scan. So, this is pretty plain——Be not too much concerned, Madam; I hope his Condition is not desperate: An Acknowledgement of Love from you, perhaps, may work a Cure; as the Fear of your Aversion occasion'd his Distemper.

Ang. [*Aside.*] Say you so; nay then I'm convinc'd: And if I don't play Trick for Trick, may I never taste the Pleasure of Revenge——Acknowledgement of Love! I find you have mistaken my Compassion, and think me guilty of a Weakness I am a Stranger to. But I have too much Sincerity to deceive you, and too much Charity to suffer him to be deluded with vain Hopes. Good Nature and Humanity oblige me to be concern'd for him; but to love is neither in my Power nor Inclination; and if he can't be cur'd without I suck the Poison from his Wounds, I'm afraid he won't recover his Senses 'till I lose mine.

Scan. Hey, brave Woman, I faith——Won't you see him then, if he desire it?

Ang. What signifie a Madman's Desires? Besides, 'twou'd make me uneasie—If I don't see him, perhaps my Concern for him may lessen—

If I forget him, 'tis no more than he has done by himself; and now the Surprize is over, methinks I am not half so sorry as I was——

Scan. So, faith good Nature works apace; you were confessing just now an Obligation to his Love.

Ang. But I have consider'd that Passions are unreasonable and involuntary; if he loves, he can't help it; and if I don't love, I can't help it; no more than he can help his being a Man, or I my being a Woman; or no more than I can help my want of Inclination to stay longer here—Come, *Jenny.*

SCENE IV.

SCANDAL, JEREMY.

Scan. Humh!—An admirable Composition, Faith, this same Womankind.

Jere. What, is she gone, Sir?

Scan. Gone; why she was never here, nor any where else; nor I don't know her if I see her; nor you neither.

Jere. Good lack! What's the matter now? Are any more of us to be mad? Why, Sir, my Master longs to see her; and is almost mad in good earnest, with the joyful News of her being here.

Scan. We are all under a Mistake——Ask no Questions, for I can't resolve you; but I'll inform your Master. In the mean time, if our Project succeed no better with his Father, than it does with his Mistress, he may descend from his Exaltation of Madness into the Road of common Sense, and be content only to be made a Fool with other reasonable People. I hear Sir *Sampson.* You know your Cue; I'll to your Master.

SCENE V.

JEREMY, *Sir* SAMPSON LEGEND, *with a* LAWYER.

Sir *Samp*. D'ye see, Mr. *Buckram*, here's the Paper sign'd with his own Hand.

Buck. Good, Sir. And the Conveyance is ready drawn in this Box, if he be ready to sign and seal.

Sir *Samp*. Ready, Body o'me, he must be ready: His Sham-Sickness shan't excuse him—O, here's his Scoundrel. Sirrah, where's your Master?

Jere. Ah, Sir, he's quite gone.

Sir *Samp*. Gone! What, he is not dead?

Jere. No, Sir, not dead.

Sir *Samp*. What, is he gone out of Town, run away, ha! has he trick'd me? speak, Varlet.

Jere. No, no, Sir, he's safe enough, Sir, an he were but as sound, poor Gentleman. He is indeed here, Sir, and not here, Sir.

Sir *Samp*. Hey day, Rascal, do you banter me? Sirrah, d'ye banter me,——Speak Sirrah, where is he, for I will find him.

Jere. Would you could, Sir; for he has lost himself. Indeed, Sir, I have a most broke my Heart about him—I can't refrain Tears when I think of him, Sir: I'm as melancholy for him as a Passing-Bell, Sir; or a Horse in a Pound.

Sir *Samp*. A Pox confound your Similitudes, Sir——Speak to be understood, and tell me in plain Terms what the Matter is with him, or I'll crack your Fool's Scull.

Jere. Ah, you've hit it, Sir; that's the Matter with him, Sir; his Skull's crack'd, poor Gentleman; he's stark mad, Sir.

Sir *Samp*. Mad!

Buck. What, is he *Non Compos*?

Jere. Quite *Non Compos*, Sir.

Buck. Why then all's obliterated, Sir *Sampson*,

if he be *Non Compos mentis*, his Act and Deed will be of no Effect, it is not good in Law.

Sir *Samp*. Oons, I won't believe it ; let me see him, Sir—Mad, I'll make him find his Senses.

Jere. Mr. *Scandal* is with him, Sir ; I'll knock at the Door.

[*Goes to the Scene, which opens.*

SCENE VI.

Sir SAMPSON, VALENTINE, SCANDAL, JEREMY, *and* LAWYER. (Valentine *upon a Couch disorderly dress'd.*)

Sir *Samp*. How now, what's here to do ?

Val. Ha ! Who's that ? [*Starting.*

Scan. For Heav'ns sake softly, Sir, and gently ; don't provoke him.

Val. Answer me ; Who is that ? and that ?

Sir *Samp*. Gads bobs, does he not know me ? Is he mischievous ? I'll speak gently—*Val*, *Val*, do'st thou not know me, Boy ? Not know thy own Father, *Val* ! I am thy own Father, and this is honest *Brief Buckram* the Lawyer.

Val. It may be so——I did not know you——the World is full——There are People that we do know, and People that we do not know ; and yet the Sun shines upon all alike——There are Fathers that have many Children ; and there are Children that have many Fathers——'tis strange ! But I am Truth, and come to give the World the Lie.

Sir *Samp*. Body o'me, I know not what to say to him.

Val. Why does that Lawyer wear black ?——Does he carry his Conscience withoutside ?—Lawyer, what art thou ? Dost thou know me ?

Buckr. O Lord, what must I say ?——Yes, Sir.

Val. Thou liest, for I am Truth. 'Tis hard I cannot get a Livelyhood amongst you. I have been sworn out of *Westminster-Hall* the first Day of every Term—Let me see—No matter how long ——But I'll tell you one thing; it's a Question that would puzzle an Arithmetician, if you should ask him, whether the Bible saves more Souls in *Westminster-Abby*, or damns more in *Westminster-Hall*: For my part, I am Truth, and can't tell; I have very few Acquaintance.

Sir *Samp*. Body o'me, he talks sensibly in his Madness——Has he no Intervals?

Jere. Very short, Sir.

Buckr. Sir, I can do you no Service while he's in this Condition: Here's your Paper, Sir——He may do me a Mischief if I stay——The Conveyance is ready, Sir. If he recovers his Senses.

SCENE VII.

Sir SAMPSON, VALENTINE, SCANDAL, JEREMY.

Sir *Samp*. Hold, hold, don't you go yet.

Scan. You'd better let him go, Sir; and send for him if there be Occasion; for I fancy his Presence provokes him more.

Val. Is the Lawyer gone? 'Tis well, then we may drink about without going together by the Ears—heigh ho! What a Clock is't? My Father here! Your Blessing, Sir?

Sir *Samp*. He recovers——bless thee, *Val*.—How dost thou do, Boy?

Val. Thank you, Sir, pretty well——I have been a little out of Order; won't you please to sit, Sir?

Sir *Samp*. Ay, Boy,—Come, thou shalt sit down by me.

Val. Sir, 'tis my Duty to wait.

Sir *Samp*. No, no, come, come, sit thee down, honest *Val*: How do'st thou do? let me feel thy Pulse—Oh, pretty well now, *Val*: Body o'me, I was sorry to see thee indisposed: But I'm glad thou art better, honest *Val*.

26 *Westminster-Hall*] Then the law court.

Val. I thank you, Sir.

Scan. Miracle! the Monster grows loving. [*Aside.*

Sir *Samp.* Let me feel thy Hand again, *Val*: It does not shake—I believe thou canst write, *Val*: Ha, Boy? thou canst write thy Name, *Val*?——*Jeremy*, step and overtake Mr. *Buckram*, bid him make haste back with the Conveyance—quick—quick. [*In Whisper to* Jeremy.

SCENE VIII.

Sir SAMPSON, VALENTINE, SCANDAL.

Scan. That ever I shou'd suspect such a Heathen of any Remorse! [*Aside.*

Sir *Samp.* Do'st thou know this Paper, *Val*? I know thou'rt honest, and wilt perform Articles.

[*Shews him the Paper, but holds it out of his Reach.*

Val. Pray let me see it, Sir. You hold it so far off, that I can't tell whether I know it or no. 6

Sir *Samp.* See it, Boy? Ay, ay, why thou do'st see it—'tis thy own Hand, *Vally*. Why, let me see, I can read it as plain as can be: Look you here [*Reads.*] *The Condition of this Obligation*——Look you, as plain as can be, so it begins——And then at the Bottom——*As witness my Hand*, VALENTINE LEGEND, in great Letters. Why, 'tis as plain as the Nose in one's Face: What, are my Eyes better than thine? I believe I can read it farther off yet—let me see.

[*Stretches his Arm as far as he can.*

Val. Will you please let me hold it, Sir? 17

Sir *Samp.* Let thee hold it, say'st thou——Ay, with all my Heart——What matter is it who holds it? What need any body hold it?—I'll put it up in my Pocket, *Val.* and then no body need hold it [*Puts the Paper in his Pocket.*] There *Val*: it's safe enough, Boy——But thou shalt have it as soon as thou hast set thy Hand to another Paper, little *Val*.

SCENE IX.

[*To them*] JEREMY *with* BUCKRAM.

Val. What, is my bad Genius here again! Oh no, 'tis the Lawyer with an itching Palm; and he's come to be scratch'd—My Nails are not long enough—Let me have a Pair of Red-hot Tongs quickly, quickly, and you shall see me act St. *Dunstan*, and lead the Devil by the Nose.

Buckr. O Lord, let me be gone; I'll not venture my self with a Madman.

SCENE X.

Sir SAMPSON, VALENTINE, SCANDAL, JEREMY.

Val. Ha, ha, ha; you need not run so fast, Honesty will not overtake you——Ha, ha, ha, the Rogue found me out to be in *Forma Pauperis* presently.

Sir *Samp*. Oons! What a Vexation is here! I know not what to do, or say, nor which way to go.

Val. Who's that, that's out of his way?——I am Truth, and can set him right——Harkee, Friend, the strait Road is the worst way you can go——He that follows his Nose always, will very often be led into a Stink. *Probatum est*. But what are you for? Religion or Politicks? There's a couple of Topicks for you, no more like one another than Oil and Vinegar; and yet those two beaten together by a State-Cook, make Sauce for the whole Nation.

Sir *Samp*. What the Devil had I to do, ever to beget Sons? Why did I ever marry?

Val. Because thou wert a Monster; old Boy?

The two greatest Monsters in the World, are a Man and a Woman? What's thy Opinion?

Sir *Samp.* Why, my Opinion is, that those two Monsters join'd together, make yet a greater, that's a Man and his Wife.

Val. A ha! Old True-penny, say'st thou so: thou hast nick'd it——But it's wonderful strange, *Jeremy.*

Jere. What is, Sir? 29

Val. That gray Hairs shou'd cover a green Head—and I make a Fool of my Father. What's here! *Erra Pater*: or a bearded Sybil? If Prophecy comes Truth must give place.

SCENE XI.

Sir SAMPSON, SCANDAL, FORESIGHT, *Mrs.* FORESIGHT, *Mrs.* FRAIL.

Fore. What says he? What, did he prophesie? Ha, Sir *Sampson*, bless us! How are we?

Sir *Samp.* Are we? A Pox o'your Prognostication—Why, we are Fools as we use to be—Oons, that you cou'd not foresee, that the Moon wou'd predominate, and my Son be mad—Where's your Oppositions, your Trines, and your Quadrates? ——What did your *Cardan* and your *Ptolome* tell you? Your *Messahalah* and your *Longomontanus*, your Harmony of Chiromancy with Astrology. Ah! pox on't, that I that know the World, and Men and Manners, that don't believe a Syllable in the Sky and Stars, and Sun and Almanacks, and trash, should be directed by a Dreamer, an Omen-hunter, and defer Business in Expectation of a lucky Hour. When, Body o'me, there never was a lucky Hour after the first Opportunity.

SCENE XII.

Scandal, Foresight, *Mrs.* Foresight, *Mrs.* Frail.

Fore. Ah, Sir *Sampson*, Heav'n help your Head——This is none of your lucky Hour; *Nemo omnibus horis sapit.* What, is he gone, and in contempt of Science! Ill Stars, and unconvertible Ignorance attend him.

Scan. You must excuse his Passion, Mr. *Foresight*; for he has been heartily vex'd—His Son is *Non compos mentis*, and thereby incapable of making any Conveyance in Law; so that all his Measures are disappointed. 10

Fore. Ha! say you so?

Mrs. *Frail.* What, has my Sea-Lover lost his Anchor of Hope then?

[*Aside to Mrs.* Foresight.

Mrs. *Fore.* Oh Sister, what will you do with him?

Mrs. *Frail.* Do with him, send him to Sea again in the next foul Weather——He's us'd to an inconstant Element, and won't be surpriz'd to see the Tide turn'd. 19

Fore. Wherein was I mistaken, not to foresee this? [*Considers.*

Scan. Madam, you and I can tell him something else, that he did not foresee, and more particularly relating to his own Fortune.

[*Aside to Mrs.* Foresight.

Mrs. *Fore.* What do you mean? I don't understand you.

Scan. Hush, softly—the Pleasures of last Night, my Dear, too considerable to be forgot so soon.

Mrs. *Fore.* Last Night! and what wou'd your Impudence infer from last Night? last Night was like the Night before, I think. 31

Scan. 'S'death, do you make no difference between me and your Husband?

Mrs. *Fore.* Not much,——he's superstitious; and you are mad in my Opinion.

Scan. You make me mad——You are not serious—Pray recollect your self.

Mrs. *Fore.* O yes, now I remember, you were very impertinent and impudent,—and would have come to Bed to me.

Scan. And did not?

Mrs. *Fore.* Did not! With what Face can you ask the Question?

Scan. This I have heard of before, but never believ'd. I have been told, she had that admirable Quality of forgetting to a Man's Face in the Morning, that she had lain with him all Night, and denying that she had done Favours with more Impudence, than she cou'd grant 'em—Madam, I'm your humble Servant, and honour you.—You look pretty well, Mr. *Foresight.*—How did you rest last Night?

Fore. Truly Mr. *Scandal*, I was so taken up with broken Dreams and distracted Visions, that I remember little.

Scan. 'Twas a very forgetting Night.—But would you not talk with *Valentine*, perhaps you may understand him; I'm apt to believe, there is something mysterious in his Discourses, and sometimes rather think him inspir'd than mad.

Fore. You speak with singular good Judgment, Mr. *Scandal*, truly,——I am inclining to your *Turkish* Opinion in this Matter, and do reverence a Man whom the vulgar think mad. Let us go to him.

Mrs. *Frail.* Sister, do you stay with them; I'll find out my Lover, and give him his Discharge, and come to you. O'my Conscience here he comes.

SCENE XIII.

Mrs. FRAIL, BEN.

Ben. All mad, I think—Flesh, I believe all the

Calentures of the Sea are come ashore, for my part.

Mrs. *Frail*. Mr. *Benjamin* in Choler!

Ben. No, I'm pleased well enough, now I have found you,——Mess, I have had such a Hurricane upon your Account yonder.—

Mrs. *Frail*. My Account, pray what's the Matter?

Ben. Why, Father came and found me squabling with yon chitty-fac'd thing, as he would have me marry,—so he ask'd what was the Matter.—He ask'd in a surly sort of a way—(It seems Brother *Val*. is gone mad, and so that put'n into a Passion; but what did I know that, what's that to me?)—So he ask'd in a surly sort of manner,—and Gad I answer'd 'en as surlily, What tho'f he be my Father, I an't bound Prentice to 'en:—so faith I told'n in plain Terms, if I were minded to marry, I'd marry to please my self, not him: And for the young Woman that he provided for me, I thought it more fitting for her to learn her Sampler, and make Dirt-Pies, than to look after a Husband; for my part I was none of her Man.——I had another Voyage to make, let him take it as he will.

Mrs. *Frail*. So then, you intend to go to Sea again?

Ben. Nay, nay, my Mind run upon you,—but I wou'd not tell him so much—So he said he'd make my Heart ake; and if so be that he cou'd get a Woman to his Mind, he'd marry himself. Gad, says I, an you play the Fool and marry at these Years, there's more Danger of your Head's aking than my Heart.—He was woundy angry when I gav'n that wipe.—He hadn't a Word to say, and so I left'n, and the green Girl together; may-hap the Bee may bite, and he'll marry her himself, with all my Heart.

2 Calenture] a delirious fever common at sea in hot latitudes.

Mrs. *Frail.* And were you this undutiful and graceless Wretch to your Father?

Ben. Then why was he graceless first,——If I am undutiful and graceless, why did he beget me so? I did not get my self.

Mrs. *Frail.* O Impiety! How have I been mistaken! What an inhuman merciless Creature have I set my Heart upon? O I am happy to have discover'd the Shelves and Quicksands that lurk beneath that faithless smiling Face.

Ben. Hey toss! What's the Matter now? Why you ben't angry, be you?

Mrs. *Frail.* O see me no more,——for thou wert born amongst Rocks, suckl'd by Whales, cradled in a Tempest, and whistled to by Winds; and thou art come forth with Fins and Scales, and three Rows of Teeth, a most outragious Fish of Prey.

Ben. O Lord, O Lord, she's mad, poor young Woman, Love has turn'd her Senses, her Brain is quite overset. Well-a-day, how shall I do to set her to rights.

Mrs. *Frail.* No, no, I am not mad, Monster, I am wise enough to find you out.——Hadst thou the Impudence to aspire at being a Husband with that stubborn and disobedient Temper?——You that know not how to submit to a Father, presume to have sufficient Stock of Duty to undergo a Wife? I should have been finely fobb'd indeed, very finely fobb'd.

Ben. Harkee Forsooth; if so be that you are in your right Senses, d'ye see; for ought as I perceive I'm like to be finely fobb'd,——if I have got Anger here upon your Account, and you are tack'd about already.——What d'ye mean, after all your fair Speeches, and stroaking my Cheeks, and kissing and hugging, what wou'd you sheer off so? Wou'd you, and leave me aground?

Mrs. *Frail.* No, I'll leave you a-drift, and go which way you will.

Ben. What, are you false-hearted then?

Mrs. *Frail.* Only the Wind's chang'd.

Ben. More shame for you,——the Wind's chang'd?—It's an ill Wind blows no Body good,—may-hap I have a good riddance on you, if these be your Tricks,——what did you mean all this while, to make a Fool of me?

Mrs. *Frail.* Any Fool, but a Husband.

Ben. Husband! Gad I wou'd not be your Husband, if you wou'd have me; now I know your Mind, tho'f you had your Weight in Gold and Jewels, and tho'f I lov'd you never so well.

Mrs. *Frail.* Why, can'st thou love, *Porpusse*?

Ben. No matter what I can do; don't call Names,——I don't love you so well as to bear that, whatever I did,——I'm glad you shew your self, Mistress:—Let them marry you, as don't know you:—Gad I know you too well, by sad Experience; I believe he that marries you will go to Sea in a Hen-peck'd Frigat—I believe that, young Woman——and may-hap may come to an Anchor at *Cuckolds-Point*; so there's a Dash for you, take it as you will, may-hap you may holla after me when I won't come too.

Mrs. *Frail.* Ha, ha, ha, no doubt on't,—*My true Love is gone to Sea*—— [*Sings.*

SCENE XIV.

Mrs. FRAIL, *Mrs.* FORESIGHT.

Mrs. *Frail.* O Sister, had you come a Minute sooner, you would have seen the Resolution of a Lover,——Honest *Tarr* and I are parted;——and with the same Indifference that we met:——O' my Life I am half vex'd at the insensibility of a Brute that I despis'd.

Mrs. *Fore.* What then, he bore it most heroically?

Mrs. *Frail.* Most Tyrannically,——for you see

he has got the start of me ; and I the poor forsaken Maid am left complaining on the Shoar. But I'll tell you a Hint that he has given me ; Sir *Sampson* is enraged, and talks desperately of committing Matrimony himself.——If he has a Mind to throw himself away, he can't do it more effectually than upon me, if we could bring it about.

Mrs. *Fore.* Oh hang him old Fox, he's too cunning, besides he hates both you and me.——But I have a Project in my Head for you, and I have gone a good way towards it. I have almost made a Bargain with *Jeremy*, *Valentine*'s Man, to
sell his Master to us. 22

Mrs. *Frail.* Sell him, how?

Mrs. *Fore.* *Valentine* raves upon *Angelica*, and took me for her, and *Jeremy* says will take any body for her that he imposes on him.——Now I have promised him Mountains ; if in one of his mad fits he will bring you to him in her stead, and get you marry'd together, and put to Bed together ; and after Consummation, Girl, there's no revoking. And if he should recover his Senses, he'll be glad at least to make you a good Settlement—Here they come, stand aside a little, and tell me how you like the Design.

SCENE XV.

Mrs. Foresight, *Mrs.* Frail, Valentine, Scandal, Foresight, *and* Jeremy.

Scan. And have you given your Master a hint of their Plot upon him? [*To* Jere.

Jere. Yes, Sir ; he says he'll favour it, and mistake her for *Angelica*.

Scan. It may make us sport.

Fore. Mercy on us!

Val. Husht——Interrupt me not——I'll whisper Prediction to thee, and thou shalt Prophesie ;——I am Truth, and can teach thy Tongue a new

Trick,——I have told thee what's past,——Now I'll tell you what's to come ;——Dost thou know what will happen to Morrow ?——Answer me not ——for I will tell thee. To Morrow, Knaves will thrive thro' Craft, and Fools thro' Fortune ; and Honesty will go as it did, Frost-nipt in a Summer Suit. Ask me Questions concerning to Morrow ?

Scan. Ask him, Mr. *Foresight.*

Fore. Pray what will be done at Court ?

Val. Scandal will tell you ;——I am Truth, I never come there.

Fore. In the City ?

Val. Oh, Prayers will be said in empty Churches, at the usual Hours. Yet you will see such zealous Faces behind Counters, as if Religion were to be sold in every Shop. Oh things will go methodically in the City, the Clocks will strike twelve at Noon, and the horn'd Herd Buz in the Exchange at Two. Wives and Husbands will drive distinct Trades, and Care and Pleasure separately occupy the Family. Coffee-Houses will be full of Smoak and Stratagem. And the cropt Prentice, that sweeps his Master's Shop in the Morning, may ten to one dirty his Sheets before Night. But there are two things that you will see very strange ; which are wanton Wives, with their Legs at Liberty, and tame Cuckolds, with Chains about their Necks. But hold, I must examine you before I go further ; you look suspiciously. Are you a Husband ?

Fore. I am married.

Val. Poor Creature ! Is your Wife of *Covent-Garden* Parish !

Fore. No ; St. *Martins* in the Fields.

Val. Alas ; poor Man ; his Eyes are sunk, and his Hands shrivell'd : his Legs dwindl'd, and his Back bow'd, pray, pray, for a Metamorphosis—— Change thy Shape, and shake off Age ; get thee *Medea*'s Kettle, and be boil'd a-new ; come forth with lab'ring Callous Hands, a Chine of Steel, and

Atlas Shoulders. Let *Taliacotius* trim the Calves of twenty Chairmen, and make thee Pedestals to stand erect upon, and look Matrimony in the Face. Ha, ha, ha! That a Man shou'd have a Stomach to a Wedding Supper, when the Pidgeons ought rather to be laid to his Feet, ha, ha, ha.

Fore. His frenzy is very high now, Mr. *Scandal.*

Scan. I believe it is a Spring Tide.

Fore. Very likely truly; you understand these
Matters——Mr. *Scandal*, I shall be very glad to
confer with you about these things which he has
utter'd.—His Sayings are very Mysterious and
Hieroglyphical. 62

Val. Oh, why would *Angelica* be absent from my Eyes so long?

Jere. She's here, Sir.

Mrs. *Fore.* Now, Sister.

Mrs. *Frail.* O Lord, what must I say?

Scan. Humour him, Madam, by all means.

Val. Where is she? Oh I see her——she comes,
like Riches, Health and Liberty at once, to a
despairing, starving, and abandon'd Wretch, 71
Oh welcome, welcome.

Mrs. *Frail.* How d'ye you, Sir? Can I serve you?

Val. Harkee;——I have a Secret to tell you—
Endymion and the Moon shall meet us upon
Mount *Latmos*, and we'll be marry'd in the dead of
Night.——But say not a Word. *Hymen* shall put
his Torch into a dark Lanthorn, that it may be
secret; and *Juno* shall give her *Peacock* Poppy-
Water, that he may fold his ogling Tail, and
Argus's hundred Eyes be shut, ha? No body shall
know, but *Jeremy.* 83

Mrs. *Frail.* No, no, we'll keep it secret, it shall be done presently.

Val. The sooner the better——*Jeremy*, come hither——closer——that none may over-hear us; ——*Jeremy*, I can tell you News; *Angelica* is turn'd Nun; and I am turning Fryar, and yet we'll marry one another in spite of the Pope——Get me a Coul and Beads, that I may play my part,——For she'll meet me two Hours hence in black and white, and a long Veil to cover the Project, and we won't see one anothers Faces, 'till we have done something to be asham'd of; and then we'll blush once for all.

SCENE XVI.

[*To them*] TATTLE *and* ANGELICA.

Jere. I'll take care, and——

Val. Whisper.

Ang. Nay, Mr. *Tattle*, if you make Love to me, you spoil my Design, for I intend to make you my Confident.

Tatt. But, Madam, to throw away your Person, such a Person! and such a Fortune on a Madman!

Ang. I never lov'd him 'till he was mad; but don't tell any Body so.

Scan. How's this! *Tattle* making Love to *Angelica!*

Tatt. Tell, Madam! alas you don't know me——I have much ado to tell your Ladyship, how long I have been in Love with you—but encourag'd by the Impossibility of *Valentine*'s making any more Addresses to you, I have ventur'd to declare the very inmost Passion of my Heart. Oh, Madam, look upon us both. There you see the Ruins of a poor decay'd Creature——Here, a compleat and lively Figure, with Youth and Health, and all his five Senses in perfection, Madam, and to all this, the most passionate Lover——

Ang. O fie for shame, hold your Tongue, A passionate Lover, and five Senses in perfection! when you are as mad as *Valentine*, I'll believe you love me, and the maddest shall take me.

Val. It is enough. Ha! Who's here?

Frail. O Lord, her coming will spoil all. [*To* Jeremy.

Jere. No, no, Madam, he won't know her; if he shou'd, I can perswade him. 31

Val. Scandal, who are these? Foreigners? If they are, I'll tell you what I think——get away all the Company but *Angelica,* that I may discover my Design to her. [*Whisper.*

Scan. I will——I have discover'd something of *Tattle,* that is of a piece with Mrs. *Frail.* He courts *Angelica*; if we cou'd contrive to couple 'em together—Hark'ee—— [*Whisper.*

Mrs. *Fore.* He won't know you, Cousin, he knows no body. 41

Fore. But he knows more than any body,——Oh Neice, he knows things past and to come, and all the profound Secrets of Time.

Tatt. Look you, Mr. *Foresight,* it is not my way to make many Words of Matters, and so I shan't say much,—But in short, d'ye see, I will hold you a hundred Pound now, that I know more Secrets than he. 49

Fore. How! I cannot read that Knowledge in your Face, Mr. *Tattle*——Pray, what do you know?

Tatt. Why, d'ye think I'll tell you, Sir! Read it in my Face? No, Sir, 'tis written in my Heart; and safer there, Sir, than Letters writ in Juice of Lemon, for no Fire can fetch it out. I am no Blab, Sir. 57

Val. Acquaint *Jeremy* with it, he may easily bring it about.——They are welcome, and I'll tell 'em so my self. [*To* Scandal.] What, do you look strange upon me?—Then I must be plain. [*Coming up to them.*] I am Truth, and hate an old Acquaintance with a new Face.

[Scandal *goes aside with* Jeremy.

Tatt. Do you know me, *Valentine*?

Val. You? Who are you? No, I hope not.

Tatt. I am *Jack Tattle,* your Friend. 66

Val. My Friend, what to do? I am no married Man, and thou canst not lye with my Wife: I am very poor, and thou canst not borrow Mony of me: Then what Employment have I for a Friend?

Tatt. Hah! A good open Speaker, and not to be trusted with a Secret.

Ang. Do you know me, *Valentine*?

Val. Oh very well.

Ang. Who am I?

Val. You're a Woman,—One to whom Heav'n gave Beauty, when it grafted Roses on a Briar. You are the Reflection of Heav'n in a Pond, and he that leaps at you is sunk. You are all white, a Sheet of lovely spotless Paper, when you first are born; but you are to be scrawl'd and blotted by every Goose's Quill. I know you; for I lov'd a Woman, and lov'd her so long, that I found out a strange thing: I found out what a Woman was good for.

Tatt. Ay, prithee, what's that?

Val. Why, to keep a Secret.

Tatt. O Lord!

Val. O exceeding good to keep a Secret: For tho' she should tell, yet she is not to be believ'd.

Tatt. Hah! good again, faith.

Val. I would have Musick——Sing me the Song that I like——

SONG.

Set by Mr. *Finger*.

I.

I tell thee, Charmion, *could I Time retrieve,*
And could again begin to Love and Live,
To you I should my earliest Off'ring give;
  I know, my Eyes would lead my Heart to you,
  And I should all my Vows and Oaths renew,
  But to be plain, I never would be true.

II.

For by our weak and weary Truth, I find,
Love hates to center in a Point assign'd;
But runs with Joy the Circle of the Mind.
Then never let us chain what shou'd be free,
But for Relief of either Sex agree:
Since Women love to change, and so do we.

No more, for I am melancholly. [*Walks musing.*

Jere. I'll do't, Sir. [*To* Scandal.

Scan. Mr. *Foresight,* we had best leave him. He may grow outragious, and do Mischief.

Fore. I will be directed by you.

Jere. to Mrs. *Frail.*] You'll meet, Madam;—— I'll take care every thing shall be ready.

Mrs. *Frail.* Thou shalt do what thou wilt, in short, I will deny thee nothing.

Tatt. Madam, shall I wait upon you? [*To* Angelica.

Ang. No, I'll stay with him—Mr. *Scandal* will protect me. Aunt, Mr. *Tattle* desires you would give him leave to wait on you.

Tatt. Pox on't, there's no coming off, now she has said that——Madam, will you do me the Honour?

Mrs. *Fore.* Mr. *Tattle* might have us'd less Ceremony.

SCENE XVII.

ANGELICA, VALENTINE, SCANDAL.

Scan. Jeremy, follow *Tattle.*

Ang. Mr. *Scandal,* I only stay 'till my Maid comes, and because I had a mind to be rid of Mr. *Tattle.*

Scan. Madam, I am very glad that I over-heard a better Reason, which you gave to Mr. *Tattle;* for his Impertinence forc'd you to acknowledge a Kindness for *Valentine,* which you deny'd to all his Sufferings and my Sollicitations. So I'll leave him to make use of the Discovery; and your Ladyship to the free Confession of your Inclinations. 12

Ang. Oh Heav'ns! You won't leave me alone with a Madman?

Scan. No, Madam; I only leave a Madman to his Remedy.

SCENE XVIII.

ANGELICA, VALENTINE.

Val. Madam, you need not be very much afraid, for I fancy I begin to come to my self.

Ang. Ay, but if I don't fit you, I'll be hang'd. [*Aside.*

Val. You see what Disguises Love makes us put on; Gods have been in counterfeited Shapes for the same Reason; and the divine Part of me, my Mind, has worn this Masque of Madness, and this motly Livery, only as the Slave of Love, and menial Creature of your Beauty. 9

Ang. Mercy on me, how he talks! poor *Valentine*.

Val. Nay Faith, now let us understand one another, Hypocrisie apart——The Comedy draws toward an end, and let us think of leaving acting, and be our selves; and since you have lov'd me, you must own, I have at length deserv'd you shou'd confess it. 17

Ang. *Sighs.*] I would I had lov'd you——for Heav'n knows I pity you; and could I have foreseen the bad Effects, I wou'd have striven; but that's too late. [*Sighs.*

Val. What sad Effects?——What's too late? my seeming Madness has deceiv'd my Father, and procur'd me time to think of Means to reconcile me to him; and preserve the right of my Inheritance to his Estate; which otherwise by Articles, I must this Morning have resign'd: And this

I had inform'd you of to Day, but you were gone, before I knew you had been here.

Ang. How! I thought your Love of me had caus'd this Transport in your Soul; which, it seems, you only counterfeited; for mercenary Ends, and sordid Interest.

Val. Nay, now you do me Wrong; for if any Interest was consider'd it was yours; since I thought I wanted more than Love, to make me worthy of you.

Ang. Then you thought me mercenary——But how am I deluded by this interval of Sense, to reason with a Madman?

Val. Oh, 'tis barbarous to misunderstand me longer.

SCENE XIX.

[*To them*] JEREMY.

Ang. Oh here's a reasonable Creature——sure he will not have the Impudence to persevere——Come *Jeremy*, acknowledge your Trick, and confess your Master's Madness counterfeit.

Jere. Counterfeit, Madam! I'll maintain him to be as absolutely and substantially mad, as any Freeholder in *Bethlehem*; Nay, he's as mad as any Projector, Fanatick, Chymist, Lover, or Poet in *Europe*.

Val. Sirrah, you lie; I am not mad.

Ang. Ha, ha, ha, you see he denies it.

Jere. O Lord, Madam, did you ever know any Madman mad enough to own it?

Val. Sot, can't you apprehend?

Ang. Why he talk'd very sensibly just now.

Jere. Yes, Madam; he has Intervals: But you see he begins to look wild again now.

Val. Why you thick-skull'd Rascal, I tell you the Farce is done, and I will be mad no longer.

[*Beats him.*

7 *Bethlehem*] Bedlam, the lunatic asylum.

Ang. Ha, ha, ha, is he mad, or no, *Jeremy*?

Jere. Partly I think—for he does not know his own mind two Hours—I'm sure I left him just now, in the Humour to be mad: And I think I have not found him very quiet at this present. Who's there? [*One knocks.*

Val. Go see, you Sot. I'm very glad that I can move your Mirth, tho' not your Compassion.

Ang. I did not think you had Apprehension enough to be exceptious: But Madmen shew themselves most, by over-pretending to a sound Understanding; as drunken Men do by over-acting Sobriety; I was half inclining to believe you, 'till I accidently touch'd upon your tender Part: But now you have restor'd me to my former Opinion and Compassion.

Jere. Sir, your Father has sent to know if you are any better yet——Will you please to be mad, Sir, or how?

Val. Stupidity! You know the Penalty of all I'm worth must pay for the Confession of my Senses; I'm mad, and will be mad to every Body but this Lady.

Jere. So——Just the very backside of Truth—, But lying is a Figure in Speech, that interlards the greatest part of my Conversation——Madam, your Ladyship's Woman.

SCENE XX.

VALENTINE, ANGELICA, JENNY.

Ang. Well, have you been there?——Come hither.

Jenny. Yes, Madam, Sir *Sampson* will wait upon you presently. [*Aside to* Angelica.

Val. You are not leaving me in this Uncertainty?

Ang. Wou'd any thing, but a Madman, complain of Uncertainty? Uncertainty and Expectation are the Joys of Life. Security is an insipid thing, and the overtaking and possessing of a Wish, discovers the Folly of the Chase. Never let us know one another better; for the Pleasure of a Masquerade is done, when we come to shew our Faces; but I'll tell you two things before I leave you; I am not the Fool you take me for; and you are mad, and don't know it.

SCENE XXI.

VALENTINE, JEREMY.

Val. From a Riddle, you can expect nothing but a Riddle. There's my Instruction, and the Moral of my Lesson.

Jere. What, is the Lady gone again, Sir? I hope you understood one another before she went?

Val. Understood! She is harder to be understood than a Piece of *Ægyptian* Antiquity, or an *Irish* Manuscript; you may pore 'till you spoil your Eyes, and not improve your Knowledge.

Jere. I have heard 'em say, Sir, they read hard *Hebrew* Books backwards; may be you begin to read at the wrong end.

Val. They say so of a Witches Prayer, and Dreams and *Dutch* Almanacks are to be understood by contraries. But there's Regularity and Method in that; she is a Medal without a Reverse or Inscription, for Indifference has both sides alike. Yet while she does not seem to hate me, I will pursue her, and know her if it be possible, in spight of the Opinion of my Satirical Friend, *Scandal*, who says,

That Women are like Tricks by slight of Hand,
Which, to admire, we should not understand.

End of the Fourth Act.

ACT V. SCENE I.

A Room in Foresight's *House.*

Angelica, *and* Jenny.

Angelica.

Where is Sir *Sampson*? Did you not tell me, he would be here before me?

Jenny. He's at the great Glass in the Dining Room, Madam, setting his Cravat and Wig.

Ang. How! I'm glad on't—If he has a mind I should like him, it's a sign he likes me; and that's more than half my Design.

Jenny. I hear him, Madam.

Ang. Leave me, and d'ye hear, if *Valentine* shou'd come, or send, I am not to be spoken with.

SCENE II.

Angelica, *Sir* Sampson.

Sir *Samp*. I have not been honour'd with the Commands of a fair Lady, a great while—odd, Madam, you have reviv'd me—Not since I was five and thirty.

Ang. Why, you have no great Reason to complain, Sir *Sampson*, that is not long ago.

Sir *Samp*. Zooks, but it is, Madam, a very great while; to a Man that admires a fine Woman, as
much as I do. 9

Ang. You're an absolute Courtier, Sir *Sampson*.

Sir *Samp*. Not at all, Madam: Ods-bud you wrong me; I am not so old neither, to be a bare Courtier, only a Man of Words: Odd, I have warm Blood about me yet, and can serve a Lady any way—Come, come, let me tell you, you Women think a Man old too soon, faith and troth you do——Come, don't despise fifty; odd fifty, in a hale Constitution, is no such Contemptible Age.

Ang. Fifty a contemptible Age! Not at all, a very fashionable Age I think——I assure you, I know very considerable Beaus, that set a good Face upon fifty, fifty! I have seen fifty in a side Box by Candle-Light, out-blossom five and twenty.

Sir *Samp.* Outsides, Outsides; a pize take 'em, meer Outsides: Hang your Side-Box Beaus; no, I'm none of those, none of your forc'd Trees, that pretend to blossom in the Fall; and Bud when they should bring forth Fruit: I am of a long liv'd Race, and inherit Vigour, none of my Ancestors marry'd 'till fifty; yet they begot Sons and Daughters 'till fourscore: I am of your Patriarchs, I, a Branch of one of your *Antideluvian* Families, Fellows, that the Flood could not wash away. Well, Madam, what are your Commands? Has any young Rogue affronted you, and shall I cut his Throat? or——

Ang. No, Sir *Sampson*, I have no Quarrel upon my Hands—I have more Occasion for your Conduct than your Courage at this time. To tell you the Truth, I'm weary of living single, and want a Husband.

Sir *Samp.* Odsbud, and 'tis pity you should—Odd, wou'd she wou'd like me, then I shou'd hamper my young Rogues: Odd, wou'd she wou'd; faith and troth she's devilish handsome. [*Aside.*] Madam, you deserve a good Husband, and 'twere pity you shou'd be thrown away upon any of these young idle Rogues about the Town. Odd, there's ne'er a young Fellow worth hanging, —that is a very young Fellow—Pize on 'em, they never think beforehand of any thing;—And if they commit Matrimony, 'tis as they commit Murder; out of a Frolick: And are ready to hang themselves, or to be hang'd by the Law, the next Morning:—Odso, have a care, Madam.

Ang. Therefore I ask your Advice, Sir *Sampson*: I have Fortune enough to make any Man easie that I can like; If there were such a thing as a young agreeable Man, with a reasonable Stock of good Nature and Sense——For I would neither have an absolute Wit, nor a Fool.

Sir *Samp.* Odd, you are hard to please, Madam; to find a young Fellow that is neither a Wit in his own Eye, nor a Fool in the Eye of the World, is a very hard Task. But, faith and troth, you speak very discreetly; for I hate both a Wit and a Fool.

Ang. She that marries a Fool, Sir *Sampson*, forfeits the Reputation of her Honesty or Understanding: And she that marries a very witty Man is a Slave to the Severity and insolent Conduct of her Husband. I should like a Man of Wit for a Lover, because I would have such an one in my Power; but I would no more be his Wife, than his Enemy. For his Malice is not a more terrible Consequence of his Aversion, than his Jealousie is of his Love. 78

Sir *Samp.* None of old *Foresight*'s *Sybils* ever utter'd such a Truth. Odsbud, you have won my Heart: I hate a Wit; I had a Son that was spoil'd among 'em; a good hopeful Lad, 'till he learn'd to be a Wit——And might have risen in the State——But, a pox on't, his Wit run him out of his Mony, and now his Poverty has run him out of his Wits.

Ang. Sir *Sampson*, as your Friend, I must tell you, you are very much abus'd in that matter; he's no more mad than you are. 89

Sir *Samp.* How, Madam! Wou'd I cou'd prove it.

Ang. I can tell you how that may be done——But it is a thing that wou'd make me appear to be too much concern'd in your Affairs.

Sir *Samp.* Odsbud, I believe she likes me—[*Aside.*]——Ah, Madam, all my Affairs are scarce worthy to be laid at your Feet; and I wish,

Madam, they were in a better Posture, that I might make a more becoming Offer to a Lady of your incomparable Beauty and Merit.—If I had *Peru* in one Hand, and *Mexico* in t'other, and the *Eastern* Empire under my Feet; it would make me only a more glorious Victim to be offer'd at the Shrine of your Beauty.

Ang. Bless me, Sir *Sampson*, what's the Matter?

Sir *Samp.* Odd, Madam, I love you—And if you wou'd take my Advice in a Husband——

Ang. Hold, hold, Sir *Sampson*. I ask'd your Advice for a Husband, and you are giving me your Consent—I was indeed thinking to propose something like it in Jest, to satisfie you about *Valentine*: For if a Match were seemingly carried on, between you and me, it would oblige him to throw off his Disguise of Madness, in Apprehension of losing me: For you know he has long pretended a Passion for me.

Sir *Samp.* Gadzooks, a most ingenious Contrivance—If we were to go through with it. But why must the Match only be seemingly carry'd on?——Odd, let it be a real Contract.

Ang. O fie, Sir *Sampson*, what would the World say?

Sir *Samp.* Say, they would say, you were a wise Woman, and I a happy Man. Odd, Madam, I'll love you as long as I live; and leave you a good Jointure when I die.

Ang. Ay; but that is not in your Power, Sir *Sampson*; for when *Valentine* confesses himself in his Senses, he must make over his Inheritance to his younger Brother.

Sir *Samp.* Odd, you're cunning, a wary Baggage! Faith and Troth I like you the better—But, I warrant you, I have a Proviso in the Obligation in favour of my self——Body o'me, I have a Trick to turn the Settlement upon the Issue Male of our two Bodies begotten. Odsbud, let us find Children, and I'll find an Estate!

Ang. Will you? Well, do you find the Estate, and leave the t'other to me——

Sir *Samp.* O Rogue! But I'll trust you. And will you consent? Is it a Match then?

Ang. Let me consult my Lawyer concerning this Obligation; and if I find what you propose practicable; I'll give you my Answer.

Sir *Samp.* With all my Heart;—Come in with me, and I'll lend you the Bond——You shall consult your Lawyer, and I'll consult a Parson; Odzooks I'm a young Man: Odzooks I'm a young Man, and I'll make it appear—Odd, you're devilish handsome: Faith and Troth, you're very handsome, and I'm very young, and very lusty——Odsbud, Hussy, you know how to chuse, and so do I;——Odd, I think we are very well met;—Give me your Hand, odd, let me kiss it; 'tis as warm and as soft—as what?——Odd, as t'other Hand—give me t'other Hand, and I'll mumble 'em, and kiss 'em 'till they melt in my Mouth.

Ang. Hold, Sir *Sampson*——You're profuse of your Vigour before your time: You'll spend your Estate before you come to it.

Sir *Samp.* No, no, only give you a Rent-Roll of my Possessions—Ah! Baggage——I warrant you for little *Sampson*: Odd, *Sampson*'s a very good Name for an able Fellow: Your *Sampsons* were strong Dogs from the Beginning.

Ang. Have a care, and don't over-act your Part—If you remember, *Sampson*, the strongest of the Name, pull'd an old House over his Head at last.

Sir *Samp.* Say you so Hussy?—Come, let's go then; odd, I long to be pulling too, come away——Odso, here's some body coming.

SCENE III.

TATTLE, JEREMY.

Tatt. Is not that she, gone out just now?

Jere. Ay, Sir, she's just going to the Place of Appointment. Ah Sir, if you are not very faithful and close in this Business, you'll certainly be the Death of a Person that has a most extraordinary Passion for your Honour's Service.

Tatt. Ay, who's that?

Jere. Even my unworthy self, Sir——Sir, I have had an Appetite to be fed with your Commands a great while;——And now, Sir, my former Master, having much troubled the Fountain of his Understanding; it is a very plausible Occasion for me to quench my Thirst at the Spring of your Bounty—I thought I could not recommend my self better to you, Sir, than by the Delivery of a great Beauty and Fortune into your Arms, whom I have heard you sigh for.

Tatt. I'll make thy Fortune; say no more——Thou art a pretty Fellow, and canst carry a Message to a Lady, in a pretty soft kind of Phrase, and with a good perswading Accent.

Jere. Sir, I have the Seeds of Rhetorick and Oratory in my Head——I have been at *Cambridge.*

Tatt. Ay: 'tis well enough for a Servant to be bred at an University: But the Education is a little too pedantick for a Gentleman. I hope you are secret in your Nature, private, close, ha?

Jere. O Sir, for that Sir, 'tis my chief Talent; I'm as secret as the Head of *Nilus.*

Tatt. Ay? Who's he, tho'? A Privy Counsellor?

Jere. O Ignorance! [*Aside.*] A cunning *Ægyptian*, Sir, that with his Arms would over-run the Country, yet no Body could ever find out his Head-Quarters.

Tatt. Close Dog! A good Whoremaster, I warrant him——the time draws nigh, *Jeremy. Angelica* will be veil'd like a Nun; and I must be hooded like a Friar; ha, *Jeremy*?

Jere. Ay, Sir, hooded like a Hawk, to seize at first Sight upon the Quarry. It is the Whim of my Master's Madness to be so dress'd; and she is so in Love with him, she'll comply with any thing to please him. Poor Lady, I'm sure she'll have reason to pray for me, when she finds what a happy Exchange she has made, between a Madman and so accomplish'd a Gentleman.

Tatt. Ay Faith, so she will, *Jeremy*: You're a good Friend to her, poor Creature——I swear I do it hardly so much in consideration of my self, as compassion to her.

Jere. 'Tis an Act of Charity, Sir, to save a fine Woman with thirty thousand Pound, from throwing her self away.

Tatt. So 'tis, faith——I might have sav'd several others in my time; but I Gad I could never find in my Heart to marry any body before.

Jere. Well, Sir, I'll go and tell her my Master's coming; and meet you in half a Quarter of an Hour, with your Disguise, at your own Lodgings. You must talk a little madly, she won't distinguish the Tone of your Voice.

Tatt. No, no, let me alone for a Counterfeit; ——I'll be ready for you.

SCENE IV.

Tattle, *Miss* Prue.

Miss. O Mr. *Tattle*, are you here! I'm glad I have found you; I have been looking up and down for you like any thing, 'till I'm as tired as any thing in the World.

Tatt. O Pox how shall I get rid of this foolish Girl? [*Aside.*

Miss. O I have pure News, I can tell you pure News——I must not marry the Seaman now—my Father says so. Why won't you be my Husband? You say you love me, and you won't be my Husband. And I know you may be my Husband now if you please.

Tatt. O fie, Miss: Who told you so, Child?

Miss. Why, my Father—I told him that you lov'd me.

Tatt. O fie, Miss, why did you do so? And who told you so, Child?

Miss. Who? Why you did; did not you?

Tatt. O Pox, that was yesterday, Miss, that was a great while ago, Child. I have been asleep since; slept a whole Night, and did not so much as dream of the Matter. 22

Miss. Pshaw, O but I dream't that it was so tho'.

Tatt. Ay, but your Father will tell you that Dreams come by Contraries, Child——O fie; what, we must not love one another now——Pshaw, that would be a foolish thing indeed——Fie, fie, you're a Woman now, and must think of a new Man every Morning, and forget him every Night——No, no, to marry is to be a Child again, and play with the same Rattle always: O fie, marrying is a paw thing. 33

Miss. Well, but don't you love me as well as you did last Night then?

Tatt. No, no, Child, you would not have me.

Miss. No? Yes but I would tho'.

Tatt. Pshaw, but I tell you, you would not——You forget you're a Woman, and don't know your own Mind. 40

Miss. But here's my Father, and he knows my Mind.

SCENE V.

[*To them*] FORESIGHT.

Fore. O, Mr. *Tattle*, your Servant, you are a close Man; but methinks your Love to my Daughter was a Secret I might have been trusted with,——Or had you a Mind to try if I could discover it by my Art——hum, ha! I think there is something in your Physiognomy, that has a Resemblance of her; and the Girl is like me.

Tatt. And so you wou'd infer, that you and I are alike——what does the old Prig mean? I'll banter him, and laugh at him, and leave him. [*Aside.*] I fancy you have a wrong Notion of Faces.

Fore. How? What? a wrong Notion! How so?

Tatt. In the way of Art: I have some taking Features, not obvious to vulgar Eyes; that are Indications of a sudden turn of good Fortune, in the Lottery of Wives; and promise a great Beauty and great Fortune reserved alone for me, by a private Intrigue of Destiny, kept secret from the piercing Eye of Perspicuity; from all Astrologers, and the Stars themselves.

Fore. How! I will make it appear, that what you say is impossible.

Tatt. Sir, I beg your Pardon, I'm in haste——

Fore. For what?

Tatt. To be marry'd, Sir, marry'd.

Fore. Ay, but pray take me along with you, Sir——

Tatt. No, Sir; 'tis to be done privately——I never make Confidents.

Fore. Well; but my Consent I mean—You won't marry my Daughter without my Consent?

Tatt. Who I, Sir? I'm an absolute Stranger to you and your Daughter, Sir.

Fore. Hey day! What time of the Moon is this?

Tatt. Very true, Sir, and desire to continue so. I have no more Love for your Daughter, than I have Likeness of you; and I have a Secret in my Heart, which you wou'd be glad to know, and shan't know; and yet you shall know it too, and be sorry for't afterwards. I'd have you to know, Sir, that I am as knowing as the Stars, and as secret as the Night. And I'm going to be married

27 take me along] i. e. mentally. Please inform me.

just now, yet did not know of it half an Hour ago; and the Lady stays for me, and does not know of it yet—There's a Mystery for you,——I know you love to untie Difficulties——Or if you can't solve this; stay here a Quarter of an Hour, and I'll come and explain it to you.

SCENE VI.

FORESIGHT, *Miss* PRUE.

Miss. O father, why will you let him go? Won't you make him to be my Husband?

Fore. Mercy on us, what do these Lunacies portend? Alas! he's mad, Child, stark wild.

Miss. What, and must not I have e'er a Husband then? What, must I go to Bed to Nurse again, and be a Child as long as she's an old Woman? Indeed but I won't. For now my mind is set upon a Man, I will have a Man some way or other. Oh! methinks I'm sick when I think of a Man; and if I can't have one, I wou'd go to sleep all my Life: For when I'm awake it makes me wish and long, and I don't know for what——And I'd rather be always asleep, than sick with thinking.

Fore. O fearful! I think the Girl's influenc'd too,——Hussy, you shall have a Rod.

Miss. A Fiddle of a Rod, I'll have a Husband; and if you won't get me one, I'll get one for my self: I'll marry our *Robin* the Butler, he says he loves me, and he's a handsome Man, and shall be my Husband: I warrant he'll be my Husband, and thank me too, for he told me so.

SCENE VII.

[*To them*] SCANDAL, *Mrs.* FORESIGHT, *and* NURSE.

Fore. Did he so——I'll dispatch him for't presently; Rogue! Oh, Nurse, come hither.

Nurse. What is your Worship's Pleasure?

Fore. Here take your young Mistress, and lock her up presently, 'till farther Orders from me—— not a word, Hussy——Do what I bid you, no Reply, away. And bid *Robin* make ready to give an Account of his Plate and Linnen, d'ye hear, be gone when I bid you.

Mrs. *Fore.* What's the matter, Husband?

Fore. 'Tis not convenient to tell you now—— Mr. *Scandal*, Heav'n keep us all in our Senses—— I fear there is a contagious Frenzy abroad. How does *Valentine*?

Scan. O I hope he will do well again—I have a Message from him to your Neice *Angelica*.

Fore. I think she has not return'd, since she went abroad with Sir *Sampson*. Nurse, why are you not gone?

SCENE VIII.

FORESIGHT, SCANDAL, *Mrs.* FORESIGHT, BEN.

Mrs. *Fore.* Here's Mr. *Benjamin*, he can tell us if his Father be come home.

Ben. Who, Father? ay, he's come home with a Vengeance.

Mrs. *Fore.* Why, what's the matter?

Ben. Matter! Why he's mad.

Fore. Mercy on us, I was afraid of this.

Ben. And there's the handsome young Woman, she, as they say, Brother *Val.* went mad for, she's mad too, I think.

Fore. O my poor Neice, my poor Neice, is she gone too? Well, I shall run mad next.

Mrs. *Fore.* Well, but how mad? how d'ye mean?

Ben. Nay, I'll give you leave to guess——I'll undertake to make a Voyage to *Antegoa*——No, hold, I mayn't say so neither——But I'll sail as far as *Leghorn*, and back again, before you shall guess at the matter, and do nothing else; Mess, you may take in all the Points of the Compass, and not hit right.

Mrs. *Fore*. Your Experiment will take up a little too much time.

Ben. Why then I'll tell you; there's a new Wedding upon the Stocks, and they two are a going to be married to rights.

Scan. Who?

Ben. Why Father, and——the young Woman. I can't hit of her Name.

Scan. *Angelica?*

Ben. Ay, the same.

Mrs. *Fore*. Sir *Sampson* and *Angelica*, impossible!

Ben. That may be——but I'm sure it is as I tell you.

Scan. 'Sdeath, it's a Jest. I can't believe it.

Ben. Look you, Friend, it's nothing to me, whether you believe it or no. What I say is true; d'ye see, they are married, or just going to be married, I know not which.

Fore. Well, but they are not mad, that is, not Lunatick?

Ben. I don't know what you call Madness——But she's mad for a Husband, and he's horn mad, I think, or they'd ne'er make a Match together——Here they come.

SCENE IX.

[*To them*] *Sir* SAMPSON, ANGELICA, BUCKRAM.

Sir *Samp*. Where is this old Soothsayer? this Uncle of mine elect? A ha, old *Foresight*, Uncle *Foresight*, wish me Joy, Uncle *Foresight*, double Joy, both as Uncle and Astrologer; here's a Conjunction that was not foretold in all your *Ephemeris*——The brightest Star in the blue Firmament——is *shot from above, in a Jelly of*

Love, and so forth; and I'm Lord of the Ascendant. Odd, you're an old Fellow, *Foresight*; Uncle I mean, a very old Fellow, Uncle *Foresight*; and yet you shall live to dance at my Wedding; faith and troth you shall. Odd, we'll have the Musick of the Spheres for thee, old *Lilly*, that we will, and thou shalt lead up a Dance in *Via Lactea.*

Fore. I'm Thunder-struck! You are not married to my Neice? 17

Sir *Samp.* Not absolutely marry'd, Uncle; but very near it, within a Kiss of the Matter, as you see. [*Kisses* Angelica.

Ang. 'Tis very true indeed, Uncle; I hope you'll be my Father, and give me.

Sir *Samp.* That he shall, or I'll burn his Globes ——Body o'me, he shall be thy Father, I'll make him thy Father, and thou shalt make me a Father, and I'll make thee a Mother, and we'll beget Sons and Daughters enough to put the weekly Bills out of Countenance. 28

Scan. Death and Hell! Where's *Valentine*?

SCENE X.

Sir SAMPSON, ANGELICA, FORESIGHT, *Mrs.* FORESIGHT, BEN, BUCKRAM.

Mrs. *Fore.* This is so surprizing——

Sir *Samp.* How! What does my Aunt say? Surprizing, Aunt? Not at all, for a young Couple to make a Match in Winter? Not at all—It's a Plot to undermine cold Weather; and destroy that Usurper of a Bed call'd a Warming-Pan.

Mrs. *Fore.* I'm glad to hear you have so much Fire in you, Sir *Sampson*. 8

Ben. Mess, I fear his Fire's little better than Tinder; may-hap it will only serve to light up a Match for some Body else. The young Woman's a handsome young Woman, I can't deny it: But

Father, if I might be your Pilot in this Case, you should not marry her. It's just the same thing, as if so be you should sail so far as the *Straights* without Provision.

Sir *Samp*. Who gave you Authority to speak, Sirrah? To your Element, Fish, be mute, Fish, and to Sea, rule your Helm, Sirrah, don't direct me.

Ben. Well, well, take you care of your own Helm, or you mayn't keep your new Vessel steddy.

Sir *Samp*. Why, you impudent Tarpaulin! Sirrah, do you bring your Forecastle Jests upon your Father? But I shall be even with you, I won't give you a Groat. Mr. *Buckram*, is the Conveyance so worded, that nothing can possibly descend to this Scoundrel? I would not so much as have him have the Prospect of an Estate; tho' there were no way to come to it, but by the *North-East* Passage.

Buckr. Sir, it is drawn according to your Directions; there is not the least Cranny of the Law unstopt.

Ben. Lawyer, I believe there's many a Cranny and Leak unstopt in your Conscience——If so be that one had a Pump to your Bosom, I believe we shou'd discover a foul Hold. They say a Witch will sail in a Sieve——But I believe the Devil wou'd not venture aboard o'your Conscience. And that's for you.

Sir *Samp*. Hold your Tongue, Sirrah. How now, who's here?

SCENE XI.

[*To them*] TATTLE *and* Mrs. FRAIL.

Mrs. *Frail*. O, Sister, the most unlucky Accident.

Mrs. *Fore*. What's the Matter?

Tatt. O, the two most unfortunate poor Creatures in the World we are.

Fore. Bless us! How so?

Mrs. *Frail.* Ah Mr. *Tattle* and I, poor Mr. *Tattle* and I are——I can't speak it out.

Tatt. Nor I——poor Mrs. *Frail* and I are——

Mrs. *Frail.* Married.

Mrs. *Fore.* Married! How?

Tatt. Suddenly——before we knew where we were—that Villain *Jeremy*, by the help of Disguises, trickt us into one another.

Fore. Why, you told me just now, you went hence in haste to be married.

Ang. But I believe Mr. *Tattle* meant the Favour to me, I thank him.

Tatt. I did, as I hope to be sav'd, Madam, my Intentions were good——But this is the most cruel thing, to marry one does not know how, nor why, nor wherefore—The Devil take me if ever I was so much concern'd at any thing in my Life.

Ang. Tis very unhappy, if you don't care for one another.

Tatt. The least in the World—That is for my Part, I speak for my self. Gad, I never had the least Thought of serious Kindness——I never lik'd any Body less in my Life. Poor Woman! Gad I'm sorry for her too; for I have no reason to hate her neither; but I believe I shall lead her a damn'd sort of a Life.

Mrs. *Fore.* He's better than no Husband at all—tho' he's a Coxcomb. [*To* Frail.

Mrs. *Frail to her.* Ay, ay, it's well it's no worse ——Nay, for my part I always despised Mr. *Tattle* of all things; nothing but his being my Husband could have made me like him less.

Tatt. Look you there, I thought as much——Pox on't, I wish we could keep it secret, why I don't believe any of this Company wou'd speak of it.

Mrs. *Frail.* But, my Dear, that's impossible; the Parson and that Rogue *Jeremy* will publish it.

Tatt. Ay, my Dear, so they will, as you say.

Ang. O you'll agree very well in a little time; Custom will make it easie to you.

Tatt. Easie! Pox on't, I don't believe I shall sleep to Night.

Sir *Samp.* Sleep, Quotha! No, why you would not sleep o' your Wedding-Night? I'm an older Fellow than you, and don't mean to sleep.

Ben. Why there's another Match now, as thof' a couple of Privateers were looking for a Prize, and should fall foul of one another. I'm sorry for the young Man with all my Heart. Look you, Friend, if I may advise you, when she's going, for that you must expect, I have Experience of her, when she's going, let her go. For no Matrimony is tough enough to hold her, and if she can't drag her Anchor along with her, she'll break her Cable, I can tell you that. Who's here? the Madman?

SCENE, *The Last.*

VALENTINE, SCANDAL, *Sir* SAMPSON, ANGELICA, FORESIGHT, *Mrs.* FORESIGHT, TATTLE, *Mrs.* FRAIL, BEN, JEREMY, BUCKRAM.

Val. No; here's the Fool; and if occasion be, I'll give it under my Hand.

Sir *Samp.* How now?

Val. Sir, I'm come to acknowledge my Errors, and ask your Pardon.

Sir *Samp.* What, have you found your Senses at last then? In good time, Sir.

Val. You were abus'd, Sir, I never was distracted.

Fore. How! Not Mad! Mr. *Scandal.*

Scan. No really, Sir; I'm his Witness, it was all Counterfeit.

Val. I thought I had Reasons——But it was a poor Contrivance, the Effect has shewn it such.

Sir *Samp.* Contrivance, what to cheat me? to cheat your Father! Sirrah, could you hope to prosper?

Val. Indeed, I thought, Sir, when the Father endeavoured to undo the Son, it was a reasonable return of Nature.

Sir *Samp.* Very good, Sir—Mr. *Buckram*, are you ready?——Come, Sir, will you sign and seal?

Val. If you please, Sir; but first I would ask this Lady one Question.

Sir *Samp.* Sir, you must ask me leave first; that Lady? No, Sir; you shall ask that Lady no Questions, 'till you have ask'd her Blessing, Sir; that Lady is to be my Wife.

Val. I have heard as much, Sir; but I wou'd have it from her own Mouth.

Sir *Samp.* That's as much as to say, I lie, Sir, and you don't believe what I say.

Val. Pardon me, Sir. But I reflect that I very lately counterfeited Madness; I don't know but the Frolick may go round.

Sir *Samp.* Come, Chuck, satisfie him, answer him;——Come, come, Mr. *Buckram*, the Pen and Ink.

Buckr. Here it is, Sir, with the Deed, all is ready. [Val. *goes to* Ang.

Ang. 'Tis true, you have a great while pretended Love to me; nay, what if you were sincere? still you must pardon me, if I think my own Inclinations have a better Right to dispose of my Person, than yours.

Sir *Samp.* Are you answer'd now, Sir?

Val. Yes, Sir.

Sir *Samp.* Where's your Plot, Sir? and your Contrivance now, Sir? Will you sign, Sir? Come, will you sign and seal?

Val. With all my Heart, Sir.

Scan. 'Sdeath, you are not mad indeed, to ruin your self?

Val. I have been disappointed of my only Hope; and he that loses Hope may part with any thing. I never valu'd Fortune, but as it was subservient to my Pleasure; and my only Pleasure was to please this Lady: I have made many vain Attempts, and find at last that nothing but my Ruin can effect it: Which, for that Reason, I will sign to——Give me the Paper.

Ang. Generous *Valentine*! [*Aside.*

Buckr. Here is the Deed, Sir.

Val. But where is the Bond, by which I am oblig'd to sign this?

Buckr. Sir *Sampson*, you have it.

Ang. No, I have it; and I'll use it, as I wou'd every thing that is an Enemy to *Valentine*.

[*Tears the Paper.*

Sir *Samp.* How now!

Val. Ha!

Ang. Had I the World to give you, it cou'd not make me worthy of so generous and faithful a Passion: Here's my Hand, my Heart was always yours, and struggl'd very hard to make this utmost Trial of your Vertue. [*To* Val.

Val. Between Pleasure and Amazement, I am lost——But on my Knees I take the Blessing.

Sir *Samp.* Oons, what is the Meaning of this?

Ben. Mess here's the Wind chang'd again. Father, you and I may make a Voyage together now.

Ang. Well, Sir *Sampson*, since I have plaid you a Trick, I'll advise you, how you may avoid such another. Learn to be a good Father, or you'll never get a second Wife. I always lov'd your Son, and hated your unforgiving Nature. I was resolv'd to try him to the utmost; I have try'd you too, and know you both. You have not more Faults than he has Virtues; and 'tis hardly more Pleasure to me, that I can make him and my self happy, than that I can punish you.

Val. If my Happiness cou'd receive Addition, this kind Surprize wou'd make it double.

Sir *Samp.* Oons you're a *Crocodile*.

Fore. Really, Sir *Sampson*, this is a sudden Eclipse.

Sir *Samp*. You're an illiterate old Fool, and I'm another.

Tatt. If the Gentleman is in Disorder for want of a Wife, I can spare him mine. Oh are you there, Sir? I'm indebted to you for my Happiness. 101
[*To* Jere.

Jere. Sir, I ask you ten thousand Pardons, 'twas an errant Mistake——You see, Sir, my Master was never mad, nor any thing like it——Then how cou'd it be otherwise?

Val. *Tattle*, I thank you, you would have interposed between me and Heav'n; but Providence laid Purgatory in your way——You have but Justice. 109

Scan. I hear the Fiddles that Sir *Sampson* provided for his own Wedding; methinks 'tis pity they shou'd not be employ'd when the Match is so much mended. *Valentine*, tho' it be Morning, we may have a Dance.

Val. Any thing, my Friend, every thing that looks like Joy and Transport.

Scan. Call 'em, *Jeremy*.

Ang. I have done dissembling now, *Valentine*; and if that Coldness which I have always worn before you, should turn to an extream Fondness, you must not suspect it. 121

Val. I'll prevent that Suspicion——For I intend to doat to that immoderate degree, that your Fondness shall never distinguish it self enough to be taken notice of. If ever you seem to love too much, it must be only when I can't love enough.

Ang. Have a Care of Promises; you know you are apt to run more in Debt than you are able to pay. 130

Val. Therefore I yield my Body as your Prisoner, and make your best on't.

Scan. The Musick stays for you. [*Dance*.

Scan. Well, Madam, you have done Exemplary Justice, in punishing an inhuman Father, and rewarding a faithful Lover: But there is a third good Work, which I, in particular, must thank you for; I was an Infidel to your Sex, and you have converted me——For now I am convinc'd that all Women are not like Fortune, blind in bestowing Favours, either on those who do not merit, or who do not want 'em. 142

Ang. 'Tis an unreasonable Accusation, that you lay upon our Sex: You tax us with Injustice, only to cover your own want of Merit. You would all have the Reward of Love; but few have the Constancy to stay 'till it becomes your due. Men are generally Hypocrites and Infidels, they pretend to Worship, but have neither Zeal nor Faith: How few, like *Valentine*, would persevere even to Martyrdom, and sacrifice their Interest to their Constancy! In admiring me, you misplace the Novelty. 153

The Miracle to Day is, that we find
A Lover true: Not that a Woman's Kind.

EPILOGUE,

Spoken at the Opening of the New House.

By Mrs. *Bracegirdle.*

Sure Providence at first design'd this Place
To be the Player's Refuge in Distress;
For still in every Storm, they all run hither,
As to a Shed, that shields 'em from the Weather.
But thinking of this Change which last befell us,
It's like what I have heard our Poets tell us:
For when behind our Scenes their Suits are pleading,
To help their Love, sometimes they show their Reading;
And wanting ready cash to pay for Hearts,
They top their Learning on us, and their Parts.

Once of Philosophers they told us Stories,
Whom, as I think, they call'd—Py—Pythagories,
I'm sure 'tis some such Latin *Name they give 'em,*
And we, who know no better, must believe 'em.
Now to these Men (say they) such Souls were giv'n,
That after Death, ne'er went to Hell, nor Heav'n,
But liv'd, I know not how, in Beasts ; and then
When many Years were past, in Men again.
Methinks, we Players *resemble such a Soul,*
That, does from Bodies, we from Houses strole.
Thus Aristotle's *Soul, of old that was,*
May now be damn'd to animate an Ass ;
Or in this very House, for ought we know,
Is doing painful Penance in some Beau :
And thus, our Audience, which did once resort
To shining Theatres to see our Sport,
Now find us toss'd into a Tennis-Court.
These Walls but t'other Day were fill'd with Noise
Of Roaring Gamesters, and your Damme Boys ;
Then bounding Balls and Rackets they encompast,
And now they're fill'd with Jests, and Flights, and Bombast !
I vow, I dont much like this Transmigration,
Stroling from Place to Place, by Circulation,
Grant Heav'n, we don't return to our first Station.
I know not what these think, but for my Part,
I can't reflect without an aking Heart,
How we shou'd end in our Original, a Cart.
But we can't fear, since you're so good to save us,
That you have only set us up, to leave us.
Thus from the past, we hope for future Grace,
I beg it——
And some here know I have a begging Face.
Then pray continue this your kind Behaviour,
For a clear Stage won't do, without your Favour.

27 *Tennis-Court*] within the walls of which the new theatre was built.

37 *Cart*] a reference to the actors of the fourteenth and fifteenth-century cycle and other plays, who often performed from carts.

THE

WAY of the WORLD.

A

COMEDY.

Audire est Operæ pretium, procedere recte
Qui mæchis non vultis —— Hor. Sat. 2. l. 1.
—— *Metuat doti deprensa.* —— Ibid.

Printed in the YEAR 1710.

TO

Mr. *C O N G R E V E*,

Occasion'd by his

C O M E D Y

CALL'D

The WAY *of the* WORLD.

When Pleasure's falling to the low Delight,
In the vain Joys of the uncertain Sight,
No sense of Wit when rude Spectators know,
But in distorted Gesture, Farce and Show;
How could, Great Author, your Aspiring Mind
Dare to Write only to the Few Refin'd!
Yet tho' that nice Ambition you pursue,
'Tis not in Congreve's *Power to please but few.*
Implicitly devoted to his Fame,
Well-dress'd Barbarians know his awful Name;
Tho' senseless they're of Mirth, but when they laugh,
As they feel Wine, but when, 'till drunk, they quaff.

On you, from Fate, a lavish Portion fell
In ev'ry way of Writing to excell.
Your Muse Applause to Arabella *brings,*
In Notes as sweet as Arabella *Sings.*
When e'er you draw an undissembled Woe,
With sweet Distress your Rural Numbers flow
Pastora's *the Complaint of ev'ry Swain,*
Pastora *still the Eccho of the Plain!*
Or if your Muse describe, with warming Force,
The wounded Frenchman *falling from his Horse;*

And her own William *glorious in the Strife,*
Bestowing on the prostrate Foe his Life :
You the great Act as gen'rously rehearse,
And all the English *Fury's in your Verse.*
By your selected Scenes, and handsome Choice,
Ennobled Comedy exalts her Voice ;
You check unjust Esteem and fond Desire,
And teach to Scorn, what else we should Admire ;
The just Impression taught by you we bear,
The Player acts the World, the World the Player,
Whom still that World unjustly disesteems,
Tho' he, alone, professes what he seems :
But when your Muse assumes her Tragick Part,
She conquers and she reigns in ev'ry Heart ;
To mourn with her Men cheat their private Woe,
And gen'rous Pity's all the Grief they know ;
The Widow, who impatient of Delay,
From the Town-joys must mask it to the Play,
Joyns with your Mourning-Bride's resistless Moan,
And weeps a Loss she slighted, when her own ;
You give us Torment, and you give us Ease,
And vary our Afflictions as you please ;
Is not a Heart so kind as yours in Pain,
To load your Friends with Cares you only feign ;
Your Friends in Grief, compos'd your self, to leave ?
But 'tis the only way you'll e'er deceive.
Then still, great Sir, your moving Pow'r employ,
To lull our Sorrow, and correct our Joy.

R. STEELE.

To the Right Honourable

R A L P H,

Earl of *MOUNTAGUE*, &c.

My LORD,

Whether the World will arraign me of Vanity, or not, that I have presum'd to Dedicate this Comedy to Your Lordship, I am yet in Doubt: Tho' it may be it is some degree of Vanity even to doubt of it. One who has at any time had the Honour of Your Lordship's Conversation, cannot be suppos'd to think very meanly of that which he wou'd prefer to Your Perusal: Yet it were to incur the Imputation of too much Sufficiency, to pretend to such a Merit as might abide the Test of Your Lordship's Censure.

Whatever Value may be wanting to this Play while yet it is mine, will be sufficiently made up to it, when it is once become Your Lordship's; and it is my Security, that I cannot have overrated it more by my Dedication, than Your Lordship will dignifie it by Your Patronage.

That it succeeded on the Stage, was almost beyond my Expectation; for but little of it was prepar'd for that general Taste which seems now to be predominant in the Pallats of our Audience.

Those Characters which are meant to be ridicul'd in most of our Comedies, are of Fools so gross, that in my humble Opinion, they shou'd rather disturb than divert the well-natur'd and reflecting Part of an Audience; they are rather

Dedication. Mountague] Afterwards first Duke. A successful patron of the arts.

Objects of Charity than Contempt; and instead of moving our Mirth, they ought very often to excite our Compassion.

This Reflection mov'd me to design some Characters, which shou'd appear ridiculous not so much thro' a natural Folly (which is incorrigible, and therefore not proper for the Stage) as thro' an affected Wit; a Wit, which at the same time that it is affected, is also false. As there is some Difficulty in the Formation of a Character of this Nature, so there is some Hazard which attends the Progress of its Success, upon the Stage: For many come to a Play, so over-charg'd with Criticism, that they very often let fly their Censure, when thro' their Rashness they have mistaken their Aim. This I had Occasion lately to observe: For this Play had been acted two or three Days, before some of these hasty Judges cou'd find the leisure to distinguish betwixt the Character of a *Witwoud* and a *Truewit.*

I must beg Your Lordship's Pardon for this Digression from the true Course of this Epistle; but that it may not seem altogether impertinent, I beg, that I may plead the Occasion of it, in part of that Excuse of which I stand in need, for recommending this Comedy to Your Protection. It is only by the Countenance of Your Lordship, and the *Few* so qualify'd, that such who write with Care and Pains can hope to be distinguish'd: For the Prostituted Name of *Poet* promiscuously levels all that bear it.

Terence, the most correct Writer in the World, had a *Scipio* and a *Lelius*, if not to assist him, at least to support him in his Reputation: And notwithstanding his extraordinary Merit, it may be, their Countenance was not more than necessary.

The purity of his Stile, the Delicacy of his Turns, and the Justness of his Characters, were all of them Beauties, which the greater Part of his Audience were incapable of Tasting: Some of the coursest Strokes of *Plautus*, so severely censur'd by *Horace*, were more likely to affect the Multitude; such, who come with expectation to laugh at the last Act of a Play, and are better entertain'd with two or three unseasonable Jests, than with the artful Solution of the *Fable*.

As *Terence* excell'd in his Performances, so had he great Advantages to encourage his Undertakings; for he built most on the Foundations of *Menander*: His Plots were generally modell'd, and his Characters ready drawn to his Hand. He copied *Menander*; and *Menander* had no less Light in the Formation of his Characters, from the Observations of *Theophrastus*, of whom he was a Disciple; and *Theophrastus* it is known was not only the Disciple, but the immediate Successor of *Aristotle*, the first and greatest Judge of Poetry. These were great Models to design by; and the further Advantage which *Terence* possess'd, towards giving his Plays the due Ornaments of Purity of Stile, and Justness of Manners, was not less Considerable, from the Freedom of Conversation, which was permitted him with *Lelius* and *Scipio*, two of the greatest and most polite Men of his Age. And indeed, the Privilege of such a Conversation, is the only certain Means of attaining to the Perfection of Dialogue.

If it has happen'd in any Part of this Comedy, that I have gain'd a Turn of Stile, or Expression more Correct, or at least more Corrigible than in those which I have formerly written, I must, with equal Pride and Gratitude, ascribe it to the Honour of Your Lordship's admitting me into Your Conversation, and that of a Society where every body else was so well worthy of You, in Your Retirement last Summer from the Town: For it was immediately after, that this Comedy was written. If I have fail'd in my Performance, it is only to be regretted, where there were so many,

6 *Fable.*] Plot.

not inferior either to a *Scipio* or a *Lelius*, that there shou'd be one wanting, equal in Capacity to a *Terence*.

If I am not mistaken, Poetry is almost the only Art, which has not yet laid Claim to your Lordship's Patronage. Architecture, and Painting, to the great Honour of our Country, have flourish'd under Your Influence and Protection. In the mean time, Poetry, the eldest Sister of all Arts, and Parent of most, seems to have resign'd her Birth-right, by having neglected to pay her Duty to Your Lordship; and by permitting others of a later Extraction, to prepossess that Place in Your Esteem, to which none can pretend a better Title. Poetry, in its Nature, is sacred to the Good and Great; the Relation between them is reciprocal, and they are ever propitious to it. It is the Privilege of Poetry to address to them, and it is their Prerogative alone to give it Protection.

This receiv'd Maxim is a general Apology for all Writers who Consecrate their Labours to great Men: But I could wish, at this time, that this Address were exempted from the common Pretence of all Dedications; and that as I can distinguish Your Lordship even among the most Deserving, so this Offering might become remarkable by some particular Instance of Respect, which should assure Your Lordship, that I am, with all due sense of Your extream Worthiness and Humanity,

My LORD,

Your Lordship's most Obedient

and most Oblig'd Humble Servant,

Will. Congreve.

17 propitious to it] A sly dig at Collier.

PROLOGUE,

Spoken by Mr. *Betterton.*

Of those few Fools, who with ill Stars are curst,
Sure scribling Fools, call'd Poets, fare the worst:
For they're a sort of Fools which Fortune *makes,*
And after she has made 'em Fools, forsakes.
With Nature's *Oafs 'tis quite a diff'rent Case,*
For Fortune *favours all her* Idiot-Race*:*
In her own Nest the Cuckow-Eggs *we find,*
O'er which she broods to hatch the Changling-Kind.
No Portion for her own she has to spare,
So much she doats on her adopted Care.
Poets are Bubbles, by the Town drawn in,
Suffer'd at first some trifling Stakes to win:
But what unequal Hazards do they run!
Each time they write they venture all they've won:
The Squire that's butter'd still, is sure to be undone.
This Author, heretofore, has found your Favour,
But pleads no Merit from his past Behaviour;
To build on that might prove a vain Presumption,
Shou'd Grants to Poets made, admit Resumption:
And in Parnassus *he must lose his Seat,*
If that be found a forfeited Estate.
He owns, with Toil, he wrought the following Scenes,
But if they're naught ne'er spare him for his Pains:
Damn him the more; have no Commiseration
For Dulness on mature Deliberation.
He swears he'll not resent one hiss'd-off Scene
Nor, like those peevish Wits, his Play maintain,
Who, to assert their Sense, your Taste arraign.
Some Plot we think he has, and some new Thought;
Some Humour too, no Farce; but that's a Fault.

Satire, he thinks, you ought not to expect ;
For so Reform'd a Town, who dares Correct ?
To Please, this Time, has been his sole Pretence,
He'll not instruct, lest it shou'd give Offence.
Shou'd he by chance a Knave or Fool expose,
That hurts none here, sure here are none of those.
In short, our Play shall (with your leave to shew it)
Give you one Instance of a Passive Poet.
Who to your Judgments yields all Resignation ;
So Save or Damn, after your own Discretion.

Dramatis Personae.

MEN.

Fainall, In Love with Mrs. *Marwood*.	Mr. *Betterton*.
Mirabell, In Love with Mrs. *Millamant*.	Mr. *Verbruggen*.
Witwoud, *Petulant*, } Followers of Mrs. *Millamant*.	Mr. *Bowen*. Mr. *Bowman*.
Sir *Wilfull Witwoud*, Half Brother to *Witwoud*, and Nephew to Lady *Wishfort*.	Mr. *Underhill*.
Waitwell, Servant to *Mirabell*.	Mr. *Bright*.

WOMEN.

Lady *Wishfort*, Enemy to *Mirabell*, for having falsly pretended Love to her.	Mrs. *Leigh*.
Mrs. *Millamant*, A fine Lady, Neice to Lady *Wishfort*, and loves *Mirabell*.	Mrs. *Bracegirdle*.
Mrs. *Marwood*, Friend to Mr. *Fainall*, and likes *Mirabell*.	Mrs. *Barry*.
Mrs. *Fainall*, Daughter to Lady *Wishfort*, and Wife to *Fainall*, formerly Friend to *Mirabell*.	Mrs. *Bowman*.
Foible, Woman to Lady *Wishfort*.	Mrs. *Willis*.
Mincing, Woman to Mrs. *Millamant*.	Mrs. *Prince*.

Dancers, Footmen, *and* Attendants.

SCENE *LONDON*.

The Time equal to that of the Presentation.

THE

WAY *of the* WORLD.

ACT I. SCENE I.

A Chocolate-House.

MIRABELL *and* FAINALL [*Rising from Cards.*] BETTY *waiting.*

MIRABELL.

You are a fortunate Man, Mr. *Fainall.*

Fain. Have we done?

Mira. What you please. I'll play on to entertain you.

Fain. No, I'll give you your Revenge another time, when you are not so indifferent; you are thinking of something else now, and play too negligently; the Coldness of a losing Gamester lessens the Pleasure of the Winner. I'd no more play with a Man that slighted his ill Fortune, than I'd make Love to a Woman who undervalu'd the Loss of her Reputation.

Mira. You have a Taste extreamly delicate, and are for refining on your Pleasures.

Fain. Prithee, why so reserv'd? Something has put you out of Humour.

Mira. Not at all: I happen to be grave to Day; and you are gay; that's all.

Fain. Confess, *Millamant* and you quarrell'd last Night, after I left you; my fair Cousin has some Humours that wou'd tempt the Patience of a Stoick. What, some Coxcomb came in, and was well receiv'd by her, while you were by.

Mira. Witwoud and *Petulant*; and what was worse, her Aunt, your Wife's Mother, my evil Genius; or to sum up all in her own Name, my old Lady *Wishfort* came in.——

Fain. O there it is then——She has a lasting Passion for you, and with Reason.——What, then my Wife was there?

Mira. Yes, and Mrs. *Marwood* and three or four more, whom I never saw before; seeing me, they all put on their grave Faces, whisper'd one another; then complain'd aloud of the Vapours, and after fell into a profound Silence.

Fain. They had a mind to be rid of you.

Mira. For which good Reason I resolv'd not to stir. At last the good old Lady broke thro' her painful Taciturnity, with an Invective against long Visits. I would not have understood her, but *Millamant* joining in the Argument, I rose and with a constrain'd Smile told her, I thought nothing was so easie as to know when a Visit began to be troublesome; she reden'd and I withdrew, without expecting her reply.

Fain. You were to blame to resent what she spoke only in Compliance with her Aunt.

Mira. She is more Mistress of her self, than to be under the necessity of such a Resignation.

Fain. What? tho' half her Fortune depends upon her Marrying with my Lady's Approbation?

Mira. I was then in such a Humour, that I shou'd have been better pleas'd if she had been less discreet.

Fain. Now I remember, I wonder not they were weary of you; last Night was one of their Cabal-Nights; they have 'em three times a Week, and meet by turns, at one another's Apartments, where

45 expecting] awaiting.

they come together like the Coroner's Inquest, to sit upon the murder'd Reputations of the Week. You and I are excluded; and it was once propos'd that all the Male Sex shou'd be excepted; but some body mov'd that to avoid Scandal there might be one Man of the Community; upon which *Witwoud* and *Petulant* were enroll'd Members.

Mira. And who may have been the Foundress of this Sect? My Lady *Wishfort*, I warrant, who publishes her Detestation of Mankind; and full of the Vigour of Fifty five, declares for a Friend and *Ratafia*; and let Posterity shift for it self, she'll breed no more.

Fain. The Discovery of your sham Addresses to her, to conceal your Love to her Neice, has provok'd this Separation: Had you dissembl'd better, Things might have continu'd in the State of Nature.

Mira. I did as much as Man cou'd, with any reasonable Conscience; I proceeded to the very last Act of Flattery with her, and was guilty of a Song in her Commendation. Nay, I got a Friend to put her into a Lampoon, and compliment her with the Imputation of an Affair with a young Fellow, which I carry'd so far, that I told her the malicious Town took notice that she was grown fat of a sudden; and when she lay in of a Dropsie, persuaded her she was reported to be in Labour. The Devil's in't, if an old Woman is to be flatter'd further, unless a Man shou'd endeavour downright personally to debauch her; and that my Vertue forbad me. But for the Discovery of this Amour, I am indebted to your Friend, or your Wife's Friend, Mrs. *Marwood*.

Fain. What shou'd provoke her to be your Enemy, unless she has made you Advances, which you have slighted? Women do not easily forgive Omissions of that Nature.

70 *Ratafia*] a liqueur scented with fruit.

Mira. She was always civil to me, 'till of late; I confess I am not one of those Coxcombs who are apt to interpret a Woman's good Manners to her Prejudice; and think that she who does not refuse 'em ev'ry thing, can refuse 'em nothing.

Fain. You are a gallant Man, *Mirabell;* and tho' you may have Cruelty enough, not to satisfie a Lady's longing; you have too much Generosity, not to be tender of her Honour. Yet you speak with an Indifference which seems to be affected; and confesses you are conscious of a Negligence.

Mira. You pursue the Argument with a Distrust that seems to be unaffected, and confesses you are conscious of a Concern for which the Lady is more indebted to you, than is your Wife.

Fain. Fie, fie Friend, if you grow censorious I must leave you;——I'll look upon the Gamesters in the next Room.

Mira. Who are they?

Fain. Petulant and *Witwoud*—Bring me some Chocolate.

Mira. Betty, what says your Clock?

Bet. Turn'd of the last Canonical Hour, Sir.

Mira. How pertinently the Jade answers me! Ha? almost one a Clock! [*Looking on his Watch.*] O, y'are come—

SCENE II.

MIRABELL *and* FOOTMAN.

Mira. Well; is the grand Affair over? You have been something tedious.

Serv. Sir, there's such Coupling at *Pancras*, that they stand behind one another, as 'twere in a Country Dance. Ours was the last Couple to lead up; and no Hopes appearing of Dispatch, besides, the Parson growing hoarse, we were afraid his Lungs wou'd have fail'd before it came to our Turn ; so we drove round to *Duke's-Place* ; and there they were rivetted in a trice.

Mira. So, so, you are sure they are married.

Serv. Married and Bedded, Sir : I am Witness.

Mira. Have you the Certificate.

Serv. Here it is, Sir.

Mira. Has the Tailor brought *Waitwell's* Cloaths home, and the new Liveries ?

Serv. Yes, Sir.

Mira. That's well. Do you go home again, d'ye hear, and adjourn the Consummation 'till farther Order ; bid *Waitwell* shake his Ears, and Dame *Partlet* rustle up her Feathers, and meet me at One a Clock by *Rosamond's* Pond ; that I may see her before she returns to her Lady : And as you tender your Ears be secret.

SCENE III.

MIRABELL, FAINALL, BETTY.

Fain. Joy of your Success, *Mirabell* ; you look pleas'd.

Mira. Ay ; I have been engag'd in a Matter of some sort of Mirth, which is not yet ripe for Discovery. I am glad this is not a Cabal-Night. I wonder, *Fainall*, that you who are married, and of consequence should be discreet, will suffer your Wife to be of such a Party.

Fain. Faith, I am not jealous. Besides, most who are engag'd are Women and Relations ; and for the Men, they are of a Kind too contemptible to give Scandal.

Mira. I am of another Opinion. The greater the Coxcomb, always the more the Scandal : For

9 *Duke's Place*] St. James's Church, notorious for irregular marriages (Summers). See also Lady Wishfort's remark at the end of v. i.

22 *Rosamond's* Pond] In St. James's Park, 'long consecrated to disastrous love and elegiac poetry' (Warburton).

a Woman who is not a Fool, can have but one Reason for associating with a Man who is one.

Fain. Are you jealous as often as you see *Witwoud* entertain'd by *Millamant*?

Mira. Of her Understanding I am, if not of her Person.

Fain. You do her wrong; for to give her her Due, she has Wit.

Mira. She has Beauty enough to make any Man think so; and Complaisance enough not to contradict him who shall tell her so.

Fain. For a passionate Lover, methinks you are a Man somewhat too discerning in the Failings of your Mistress.

Mira. And for a discerning Man, somewhat too passionate a Lover; for I like her with all her Faults; nay, like her for her Faults. Her Follies are so natural, or so artful, that they become her; and those Affectations which in another Woman wou'd be odious, serve but to make her more agreeable. I'll tell thee, *Fainall*, she once us'd me with that Insolence, that in Revenge I took her to pieces; sifted her, and separated her Failings; I study'd 'em, and got 'em by Rote. The Catalogue was so large, that I was not without Hopes, one Day or other to hate her heartily: To which end I so us'd my self to think of 'em, that at length, contrary to my Design and Expectation, they gave me ev'ry Hour less and less Disturbance; 'till in a few Days it became habitual to me, to remember 'em without being displeas'd. They are now grown as familiar to me as my own Frailties; and in all probability in a little time longer I shall like 'em as well.

Fain. Marry her, marry her; be half as well acquainted with her Charms, as you are with her Defects, and my Life on't, you are your own Man again.

Mira. Say you so?

Fain. Ay, ay, I have Experience: I have a Wife, and so forth.

SCENE IV.

[*To them*] MESSENGER.

Mess. Is one Squire *Witwoud* here?

Bet. Yes; What's your Business?

Mess. I have a Letter for him, from his Brother Sir *Wilfull*, which I am charg'd to deliver into his own Hands.

Bet. He's in the next Room, Friend—That way.

SCENE V.

MIRABELL, FAINALL, BETTY.

Mira. What, is the chief of that noble Family in Town, Sir *Wilfull Witwoud?*

Fain. He is expected to Day. Do you know him?

Mira. I have seen him, he promises to be an extraordinary Person; I think you have the Honour to be related to him.

Fain. Yes; he is half Brother to this *Witwoud* by a former Wife, who was Sister to my Lady *Wishfort*, my Wife's Mother. If you marry *Millamant*, you must call Cousins too.

Mira. I had rather be his Relation than his Acquaintance.

Fain. He comes to Town in order to Equip himself for Travel.

Mira. For Travel! Why the Man that I mean is above Forty.

Fain. No matter for that; 'tis for the Honour of *England*, that all *Europe* should know that we have Blockheads of all Ages.

Mira. I wonder there is not an Act of Parliament to save the Credit of the Nation, and prohibit the Exportation of Fools.

Fain. By no means, 'tis better as 'tis; 'tis

better to Trade with a little Loss, than to be quite eaten up, with being overstock'd.

Mira. Pray, are the Follies of this Knight-Errant, and those of the Squire his Brother, any thing related ? 29

Fain. Not at all ; *Witwoud* grows by the Knight, like a Medlar grafted on a Crab. One will melt in your Mouth, and t'other set your Teeth on edge ; one is all Pulp, and the other all Core.

Mira. So one will be Rotten before he be Ripe, and the other will be Rotten without ever being Ripe at all.

Fain. Sir *Wilfull* is an odd Mixture of Bashfulness and Obstinacy.——But when he's drunk, he's as loving as the Monster in the Tempest ; and much after the same manner. To give t'other his due ; he has something of good Nature, and does not always want Wit. 42

Mira. Not always ; but as often as his Memory fails him, and his common Place of Comparisons. He is a Fool with a good Memory, and some few Scraps of other Folks Wit. He is one whose Conversation can never be approv'd, yet it is now and then to be endur'd. He has indeed one good Quality, he is not Exceptious ; for he so passionately affects the Reputation of understanding Raillery, that he will construe an Affront into a Jest ; and call downright Rudeness and ill Language, Satire and Fire. 53

Fain. If you have a mind to finish his Picture, you have an Opportunity to do it at full length. Behold the Original.

SCENE VI.

[*To them*] WITWOUD.

Wit. Afford me your Compassion, my Dears ; pity me, *Fainall*, *Mirabell*, pity me.

Mira. I do from my Soul.

Fain. Why, what's the Matter?

Wit. No Letters for me, *Betty*?

Bet. Did not a Messenger bring you one but now, Sir?

Wit. Ay, but no other?

Bet. No, Sir.

Wit. That's hard, that's very hard;—A Mes- 9
senger, a Mule, a Beast of Burden, he has brought me a Letter from the Fool my Brother, as heavy as a Panegyrick in a Funeral Sermon, or a Copy of Commendatory Verses from one Poet to another. And what's worse, 'tis as sure a Forerunner of the Author, as an Epistle Dedicatory.

Mira. A Fool, and your Brother, *Witwoud*!

Wit. Ay, ay, my half Brother. My half Brother he is, no nearer upon Honour.

Mira. Then 'tis possible he may be but half a Fool.

Wit. Good, good, *Mirabell, le Drole!* Good, 21
good, hang him, don't let's talk of him;——*Fainall*, how does your Lady? Gad. I say any thing in the World to get this Fellow out of my Head. I beg Pardon that I shou'd ask a Man of Pleasure, and the Town, a Question at once so Foreign and Domestick. But I Talk like an old Maid at a Marriage, I don't know what I say: But she's the best Woman in the World. 30

Fain. 'Tis well you don't know what you say, or else your Commendation wou'd go near to make me either Vain or Jealous.

Wit. No Man in Town lives well with a Wife but *Fainall*. Your Judgment, *Mirabell*?

Mira. You had better step and ask his Wife; if you wou'd be credibly inform'd.

Wit. Mirabell.

Mira. Ay.

Wit. My Dear, I ask Ten Thousand Pardons; 39
——Gad I have forgot what I was going to say to you.

Mira. I thank you heartily, heartily.

Wit. No, but prithee excuse me,——my Memory is such a Memory.

Mira. Have a care of such Apologies, *Witwoud*; ——for I never knew a Fool but he affected to complain, either of the Spleen or his Memory.

Fain. What have you done with *Petulant*?

Wit. He's reckoning his Mony,——my Mony it was——I have no Luck to Day.

Fain. You may allow him to win of you at Play; ——for you are sure to be too hard for him at Repartee: Since you monopolize the Wit that is between you, the Fortune must be his of Course.

Mira. I don't find that *Petulant* confesses the Superiority of Wit to be your Talent, *Witwoud*.

Wit. Come, come, you are malicious now, and wou'd breed Debates——*Petulant*'s my Friend, and a very honest Fellow, and a very pretty Fellow, and has a smattering——Faith and Troth a pretty deal of an odd sort of a small Wit: Nay, I'll do him Justice. I'm his Friend, I won't wrong him.——And if he had any Judgment in the World,——he wou'd not be altogether contemptible. Come, come, don't detract from the Merits of my Friend.

Fain. You don't take your Friend to be over-nicely bred.

Wit. No, no, hang him, the Rogue has no Manners at all, that I must own—No more Breeding than a Bum-bailey, that I grant you,—— 'Tis pity; the Fellow has Fire and Life.

Mira. What, Courage?

Wit. Hum, faith I don't know as to that,—— I can't say as to that.——Yes, faith, in a Controversie he'll contradict any Body.

Mira. Tho' 'twere a Man whom he fear'd, or a Woman whom he lov'd.

Wit. Well, well, he does not always think before he speaks;——We have all our Failings; you are too hard upon him, you are faith. Let me excuse him,——I can defend most of his Faults, except one or two; one he has, that's the Truth on't, if he were my Brother, I cou'd not acquit him——That indeed I cou'd wish were otherwise.

Mira. Ay marry, what's that, *Witwoud*?

Wit. O pardon me——Expose the Infirmities of my Friend.——No, my Dear, excuse me there.

Fain. What I warrant he's unsincere, or 'tis some such Trifle.

Wit. No, no, what if he be? 'Tis no matter for that, his Wit will excuse that: A Wit shou'd no more be sincere, than a Woman constant; one argues a Decay of Parts, as t'other of Beauty.

Mira. May be you think him too positive?

Wit. No, no, his being positive is an Incentive to Argument, and keeps up Conversation.

Fain. Too illiterate.

Wit. That! that's his Happiness——His want of Learning gives him the more Opportunities to shew his natural Parts.

Mira. He wants Words.

Wit. Ay; but I like him for that now; for his want of Words gives me the Pleasure very often to explain his Meaning.

Fain. He's Impudent.

Wit. No, that's not it.

Mira. Vain.

Wit. No.

Mira. What, he speaks unseasonable Truths sometimes, because he has not Wit enough to invent an Evasion.

Wit. Truths! Ha, ha, ha! No, no, since you will have it,——I mean, he never speaks Truth at all,—That's all. He will lie like a Chambermaid, or a Woman of Quality's Porter. Now that is a Fault.

SCENE VII.

[*To them*] COACHMAN.

Coach. Is Master *Petulant* here, Mistress?

Bet. Yes.

Coach. Three Gentlewomen in a Coach would speak with him.

Fain. O brave *Petulant*, Three!

Bet. I'll tell him.

Coach. You must bring Two Dishes of Chocolate and a Glass of Cinnamon-water.

SCENE VIII.

Mirabell, Fainall, Witwoud.

Wit. That should be for Two fasting Strumpets, and a Bawd troubled with Wind. Now you may know what the Three are.

Mira. You are free with your Friend's Acquaintance.

Wit. Ay, ay, Friendship without Freedom is as dull as Love without Enjoyment, or Wine without Toasting; but to tell you a Secret, these are Trulls whom he allows Coach-hire, and something more by the Week, to call on him once a Day at publick Places.

Mira. How!

Wit. You shall see he won't go to 'em because there's no more Company here to take notice of him——Why this is nothing to what he us'd to do;——Before he found out this way, I have known him call for himself——

Fain. Call for himself? What dost thou mean?

Wit. Mean, why he wou'd slip you out of this Chocolate-house, just when you had been talking to him——As soon as your Back was turn'd——Whip he was gone;——Then trip to his Lodging, clap on a Hood and Scarf, and a Mask, slap into a Hackney-Coach, and drive hither to the Door again in a trice; where he wou'd send in for himself, that I mean, call for himself, wait for himself, nay and what's more, not finding himself, sometimes leave a Letter for himself.

Mira. I confess this is something extraordinary ——I believe he waits for himself now, he is so long a coming; O I ask his Pardon.

SCENE IX.

PETULANT, MIRABELL, FAINALL, WITWOUD, BETTY.

Bet. Sir, the Coach stays.

Pet. Well, well; I come——'Sbud a Man had as good be a profess'd Midwife, as a profess'd Whoremaster, at this rate; to be knock'd up and rais'd at all Hours, and in all Places. Pox on 'em, I won't come——D'ye hear, tell 'em I won't come.——Let 'em snivel and cry their Hearts out.

Fain. You are very cruel, *Petulant.*

Pet. All's one, let it pass——I have a Humour to be cruel.

Mira. I hope they are not Persons of Condition that you use at this rate.

Pet. Condition, Condition's a dry'd Fig, if I am not in Humour——By this Hand, if they were your—a—a—your What-dee-call-'ems themselves, they must wait or rub off, if I want Appetite.

Mira. What-dee-call-'ems! What are they, *Witwoud*?

Wit. Empresses, my Dear—By your What-dee-call-'ems he means Sultana Queens.

Pet. Ay, *Roxolana's.*

Mira. Cry you Mercy.

Fain. *Witwoud* says they are——

Pet. What does he say th'are?

Wit. I; fine Ladies I say.

Pet. Pass on, *Witwoud*——Harkee, by this Light his Relations——Two Co-heiresses his Cousins, and an old Aunt, who loves Catterwauling better than a Conventicle.

Wit. Ha, ha, ha; I had a Mind to see how the Rogue wou'd come off——Ha, ha, ha; Gad I can't be angry with him; if he had said they were my Mother and my Sisters.

Mira. No!

Wit. No; the Rogue's Wit and Readiness of Invention charm me, dear *Petulant.*

Bet. They are gone, Sir, in great Anger.

Pet. Enough, let 'em trundle. Anger helps Complexion, saves Paint.

Fain. This Continence is all dissembled; this is in order to have something to brag of the next time he makes Court to *Millamant,* and swear he has abandoned the whole Sex for her Sake.

Mira. Have you not left off your impudent Pretensions there yet? I shall cut your Throat, sometime or other, *Petulant,* about that Business.

Pet. Ay, ay, let that pass—There are other Throats to be cut.——

Mira. Meaning mine, Sir?

Pet. Not I——I mean no Body——I know nothing.——But there are Uncles and Nephews in the World——And they may be Rivals——What then? All's one for that——

Mira. How! Harkee *Petulant,* come hither——Explain, or I shall call your Interpreter.

Pet. Explain; I know nothing—Why you have an Uncle, have you not, lately come to Town, and lodges by my Lady *Wishfort*'s?

Mira. True.

Pet. Why that's enough——You and he are not Friends; and if he shou'd marry and have a Child, you may be disinherited, ha?

Mira. Where hast thou stumbled upon all this Truth?

Pet. All's one for that; why then say I know something.

Mira. Come, thou art an honest Fellow *Petulant,* and shalt make Love to my Mistress, thou sha't, Faith. What hast thou heard of my Uncle?

Pet. I, nothing I. If Throats are to be cut, let Swords clash; snug's the Word, I shrug and am silent.

Mira. O Raillery, Raillery. Come, I know thou art in the Women's Secrets—What you're a Cabalist, I know you staid at *Millamant*'s last Night, after I went. Was there any Mention made of my Uncle, or me? Tell me; if thou hadst but good Nature equal to thy Wit *Petulant*, *Tony Witwoud*, who is now thy Competitor in Fame, would shew as dim by thee as a dead Whiting's Eye by a Pearl of Orient; he wou'd no more be seen by thee, than *Mercury* is by the Sun: Come, I'm sure thou wo't tell me.

Pet. If I do, will you grant me common Sense then, for the future?

Mira. Faith I'll do what I can for thee, and I'll pray that Heav'n may grant it thee in the mean time.

Pet. Well, harkee.

Fain. *Petulant* and you both will find *Mirabell* as warm a Rival as a Lover.

Wit. Pshaw, pshaw, that she laughs at *Petulant* is plain. And for my part——But that it is almost a Fashion to admire her, I should——Harkee——To tell you a Secret, but let it go no further—Between Friends, I shall never break my Heart for her.

Fain. How!

Wit. She's handsome; but she's a sort of an uncertain Woman.

Fain. I thought you had dy'd for her.

Wit. Umh——No——

Fain. She has Wit.

Wit. 'Tis what she will hardly allow any body else—Now, Demme, I shou'd hate that, if she were as handsome as *Cleopatra*. *Mirabell* is not so sure of her as he thinks for.

Fain. Why do you think so?

Wit. We staid pretty late there last Night;

and heard something of an Uncle to *Mirabell*, who is lately come to Town——and is between him and the best part of his Estate; *Mirabell* and he are at some Distance, as my Lady *Wishfort* has been told; and you know she hates *Mirabell*, worse than a Quaker hates a Parrot, or than a Fishmonger hates a hard Frost. Whether this Uncle has seen Mrs. *Millamant* or not, I cannot say; but there were Items of such a Treaty being in Embrio; and if it shou'd come to Life, poor *Mirabell* wou'd be in some sort unfortunately fobb'd i'faith. 122

Fain. 'Tis impossible *Millamant* shou'd harken to it.

Wit. Faith, my Dear, I can't tell; she's a Woman and a kind of a Humorist.

Mira. And this is the Sum of what you cou'd collect last Night.

Pet. The Quintessence. May be *Witwoud* knows more, he stay'd longer——Besides they never mind him; they say any thing before him.

Mira. I thought you had been the greatest Favourite. 133

Pet. Ay *tete a tete;* But not in publick, because I make Remarks.

Mira. You do?

Pet. Ay, ay, pox I'm malicious, Man. Now he's soft, you know, they are not in awe of him——The Fellow's well bred, he's what you call a——What-d'ye-call-'em. A fine Gentleman, but he's silly withal. 141

Mira. I thank you, I know as much as my Curiosity requires. *Fainall*, are you for the *Mall*?

Fain. Ay, I'll take a Turn before Dinner.

Wit. Ay, we'll all walk in the Park, the Ladies talk'd of being there.

Mira. I thought you were oblig'd to watch for your Brother Sir *Wilfull*'s Arrival. 149

Wit. No, no, he's come to his Aunt's, my Lady

Wishfort; pox on him, I shall be troubled with him too; what shall I do with the Fool?

Pet. Beg him for his Estate; that I may beg you afterwards; and so have but one Trouble with you both.

Wit. O rare *Petulant*; thou art as quick as Fire in a frosty Morning; thou shalt to the *Mall* with us; and we'll be very severe.

Pet. Enough, I'm in a Humour to be severe.

Mira. Are you? Pray then walk by your selves,——Let not us be accessary to your putting the Ladies out of Countenance, with your senseless Ribaldry; which you roar out aloud as often as they pass by you; and when you have made a handsome Woman blush, then you think you have been severe.

Pet. What, what? Then let 'em either shew their Innocence by not understanding what thy hear, or else shew their Discretion by not hearing what they wou'd not be thought to understand.

Mira. But hast not thou then Sense enough to know that thou ought'st to be most asham'd thy self, when thou hast put another out of Countenance.

Pet. Not I, by this Hand——I always take Blushing either for a Sign of Guilt, or ill Breeding.

Mira. I confess you ought to think so. You are in the right, that you may plead the Error of your Judgment in defence of your Practice.

Where Modesty's ill Manners, 'tis but fit
That Impudence and Malice pass for Wit.

End of the First Act.

ACT II. SCENE I.

St. JAMES's PARK.

Mrs. FAINALL *and Mrs.* MARWOOD.

Mrs. FAINALL.

Ay, ay, dear *Marwood*, if we will be happy, we must find the Means in our selves, and among our selves. Men are ever in Extreams ; either doating or averse. While they are Lovers, if they have Fire and Sense, their Jealousies are insupportable : And when they cease to Love, (we ought to think at least) they loath ; they look upon us with Horror and Distaste ; they meet us like the Ghosts of what we were, and as from such, fly from us.

Mrs. *Mar.* True, 'tis an unhappy Circumstance of Life, that Love shou'd ever die before us ; and that the Man so often shou'd out-live the Lover. But say what you will, 'tis better to be left, than never to have been lov'd. To pass our Youth in dull Indifference, to refuse the Sweets of Life because they once must leave us, is as preposterous, as to wish to have been born Old, because we one Day must be Old. For my part, my Youth may wear and waste, but it shall never rust in my Possession.

Mrs. *Fain.* Then it seems you dissemble an Aversion to Mankind, only in compliance to my Mother's Humour.

Mrs. *Mar.* Certainly. To be free ; I have no Taste of those insipid dry Discourses, with which our Sex of force must entertain themselves, apart from Men. We may affect Endearments to each other, profess eternal Friendships, and seem to dote like Lovers ; but 'tis not in our Natures long to persevere. Love will resume his Empire in our

Breasts, and every Heart, or soon or late, receive and readmit him as its lawful Tyrant.

Mrs. *Fain.* Bless me, how have I been deceiv'd! Why you profess a Libertine.

Mrs. *Mar.* You see my Friendship by my Freedom. Come, be as sincere, acknowledge that your Sentiments agree with mine.

Mrs. *Fain.* Never.

Mrs. *Mar.* You hate Mankind?

Mrs. *Fain.* Heartily, Inveterately.

Mrs. *Mar.* Your Husband?

Mrs. *Fain.* Most transcendently; ay, tho' I say it, meritoriously.

Mrs. *Mar.* Give me your Hand upon it.

Mrs. *Fain.* There.

Mrs. *Mar.* I join with you; what I have said has been to try you.

Mrs. *Fain.* Is it possible? Dost thou hate those Vipers Men?

Mrs. *Mar.* I have done hating 'em, and am now come to despise 'em; the next thing I have to do, is eternally to forget 'em.

Mrs. *Fain.* There spoke the Spirit of an *Amazon*, a *Penthesilea.*

Mrs. *Mar.* And yet I am thinking sometimes to carry my Aversion further.

Mrs. *Fain.* How?

Mrs. *Mar.* Faith by marrying; if I cou'd but find one that lov'd me very well, and would be throughly sensible of ill Usage, I think I should do my self the Violence of undergoing the Ceremony.

Mrs. *Fain.* You wou'd not make him a Cuckold?

Mrs. *Mar.* No; but I'd make him believe I did, and that's as bad.

Mrs. *Fain.* Why had not you as good do it?

Mrs. *Mar.* O if he shou'd ever discover it, he wou'd then know the worst, and be out of his Pain; but I wou'd have him ever to continue upon the Rack of Fear and Jealousie.

Mrs. *Fain*. Ingenious Mischief! Wou'd thou wert married to *Mirabell*.

Mrs. *Mar*. Wou'd I were.

Mrs. *Fain*. You change Colour.

Mrs. *Mar*. Because I hate him.

Mrs. *Fain*. So do I; but I can hear him nam'd. But what Reason have you to hate him in particular?

Mrs. *Mar*. I never lov'd him; he is, and always was insufferably proud.

Mrs. *Fain*. By the Reason you give for your Aversion, one wou'd think it dissembled; for you have laid a Fault to his Charge, of which his Enemies must acquit him.

Mrs. *Mar*. O then it seems you are one of his favourable Enemies. Methinks you look a little pale, and now you flush again.

Mrs. *Fain*. Do I? I think I am a little sick o' the sudden.

Mrs. *Mar*. What ails you?

Mrs. *Fain*. My Husband. Don't you see him? He turn'd short upon me unawares, and has almost overcome me.

SCENE II.

[*To them*] FAINALL *and* MIRABELL.

Mrs. *Mar*. Ha, ha, ha; he comes opportunely for you.

Mrs. *Fain*. For you, for he has brought *Mirabell* with him.

Fain. My Dear.

Mrs. *Fain*. My Soul.

Fain. You don't look well to Day, Child.

Mrs. *Fain*. D'ye think so?

Mira. He is the only Man that does, Madam.

Mrs. *Fain*. The only Man that wou'd tell me so at least; and the only Man from whom I cou'd hear it without Mortification.

Fain. O my Dear I am satisfy'd of your Tenderness ; I know you cannot resent any thing from me ; especially what is an effect of my Concern.

Mrs. *Fain.* Mr. *Mirabell*, my Mother interrupted you in a pleasant Relation last Night : I wou'd fain hear it out.

Mira. The Persons concern'd in that Affair, have yet a tolerable Reputation.——I am afraid Mr. *Fainall* will be censorious. 21

Mrs. *Fain.* He has a Humour more prevailing than his Curiosity, and will willingly dispence with the hearing of one scandalous Story, to avoid giving an Occasion to make another by being seen to walk with his Wife. This way Mr. *Mirabell*, and I dare promise you will oblige us both.

SCENE III.

FAINALL, *Mrs.* MARWOOD.

Fain. Excellent Creature ! Well, sure if I shou'd live to be rid of my Wife, I shou'd be a miserable Man.

Mrs. *Mar.* Ay !

Fain. For having only that one Hope, the accomplishment of it, of Consequence must put an end to all my Hopes ; and what a Wretch is he who must survive his Hopes ! Nothing remains when that Day comes, but to sit down and weep like *Alexander*, when he wanted other Worlds to conquer. 11

Mrs. *Mar.* Will you not follow 'em ?

Fain. Faith, I think not.

Mrs. *Mar.* Pray let us ; I have a Reason.

Fain. You are not Jealous ?

Mrs. *Mar.* Of whom ?

Fain. Of *Mirabell*.

Mrs. *Mar.* If I am, is it inconsistent with my Love to you that I am tender of your Honour ?

Fain. You wou'd intimate then, as if there were a fellow-feeling between my Wife and him.

Mrs. *Mar.* I think she does not hate him to that degree she wou'd be thought. 23

Fain. But he, I fear, is too Insensible.

Mrs. *Mar.* It may be you are deceiv'd.

Fain. It may be so. I do not now begin to apprehend it.

Mrs. *Mar.* What?

Fain. That I have been deceiv'd, Madam, and you are false. 30

Mrs. *Mar.* That I am false! What mean you?

Fain. To let you know I see through all your little Arts——Come, you both love him; and both have equally dissembl'd your Aversion. Your mutual Jealousies of one another, have made you clash 'till you have both struck Fire. I have seen the warm Confession red'ning on your Cheeks, and sparkling from your Eyes.

Mrs. *Mar.* You do me wrong. 39

Fain. I do not——'Twas for my ease to oversee and wilfully neglect the gross Advances made him by my Wife; that by permitting her to be engag'd, I might continue unsuspected in my Pleasures; and take you oftner to my Arms in full Security. But cou'd you think, because the nodding Husband wou'd not wake, that e'er the watchful Lover slept?

Mrs. *Mar.* And wherewithal can you reproach me? 49

Fain. With Infidelity, with loving another, with Love of *Mirabell*.

Mrs. *Mar.* 'Tis false. I challenge you to shew an Instance that can confirm your groundless Accusation. I hate him.

Fain. And wherefore do you hate him? He is insensible, and your Resentment follows his Neglect. An Instance! The Injuries you have done him are a Proof: Your interposing in his Love. What cause had you to make Discoveries of his pretended Passion? To undeceive the credulous Aunt, and be the officious Obstacle of his Match with *Millamant?* 62

Mrs. *Mar.* My Obligations to my Lady urg'd me: I had profess'd a Friendship to her; and cou'd not see her easie Nature so abus'd by that Dissembler.

Fain. What, was it Conscience then? Profess'd a Friendship! O the pious Friendships of the Female Sex! 69

Mrs. *Mar.* More tender, more sincere, and more enduring, than all the vain and empty Vows of Men, whether professing Love to us, or mutual Faith to one another.

Fain. Ha, ha, ha; you are my Wife's Friend too.

Mrs. *Mar.* Shame and Ingratitude! Do you reproach me? You, you upbraid me! Have I been false to her, thro' strict Fidelity to you, and sacrific'd my Friendship to keep my Love inviolate? And have you the Baseness to charge me with the Guilt, unmindful of the Merit! To you it shou'd be meritorious, that I have been vicious: And do you reflect that Guilt upon me, which shou'd lie buried in your Bosom? 84

Fain. You misinterpret my Reproof. I meant but to remind you of the slight Account you once cou'd make of strictest Ties, when set in Competition with your Love to me.

Mrs. *Mar.* 'Tis false, you urg'd it with deliberate Malice——'Twas spoke in scorn, and I never will forgive it. 91

Fain. Your Guilt, not your Resentment, begets your Rage. If yet you lov'd, you cou'd forgive a Jealousie: But you are stung to find you are discover'd.

Mrs. *Mar.* It shall be all discover'd. You too shall be discover'd; be sure you shall. I can but be expos'd——If I do it my self I shall prevent your Baseness.

Fain. Why, what will you do?

Mrs. *Mar.* Disclose it to your Wife; own what has past between us.

Fain. Frenzy!

Mrs. *Mar.* By all my Wrongs I'll do't——I'll publish to the World the Injuries you have done me, both in my Fame and Fortune: With both I trusted you, you Bankrupt in Honour, as indigent of Wealth.

Fain. Your Fame I have preserv'd. Your Fortune has been bestow'd as the Prodigality of your Love would have it, in Pleasures which we both have shar'd. Yet, had not you been false, I had e'er this repaid it——'Tis true——had you permitted *Mirabell* with *Millamant* to have stoll'n their Marriage, my Lady had been incens'd beyond all Means of Reconcilement: *Millamant* had forfeited the Moiety of her Fortune; which then wou'd have descended to my Wife;——And wherefore did I marry, but to make lawful Prize of a rich Widow's Wealth, and squander it on Love and you?

Mrs. *Mar.* Deceit and frivolous Pretence.

Fain. Death, am I not married? What's Pretence? Am I not imprison'd, fetter'd? Have I not a Wife? Nay a Wife that was a Widow, a young Widow, a handsome Widow; and wou'd be again a Widow, but that I have a Heart of Proof, and something of a Constitution to bustle thro' the ways of Wedlock and this World. Will you yet be reconcil'd to Truth and me?

Mrs. *Mar.* Impossible. Truth and you are inconsistent——I hate you, and shall for ever.

Fain. For loving you?

Mrs. *Mar.* I loath the Name of Love after such Usage; and next to the Guilt with which you wou'd asperse me, I scorn you most. Farewel.

Fain. Nay, we must not part thus.

Mrs. *Mar.* Let me go.

Fain. Come, I'm sorry.

Mrs. *Mar*. I care not——Let me go——Break my Hands, do——I'd leave 'em to get loose.

Fain. I wou'd not hurt you for the World. Have I no other Hold to keep you here?

Mrs. *Mar*. Well, I have deserv'd it all.

Fain. You know I love you.

Mrs. *Mar*. Poor dissembling!——O that——Well, it is not yet——

Fain. What? What is it not? What is it
not yet? It is not yet too late—— 149

Mrs. *Mar*. No, it is not yet too late—I have that Comfort.

Fain. It is, to love another.

Mrs. *Mar*. But not to loath, detest, abhor Mankind, my self and the whole treacherous World.

Fain. Nay, this is Extravagance——Come, I ask your Pardon——No Tears—I was to blame, I cou'd not love you and be easie in my Doubts——Pray forbear——I believe you; I'm convinc'd I've done you wrong; and any way, ev'ry way will make amends;——I'll hate my Wife yet more, Damn her, I'll part with her, rob her of all she's worth, and we'll retire somewhere, any where, to another World, I'll marry thee——Be pacify'd——'Sdeath they come, hide your Face, your Tears——You have a Mask, wear it a moment. This way, this way, be persuaded.

SCENE III.

MIRABELL *and Mrs*. FAINALL.

Mrs. *Fain*. They are here yet.

Mira. They are turning into the other Walk.

Mrs. *Fain*. While I only hated my Husband, I cou'd bear to see him; but since I have despis'd him, he's too offensive.

Mira. O you shou'd hate with Prudence.

Mrs. *Fain*. Yes, for I have lov'd with Indiscretion.

Mira. You shou'd have just so much Disgust for your Husband, as may be sufficient to make you relish your Lover.

Mrs. *Fain.* You have been the Cause that I have lov'd without Bounds, and wou'd you set Limits to that Aversion, of which you have been the Occasion? Why did you make me marry this Man?

Mira. Why do we daily commit disagreeable and dangerous Actions? To save that Idol Reputation. If the Familiarities of our Loves had produc'd that Consequence, of which you were apprehensive, where cou'd you have fix'd a Father's Name with Credit, but on a Husband? I knew *Fainall* to be a Man lavish of his Morals, an interested and professing Friend, a false and a designing Lover; yet one whose Wit and outward fair Behaviour, have gain'd a Reputation with the Town, enough to make that Woman stand excus'd, who has suffer'd her self to be won by his Addresses. A better Man ought not to have been sacrific'd to the Occasion; a worse had not answer'd to the Purpose. When you are weary of him, you know your Remedy.

Mrs. *Fain.* I ought to stand in some Degree of Credit with you, *Mirabell.*

Mira. In Justice to you, I have made you privy to my whole Design, and put it in your Pow'r to ruin or advance my Fortune.

Mrs. *Fain.* Whom have you instructed to represent your pretended Uncle?

Mira. Waitwell, my Servant.

Mrs. *Fain.* He is an humble Servant to *Foible* my Mother's Woman, and may win her to your Interest.

Mira. Care is taken for that——She is won and worn by this time. They were married this Morning.

Mrs. *Fain.* Who?

Mira. Waitwell and *Foible.* I wou'd not tempt

my Servant to betray me by trusting him too tar. If your Mother, in hopes to ruin me, shou'd consent to marry my pretended Uncle, he might, like *Mosca* in the *Fox*, stand upon Terms ; so I made him sure before-hand.

Mrs. *Fain*. So, if my poor Mother is caught in a Contract, you will discover the Imposture betimes ; and release her by producing a Certificate of her Gallant's former Marriage.

Mira. Yes, upon Condition that she consent to my Marriage with her Neice, and surrender the Moiety of her Fortune in her Possession.

Mrs. *Fain*. She talk'd last Night of endeavouring at a Match between *Millamant* and your Uncle.

Mira. That was by *Foible*'s Direction, and my Instruction, that she might seem to carry it more privately.

Mrs. *Fain*. Well, I have an Opinion of your Success ; for I believe my Lady will do any thing to get an Husband ; and when she has this, which you have provided for her, I suppose she will submit to any thing to get rid of him.

Mira. Yes, I think the good Lady wou'd marry any thing that resembl'd a Man, though 'twere no more than what a Butler could pinch out of a Napkin.

Mrs. *Fain*. Female Frailty ! We must all come to it, if we live to be Old, and feel the craving of a false Appetite when the true is decay'd.

Mira. An old Woman's Appetite is deprav'd like that of a Girl——'Tis the Green-Sickness of a second Childhood ; and like the faint Offer of a latter Spring, serves but to usher in the Fall ; and withers in an affected Bloom.

Mrs. *Fain*. Here's your Mistress.

SCENE IV.

[*To them*] *Mrs.* MILLAMANT, WITWOUD, MINCING.

Mira. Here she comes i'faith full Sail, with her Fan spread and Streamers out, and a Shoal of Fools for Tenders——Ha, no, I cry her Mercy.

Mrs. *Fain.* I see but one poor empty Sculler; and he tows her Woman after him.

Mira. You seem to be unattended, Madam,——You us'd to have the *Beau-mond* Throng after you; and a Flock of gay fine Perukes hovering round you.

Wit. Like Moths about a Candle——I had like to have lost my Comparison for want of Breath.

Milla. O I have deny'd my self Airs to Day. I have walk'd as fast through the Croud—— 12

Wit. As a Favourite just disgrac'd; and with as few Followers.

Milla. Dear Mr. *Witwoud*, Truce with your Similitudes: For I am as Sick of 'em—

Wit. As a Physician of a good Air——I cannot help it, Madam, tho' 'tis against my self.

Milla. Yet again! *Mincing*, stand between me and his Wit. 20

Wit. Do, Mrs. *Mincing*, like a Skreen before a great Fire. I confess I do blaze to Day, I am too bright.

Mrs. *Fain.* But dear *Millamant*, why were you so long?

Milla. Long! Lord, have I not made violent haste? I have ask'd every living Thing I met for you; I have enquir'd after you, as after a new Fashion. 29

Wit. Madam, Truce with your Similitudes——No, you met her Husband, and did not ask him for her.

Mira. By your leave *Witwoud*, that were like enquiring after an old Fashion, to ask a Husband for his Wife.

Wit. Hum, a hit, a hit, a palpable hit, I confess it.

Mrs. *Fain.* You were dress'd before I came abroad.

Milla. Ay, that's true——O but then I had——*Mincing*, what had I? Why was I so long?

Minc. O Mem, your Laship staid to peruse a Pacquet of Letters.

Milla. O ay, Letters——I had Letters——I am persecuted with Letters——I hate Letters——No Body knows how to write Letters; and yet one has 'em, one does not know why——They serve one to pin up one's Hair.

Wit. Is that the way? Pray, Madam, do you pin up your Hair with all your Letters; I find I must keep Copies.

Milla. Only with those in Verse, Mr. *Witwoud.* I never pin up my Hair with Prose. I think I try'd once, *Mincing*.

Minc. O Mem, I shall never forget it.

Milla. Ay, poor *Mincing* tift and tift all the Morning.

Minc. 'Till I had the Cramp in my Fingers, I'll vow Mem. And all to no purpose. But when your Laship pins it up with Poetry, it sits so pleasant the next Day as any Thing, and is so pure and so crips.

Wit. Indeed, so crips?

Minc. You're such a Critick, Mr. *Witwoud.*

Milla. Mirabell, Did you take Exceptions last Night? O ay, and went away——Now I think on't I'm angry——No, now I think on't I'm pleas'd——For I believe I gave you some Pain.

Mira. Does that please you?

Milla. Infinitely; I love to give Pain.

Mira. You wou'd affect a Cruelty which is not in your Nature; your true Vanity is in the Power of pleasing.

Milla. O I ask your Pardon for that—Ones Cruelty is ones Power, and when one parts with ones Cruelty, one parts with ones Power; and when one has parted with that, I fancy one's old and ugly. 78

Mira. Ay, ay, suffer your Cruelty to ruin the Object of your Power, to destroy your Lover— And then how vain, how lost a Thing you'll be? Nay, 'tis true: You are no longer handsome when you've lost your Lover; your Beauty dies upon the Instant: For Beauty is the Lover's Gift; 'tis he bestows your Charms——Your Glass is all a Cheat. The Ugly and the Old, whom the Looking-glass mortifies, yet after Commendation can be flatter'd by it, and discover Beauties in it: For that reflects our Praises, rather than your Face. 90

Milla. O the Vanity of these Men! *Fainall*, d'ye hear him? If they did not commend us, we were not handsome! Now you must know they cou'd not commend one, if one was not handsome. Beauty the Lover's Gift——Lord, what is a Lover, that it can give? Why one makes Lovers as fast as one pleases, and they live as long as one pleases, and they die as soon as one pleases: And then if one pleases one makes more. 99

Wit. Very pretty. Why you make no more of making of Lovers, Madam, than of making so many Card-matches.

Milla. One no more owes ones Beauty to a Lover, than ones Wit to an Eccho: They can but reflect what we look and say; vain empty Things if we are silent or unseen, and want a Being.

Mira. Yet, to those two vain empty Things, you owe two of the greatest Pleasures of your Life.

Milla. How so? 109

Mira. To your Lover you owe the Pleasure of hearing your selves prais'd; and to an Eccho the Pleasure of hearing your selves talk.

Wit. But I know a Lady that loves Talking so incessantly, she won't give an Eccho fair play; she has that everlasting Rotation of Tongue, that an Eccho must wait 'till she dies, before it can catch her last Words.

Milla. O Fiction; *Fainall,* let us leave these Men.

Mira. Draw off *Witwoud.* [*Aside to Mrs.* Fainall.

Mrs. *Fain.* Immediately; I have a Word or two for Mr. *Witwoud.*

SCENE V.

MILLAMANT, MIRABELL, MINCING.

Mira. I wou'd beg a little private Audience too ——You had the Tyranny to deny me last Night; tho' you knew I came to impart a Secret to you that concern'd my Love.

Milla. You saw I was engag'd.

Mira. Unkind. You had the leisure to entertain a Herd of Fools; Things who visit you from their excessive Idleness; bestowing on your Easiness that Time, which is the Incumbrance of their Lives. How can you find Delight in such Society? It is impossible they shou'd admire you, they are not capable: Or if they were, it shou'd be to you as a Mortification; for sure to please a Fool is some degree of Folly.

Milla. I please my self——Besides, sometimes to converse with Fools is for my Health.

Mira. Your Health! Is there a worse Disease than the Conversation of Fools?

Milla. Yes, the Vapours; Fools are Physick for it, next to *Assa-fœtida.*

Mira. You are not in a Course of Fools?

Milla. *Mirabell,* if you persist in this offensive Freedom—you'll displease me——I think I must resolve after all, not to have you——We shan't agree.

Mira. Not in our Physick it may be.

Milla. And yet our Distemper in all likelihood

will be the same; for we shall be sick of one another. I shan't endure to be reprimanded, nor instructed; 'tis so dull to act always by Advice, and so tedious to be told of ones Faults——I can't bear it. Well, I won't have you *Mirabell*——I'm resolv'd—I think——You may go—Ha, ha, ha. What wou'd you give, that you cou'd help loving me?

Mira. I wou'd give something that you did not know, I cou'd not help it.

Milla. Come, don't look grave then. Well,
what do you say to me? 39

Mira. I say that a Man may as soon make a Friend by his Wit, or a Fortune by his Honesty, as win a Woman with Plain-dealing and Sincerity.

Milla. Sententious *Mirabell!* Prithee don't look with that violent and inflexible wise Face, like *Solomon* at the dividing of the Child in an old Tapestry Hanging.

Mira. You are merry, Madam, but I would
persuade you for a Moment to be serious. 48

Milla. What, with that Face? No, if you keep your Countenance, 'tis impossible I shou'd hold mine. Well, after all, there is something very moving in a Lovesick Face. Ha, ha, ha——Well I won't laugh, don't be peevish——Heigho! Now I'll be melancholy, as melancholy as a Watch-light. Well *Mirabell*, if ever you will win me woo me now——Nay, if you are so tedious, fare you well;——I see they are walking away.

Mira. Can you not find in the variety of your
Disposition one Moment—— 59

Milla. To hear you tell me *Foible*'s Marry'd, and your Plot like to speed——No.

Mira. But how you came to know it——

Milla. Without the help of the Devil, you can't imagine; unless she should tell me her self. Which of the two it may have been, I will leave you to consider; and when you have done thinking of that, think of me.

SCENE VI.

MIRABELL *alone.*

Mira. I have something more——Gone——Think of you! To think of a Whirlwind, tho' 'twere in a Whirlwind, were a Case of more steady Contemplation; a very Tranquility of Mind and Mansion. A Fellow that lives in a Windmill, has not a more whimsical Dwelling than the Heart of a Man that is lodg'd in a Woman. There is no Point of the Compass to which they cannot turn, and by which they are not turn'd; and by one as well as another; for Motion not Method is their Occupation. To know this, and yet continue to be in Love, is to be made wise from the Dictates of Reason, and yet persevere to play the Fool by the force of Instinct.——O here come my Pair of Turtles,——What, billing so sweetly! Is not *Valentine*'s Day over with you yet?

SCENE VII.

[*To him*] WAITWELL, FOIBLE.

Mira. Sirrah, *Waitwell,* why sure you think you were marry'd for your own Recreation, and not for my Conveniency.

Wait. Your Pardon, Sir. With Submission, we have indeed been solacing in lawful Delights; but still with an Eye to Business, Sir. I have instructed her as well as I could. If she can take your Directions as readily as my Instructions, Sir, your Affairs are in a prosperous way.

Mira. Give you Joy, Mrs. *Foible.*

Foib. O-las, Sir, I'm so asham'd——I'm afraid my Lady has been in a Thousand Inquietudes for me. But I protest, Sir, I made as much haste as I could.

Wait. That she did indeed, Sir. It was my Fault that she did not make more.

Mira. That I believe.

Foib. But I told my Lady as you instructed me, Sir. That I had a prospect of seeing Sir *Rowland* your Uncle ; and that I wou'd put her Ladiship's Picture in my Pocket to shew him : which I'll be sure to say has made him so enamour'd of her Beauty, that he burns with Impatience to lye at her Ladiship's Feet and worship the Original. 23

Mira. Excellent *Foible* ! Matrimony has made you eloquent in Love.

Wait. I think she has profited, Sir. I think so.

Foib. You have seen Madam *Millamant*, Sir ?

Mira. Yes.

Foib. I told her, Sir, because I did not know that you might find an Opportunity ; she had so much Company last Night. 31

Mira. Your Diligence will merit more—In the mean time— [*Gives Mony.*

Foib. O dear Sir, your humble Servant.

Wait. Spouse.

Mira. Stand off Sir, not a Penny——Go on and prosper, *Foible*——The Lease shall be made good and the Farm stock'd, if we succeed. 38

Foib. I don't question your Generosity, Sir : And you need not doubt of Success. If you have no more Commands, Sir, I'll be gone ; I'm sure my Lady is at her Toilet, and can't dress 'till I come.——O dear, I'm sure that [*Looking out.*] was Mrs. *Marwood* that went by in a Mask ; if she has seen me with you I'm sure she'll tell my Lady. I'll make haste home and prevent her. Your Servant Sir. B'w'y *Waitwell.*

SCENE VIII.

MIRABELL, WAITWELL.

Wait. Sir *Rowland* if you please. The Jade's so pert upon her Preferment she forgets her self.

Mira. Come Sir, will you endeavour to forget your self——and transform into Sir *Rowland.*

Wait. Why Sir ; it will be impossible I shou'd remember my self——Marry'd, Knighted and attended all in one Day ! 'Tis enough to make any Man forget himself. The Difficulty will be how to recover my Acquaintance and Familiarity with my former self ; and fall from my Transformation to a Reformation into *Waitwell.* Nay, I shan't be quite the same *Waitwell* neither——for now I remember me, I'm marry'd, and can't be my own Man again. 14

Ay there's my Grief ; that's the sad Change
of Life ;
To lose my Title, and yet keep my Wife.

End of the Second Act.

ACT III. SCENE I.

A Room in Lady Wishfort's *House.*

Lady WISHFORT *at her Toilet,* PEG *waiting*

LADY.

Merciful, no news of *Foible* yet ?

Peg. No, Madam.

Lady. I have no more Patience—If I have not fretted my self 'till I am pale again, there's no Veracity in me. Fetch me the Red——the Red, do you hear, Sweet-heart ? An errant Ash colour, as I'm a Person. Look you how this Wench stirs ! Why dost thou not fetch me a little Red ? Didst thou not hear me, Mopus ? 9

Peg. The red *Ratafia* does your Ladiship mean, or the Cherry-Brandy ?

Lady. Ratafia, Fool. No, Fool. Not the *Ratafia,* Fool——Grant me Patience ! I mean the *Spanish* Paper, Idiot, Complexion Darling.

Paint, Paint, Paint, dost thou understand that, Changeling, dangling thy Hands like Bobbins before thee? Why dost thou not stir, Puppet? thou wooden Thing upon Wires. 18

Peg. Lord, Madam, your Ladiship is so impatient——I cannot come at the Paint, Madam, Mrs. *Foible* has lock'd it up, and carry'd the Key with her.

Lady. A Pox take you both—Fetch me the Cherry-Brandy then.

SCENE II.

Lady WISHFORT.

I'm as pale and as faint, I look like Mrs. *Qualmsick* the Curate's Wife, that's always breeding—Wench, come, come, Wench, what art thou doing, Sipping? Tasting? Save thee, dost thou not know the Bottle?

SCENE III.

Lady WISHFORT, PEG *with a Bottle and* China *Cup.*

Peg. Madam, I was looking for a Cup.

Lady. A Cup, save thee, and what a Cup hast thou brought! Dost thou take me for a *Fairy*, to drink out of an *Acorn*? Why didst thou not bring thy Thimble? Hast thou ne'er a Brass-Thimble clinking in thy Pocket with a bit of Nutmeg? I warrant thee. Come, fill, fill.——So——again. See who that is——[*One knocks.*] Set down the Bottle first. Here, here, under the Table——What, wou'dst thou go with the Bottle in thy Hand like a Tapster. As I'm a Person, this Wench has liv'd in an Inn upon the Road, before she came to me, like *Maritornes* the *Asturian* in *Don Quixote*. No *Foible* yet? 14

Peg. No Madam, Mrs. *Marwood.*

Lady. O *Marwood,* let her come in. Come in good *Marwood.*

SCENE IV.

[*To them*] *Mrs.* MARWOOD.

Mrs. *Mar.* I'm surpriz'd to find your Ladiship in *dishabillé* at this time of Day.

Lady. Foible's a lost Thing; has been abroad since Morning, and never heard of since.

Mrs. *Mar.* I saw her but now, as I came mask'd through the Park, in Conference with *Mirabell.*

Lady. With *Mirabell!* You call my Blood into my Face, with mentioning that Traitor. She durst not have the Confidence. I sent her to negotiate an Affair, in which if I'm detected I'm undone. If that wheadling Villain has wrought upon *Foible* to detect me, I'm ruin'd. Oh my dear Friend, I'm a Wretch of Wretches if I'm detected.

Mrs. *Mar.* O Madam, you cannot suspect Mrs. *Foible*'s Integrity.

Lady. O, he carries Poison in his Tongue that wou'd corrupt Integrity it self. If she has given him an Opportunity, she has as good as put her Integrity into his Hands. Ah dear *Marwood,* what's Integrity to an Opportunity?——Hark! I hear her——Dear Friend retire into my Closet, that I may examine her with more Freedom——You'll pardon me, dear Friend, I can make bold with you——There are Books over the Chimney——*Quarles* and *Pryn*, and the *Short View of the Stage*, with *Bunyan*'s Works to entertain you.——Go, you Thing, and send her in. [*To* Peg.

27 entertain you] Quarles, 'that makes God speak so big in's poetry'. Prynne, *Histriomastix, or the Players' Scourge.* Collier, the notorious, and then much-read attack, *A Short View of the Stage,* &c.

SCENE V.

Lady WISHFORT, FOIBLE.

Lady. O *Foible*, where hast thou been? what hast thou been doing?

Foib. Madam, I have seen the Party.

Lady. But what hast thou done?

Foib. Nay, 'tis your Ladiship has done, and are to do; I have only promis'd. But a Man so enamour'd——so transported! Well, if worshipping of Pictures be a Sin——Poor Sir *Rowland*, I say.

Lady. The Miniature has been counted like——But hast thou not betray'd me, *Foible*? Hast thou not detected me to that faithless *Mirabell*?——What hadst thou to do with him in the Park? Answer me, has he got nothing out of thee?

Foib. So, the Devil has been beforehand with me, what shall I say?——Alas, Madam, cou'd I help it, if I met that confident Thing? Was I in Fault? If you had heard how he us'd me, and all upon your Ladiship's Account, I'm sure you wou'd not suspect my Fidelity. Nay, if that had been the worst I cou'd have born: But he had a Fling at your Ladiship too; and then I cou'd not hold: But i'faith I gave him his own.

Lady. Me? What did the filthy Fellow say?

Foib. O Madam; 'tis a Shame to say what he said——With his Taunts and his Fleers, tossing up his Nose. Humh (says he) what you are a hatching some Plot (says he) you are so early abroad, or Catering (says he) ferreting for some disbanded Officer, I warrant——Half Pay is but thin Subsistance (says he)——Well, what Pension does your Lady propose? Let me see (says he) what she must come down pretty deep now, she's superannuated (says he) and——

Lady. Ods my Life, I'll have him, I'll have him

murder'd. I'll have him poison'd. Where does he eat? I'll marry a Drawer to have him poison'd in his Wine. I'll send for *Robin* from *Lockets*—Immediately. 39

Foib. Poison him? Poisoning's too good for him. Starve him, Madam, starve him; marry Sir *Rowland*, and get him disinherited. O you wou'd bless your self, to hear what he said.

Lady. A Villain, superannuated!

Foib. Humh (says he) I hear you are laying Designs against me too (says he) and Mrs. *Millamant* is to marry my Uncle; (he does not suspect a Word of your Ladiship;) but (says he) I'll fit you for that, I warrant you (says he) I'll hamper you for that (says he) you and your old Frippery too (says he) I'll handle you— 51

Lady. Audacious Villain! handle me, wou'd he durst——Frippery? old Frippery! Was there ever such a foul-mouth'd Fellow? I'll be marry'd to Morrow, I'll be contracted to Night.

Foib. The sooner the better, Madam.

Lady. Will Sir *Rowland* be here, say'st thou? when, *Foible*? 58

Foib. Incontinently, Madam. No new Sheriff's Wife expects the Return of her Husband after Knighthood, with that Impatience in which Sir *Rowland* burns for the dear Hour of kissing your Ladiship's Hand after Dinner.

Lady. Frippery! superannuated Frippery! I'll Frippery the Villain; I'll reduce him to Frippery and Rags: A Tatterdemallion——I hope to see him hung with Tatters, like a *Long-Lane* Pent-house, or a Gibbet-Thief. A slander-mouth'd Railer: I warrant the Spendthrift Prodigal's in Debt as much as the Million Lottery, or the whole Court upon a Birth-Day. I'll spoil his Credit with his Tailor. Yes, he shall have my Neice with her Fortune, he shall. 73

67 *Long-Lane*] Where old clothes were sold.

Foib. He! I hope to see him lodge in *Ludgate* first, and angle into *Black-Fryars* for Brass Farthings, with an old Mitten.

Lady. Ay dear *Foible*; thank thee for that, dear *Foible.* He has put me out of all Patience. I shall never recompose my Features, to receive Sir *Rowland* with any Oeconomy of Face. This Wretch has fretted me that I am absolutely decay'd. Look *Foible.*

Foib. Your Ladiship has frown'd a little too rashly, indeed Madam. There are some Cracks discernable in the white Vernish.

Lady. Let me see the Glass—Cracks, say'st thou? Why I am arrantly flea'd—I look like an old peel'd Wall. Thou must repair me, *Foible,* before Sir *Rowland* comes; or I shall never keep up to my Picture.

Foib. I warrant you, Madam; a little Art once made your Picture like you; and now a little of the same Art must make you like your Picture. Your Picture must sit for you, Madam.

Lady. But art thou sure Sir *Rowland* will not fail to come? Or will a not fail when he does come? Will he be Importunate, *Foible,* and push? For if he shou'd not be importunate—I shall never break Decorums——I shall die with Confusion, if I am forc'd to advance——Oh no, I can never advance——I shall swoon if he should expect Advances. No, I hope Sir *Rowland* is better bred, than to put a Lady to the Necessity of breaking her Forms. I won't be too coy neither.——I won't give him Despair——But a little Disdain is not amiss; a little Scorn is alluring.

Foib. A little Scorn becomes your Ladiship.

Lady. Yes, but Tenderness becomes me best——A sort of Dyingness——You see that Picture has a sort of a——Ha *Foible*? A Swimmingness in the Eyes——Yes, I'll look so——My Neice affects it; but she wants Features. Is Sir *Rowland* handsome?

74 *Ludgate*] the debtors' prison.

Let my Toilet be remov'd——I'll dress above. I'll receive Sir *Rowland* here. Is he handsome? Don't answer me. I won't know: I'll be surpriz'd. I'll be taken by Surprize.

Foib. By Storm, Madam. Sir *Rowland*'s a brisk Man.

Lady. Is he! O then he'll importune, if he's a brisk Man. I shall save Decorums if Sir *Rowland* importunes. I have a mortal Terror at the Apprehension of offending against Decorums. O I'm glad he's a brisk Man. Let my Things be remov'd, good *Foible*.

SCENE VI.

Mrs. FAINALL, FOIBLE.

Mrs. *Fain*. O *Foible*, I have been in a Fright, lest I shou'd come too late. That Devil, *Marwood*, saw you in the Park with *Mirabell*, and I'm afraid will discover it to my Lady.

Foib. Discover what, Madam?

Mrs. *Fain*. Nay, nay, put not on that strange Face. I am privy to the whole Design, and know *Waitwell*, to whom thou wert this Morning marry'd, is to personate *Mirabell*'s Uncle, and as such, winning my Lady, to involve her in those Difficulties from which *Mirabell* only must release her, by his making his Conditions to have my Cousin and her Fortune left to her own Disposal.

Foib. O dear Madam, I beg your Pardon. It was not my Confidence in your Ladiship that was deficient; but I thought the former good Correspondence between your Ladiship and Mr. *Mirabell*, might have hinder'd his communicating this Secret.

Mrs. *Fain*. Dear *Foible*, forget that.

Foib. O dear Madam, Mr. *Mirabell* is such a sweet winning Gentleman——But your Ladiship is the Pattern of Generosity.——Sweet Lady, to be so good! Mr. *Mirabell* cannot chuse but to be grateful. I find your Ladiship has his Heart still. Now, Madam, I can safely tell your Ladiship our Success, Mrs. *Marwood* had told my Lady; but I warrant I manag'd my self. I turn'd it all for the better. I told my Lady that Mr. *Mirabell* rail'd at her. I laid horrid Things to his Charge, I'll vow; and my Lady is so incens'd, that she'll be contracted to Sir *Rowland* to Night, she says; ——I warrant I work'd her up, that he may have her for asking for, as they say of a *Welsh* Maidenhead.

Mrs. *Fain.* O rare *Foible*!

Foib. Madam, I beg your Ladiship to acquaint Mr. *Mirabell* of his Success. I would be seen as little as possible to speak to him——besides, I believe Madam *Marwood* watches me.——She has a Month's Mind; but I know Mr. *Mirabell* can't abide her.——[*Calls.*] *John*—remove my Lady's Toilet. Madam, your Servant. My Lady is so impatient, I fear she'll come for me, if I stay.

Mrs. *Fain.* I'll go with you up the back Stairs, lest I shou'd meet her.

SCENE VII.

Mrs. MARWOOD *alone.*

Mrs. *Mar.* Indeed, Mrs. Engine, is it thus with you? Are you become a go-between of this Importance? Yes, I shall watch you. Why this Wench is the *Pass-par-toute*, a very Master-Key to every Body's strong Box. My Friend *Fainall*, have you carry'd it so swimmingly? I thought there was something in it; but it seems it's over with you. Your Loathing is not from a want of Appetite then, but from a Surfeit. Else you could

41 a Month's Mind] a longing.

never be so cool to fall from a Principal to be an Assistant; to procure for him! A Pattern of Generosity, that I confess. Well, Mr. *Fainall*, you have met with your Match.——O Man, Man! Woman, Woman! The Devil's an Ass: If I were a Painter, I would draw him like an Idiot, a Driveler with a Bib and Bells. Man shou'd have his Head and Horns, and Woman the rest of him. Poor simple Fiend! Madam *Marwood* has a Month's Mind, but he can't abide her——'Twere better for him you had not been his Confessor in that Affair; without you could have kept his Counsel closer. I shall not prove another Pattern of Generosity ——he has not oblig'd me to that with those Excesses of himself; and now I'll have none of him. Here comes the good Lady, panting ripe; with a Heart full of Hope, and a Head full of Care, like any Chymist upon the Day of Projection.

SCENE VIII.

[*To her*] *Lady* WISHFORT.

Lady. O dear *Marwood*, what shall I say for this rude Forgetfulness——But my dear Friend is all Goodness.

Mrs. *Mar*. No Apologies, dear Madam. I have been very well entertain'd.

Lady. As I'm a Person I am in a very Chaos to think I shou'd so forget my self——But I have such an Olio of Affairs really I know not what to do——[*Calls*]——*Foible*——I expect my Nephew Sir *Wilfull* ev'ry Moment too:—Why *Foible*—— He means to travel for Improvement. 11

Mrs. *Mar*. Methinks Sir *Wilfull* shou'd rather think of marrying than travelling at his Years. I hear he is turn'd of forty.

Lady. O he's in less Danger of being spoil'd by his Travels——I am against my Nephew's marrying too Young. It will be time enough when he comes back, and has acquir'd Discretion to chuse for himself.

Mrs. *Mar.* Methinks Mrs. *Millamant* and he wou'd make a very fit Match. He may travel afterwards. 'Tis a Thing very usual with young Gentlemen.

Lady. I promise you I have thought on't——And since 'tis your Judgment, I'll think on't again. I assure you I will; I value your Judgment extreamly. On my Word I'll propose it.

SCENE IX.

[*To them*] FOIBLE.

Lady. Come, come *Foible*—I had forgot my Nephew will be here before Dinner——I must make haste.

Foib. Mr. *Witwoud* and Mr. *Petulant* are come to dine with your Ladiship.

Lady. O Dear, I can't appear 'till I am dress'd. Dear *Marwood* shall I be free with you again, and beg you to entertain 'em. I'll make all imaginable haste. Dear Friend excuse me.

SCENE X.

Mrs. MARWOOD, *Mrs.* MILLAMANT, MINCING.

Milla. Sure never any thing was so Unbred as that odious Man.—*Marwood,* your Servant.

Mrs. *Mar.* You have a Colour, what's the matter?

Milla. That horrid Fellow *Petulant* has provok'd me into a Flame——I have broke my Fan——*Mincing,* lend me yours;——Is not all the Powder out of my Hair?

Mrs. *Mar.* No. What has he done?

Milla. Nay, he has done nothing; he has only talk'd——Nay, he has said nothing neither;

but he has contradicted ev'ry Thing that has been said. For my part, I thought *Witwoud* and he wou'd have quarrell'd.

Minc. I vow Mem, I thought once they wou'd have fitt.

Milla. Well, 'tis a lamentable thing I swear, that one has not the Liberty of chusing one's Acquaintance as one does ones Cloaths.

Mrs. *Mar.* If we had that Liberty, we shou'd be as weary of one Set of Acquaintance, tho' never so good, as we are of one Suit, tho' never so fine. A Fool and a *Doily* Stuff wou'd now and then find Days of Grace, and be worn for Variety.

Milla. I could consent to wear 'em, if they would wear alike; but Fools never wear out—— They are such *Drap-de-berry* Things! Without one cou'd give 'em to ones Chamber-Maid after a Day or two.

Mrs. *Mar.* 'Twere better so indeed. Or what think you of the Play-house? A fine gay glossy Fool shou'd be given there, like a new masking Habit, after the Masquerade is over, and we have done with the Disguise. For a Fool's Visit is always a Disguise; and never admitted by a Woman of Wit, but to blind her Affair with a Lover of Sense. If you wou'd but appear bare-fac'd now, and own *Mirabell*; you might as easily put off *Petulant* and *Witwoud*, as your Hood and Scarf. And indeed 'tis time, for the Town has found it: The Secret is grown too big for the Pretence: 'Tis like Mrs. *Primly*'s great Belly; she may lace it down before, but it burnishes on her Hips. Indeed, *Millamant*, you can no more conceal it, than my Lady *Strammel* can her Face, that goodly Face, which in Defiance of her Rhenish-wine Tea, will not be comprehended in a Mask.

Milla. I'll take my Death, *Marwood*, you are

16 fitt] Mincing's conjugation of the verb 'to fight'.

more Censorious than a decay'd Beauty, or a discarded Toast; *Mincing*, tell the Men they may come up. My Aunt is not dressing here; their Folly is less provoking than your Malice.

SCENE XI.

MILLAMANT, MARWOOD.

Milla. The Town has found it. What has it found? That *Mirabell* loves me is no more a Secret, than it is a Secret that you discover'd it to my Aunt, or than the Reason why you discover'd it is a Secret.

Mrs. *Mar.* You are nettl'd.

Milla. You're mistaken. Ridiculous!

Mrs. *Mar.* Indeed, my Dear, you'll tear another Fan, if you don't mitigate those violent Airs.

Milla. O silly! Ha, ha, ha. I cou'd laugh immoderately. Poor *Mirabell*! His Constancy to me has quite destroy'd his Complaisance for all the World beside. I swear, I never enjoin'd it him, to be so coy——If I had the Vanity to think he wou'd obey me; I wou'd command him to shew more Gallantry——'Tis hardly well bred to be so particular on one Hand, and so insensible on the other. But I despair to prevail, and so let him follow his own Way. Ha, ha, ha. Pardon me, dear Creature, I must laugh, ha, ha, ha; tho' I grant you 'tis a little barbarous, ha, ha, ha.

Mrs. *Mar.* What pity 'tis, so much fine Railery, and deliver'd with so significant Gesture, shou'd be so unhappily directed to miscarry.

Milla. Hæ? Dear Creature I ask your Pardon ——I swear I did not mind you.

Mrs. *Mar.* Mr. *Mirabell* and you both may think it a Thing impossible, when I shall tell him by telling you——

Milla. O dear, what? for it is the same thing, if I hear it——Ha, ha, ha.

Mrs. *Mar.* That I detest him, hate him, Madam.

Milla. O Madam, why so do I——And yet the Creature loves me, ha, ha, ha. How can one forbear laughing to think of it—I am a Sybil if I am not amaz'd to think what he can see in me. I'll take my Death, I think you are handsomer—and within a Year or two as young.——If you cou'd but stay for me, I shou'd overtake you——But that cannot be——Well, that Thought makes me melancholick——Now I'll be sad. 41

Mrs. *Mar.* Your merry Note may be chang'd sooner than you think.

Milla. D'ye say so? Then I'm resolv'd I'll have a Song to keep up my Spirits.

SCENE XII.

[*To them*] MINCING.

Minc. The Gentlemen stay but to Comb, Madam; and will wait on you.

Milla. Desire Mrs.——that is in the next Room to sing the Song I wou'd have learnt Yesterday. You shall hear it, Madam——Not that there's any great Matter in it——But 'tis agreeable to my Humour.

SONG.

Set by Mr. JOHN ECCLES.

I.

Love's but the Frailty of the Mind,
When 'tis not with Ambition join'd;
A sickly Flame, which if not fed expires; 10
And feeding, wastes in Self-consuming Fires.

II.

'Tis not to wound a wanton Boy
Or am'rous Youth, that gives the Joy;
But 'tis the Glory to have pierc'd a Swain,
For whom inferior Beauties sigh'd in vain.

III.

Then I alone the Conquest prize,
When I insult a Rival's Eyes:
If there's Delight in Love, 'tis when I see
That Heart which others bleed for, bleed for me.

SCENE XIII.

[*To them*] PETULANT, WITWOUD.

Milla. Is your Animosity compos'd, Gentlemen?

Wit. Raillery, Raillery, Madam, we have no Animosity——We hit off a little Wit now and then, but no Animosity——The falling out of Wits is like the falling out of Lovers——We agree in the main, like Treble and Base. Ha, *Petulant*!

Pet. Ay in the main—But when I have a Humour to contradict——

Wit. Ay, when he has a Humour to contradict, then I contradict too. What, I know my Cue. Then we contradict one another like two Battledores; For Contradictions beget one another like *Jews*.

Pet. If he says Black's Black—If I have a Humour to say 'tis Blue——Let that pass——All's one for that. If I have a Humour to prove it, it must be granted.

Wit. Not positively must—But it may—It may.

Pet. Yes, it positively must, upon Proof positive.

Wit. Ay, upon Proof positive it must; but upon Proof presumptive it only may. That's a Logical Distinction now, Madam.

Mrs. *Mar.* I perceive your Debates are of Importance, and very learnedly handled.

Pet. Importance is one Thing, and Learning's another; but a Debate's a Debate, that I assert.

Wit. Petulant's an Enemy to Learning; he relies altogether on his Parts.

Pet. No, I'm no Enemy to Learning; it hurts not me.

Mrs. *Mar.* That's a Sign indeed its no Enemy to you.

Pet. No, no, it's no Enemy to any Body, but them that have it.

Milla. Well, an illiterate Man's my Aversion, I wonder at the Impudence of any illiterate Man, to offer to make Love.

Wit. That I confess I wonder at too.

Milla. Ah! to marry an Ignorant! that can hardly Read or Write.

Pet. Why should a Man be any further from being Marry'd tho' he can't read, than he is from being Hang'd. The Ordinary's paid for setting the *Psalm*, and the Parish-Priest for reading the Ceremony. And for the rest which is to follow in both Cases, a Man may do it without Book——So all's one for that.

Milla. D'ye hear the Creature? Lord, here's Company, I'll be gone.

SCENE XIV.

Sir WILFULL WITWOUD *in a riding Dress, Mrs.* MARWOOD, PETULANT, WITWOUD, FOOTMAN.

Wit. In the Name of *Bartlemew* and his Fair, what have we here?

Mrs. *Mar.* 'Tis your Brother, I fancy. Don't you know him?

Wit. Not I—Yes, I think it is he—I've almost forgot him; I have not seen him since the Revolution.

Foot. Sir, my Lady's dressing. Here's Com-

1 *Bartlemew*] Bartholomew Fair was held at Smithfield until 1855.

pany; if you please to walk in, in the mean time.

Sir *Wil.* Dressing! What, it's but Morning here I warrant with you in *London;* we shou'd count it towards Afternoon in our Parts, down in *Shropshire*—Why then belike my Aunt han't din'd yet——Ha, Friend?

Foot. Your Aunt, Sir?

Sir *Wil.* My Aunt, Sir, yes my Aunt, Sir, and your Lady, Sir; your Lady is my Aunt, Sir——Why, what do'st thou not know me, Friend? Why then send some Body hither that does. How long hast thou liv'd with thy Lady, Fellow, ha?

Foot. A Week, Sir; longer than any Body in the House, except my Lady's Woman.

Sir *Wil.* Why then belike thou dost not know thy Lady, if thou see'st her, ha Friend?

Foot. Why truly Sir, I cannot safely swear to her Face in a Morning, before she is dress'd. 'Tis like I may give a shrewd guess at her by this time.

Sir *Wil.* Well, prithee try what thou canst do; if thou canst not guess, enquire her out, do'st hear, Fellow? And tell her, her Nephew, Sir *Wilfull Witwoud*, is in the House.

Foot. I shall, Sir.

Sir *Wil.* Hold ye, hear me, Friend; a Word with you in your Ear, prithee who are these Gallants?

Foot. Really, Sir, I can't tell; here come so many here, 'tis hard to know 'em all.

SCENE XV.

Sir WILFULL WITWOUD, PETULANT, WITWOUD, *Mrs.* MARWOOD.

Sir *Wil.* Oons this Fellow knows less than a Starling; I don't think a'knows his own Name.

Mrs. *Mar*. Mr. *Witwoud*, your Brother is not behind hand in Forgetfulness——I fancy he has forgot you too.

Wit. I hope so——The Devil take him that remembers first, I say.

Sir *Wil*. Save you Gentlemen and Lady.

Mrs. *Mar*. For shame, Mr. *Witwoud*; why don't you speak to him?——And you, Sir.

Wit. *Petulant* speak.

Pet. And you, Sir.

Sir *Wil*. No Offence, I hope.

[*Salutes* Marwood.

Mrs. *Mar*. No sure, Sir.

Wit. This is a vile Dog, I see that already. No Offence! Ha, ha, ha, to him; to him, *Petulant*, smoke him.

Pet. It seems as if you had come a Journey, Sir; hem, hem. [*Surveying him round.*

Sir *Wil*. Very likely, Sir, that it may seem so.

Pet. No Offence, I hope, Sir.

Wit. Smoke the Boots, the Boots; *Petulant*, the Boots; Ha, ha, ha.

Sir *Wil*. May be not, Sir; thereafter as 'tis meant, Sir.

Pet. Sir, I presume upon the Information of your Boots.

Sir *Wil*. Why, 'tis like you may, Sir: If you are not satisfy'd with the Information of my Boots, Sir, if you will step to the Stable, you may enquire further of my Horse, Sir.

Pet. Your Horse, Sir! Your Horse is an Ass, Sir!

Sir *Wil*. Do you speak by way of Offence, Sir?

Mrs. *Mar*. The Gentleman's merry, that's all, Sir——S'life, we shall have a Quarrel betwixt an Horse and an Ass, before they find one another out. You must not take any thing amiss from your Friends, Sir. You are among your Friends, here, tho' it may be you don't know it—If I am not mistaken, you are Sir *Wilfull Witwoud*.

Sir *Wil.* Right Lady; I am Sir *Wilfull Witwoud*, so I write my self; no Offence to any Body, I hope; and Nephew to the Lady *Wishfort* of this Mansion.

Mrs. *Mar.* Don't you know this Gentleman, Sir?

Sir *Wil.* Hum! What, sure 'tis not—Yea by'r Lady, but 'tis—'Sheart I know not whether 'tis or no——Yea but 'tis, by the *Wrekin*. Brother *Antony*! What *Tony*, i'faith! What do'st thou not know me? By'r Lady nor I thee, thou art so Becravated, and so Beperriwig'd—'Sheart why do'st not speak? Art thou o'erjoy'd?

Wit. Odso Brother, is it you? Your Servant, Brother.

Sir *Wil.* Your Servant! Why yours, Sir. Your Servant again——'Sheart, and your Friend and Servant to that——And a——(*puff*) and a Flap Dragon for your Service, Sir: And a Hare's Foot, and a Hare's Scut for your Service, Sir; an you be so cold and so courtly!

Wit. No Offence, I hope, Brother.

Sir *Wil.* 'Sheart, Sir, but there is, and much Offence.——A Pox, is this your Inns o' Court Breeding, not to know your Friends and your Relations, your Elders, and your Betters?

Wit. Why, Brother *Wilfull of Salop*, you may be as short as a *Shrewsbury* Cake, if you please. But I tell you 'tis not modish to know Relations in Town. You think you're in the Country, where great lubberly Brothers slabber and kiss one another when they meet, like a Call of Serjeants ——'Tis not the Fashion here; 'tis not indeed, dear Brother.

Sir *Wil.* The Fashion's a Fool; and you're a Fop, dear Brother. 'Sheart, I've suspected this ——By'r Lady I conjectur'd you were a Fop, since you began to change the Stile of your Letters, and write in a scrap of Paper gilt round the Edges, no bigger than a *Subpœna*. I might expect this when you left off Honour'd Brother; and hoping you are in good Health, and so forth——To begin with a Rat me, Knight, I'm so sick of a last Night's Debauch——O'ds Heart, and then tell a familiar Tale of a Cock and a Bull, and a Whore and a Bottle, and so conclude——You cou'd write News before you were out of your Time, when you liv'd with honest *Pumple-Nose* the Attorney of *Furnival*'s Inn——You cou'd intreat to be remember'd then to your Friends round the *Wrekin*. We could have Gazettes then, and *Dawks*'s Letter, and the Weekly Bill, 'till of late Days. 93

Pet. 'Slife, *Witwoud*, were you ever an Attorney's Clerk? Of the Family of the *Furnivals*. Ha, ha, ha!

Wit. Ay, ay, but that was but for a while. Not long, not long; pshaw, I was not in my own Power then. An Orphan, and this Fellow was my Guardian; ay, ay, I was glad to consent to that Man to come to *London*. He had the Disposal of me then. If I had not agreed to that, I might have been bound Prentice to a Felt-maker in *Shrewsbury*; this Fellow would have bound me to a Maker of Felts.

Sir *Wil.* 'Sheart, and better than to be bound to a Maker of Fops; where, I suppose, you have serv'd your Time; and now you may set up for your self. 109

Mrs. *Mar.* You intend to Travel, Sir, as I'm inform'd.

Sir *Wil.* Belike I may, Madam. I may chance to sail upon the salt Seas, if my Mind hold.

Pet. And the Wind serve.

Sir *Wil.* Serve or not serve, I shan't ask License of you, Sir; nor the Weather-Cock your Companion. I direct my Discourse to the Lady, Sir; 'Tis like my Aunt may have told you, Madam——Yes, I have settl'd my Concerns, I may say now, and am minded to see Foreign Parts. If an how that the Peace holds, whereby that is Taxes abate.

Mrs. *Mar*. I thought you had designed for *France* at all Adventures.

Sir *Wil*. I can't tell that; 'tis like I may, and 'tis like I may not. I am somewhat dainty in making a Resolution,——because when I make it I keep it. I don't stand shill I, shall I, then; if I say't, I'll do't: But I have Thoughts to tarry a small matter in Town, to learn somewhat of your *Lingo* first, before I cross the Seas. I'd gladly have a spice of your *French* as they say, whereby to hold Discourse in Foreign Countries.

Mrs. *Mar*. Here's an Academy in Town for that use.

Sir *Wil*. There is? 'Tis like there may.

Mrs. *Mar*. No doubt you will return very much improv'd.

Wit. Yes, refin'd like a *Dutch* Skipper from a Whale-fishing.

SCENE XVI.

[*To them*] *Lady* WISHFORT *and* FAINALL.

Lady. Nephew, you are welcome.

Sir *Wil*. Aunt, your Servant.

Fain. Sir *Wilfull*, your most faithful Servant.

Sir *Wil*. Cousin *Fainall*, give me your Hand.

Lady. Cousin *Witwoud*, your Servant; Mr. *Petulant*, your Servant——Nephew, you are welcome again. Will you drink any Thing after your Journey, Nephew, before you eat? Dinner's almost ready.

Sir *Wil*. I'm very well I thank you, Aunt——However, I thank you for your courteous Offer. 'Sheart I was afraid you wou'd have been in the Fashion too, and have remember'd to have forgot your Relations. Here's your Cousin *Tony*, belike, I mayn't call him Brother for fear of Offence.

Lady. O he's a Rallier, Nephew——My Cousin's a Wit: And your great Wits always rally their best Friends to chuse. When you have been Abroad, Nephew, you'll understand Raillery better.

[Fain. *and Mrs.* Marwood *talk apart.*

Sir *Wil.* Why then let him hold his Tongue in the mean Time ; and rail when that Day comes.

SCENE XVII.

[*To them*] MINCING.

Minc. Mem, I come to acquaint your Laship that Dinner is impatient.

Sir *Wil.* Impatient ? Why then belike it won't stay 'till I pull off my Boots. Sweet-heart, can you help me to a pair of Slippers ?——My Man's with his Horses, I warrant.

Lady. Fie, fie, Nephew, you wou'd not pull off your Boots here——Go down into the Hall——Dinner shall stay for you——My Nephew's a little unbred, you'll pardon him, Madam,——Gentlemen will you walk ? *Marwood ?* 11

Mrs. *Mar.* I'll follow you, Madam,——Before Sir *Wilfull* is ready.

SCENE XVIII.

MARWOOD, FAINALL.

Fain. Why then *Foible*'s a Bawd, an Errant, Rank, Matchmaking Bawd. And I it seems am a Husband, a Rank-Husband ; and my Wife a very Errant, Rank-Wife,—all in the Way of the *World.* 'Sdeath to be a Cuckold by Anticipation, a Cuckold in Embrio ? Sure I was born with budding Antlers like a young Satyr, or a Citizen's Child. 'Sdeath to be Out-witted, to be Out-jilted ——Out-Matrimony'd,——If I had kept my Speed like a Stag, 'twere somewhat,——but to crawl after, with my Horns like a Snail, and be out-stripp'd by my Wife—'tis Scurvy Wedlock.

Mrs. *Mar.* Then shake it off, you have often wish'd for an Opportunity to part ;——and now you have it. But first prevent their Plot,——the half of *Millamant*'s Fortune is too considerable to be parted with, to a Foe, to *Mirabell.*

Fain. Dam him, that had been mine——had you not made that fond Discovery——That had been forfeited, had they been Married. My Wife had added Lustre to my Horns, by that Encrease of Fortune, I cou'd have worn 'em tipt with Gold, tho' my Forehead had been furnish'd like a Deputy-Lieutenant's-Hall.

Mrs. *Mar.* They may prove a Cap of Maintenance to you still, if you can away with your Wife. And she's no worse than when you had her—I dare swear she had given up her Game, before she was Marry'd.

Fain. Hum ! That may be——

Mrs. *Mar.* You Married her to keep you ; and if you can contrive to have her keep you better than you expected ; why should you not keep her longer than you intended ?

Fain. The Means, the Means.

Mrs. *Mar.* Discover to my Lady your Wife's Conduct ; threaten to part with her——My Lady loves her, and will come to any Composition to save her Reputation. Take the Opportunity of breaking it, just upon the Discovery of this Imposture. My Lady will be enrag'd beyond Bounds, and sacrifice Neice, and Fortune, and all at that Conjuncture. And let me alone to keep her warm ; if she shou'd flag in her part, I will not fail to prompt her.

Fain. Faith this has an Appearance.

Mrs. *Mar.* I'm sorry I hinted to my Lady to endeavour a Match between *Millamant* and Sir *Wilfull*, that may be an Obstacle.

Fain. O for that matter leave me to manage him ; I'll disable him for that, he will drink like a *Dane* : after Dinner, I'll set his Hand in.

Mrs. *Mar*. Well, how do you stand affected towards your Lady?

Fain. Why faith I'm thinking of it.——Let me see——I am Marry'd already; so that's over—My Wife has plaid the Jade with me—Well, that's over too—I never lov'd her, or if I had, why that wou'd have been over too by this time—Jealous of her I cannot be, for I am certain; so there's an end of Jealousie. Weary of her, I am and shall be——No, there's no end of that; No, no, that were too much to hope. Thus far concerning my Repose. Now for my Reputation,——As to my own, I Marry'd not for it; so that's out of the Question.——And as to my Part in my Wife's——Why she had parted with hers before; so bringing none to me, she can take none from me; 'tis against all rule of Play, that I should lose to one, who has not wherewithal to stake.

Mrs. *Mar*. Besides you forget, Marriage is honourable.

Fain. Hum! Faith and that's well thought on; Marriage is honourable, as you say; and if so, wherefore should Cuckoldom be a Discredit, being deriv'd from so honourable a Root?

Mrs. *Mar*. Nay I know not; if the Root be honourable, why not the Branches?

Fain. So, so, why this Point's clear.——Well, how do we proceed?

Mrs. *Mar*. I will contrive a Letter which shall be deliver'd to my Lady at the time when that Rascal who is to act Sir *Rowland* is with her. It shall come as from an unknown Hand——for the less I appear to know of the Truth, the better I can play the Incendiary. Besides, I wou'd not have *Foible* provok'd if I cou'd help it,——because you know she knows some Passages——Nay I expect all will come out——But let the Mine be sprung first, and then I care not if I am discover'd.

Fain. If the worst come to the worst,——I'll turn my Wife to Grass——I have already a Deed of Settlement of the best part of her Estate; which I wheadl'd out of her; and that you shall partake at least.

Mrs. *Mar.* I hope you are convinc'd that I hate *Mirabell* now: You'll be no more Jealous? 97

Fain. Jealous, no,——by this Kiss——let Husbands be Jealous; but let the Lover still believe: Or if he doubt, let it be only to endear his Pleasure, and prepare the Joy that follows, when he proves his Mistress true. But let Husbands Doubts convert to endless Jealousie; or if they have Belief, let it corrupt to Superstition, and blind Credulity. I am single, and will herd no more with 'em. True, I wear the Badge, but I'll disown the Order. And since I take my Leave of 'em, I care not if I leave 'em a common Motto to their common Crest. 109

All Husbands must, or Pain, or Shame, endure;
The Wise too jealous are, Fools too secure.

End of the Third Act.

ACT IV. SCENE I.

[SCENE *Continues.*]

Lady WISHFORT *and* FOIBLE.

LADY.

Is Sir *Rowland* coming say'st thou, *Foible*? and are things in Order?

Foib. Yes, Madam. I have put Wax-Lights in the Sconces; and plac'd the Footmen in a Row in the Hall, in their best Liveries, with the Coachman and Postilion to fill up the Equipage.

Lady. Have you pullvill'd the Coachman and Postilion, that they may not stink of the Stable, when Sir *Rowland* comes by?

Foib. Yes, Madam.

Lady. And are the Dancers and the Musick ready, that he may be entertain'd in all Points with Correspondence to his Passion?

Foib. All is ready, Madam.

Lady. And——well——and how do I look, *Foible*?

Foib. Most killing well, Madam.

Lady. Well, and how shall I receive him? In what Figure shall I give his Heart the first Impression? There is a great deal in the first Impression. Shall I sit?——No, I won't sit——I'll walk——ay I'll walk from the Door upon his Entrance; and then turn full upon him——No, that will be too sudden. I'll lye——ay, I'll lye down——I'll receive him in my little Dressing-Room, there's a Couch—Yes, yes, I'll give the first Impression on a Couch——I won't lye neither, but loll and lean upon one Elbow; with one Foot a little dangling off, jogging in a thoughtful way—Yes—and then as soon as he appears, start, ay, start and be surpriz'd, and rise to meet him in a pretty Disorder—Yes—O, nothing is more alluring than a Levee from a Couch in some Confusion—It shews the Foot to advantage, and furnishes with Blushes, and re-composing Airs beyond Comparison. Hark! There's a Coach.

Foib. 'Tis he, Madam.

Lady. O dear, has my Nephew made his Addresses to *Millamant*? I order'd him.

Foib. Sir *Wilfull* is set in to Drinking, Madam, in the Parlour.

Lady. Ods my Life, I'll send him to her. Call her down, *Foible*; bring her hither. I'll send him as I go——When they are together, then come to me *Foible*, that I may not be too long alone with Sir *Rowland*.

SCENE II.

Mrs. MILLAMANT, *Mrs.* FAINALL, FOIBLE.

Foib. Madam, I stay'd here, to tell your Ladiship that Mr. *Mirabell* has waited this half Hour for an Opportunity to talk with you. Tho' my Lady's Orders were to leave you and Sir *Wilfull* together. Shall I tell Mr. *Mirabell* that you are at leisure ?

Milla. No——What wou'd the dear Man have ? I am thoughtful, and wou'd amuse my self,——bid him come another time.

There never yet was Woman made,
Nor shall, but to be curs'd.

[*Repeating and walking about.*

That's hard !

Mrs. *Fain.* You are very fond of Sir *John Suckling* to day, *Millamant*, and the Poets.

Milla. He ? Ay, and filthy Verses——So I am.

Foib. Sir *Wilfull* is coming, Madam. Shall I send Mr. *Mirabell* away ?

Milla. Ay, if you please, *Foible*, send him away,—Or send him hither,—just as you will, dear *Foible.*——I think I'll see him——Shall I ? Ay, let the Wretch come.

Thyrsis, *a Youth of the Inspir'd Train.*

[*Repeating.*

Dear *Fainall*, entertain Sir *Wilfull*——Thou hast Philosophy to undergo a Fool, thou art marry'd and hast Patience——I would confer with my own Thoughts.

Mrs. *Fain.* I am oblig'd to you, that you would make me your Proxy in this Affair ; but I have Business of my own.

SCENE III.

[*To them*] *Sir* WILFULL.

Mrs. *Fain.* O Sir *Wilfull* ; you are come at the

Critical Instant. There's your Mistress up to the Ears in Love and Contemplation, pursue your Point, now or never.

Sir *Wil.* Yes; my Aunt will have it so,——I would gladly have been encourag'd with a Bottle or two, because I'm somewhat wary at first, before I am acquainted;—But I *{This while* Milla. *walks about Repeating to her self.}* hope, after a time, I shall break my Mind——that is upon further Acquaintance——So for the present, Cousin, I'll take my leave——If so be you'll be so kind to make my Excuse, I'll return to my Company——

Mrs. *Fain.* O fie, Sir *Wilfull*! What, you must not be daunted. 16

Sir *Wil.* Daunted, no, that's not it, it is not so much for that——for if so be that I set on't, I'll do't. But only for the present, 'tis sufficient 'till further Acquaintance, that's all——your Servant.

Mrs. *Fain.* Nay, I'll swear you shall never lose so favourable an Opportunity, if I can help it. I'll leave you together, and lock the Door.

SCENE IV.

Sir WILFULL, MILLAMANT.

Sir *Wil.* Nay, nay Cousin,——I have forgot my Gloves,——What d'ye do? 'Sheart a'has lock'd the Door indeed, I think——Nay, Cousin *Fainall*, open the Door—Pshaw, what a Vixon Trick is this?——Nay, now a'has seen me too——Cousin, I made bold to pass thro' as it were——I think this Door's inchanted——

Milla. [*repeating.*]

I prithee spare me, gentle Boy,
Press me no more for that slight Toy.

Sir *Wil.* Anan? Cousin, your Servant. 10

Milla.—*That foolish Trifle of a Heart*——Sir *Wilfull*!

Sir *Wil.* Yes——your Servant. No Offence I hope, Cousin.

Milla. [*Repeating.*]

I swear it will not do its Part,
Tho' thou dost thine, employ'st thy Power and Art.

Natural, easie *Suckling* !

Sir *Wil.* Anan ? *Suckling* ? No such Suckling neither, Cousin, nor Stripling : I thank Heav'n I'm no Minor.

Milla. Ah Rustick, ruder than *Gothick.*

Sir *Wil.* Well, well, I shall understand your *Lingo* one of these Days, Cousin, in the mean while I must answer in plain *English.*

Milla. Have you any Business with me, Sir *Wilfull ?*

Sir *Wil.* Not at present, Cousin,——Yes, I made bold to see, to come and know if that how you were dispos'd to fetch a Walk this Evening, if so be that I might not be troublesome, I would have sought a Walk with you.

Milla. A Walk ? What then ?

Sir *Wil.* Nay nothing——Only for the Walk's sake, that's all——

Milla. I nauseate Walking ; 'tis a Country Diversion, I loath the Country and every thing that relates to it.

Sir *Wil.* Indeed ! Hah ! Look ye, look ye, you do ? Nay, 'tis like you may——Here are choice of Pastimes here in Town, as Plays and the like, that must be confess'd indeed.——

Milla. Ah l'etourdie ! I hate the Town too.

Sir *Wil.* Dear Heart, that's much——Hah ! that you should hate 'em both ! Hah ! 'tis like you may ; there are some can't relish the Town, and others can't away with the Country,——'tis like you may be one of those, Cousin.

17 *Suckling*] The point of the poems that Millamant quotes is that fruition is a danger owing to the inconstancy of men. Unless Congreve took for granted that his audience knew the poems, the reference is much too subtle.

Milla. Ha, ha, ha. Yes, 'tis like I may.—— You have nothing further to say to me?

Sir *Wil.* Not at present, Cousin.—'Tis like when I have an Opportunity to be more private,—I may break my Mind in some measure—I conjecture you partly guess—However that's as time shall try,—But spare to speak and spare to speed, as they say.

Milla. If it is of no great Importance, Sir *Wilfull*, you will oblige me to leave me: I have just now a little Business.—

Sir *Wil.* Enough, enough, Cousin: Yes, yes, all a case—When you're dispos'd, when you're dispos'd. Now's as well as another time; and another time as well as now. All's one for that,—Yes, yes, if your Concerns call you, there's no haste; it will keep cold as they say—Cousin, your Servant.——I think this Door's lock'd.

Milla. You may go this way, Sir.

Sir *Wil.* Your Servant, then with your leave I'll return to my Company.

Milla. Ay, ay; ha, ha, ha.

Like Phœbus *sung the no less am'rous Boy.*

SCENE V.

MILLAMANT, MIRABELL.

Mira.—Like Daphne *she, as Lovely and as Coy.* Do you lock your self up from me, to make my Search more curious? Or is this pretty Artifice contriv'd, to signifie that here the Chace must end, and my Pursuit be crown'd, for you can fly no further?—

Milla. Vanity! No——I'll fly and be follow'd to the last Moment, tho' I am upon the very Verge of Matrimony, I expect you should sollicit me as much as if I were wavering at the Grate of a Monastery, with one Foot over the Threshold. I'll be sollicited to the very last, nay and afterwards.

Mira. What, after the last?

Milla. O, I should think I was poor and had nothing to bestow, if I were reduc'd to an inglorious Ease; and freed from the agreeable Fatigues of Sollicitation.

Mira. But do not you know, that when Favours are conferr'd upon instant and tedious Sollicitation, that they diminish in their Value, and that both the Giver loses the Grace, and the Receiver lessens his Pleasure?

Milla. It may be in Things of common Application; but never sure in Love. O, I hate a Lover, that can dare to think he draws a Moment's Air, independent on the Bounty of his Mistress. There is not so impudent a Thing in Nature, as the sawcy Look of an assured Man, confident of Success. The Pedantick Arrogance of a very Husband, has not so Pragmatical an Air. Ah! I'll never marry, unless I am first made sure of my Will and Pleasure.

Mira. Would you have 'em both before Marriage? Or will you be contented with the first now, and stay for the other 'till after Grace?

Milla. Ah don't be impertinent—My dear Liberty, shall I leave thee? My faithful Solitude, my darling Contemplation, must I bid you then Adieu? Ay-h adieu—My Morning Thoughts, agreeable Wakings, indolent Slumbers, all ye *douceurs*, ye *Someils du Matin*, adieu—I can't do't, 'tis more than impossible—Positively *Mirabell*, I'll lye a-bed in a Morning as long as I please.

Mira. Then I'll get up in a Morning as early as I please.

Milla. Ah! Idle Creature, get up when you will——And d'ye hear, I won't be call'd Names after I'm Marry'd; positively I won't be call'd Names.

Mira. Names!

Milla. Ay, as Wife, Spouse, my Dear, Joy, Jewel, Love, Sweet-heart, and the rest of that nauseous Cant, in which Men and their Wives are so fulsomly familiar,——I shall never bear that——Good *Mirabell* don't let us be familiar or fond, nor kiss before Folks, like my Lady *Fadler* and Sir *Francis*: Nor go to *Hide-Park* together the first *Sunday* in a new Chariot, to provoke Eyes and Whispers; And then never be seen there together again; as if we were proud of one another the first Week, and asham'd of one another ever after. Let us never Visit together, nor go to a Play together, but let us be very strange and well bred: Let us be as strange as if we had been marry'd a great while; and as well bred as if we were not marry'd at all.

Mira. Have you any more Conditions to offer? Hitherto your Demands are pretty reasonable.

Milla. Trifles,——As Liberty to pay and receive Visits to and from whom I please; to write and receive Letters, without Interrogatories or wry Faces on your part; to wear what I please; and chuse Conversation with regard only to my own Taste; to have no Obligation upon me to converse with Wits that I don't like, because they are your Acquaintance; or to be intimate with Fools, because they may be your Relations. Come to Dinner when I please, dine in my Dressing-Room when I'm out of Humour, without giving a Reason. To have my Closet inviolate; to be sole Empress of my Tea-Table, which you must never presume to approach without first asking leave. And lastly where-ever I am, you shall always knock at the Door before you come in. These Articles subscrib'd, if I continue to endure you a little longer, I may by degrees dwindle into a Wife.

Mira. Your Bill of Fare is something advanc'd in this latter Account. Well, have I Liberty to offer Conditions——That when you are dwindled into a Wife, I may not be beyond measure enlarg'd into a Husband.

Milla. You have free leave, propose your utmost, speak and spare not.

Mira. I thank you. *Inprimis* then, I covenant that your Acquaintance be general; that you admit no sworn Confident, or Intimate of your own Sex; no she Friend to skreen her Affairs under your Countenance, and tempt you to make Trial of a mutual Secresie. No Decoy-Duck to wheadle you a *fop—scrambling* to the Play in a Mask—— Then bring you home in a pretended Fright, when you think you shall be found out—And rail at me for missing the Play, and disappointing the Frolick which you had to pick me up and prove my Constancy.

Milla. Detestable *Inprimis*! I go to the Play in a Mask! 107

Mira. Item, I Article, that you continue to like your own Face, as long as I shall: And while it passes currant with me, that you endeavour not to new Coin it. To which end, together with all Vizards for the Day, I prohibit all Masks for the Night, made of Oil'd-skins and I know not what ——Hog's Bones, Hare's Gall, Pig Water, and the Marrow of a roasted Cat. In short, I forbid all Commerce with the Gentlewoman in *what-d'ye-call-it* Court. *Item,* I shut my Doors against all Bauds with Baskets, and penny-worths of *Muslin, China, Fans, Atlasses,* &c.——*Item,* when you shall be Breeding—— 120

Milla. Ah! Name it not.

Mira. Which may be presum'd, with a Blessing on our Endeavours——

Milla. Odious Endeavours!

Mira. I denounce against all strait Lacing, squeezing for a Shape, 'till you mould my Boy's Head like a Sugar-loaf; and instead of a Man-Child, make me Father to a Crooked-billet. Lastly, to the Dominion of the *Tea-Table* I submit. ——But with *proviso,* that you exceed not in your Province; but restrain your self to native and simple *Tea-Table* Drinks, as *Tea, Chocolate,* and *Coffee.* As likewise to Genuine and Authoriz'd

Tea-Table Talk——Such as mending of Fashions, spoiling Reputations, railing at absent Friends, and so forth——But that on no Account you encroach upon the Mens Prerogative, and presume to drink Healths, or toast Fellows; for prevention of which, I banish all *Foreign Forces*, all Auxiliaries to the *Tea-Table*, as *Orange-Brandy*, all *Anniseed, Cinamon, Citron* and *Barbado*'s-*Waters*, together with *Ratafia* and the most noble Spirit of *Clary*. ——But for *Couslip-Wine, Poppy-Water*, and all *Dormitives*, those I allow.——These *Proviso*'s admitted, in other things I may prove a tractable and complying Husband.

Milla. O horrid *Proviso's*! filthy strong Waters! I toast Fellows, Odious Men! I hate your odious *Proviso's*.

Mira. Then we're agreed. Shall I kiss your Hand upon the Contract? and here comes one to be a Witness to the Sealing of the Deed.

SCENE VI.

[*To them*] *Mrs.* FAINALL.

Milla. Fainall, what shall I do? Shall I have him? I think I must have him.

Mrs. *Fain.* Ay, ay, take him, take him, what shou'd you do?

Milla. Well then—I'll take my Death I'm in a horrid Fright——*Fainall*, I shall never say it——Well——I think——I'll endure you.

Mrs. *Fain.* Fy, fy, have him, have him, and tell him so in plain Terms: For I am sure you have a Mind to him.

Milla. Are you? I think I have——and the horrid Man looks as if he thought so too——Well, you ridiculous thing you, I'll have you——I won't be kiss'd, nor I won't be thank'd——Here kiss my Hand tho'——So, hold your Tongue now, don't say a Word.

Mrs. *Fain.* *Mirabell*, there's a Necessity for your Obedience ;——You have neither time to talk nor stay. My Mother is coming ; and in my Conscience if she shou'd see you, wou'd fall into Fits, and may be not recover, time enough to return to Sir *Rowland* ; who, as *Foible* tells me, is in a fair Way to succeed. Therefore spare your Extacies for another Occasion, and slip down the back Stairs, where *Foible* waits to consult you.

Milla. Ay, go, go. In the mean time I suppose you have said something to please me.

Mira. I am all Obedience.

SCENE VII.

MILLAMANT, *Mrs.* FAINALL.

Mrs. *Fain.* Yonder Sir *Wilfull*'s drunk ; and so noisie that my Mother has been forc'd to leave Sir *Rowland* to appease him ; but he answers her only with Singing and Drinking——What they may have done by this time I know not ; but *Petulant* and he were upon quarrelling as I came by.

Milla. Well, If *Mirabell* should not make a good Husband, I am a lost thing ;——for I find I love him violently.

Mrs. *Fain.* So it seems ; for you mind not what's said to you.——If you doubt him, you had best take up with Sir *Wilfull.*

Milla. How can you name that superannuated Lubber ? foh !

SCENE VIII.

[*To them*] WITWOUD *from drinking.*

Mrs. *Fain.* So, is the Fray made up, that you have left 'em ?

Wit. Left 'em ? I could stay no longer——I have laugh'd like ten Christnings——I am tipsie with laughing——If I had staid any longer

I should have burst,——I must have been let out and piec'd in the Sides like an unsiz'd Camlet——Yes, yes, the Fray is compos'd ; my Lady came in like a *Noli prosequi*, and stopt the Proceedings.

Milla. What was the Dispute ?

Wit. That's the Jest ; there was no Dispute. They could neither of 'em speak for Rage ; and so fell a sputt'ring at one another like two roasting Apples.

SCENE IX.

[*To them*] PETULANT *Drunk.*

Wit. Now *Petulant*? all's over, all's well ? Gad my Head begins to whim it about——Why dost thou not speak ? thou art both as drunk and as mute as a Fish.

Pet. Look you, Mrs. *Millamant*——if you can love me, dear Nymph—say it—and that's the Conclusion—pass on, or pass off,——that's all.

Wit. Thou hast utter'd *Volumes*, *Folio's*, in less than *Decimo Sexto*, my dear *Lacedemonian*. Sirrah, *Petulant*, thou art an Epitomizer of Words.

Pet. *Witwoud*——You are an Annihilator of Sense.

Wit. Thou art a Retailer of Phrases ; and dost deal in Remnants of Remnants, like a Maker of Pincushions—thou art in truth (metaphorically speaking) a Speaker of Short-hand.

Pet. Thou art (without a Figure) just one half of an Ass, and *Baldwin* yonder, thy half Brother, is the rest—A *Gemini* of Asses split, would make just four of you.

Wit. Thou dost bite, my dear Mustard-seed ; kiss me for that.

Pet. Stand off——I'll kiss no more Males,——I have kiss'd your *Twin* yonder in a humour of Reconciliation, 'till he (*hiccup*) rises upon my Stomach like a Radish.

18 *Baldwin*] The ass in *Reynard the Fox.*

Milla. Eh! filthy Creature—what was the Quarrel?

Pet. There was no Quarrel—there might have been a Quarrel.

Wit. If there had been Words enow between 'em to have express'd Provocation, they had gone together by the Ears like a pair of Castanets.

Pet. You were the Quarrel.

Milla. Me!

Pet. If I have a Humour to quarrel, I can make less Matters conclude Premises,—If you are not handsom, what then; If I have a Humour to prove it?—If I shall have my Reward, say so; if not, fight for your Face the next time your self—I'll go sleep.

Wit. Do, wrap thy self up like a *Woodlouse*, and dream Revenge—And hear me, if thou canst learn to write by to Morrow Morning, pen me a Challenge—I'll carry it for thee.

Pet. Carry your Mistress's *Monkey* a *Spider*,——go flea Dogs, and read Romances——I'll go to Bed to my Maid.

Mrs. *Fain.* He's horridly Drunk——how came you all in this Pickle?

Wit. A Plot, a Plot, to get rid of the Knight,——Your Husband's Advice; but he sneak'd off.

SCENE X.

Sir WILFULL *Drunk*, *Lady* WISHFORT,
WITWOUD, MILLAMANT, *Mrs.* FAINALL.

Lady. Out upon't, out upon't, at Years of Discretion, and comport your self at this Rantipole rate.

Sir *Wil.* No Offence, Aunt.

Lady. Offence? As I'm a Person, I'm asham'd of you——Fogh! how you stink of Wine! D'ye think my Neice will ever endure such a *Borachio*! you're an absolute *Borachio*.

7 *Borachio*] Pottle-pot. Literally wine-skin.

Sir *Wil. Borachio !*

Lady. At a time when you shou'd commence an Amour, and put your best Foot foremost——

Sir *Wil.* 'Sheart, an you grutch me your Liquor, make a Bill——Give me more Drink, and take my Purse.

Sings. *Prithee fill me the Glass*
'Till it laugh in my Face,
With Ale that is Potent and Mellow ;
He that whines for a Lass
Is an ignorant Ass,
For a Bumper *has not its Fellow.*

But if you wou'd have me marry my Cousin,——say the Word, and I'll do't——*Wilfull* will do't, that's the Word——*Wilfull* will do't, that's my Crest——my Motto I have forgot.

Lady. My Nephew's a little overtaken, Cousin——but 'tis with drinking your Health——O' my Word you are oblig'd to him——

Sir *Wil. In Vino Veritas,* Aunt :——If I drunk your Health to Day, Cousin,——I am a *Borachio.* But if you have a Mind to be marry'd, say the Word, and send for the Piper, *Wilfull* will do't. If not, dust it away, and let's have t'other Round——*Tony,* Ods-heart where's *Tony*——*Tony*'s an honest Fellow, but he spits after a Bumper, and that's a Fault,

Sings. *We'll drink and we'll never ha' done Boys,*
Put the Glass then around with the Sun Boys,
Let Apollo's *Example invite us ;*
For he's drunk ev'ry Night,
And that makes him so bright,
That he's able next Morning to light us.

The Sun's a good Pimple, an honest Soaker, he has a Cellar at your *Antipodes.* If I travel, Aunt,

I touch at your *Antipodes*——your *Antipodes* are a good rascally sort of topsie turvy Fellows——If I had a Bumper I'd stand upon my Head and drink a Health to 'em——A Match or no Match, Cousin, with the hard Name——Aunt, *Wilfull* will do't. If she has her Maidenhead let her look to't; if she has not, let her keep her own Counsel in the mean time, and cry out at the Nine Months End.

Milla. Your Pardon, Madam, I can stay no longer——Sir *Wilfull* grows very powerful, Egh! how he smells! I shall be overcome if I stay. Come, Cousin.

SCENE XI.

Lady WISHFORT, *Sir* WILFULL WITWOUD, *Mr.* WITWOUD, FOIBLE.

Lady. Smells! he would poison a Tallow-Chandler and his Family. Beastly Creature, I know not what to do with him.——Travel quoth a; ay travel, travel, get thee gone, get thee but far enough, to the *Saracens*, or the *Tartars*, or the *Turks*——for thou art not fit to live in a Christian Commonwealth, thou beastly Pagan.

Sir *Wil. Turks*, no; no *Turks*, Aunt: Your *Turks* are Infidels, and believe not in the Grape. Your *Mahometan*, your *Mussulman* is a dry Stinkard——No Offence, Aunt. My Map says that your *Turk* is not so honest a Man as your Christian ——I cannot find by the Map that your *Mufti* is Orthodox——Whereby it is a plain Case, that Orthodox is a hard Word, Aunt, and (*hiccup*) Greek for Claret.

Sings. *To Drink is a Christian Diversion.*
Unknown to the Turk *or the* Persian*:*
Let Mahometan *Fools*
Live by Heathenish Rules,

And be damn'd over Tea-Cups and Coffee.
But let British *Lads sing,*
Crown a Health to the King,
And a Fig for your Sultan *and* Sophy.

Ah, *Tony!* [Foible *whispers Lady* W.

Lady. Sir *Rowland* impatient? Good lack! what shall I do with this beastly Tumbril?——Go lie down and sleep, you Sot——Or as I'm a Person, I'll have you bastinado'd with Broom-sticks. Call up the Wenches with Broom-sticks.

Sir *Wil.* Ahay? Wenches, where are the Wenches?

Lady. Dear Cousin *Witwoud* get him away, and you will bind me to you inviolably. I have an Affair of moment that invades me with some Precipitation——You will oblige me to all Futurity.

Wit. Come, Knight——Pox on him, I don't know what to say to him——Will you go to a Cock-match?

Sir *Wil.* With a Wench, *Tony*? Is she a shake-bag, Sirrah? Let me bite your Cheek for that.

Wit. Horrible! He has a Breath like a Bagpipe—Ay, ay, come will you march, my *Salopian*?

Sir *Wil.* Lead on, little *Tony*——I'll follow thee my *Anthony*, my *Tantony*, Sirrah thou shalt be my *Tantony*, and I'll be thy *Pig*.

——*And a Fig for your* Sultan *and* Sophy.

Lady. This will never do. It will never make a Match.——At least before he has been abroad.

SCENE XII.

Lady WISHFORT, WAITWELL *disguis'd as for Sir* ROWLAND.

Lady. Dear Sir *Rowland,* I am confounded with

24 Sophy] Cant term for the Shah of Persia, derived from the Sufi dynasty.

Confusion at the Retrospection of my own Rudeness,——I have more Pardons to ask than the *Pope* distributes in the Year of *Jubile.* But I hope where there is likely to be so near an Alliance,——we may unbend the Severity of *Decorum*——and dispense with a little Ceremony.

Wait. My Impatience, Madam, is the Effect of my Transport;——and 'till I have the Possession of your adorable Person, I am tantaliz'd on the Rack; and do but hang, Madam, on the Tenter of Expectation.

Lady. You have Excess of Gallantry, Sir *Rowland;* and press things to a Conclusion, with a most prevailing Vehemence.——But a Day or two for Decency of Marriage.——

Wait. For Decency of Funeral, Madam. The Delay will break my Heart—or if that should fail, I shall be Poison'd. My Nephew will get an inkling of my Designs, and poison me,—and I would willingly starve him before I die——I would gladly go out of the World with that Satisfaction.—That would be some Comfort to me, if I could but live so long as to be reveng'd on that unnatural Viper.

Lady. Is he so unnatural, say you? Truly I would contribute much both to the saving of your Life, and the accomplishment of your Revenge——Not that I respect my self; tho' he has been a perfidious Wretch to me.

Wait. Perfidious to you!

Lady. O Sir *Rowland,* the Hours that he has dy'd away at my Feet, the Tears that he has shed, the Oaths that he has sworn, the Palpitations that he has felt, the Trances and the Tremblings, the Ardors and the Ecstacies, the Kneelings, and the Risings, the Heart-heavings and the Hand-gripings, the Pangs and the Pathetick Regards of his protesting Eyes! Oh no Memory can Register.

Wait. What, my Rival! Is the Rebel my Rival? a'dies.

Lady. No, don't kill him at once, Sir *Rowland*, starve him gradually Inch by Inch.

Wait. I'll do't. In three Weeks he shall be bare-foot ; in a Month out at Knees with begging an Alms,——he shall starve upward and upward, 'till he has nothing living but his Head, and then go out in a Stink like a Candle's End upon a Saveall.

Lady. Well, Sir *Rowland*, you have the way,——You are no Novice in the Labyrinth of Love——You have the Clue——But as I am a Person, Sir *Rowland*, you must not attribute my yielding to any sinister Appetite, or Indigestion of Widowhood ; nor impute my Complacency to any Lethargy of Continence——I hope you do not think me prone to any Iteration of Nuptials.——

Wait. Far be it from me——

Lady. If you do, I protest I must recede——or think that I have made a Prostitution of Decorums, but in the Vehemence of Compassion, and to save the Life of a Person of so much Importance——

Wait. I esteem it so——

Lady. Or else you wrong my Condescension——

Wait. I do not, I do not——

Lady. Indeed you do.

Wait. I do not, fair Shrine of Virtue.

Lady. If you think the least Scruple of Carnality was an Ingredient——

Wait. Dear Madam, no. You are all *Camphire* and *Frankincense*, all *Chastity* and *Odour*.

Lady. Or that——

SCENE XIII.

[*To them*] FOIBLE.

Foib. Madam, the Dancers are ready, and

71 *Camphire*] That 'causeth impotency unto venery'. *Vulgar Errors*.

there's one with a Letter, who must deliver it into your own Hands.

Lady. Sir *Rowland*, will you give me leave? Think favourably, judge candidly, and conclude you have found a Person who would suffer Racks in Honour's Cause, dear Sir *Rowland*, and will wait on you incessantly.

SCENE XIV.

WAITWELL, FOIBLE.

Wait. Fie, fie!—What a Slavery have I undergone; Spouse, hast thou any *Cordial*, I want *Spirits*.

Foib. What a washy Rogue art thou, to pant thus for a Quarter of an Hours Lying and Swearing to a fine Lady?

Wait. O, she is the Antidote to Desire. Spouse, thou wilt fare the worse for't——I shall have no Appetite to Iteration of Nuptials——this eight and forty Hours——By this Hand I'd rather be a Chairman in the Dog-days——than act Sir *Rowland* 'till this time to Morrow.

SCENE XV.

[*To them*] LADY *with a Letter.*

Lady. Call in the Dancers;——Sir *Rowland*, we'll sit, if you please, and see the Entertainment. [*Dance.*

Now with your Permission, Sir *Rowland*, I will peruse my Letter—I would open it in your Presence, because I would not make you uneasie. If it should make you uneasie I would burn it——speak if it does——but you may see, the Superscription is like a Woman's Hand.

Foib. By Heav'n! Mrs. *Marwood*'s, I know it,——my Heart akes——get it from her—— [*To him.*

Wait. A Woman's Hand? No, Madam, that's no Woman's Hand, I see that already. That's some Body whose Throat must be cut.

Lady. Nay, Sir *Rowland*, since you give me a Proof of your Passion by your Jealousie, I promise you I'll make a Return, by a frank Communication——You shall see it—we'll open it together——look you here.

Reads.——*Madam, though unknown to you,* [Look you there, 'tis from no Body that I know.] ——*I have that Honour for your Character, that I think my self oblig'd to let you know you are abus'd. He who pretends to be Sir* Rowland *is a Cheat and a Rascal*——

Oh Heav'ns! what's this?

Foib. Unfortunate, all's ruin'd.

Wait. How, how, let me see, let me see——reading, *A Rascal and disguis'd, and suborn'd for that Imposture,*—O Villany! O Villany!——*by the Contrivance of*——

Lady. I shall faint, I shall die, oh!

Foib. Say, 'tis your Nephew's Hand.—Quickly, his Plot, swear, swear it.— [*To him.*

Wait. Here's a Villain! Madam, don't you perceive it, don't you see it?

Lady. Too well, too well. I have seen too much.

Wait. I told you at first I knew the Hand—A Woman's Hand? The Rascal writes a sort of a large Hand; your *Roman* Hand—I saw there was a Throat to be cut presently. If he were my Son, as he is my Nephew, I'd pistol him—

Foib. O Treachery! But are you sure, Sir *Rowland*, it is his Writing?

Wait. Sure? Am I here? do I live? do I love this Pearl of *India*? I have twenty Letters in my Pocket from him, in the same Character.

Lady. How!

Foib. O what Luck it is, Sir *Rowland*, that you were present at this Juncture! This was the

Business that brought Mr. *Mirabell* disguis'd to Madam *Millamant* this Afternoon. I thought something was contriving, when he stole by me and would have hid his Face.

Lady. How, how!—I heard the Villain was in the House indeed; and now I remember, my Neice went away abruptly, when Sir *Wilfull* was to have made his Addresses.

Foib. Then, then Madam, Mr. *Mirabell* waited for her in her Chamber; but I would not tell your Ladiship to discompose you when you were to receive Sir *Rowland.*

Wait. Enough, his Date is short.

Foib. No, good Sir *Rowland,* don't incur the Law.

Wait. Law! I care not for Law. I can but die, and 'tis in a good Cause—My Lady shall be satisfy'd of my Truth and Innocence, tho' it cost me my Life.

Lady. No, dear Sir *Rowland,* don't fight, if you should be kill'd I must never shew my Face; or hang'd,—O consider my Reputation, Sir *Rowland* —No you shan't fight,—I'll go and examine my Neice; I'll make her confess. I conjure you Sir *Rowland* by all your Love not to fight.

Wait. I am charm'd Madam, I obey. But some Proof you must let me give you;—I'll go for a black Box, which contains the Writings of my whole Estate, and deliver that into your Hands.

Lady. Ay dear Sir *Rowland,* that will be some Comfort, bring the black Box.

Wait. And may I presume to bring a Contract to be sign'd this Night? May I hope so far?

Lady. Bring what you will; but come alive, pray come alive. O this is a happy Discovery.

Wait. Dead or alive I'll come—and married we will be in spight of Treachery; ay and get an Heir that shall defeat the last remaining Glimpse of Hope in my abandon'd Nephew. Come, my Buxom Widow:

E'er long you shall substantial Proof receive
That I'm an arrant Knight——
Foib. *Or arrant Knave.*

End of the Fourth Act.

ACT V. SCENE I.

[SCENE *Continues.*]

Lady WISHFORT *and* FOIBLE.

LADY.

Out of my House, out of my House, thou *Viper*, thou *Serpent*, that I have foster'd; thou bosom Traitress, that I rais'd from nothing——Begone, begone, begone, go, go,——That I took from washing of old Gause and weaving of dead Hair, with a bleak blue Nose, over a Chafing-dish of starv'd Embers, and Dining behind a Traverse Rag, in a shop no bigger than a Bird-Cage,——go, go, starve again, do, do.

Foib. Dear Madam, I'll beg Pardon on my Knees.

Lady. Away, out, out, go set up for your self again——do, drive a Trade, do, with your Three-penny-worth of small Ware, flaunting upon a Packthread, under a Brandy-sellers Bulk, or against a dead Wall by a Ballad-monger. Go, hang out an old *Frisoneer-gorget*, with a Yard of Yellow *Colberteen* again; do; an old gnaw'd Mask, two Rows of Pins and a Child's Fiddle; A Glass Necklace with the Beads broken, and a Quilted Night-cap with one Ear. Go, go, drive

93 *arrant*] This pun is not so bad as it seems to us. Errant was usually spelt arrant in the seventeenth century.
18 *Colberteen*] A French imitation of Italian lace, of which the manufacture was encouraged by Colbert.

a Trade,——These were your Commodities, you treacherous Trull, this was the Merchandize you dealt in, when I took you into my House, plac'd you next my self, and made you Governante of my whole Family. You have forgot this, have you, now you have feather'd your Nest ? 27

Foib. No, no, dear Madam. Do but hear me, have but a Moment's Patience——I'll confess all. Mr. *Mirabell* seduc'd me ; I am not the first that he has wheadled with his dissembling Tongue ; Your Ladiship's own Wisdom has been deluded by him, then how should I, a poor Ignorant, defend my self ? O Madam, if you knew but what he promis'd me, and how he assur'd me your Ladiship should come to no Damage——Or else the Wealth of the *Indies* should not have brib'd me to conspire against so Good, so Sweet, so Kind a Lady as you have been to me. 39

Lady. No Damage ? What to betray me, to marry me to a Cast-serving-Man ; to make me a Receptacle, an Hospital for a decay'd Pimp ? No Damage ? O thou frontless Impudence, more than a big-belly'd Actress.

Foib. Pray do but hear me Madam, he could not marry your Ladiship, Madam——No indeed his Marriage was to have been void in Law ; for he was marry'd to me first, to secure your Ladiship. He could not have bedded your Ladiship ; for if he had consummated with your Ladiship, he must have run the risque of the Law, and been put upon his Clergy——Yes indeed, I enquir'd of the Law in that case before I would meddle or make. 54

Lady. What, then I have been your Property, have I ? I have been convenient to you, it seems, ——while you were catering for *Mirabell* ; I have been Broaker for you ? What, have you made a passive Bawd of me ?——this exceeds all Prece-

54 *make*] Cf. Pandarus in Shakespeare's *Troilus and Cressida*: 'I'll not meddle nor make no further '.

dent; I am brought to fine Uses, to become a Botcher of second-hand Marriages between *Abigails* and *Andrews*! I'll couple you. Yes, I'll baste you together, you and your *Philander*. I'll *Duke's-Place* you, as I'm a Person. Your Turtle is in Custody already: You shall Coo in the same Cage, if there be Constable or Warrant in the Parish.

Foib. O that ever I was born, O that I was ever marry'd,——a Bride, ay I shall be a *Bridewell*-Bride. Oh!

SCENE II.

Mrs. FAINALL, FOIBLE.

Mrs. *Fain.* Poor *Foible*, what's the matter?

Foib. O Madam, my Lady's gone for a Constable; I shall be had to a Justice, and put to *Bridewell* to beat Hemp; poor *Waitwell*'s gone to Prison already.

Mrs. *Fain.* Have a good Heart, *Foible*, *Mirabell*'s gone to give Security for him. This is all *Marwood*'s and my Husband's doing.

Foib. Yes, yes, I know it, Madam; she was in my Lady's Closet, and overheard all that you said to me before Dinner. She sent the Letter to my Lady; and that missing Effect, Mr. *Fainall* laid this Plot to arrest *Waitwell*, when he pretended to go for the Papers; and in the mean time Mrs. *Marwood* declar'd all to my Lady.

Mrs. *Fain.* Was there no Mention made of me in the Letter?——My Mother does not suspect my being in the Confederacy? I fancy *Marwood* has not told her, tho' she has told my Husband.

Foib. Yes, Madam; but my Lady did not see that Part: We stifled the Letter before she read so far. Has that mischievous Devil told Mr. *Fainall* of your Ladiship then?

69 *Bridewell*-] Bridewell was a house of correction for vagabonds and loose women.

Mrs. *Fain.* Ay, all's out, my Affair with *Mirabell,* every thing discover'd. This is the last Day of our living together, that's my Comfort.

Foib. Indeed Madam, and so 'tis a Comfort if you knew all,——he has been even with your Ladiship; which I cou'd have told you long enough since, but I love to keep Peace and Quietness by my good Will: I had rather bring Friends together, than set 'em at Distance. But Mrs. *Marwood* and he are nearer related than ever their Parents thought for.

Mrs. *Fain.* Say'st thou so, *Foible*? Canst thou prove this?

Foib. I can take my Oath of it, Madam, so can Mrs. *Mincing*; we have had many a fair Word from Madam *Marwood,* to conceal something that passed in our Chamber one Evening when you were at *Hide-Park;*——and we were thought to have gone a Walking: But we went up unawares, ——tho' we were sworn to Secresie too; Madam *Marwood* took a Book and swore us upon it: But it was but a Book of Poems,——So long as it was not a Bible-Oath, we may break it with a safe Conscience.

Mrs. *Fain.* This Discovery is the most opportune Thing I cou'd wish. Now *Mincing*?

SCENE III.

[*To them*] MINCING.

Minc. My Lady wou'd speak with Mrs. *Foible, Mem.* Mr. *Mirabell* is with her; he has set your Spouse at liberty, Mrs. *Foible,* and wou'd have you hide your self in my Lady's Closet, 'till my old Lady's Anger is abated. O, my old Lady is in a perilous Passion, at something Mr. *Fainall* has said; he swears, and my old Lady cries. There's a fearful Hurricane I vow. He says *Mem,* how that he'll have my Lady's Fortune made over to him. or he'll be divorc'd.

Mrs. *Fain.* Does your Lady or *Mirabell* know that?

Minc. Yes *Mem,* they have sent me to see if Sir *Wilfull* be sober, and to bring him to them. My Lady is resolved to have him I think, rather than lose such a vast Sum as Six Thousand Pound. O, come Mrs. *Foible,* I hear my old Lady.

Mrs. *Fain. Foible,* you must tell *Mincing,* that she must prepare to vouch when I call her.

Foib. Yes, yes, Madam.

Minc. O yes *Mem,* I'll vouch any thing for your Ladiship's Service, be what it will.

SCENE IV.

Mrs. FAINALL, *Lady* WISHFORT, MARWOOD.

Lady. O my dear Friend, how can I enumerate the Benefits that I have receiv'd from your Goodness? To you I owe the timely Discovery of the false Vows of *Mirabell*; to you I owe the Detection of the Impostor Sir *Rowland.* And now you are become an Intercessor with my Son-in-Law, to save the Honour of my House, and compound for the Frailties of my Daughter. Well Friend, You are enough to reconcile me to the bad World, or else I would retire to Desarts and Solitudes; and feed harmless Sheep by Groves and purling Streams. Dear *Marwood,* let us leave the World, and retire by our selves and be Shepherdesses.

Mrs. *Mar.* Let us first dispatch the Affair in Hand, Madam. We shall have Leisure to think of Retirement afterwards. Here is one who is concerned in the Treaty.

Lady. O Daughter, Daughter, is it possible thou should'st be my Child, Bone of my Bone, and Flesh of my Flesh, and as I may say, another Me, and yet trangress the most minute Particle of severe Virtue? Is it possible you should lean aside to Iniquity, who have been cast in the direct Mold of Virtue? I have not only been a Mold but a Pattern for you, and a Model for you, after you were brought into the World.

Mrs. *Fain.* I don't understand your Ladiship.

Lady. Not understand? Why have you not been Naught? Have you not been Sophisticated? Not understand? Here I am ruin'd to compound for your *Caprices* and your *Cuckoldoms.* I must pawn my Plate and my Jewels, and ruin my Neice, and all little enough——

Mrs. *Fain.* I am wrong'd and abus'd, and so are you. 'Tis a false Accusation, as false as Hell, as false as your Friend there, ay or your Friend's Friend, my false Husband.

Mrs. *Mar.* My Friend, Mrs. *Fainall*? Your Husband my Friend, what do you mean?

Mrs. *Fain.* I know what I mean, Madam, and so do you; and so shall the World at a Time convenient.

Mrs. *Mar.* I am sorry to see you so passionate, Madam. More Temper would look more like Innocence. But I have done. I am sorry my Zeal to serve your Ladiship and Family, should admit of Misconstruction, or make me liable to Affront. You will pardon me, Madam, if I meddle no more with an Affair, in which I am not personally concern'd.

Lady. O dear Friend, I am so asham'd that you should meet with such Returns;——You ought to ask Pardon on your Knees, ungrateful Creature; she deserves more from you, than all your Life can accomplish——O don't leave me destitute in this Perplexity;——No, stick to me, my good Genius.

Mrs. *Fain.* I tell you, Madam, you're abus'd—Stick to you? ay, like a Leach, to suck your best Blood——she'll drop off when she's full. Madam, you shan't pawn a Bodkin, nor part with a Brass

45 Temper] Moderation.

Counter, in Composition for me. I defie 'em all. Let 'em prove their Aspersions : I know my own Innocence, and dare stand a Trial.

SCENE V.

Lady WISHFORT, MARWOOD.

Lady. Why, if she should be innocent, if she should be wrong'd after all, ha ? I don't know what to think,——and I promise you, her Education has been unexceptionable——I may say it ; for I chiefly made it my own Care to initiate her very Infancy in the Rudiments of Virtue, and to impress upon her tender Years a young Odium and Aversion to the very sight of Men,——ay Friend, she would have shriek'd if she had but seen a Man, 'till she was in her Teens. As I'm a Person 'tis true——She was never suffer'd to play with a Male-Child, tho' but in Coats ; Nay her very Babies were of the *Feminine Gender*,——O, she never look'd a Man in the Face but her own Father, or the Chaplain, and him we made a shift to put upon her for a Woman, by the help of his long Garments, and his sleek Face ; 'till she was going in her Fifteen.

Mrs. *Mar*. 'Twas much she should be deceiv'd so long.

Lady. I warrant you, or she would never have born to have been catechiz'd by him ; and have heard his long Lectures against Singing and Dancing, and such Debaucheries ; and going to filthy Plays ; and prophane Musick-meetings, where the lewd Trebles squeek nothing but Bawdy, and the Bases roar Blasphemy. O, she would have swoon'd at the Sight or Name of an obscene Play-Book——and can I think after all this, that my Daughter can be Naught ? What, a Whore ? And thought it Excommunication to set her Foot within the Door of a Play-house. O dear Friend,

I can't believe it, no, no; as she says, let him prove it, let him prove it.

Mrs. *Mar.* Prove it, Madam? What, and have your Name prostituted in a publick Court; yours and your Daughter's Reputation worry'd at the Bar by a Pack of bawling Lawyers? To be usher'd in with an *O Yes* of Scandal; and have your Case open'd by an old fumbler Leacher in a Quoif like a Man Midwife, to bring your Daughter's Infamy to Light; to be a Theme for legal Punsters, and Quiblers by the Statute; and become a Jest, against a Rule of Court, where there is no Precedent for a Jest in any Record; not even in *Dooms-day-Book*: To discompose the Gravity of the Bench, and provoke naughty Interrogatories in more naughty Law *Latin*; while the good Judge, tickl'd with the Proceeding, simpers under a Grey Beard, and figes off and on his Cushion as if he had swallow'd *Cantharides*, or sate upon *Cow-Itch*.

Lady. O, 'tis very hard!

Mrs. *Mar.* And then to have my young Revellers of the *Temple* take Notes, like Prentices at a Conventicle; and after talk it over again in Commons, or before Drawers in an Eating-House.

Lady. Worse and worse.

Mrs. *Mar.* Nay this is nothing; if it would end here 'twere well. But it must after this be consign'd by the Short-hand Writers to the publick Press; and from thence be transferr'd to the Hands nay into the Throats and Lungs of Hawkers, with Voices more licentious than the loud Flounder-man's: And this you must hear 'till you are stunn'd; nay, you must hear nothing else for some Days.

Lady. O, 'tis insupportable. No, no, dear Friend, make it up, make it up; ay, ay, I'll Compound. I'll give up all, my self and my all, my Neice and her all——any thing, every thing for Composition.

Mrs. *Mar.* Nay, Madam, I advise nothing, I only lay before you, as a Friend, the Inconveniencies which perhaps you have overseen. Here comes Mr. *Fainall,* if he will be satisfy'd to huddle up all in Silence, I shall be glad. You must think I would rather Congratulate than Condole with you.

SCENE VI.

FAINALL, *Lady* WISHFORT, *Mrs.* MARWOOD.

Lady. Ay, ay, I do not doubt it, dear *Marwood* : No, no, I do not doubt it.

Fain. Well, Madam ; I have suffer'd my self to be overcome by the Importunity of this Lady your Friend ; and am content you shall enjoy your own proper Estate during Life ; on Condition you oblige your self never to marry, under such Penalty as I think convenient.

Lady. Never to marry ?

Fain. No more Sir *Rowlands,*——the next Imposture may not be so timely detected.

Mrs. *Mar.* That Condition, I dare answer, my Lady will consent to, without Difficulty ; she has already but too much experienc'd the Perfidiousness of Men. Besides, Madam, when we retire to our Pastoral Solitude we shall bid adieu to all other Thoughts.

Lady. Ay, that's true ; but in case of Necessity ; as of Health, or some such Emergency——

Fain. O, if you are prescrib'd Marriage, you shall be consider'd ; I will only reserve to my self the Power to chuse for you. If your Physick be wholsome, it matters not who is your Apothecary. Next, my Wife shall settle on me the Remainder of her Fortune, not made over already ; and for her Maintenance depend entirely on my Discretion.

Lady. This is most inhumanly savage ; exceeding the Barbarity of a *Muscovite* Husband.

Fain. I learn'd it from his *Czarish* Majesty's

Retinue, in a Winter Evening's Conference over Brandy and Pepper, amongst other Secrets of Matrimony and Policy, as they are at present practis'd in the Northern Hemisphere. But this must be agreed unto, and that positively. Lastly, I will be endow'd, in right of my Wife, with that six thousand Pound, which is the Moiety of Mrs. *Millamant*'s Fortune in your Possession; and which she has forfeited (as will appear by the last Will and Testament of your deceas'd Husband, Sir *Jonathan Wishfort*) by her Disobedience in Contracting her self against your Consent or Knowledge; and by refusing the offer'd Match with Sir *Wilfull Witwoud*, which you, like a careful Aunt, had provided for her.

Lady. My Nephew was *non Compos*; and could not make his Addresses.

Fain. I come to make Demands——I'll hear no Objections.

Lady. You will grant me Time to consider?

Fain. Yes, while the Instrument is drawing, to which you must set your Hand 'till more sufficient Deeds can be perfected: which I will take Care shall be done with all possible speed. In the mean while I will go for the said Instrument, and 'till my Return you may ballance this Matter in your own Discretion.

SCENE VII.

Lady WISHFORT, *Mrs.* MARWOOD.

Lady. This Insolence is beyond all Precedent, all Parallel; must I be subject to this merciless Villain?

Mrs. *Mar*. 'Tis severe indeed, Madam, that you shou'd smart for your Daughter's Wantonness.

Lady. 'Twas against my Consent that she

30 Retinue] Peter the Great paid his famous visit to England in 1697.

marry'd this Barbarian, but she wou'd have him, tho' her Year was not out.—Ah! her first Husband, my Son *Languish*, wou'd not have carry'd it thus. Well, that was my Choice, this is hers; she is match'd now with a Witness——I shall be mad, dear Friend, is there no Comfort for me? Must I live to be confiscated at this Rebel-rate?——Here comes two more of my *Egyptian* Plagues too.

SCENE VIII.

[*To them*] MILLAMANT, *Sir* WILFULL.

Sir *Wil.* Aunt, your Servant.

Lady. Out *Caterpillar*, call not me Aunt; I know thee not.

Sir *Wil.* I confess I have been a little in Disguise, as they say,——'Sheart! and I'm sorry for't. What wou'd you have? I hope I committed no Offence, Aunt—and if I did I am willing to make Satisfaction; and what can a Man say fairer? If I have broke any thing I'll pay for't, an it cost a Pound. And so let that content for what's past, and make no more Words. For what's to come, to pleasure you I'm willing to marry my Cousin. So pray let's all be Friends, she and I are agreed upon the Matter before a Witness.

Lady. How's this, dear Neice? Have I any Comfort? Can this be true?

Milla. I am content to be a Sacrifice to your Repose, Madam; and to convince you that I had no Hand in the Plot, as you were misinform'd, I have laid my Commands on *Mirabell* to come in Person, and be a Witness that I give my Hand to this Flower of *Knighthood*; and for the Contract that pass'd between *Mirabell* and me, I have oblig'd him to make a Resignation of it in your Ladiship's Presence;——He is without, and waits your leave for Admittance.

Lady. Well, I'll swear I am something reviv'd

at this Testimony of your Obedience; but I cannot admit that Traitor,——I fear I cannot fortifie my self to support his Appearance. He is as terrible to me as a *Gorgon*; if I see him I fear I shall turn to Stone, petrifie incessantly.

Milla. If you disoblige him he may resent your Refusal, and insist upon the Contract still. Then 'tis the last time he will be offensive to you.

Lady. Are you sure it will be the last time?—— If I were sure of that——shall I never see him again?

Milla. Sir *Wilfull*, you and he are to Travel together, are you not?

Sir *Wil.* 'Sheart the Gentleman's a Civil Gentleman, Aunt, let him come in; why we are sworn Brothers and Fellow-Travellers.——We are to be *Pylades* and *Orestes*, he and I——He is to be my Interpreter in Foreign Parts. He has been Overseas once already; and with *proviso* that I marry my Cousin, will cross 'em once again, only to bear me Company.—'Sheart, I'll call him in,——an I set on't once, he shall come in; and see who'll hinder him. [*Goes to the Door and hems.*

Mrs. *Mar.* This is precious Fooling, if it wou'd pass; but I'll know the Bottom of it.

Lady. O dear *Marwood*, you are not going?

Mar. Not far, Madam; I'll return immediately.

SCENE IX.

Lady WISHFORT, MILLAMANT, *Sir* WILFULL, MIRABELL.

Sir *Wil.* Look up, Man, I'll stand by you, 'sbud an she do frown, she can't kill you;——Besides— harkee she dare not frown desperately, because her Face is none of her own; 'Sheart, and she shou'd her Forehead wou'd wrinkle like the Coat of a Cream-cheese; but mum for that, Fellow-Traveller.

Mira. If a deep Sense of the many Injuries I have offer'd to so good a Lady, with a sincere Remorse, and a hearty Contrition, can but obtain the least Glance of Compassion, I am too happy, ——Ah Madam, there was a time——But let it be forgotten——I confess I have deservedly forfeited the high Place I once held, of sighing at your Feet; nay kill me not, by turning from me in Disdain—I come not to plead for Favour;—Nay not for Pardon; I am a Suppliant only for Pity—I am going where I never shall behold you more——

Sir *Wil.* How, Fellow-Traveller!——You shall go by your self then.

Mira. Let me be pitied first; and afterwards forgotten——I ask no more.

Sir *Wil.* By'r Lady a very reasonable Request, and will cost you nothing, Aunt,—Come, come, forgive and forget Aunt, why you must an you are a Christian.

Mira. Consider Madam, in reality, you cou'd not receive much Prejudice; it was an innocent Device; tho' I confess it had a Face of Guiltiness, —it was at most an Artifice which Love contriv'd——And Errors which Love produces have ever been accounted *Venial.* At least think it is Punishment enough that I have lost what in my Heart I hold most dear that to your cruel Indignation, I have offer'd up this Beauty, and with her my Peace and Quiet; nay all my Hopes of future Comfort.

Sir *Wil.* An he does not move me, wou'd I may never be *O' the Quorum,*—An it were not as good a Deed as to drink, to give her to him again,——I wou'd I might never take Shipping——Aunt, if you don't forgive quickly; I shall melt, I can tell you that. My Contract went no farther than a little Mouth-Glew, and that's hardly dry;——One doleful Sigh more from my Fellow-Traveller and 'tis dissolv'd.

Lady. Well Nephew, upon your Account——Ah, he has a false insinuating Tongue——Well Sir, I will stifle my just Resentment at my Nephew's Request.——I will endeavour what I can to forget, ——but on *proviso* that you resign the Contract with my Neice immediately.

Mira. It is in Writing and with Papers of Concern; but I have sent my Servant for it, and will deliver it to you, with all Acknowledgments for your transcendent Goodness. 57

Lady. Oh, he has Witchcraft in his Eyes and Tongue;——When I did not see him I cou'd have brib'd a Villain to his Assassination; but his Appearance rakes the Embers which have so long lain smother'd in my Breast.—— [*Aside.*

SCENE X.

[*To them*] FAINALL, *Mrs.* MARWOOD.

Fain. Your Date of Deliberation, Madam, is expir'd. Here is the Instrument, are you prepar'd to sign?

Lady. If I were prepar'd, I am not impower'd. My Neice exerts a lawful Claim, having match'd her self by my Direction to Sir *Wilfull.*

Fain, That Sham is too gross to pass on me——tho' 'tis impos'd on you, Madam.

Milla. Sir, I have given my Consent. 9

Mira. And, Sir, I have resign'd my Pretensions.

Sir *Wil.* And, Sir, I assert my Right; and will maintain it in defiance of you, Sir, and of your Instrument. S'heart an you talk of an Instrument Sir, I have an old Fox by my Thigh shall hack your Instrument of *Ram Vellam* to Shreds, Sir. It shall not be sufficient for a *Mittimus* or a Tailor's Measure; therefore withdraw your Instrument Sir, or by'r Lady I shall draw mine.

Lady. Hold, Nephew, hold.

Milla. Good Sir *Wilfull* respite your Valour.

Fain. Indeed? Are you provided of your Guard, with your single Beef-eater there? But I'm prepared for you; and insist upon my first Proposal. You shall submit your own Estate to my Management, and absolutely make over my Wife's to my sole use; as pursuant to the Purport and Tenor of this other Covenant.——I suppose, Madam, your Consent is not requisite in this Case; nor, Mr. *Mirabell,* your Resignation; nor, Sir *Wilfull,* your Right——You may draw your Fox if you please Sir, and make a *Bear-Garden* flourish somewhere else: For here it will not avail. This, my Lady *Wishfort,* must be subscrib'd, or your Darling Daughter's turn'd a-drift, like a leaky Hulk to sink or swim, as she and the Current of this lewd Town can agree.

Lady. Is there no Means, no Remedy, to stop my Ruin? Ungrateful Wretch! dost thou not owe thy Being, thy Subsistance to my Daughter's Fortune?

Fain. I'll answer you when I have the rest of it in my Possession.

Mira. But that you wou'd not accept of a Remedy from my Hands——I own I have not deserv'd you shou'd owe any Obligation to me; or else perhaps I cou'd advise,——

Lady. O what? what? to save me and my Child from Ruin, from Want, I'll forgive all that's past; nay I'll consent to any Thing to come, to be deliver'd from this Tyranny.

Mira. Ay Madam; but that is too late, my Reward is intercepted. You have dispos'd of her, who only cou'd have made me a Compensation for all my Services;——But be it as it may, I am resolv'd I'll serve you, you shall not be wrong'd in this Savage manner.

Lady. How! Dear Mr. *Mirabell,* can you be so generous at last! But it is not possible. Harkee, I'll break my Nephew's Match, you shall have my

Neice yet, and all her Fortune; if you can but save me from this imminent Danger.

Mira. Will you? I take you at your Word. I ask no more. I must have leave for two Criminals to appear.

Lady. Ay, ay, any body, any body.

Mira. Foible is one, and a Penitent.

SCENE XI.

[*To them*] *Mrs.* FAINALL, FOIBLE, MINCING.

Mrs. *Mar.* O My Shame! these corrupt things are brought hither to expose me. [Mira. *and Lady go to Mrs.* Fain. *and* Foib.]

Fain. If it must all come out, why let 'em know it, 'tis but the *Way of the World.* That shall not urge me to relinquish or abate one Tittle of my Terms, no, I will insist the more.

Foib. Yes indeed Madam, I'll take my Bible-oath of it.

Minc. And so will I *Mem.*

Lady. O *Marwood, Marwood,* art thou false? my Friend deceive me? Hast thou been a wicked Accomplice with that profligate Man?

Mrs. *Mar.* Have you so much Ingratitude and Injustice, to give Credit against your Friend, to the Aspersions of Two such mercenary Truls?

Minc. Mercenary, *Mem*? I scorn your Words. 'Tis true we found you and Mr. *Fainall* in the blue Garret; by the same Token, you swore us to Secresie upon *Messalinas*'s Poems. Mercenary? No, if we wou'd have been Mercenary, we shou'd have held our Tongues; you wou'd have brib'd us sufficiently.

Fain. Go, you are an insignificant Thing.—— Well, what are you the better for this! Is this Mr. *Mirabell*'s Expedient? I'll be put off no

20 *Messalinas*'s] Mincing was wittier than she knew. She meant *miscellaneous*.

longer——You, Thing, that was a Wife, shall smart for this. I will not leave thee wherewithal to hide thy Shame: Your Body shall be Naked as your Reputation.

Mrs. *Fain.* I despise you, and defie your Malice——You have aspers'd me wrongfully——I have prov'd your Falsehood——Go you and your treacherous——I will not name it, but starve together——Perish.

Fain. Not while you are worth a Groat, indeed my Dear. Madam, I'll be fool'd no longer.

Lady. Ah Mr. *Mirabell*, this is small Comfort, the Detection of this Affair.

Mira. O in good time——Your leave for the other Offender and Penitent to appear, Madam.

SCENE XII.

[*To them*] Waitwell *with a Box of Writings.*

Lady. O Sir *Rowland*——Well, Rascal.

Wait. What your Ladiship pleases.——I have brought the Black-Box at last, Madam.

Mira. Give it me. Madam, you remember your Promise.

Lady. Ay, dear Sir.

Mira. Where are the Gentlemen?

Wait. At hand Sir, rubbing their Eyes,——just risen from Sleep.

Fain. S'death what's this to me? I'll not wait your private Concerns.

SCENE XIII.

[*To them*] Petulant, Witwoud.

Pet. How now? what's the matter? who's Hand's out?

Wit. Hey day! what are you all got together, like Players at the End of the last Act?

Mira. You may remember, Gentlemen, I once requested your Hands as Witnesses to a certain Parchment.

Wit. Ay I do, my Hand I remember—*Petulant* set his Mark. 9

Mira. You wrong him, his Name is fairly written, as shall appear——You do not remember, Gentlemen, any thing of what that Parchment contained—— [*Undoing the Box.*

Wit. No.

Pet. Not I. I writ, I read nothing.

Mira. Very well, now you shall know——Madam, your Promise.

Lady. Ay, ay, Sir, upon my Honour. 18

Mira. Mr. *Fainall,* it is now Time that you shou'd know, that your Lady, while she was at her own Disposal, and before you had by your Insinuations wheadl'd her out of a pretended Settlement of the greatest Part of her Fortune——

Fain. Sir! pretended!

Mira. Yes, Sir. I say that this Lady while a Widow, having it seems receiv'd some Cautions respecting your Inconstancy and Tyranny of Temper, which from her own partial Opinion and Fondness of you she cou'd never have suspected ——she did, I say, by the wholesome Advice of Friends and of Sages learn'd in the Laws of this Land, deliver this same as her Act and Deed to me in Trust, and to the Uses within mention'd. You may read if you please—[*Holding out the Parchment.*] tho' perhaps what is written on the Back may serve your Occasions.

Fain. Very likely, Sir. What's here? Damnation?

[*Reads.*] *A Deed of Conveyance of the whole Estate real of* Arabella Languish, *Widow, in Trust to* Edward Mirabell. 41

Confusion!

Mira. Even so, Sir, 'tis *the Way of the World*, Sir; of the Widows of the World. I suppose this Deed may bear an elder Date than what you have obtain'd from your Lady.

Fain. Perfidious Fiend! then thus I'll be reveng'd.— [*Offers to run at Mrs.* Fain.

Sir *Wil*. Hold, Sir, now you may make your *Bear-Garden* Flourish somewhere else, Sir.

Fain. *Mirabell*, you shall hear of this, Sir, be sure you shall.——Let me pass, Oaf.

Mrs. *Fain*. Madam, you seem to stifle your Resentment: You had better give it Vent.

Mrs. *Mar*. Yes, it shall have Vent——and to your Confusion, or I'll perish in the Attempt.

SCENE *the Last*.

Lady WISHFORT, MILLAMANT, MIRABELL, *Mrs.* FAINALL, *Sir* WILFULL, PETULANT, WITWOUD, FOIBLE, MINCING, WAITWELL.

Lady. O Daughter, Daughter, 'tis plain thou hast inherited thy Mother's Prudence.

Mrs. *Fain*. Thank Mr. *Mirabell*, a cautious Friend, to whose Advice all is owing.

Lady. Well Mr. *Mirabell*, you have kept your Promise——and I must perform mine.——First I pardon for your sake Sir *Rowland* there and *Foible*——The next thing is to break the Matter to my Nephew—and how to do that——

Mira. For that, Madam, give your self no Trouble,—let me have your Consent——Sir *Wilfull* is my Friend; he has had Compassion upon Lovers, and generously engag'd a Volunteer in this Action, for our Service; and now designs to prosecute his Travels.

Sir *Wil*. 'Sheart, Aunt, I have no mind to marry. My Cousin's a fine Lady, and the Gentleman loves her, and she loves him, and they deserve one another; my Resolution is to see Foreign Parts——I have set on't——and when I'm set on't, I must do't. And if these two Gentlemen wou'd travel too, I think they may be spar'd.

Pet. For my part, I say little—I think things are best off or on.

Wit. I gad I understand nothing of the matter,—I'm in a Maze yet, like a Dog in a Dancing-School.

Lady. Well Sir, take her, and with her all the Joy I can give you.

Milla. Why does not the Man take me? Wou'd you have me give my self to you over again?

Mira. Ay, and over and over again;

[*Kisses her Hand.*

I wou'd have you as often as possibly I can. Well, Heav'n grant I love you not too well, that's all my Fear.

Sir *Wil.* 'Sheart you'll have time enough to toy after you're marry'd; or if you will toy now, let us have a Dance in the mean time; that we who are not Lovers may have some other Employment, besides looking on.

Mira. With all my Heart, dear Sir *Wilfull.* What shall we do for Musick?

Foib. O Sir, some that were provided for Sir *Rowland*'s Entertainment are yet within Call.

[*A Dance.*

Lady. As I am a Person I can hold out no longer; ——I have wasted my Spirits so to Day already, that I am ready to sink under the Fatigue; and I cannot but have some Fears upon me yet, that my Son *Fainall* will pursue some desperate Course.

Mira. Madam, disquiet not your self on that account; to my Knowledge his Circumstances are such, he must of Force comply. For my part I will contribute all that in me lyes to a Reunion: In the mean time, Madam, [*To Mrs. Fain.*] let me before these Witnesses restore to you this Deed of Trust; it may be a Means, well manag'd, to make you live easily together.

From hence let those be warn'd, who mean to wed;
Lest mutual Falshood stain the Bridal-Bed:
For each Deceiver to his Cost may find,
That Marriage Frauds too oft are paid in kind.

[Exeunt Omnes.

EPILOGUE,

Spoken by Mrs. *Bracegirdle.*

After our Epilogue *this Crowd dismisses,*
I'm thinking how this Play'll be pull'd to Pieces.
But pray consider, e'er you doom its Fall,
How hard a thing 'twou'd be, to please you all.
There are some Criticks so with Spleen diseas'd,
They scarcely come inclining to be Pleas'd :
And sure he must have more than mortal Skill,
Who pleases any one against his Will.
Then, all bad Poets we are sure are Foes,
And how their Number's swell'd the Town well knows:
In shoals, I've mark'd 'em judging in the Pit ;
Tho' they're on no Pretence for Judgment fit,
But that they have been Damn'd for Want of Wit.
Since when, they by their own Offences taught,
Set up for Spies on Plays, and finding Fault.
Others there are, whose Malice we'd prevent ;
Such, who watch Plays, with scurrilous Intent
To mark out who by Characters *are meant.*
And tho' no perfect Likeness they can trace ;
Yet each pretends to know the Copy'd Face.
These, with false Glosses feed their own Ill-nature,
And turn to Libel, *what was meant a* Satire.
May such malicious Fops *this Fortune find,*
To think themselves alone the Fools *design'd :*
If any are so arrogantly Vain,
To think they singly *can support a* Scene,
And furnish Fool *enough to entertain.*
For well the Learn'd and the Judicious know,
That Satire *scorns to stoop so meanly low,*
As any one abstracted Fop *to show.*
For, as when Painters form a matchless Face,
They from each Fair one *catch some diff'rent Grace ;*
And shining Features in one Portrait blend,
To which no single Beauty must pretend :
So Poets oft, do in one Piece expose
Whole Belles Assemblées *of* Cocquets *and* Beaux.